"For students and colleagues to present essays to a professor is already a great honor, but for the essays to be both scholarly and pastoral is a tribute to the person of Maxwell Johnson who has consistently demonstrated that sound historical scholarship is the best approach to good pastoral praxis."

— Michael Driscoll
Co-Director of the Master in Sacred Music Program
University of Notre Dame

"[This is a] magnificent volume of equally outstanding essays. Instead of digging in the liturgical past as nostalgic antiquarians intent on restoring authenticity and purity, the contributors have ingeniously focused on three main categories—liturgical year, Christian initiation, and Eucharist—and used three innovative approaches that address primarily the pastoral role of liturgical history. In so doing, they have produced an extraordinary work of scholarship, which not only does justice to the research of one of the most prominent liturgical historians living today, but to the field as a whole."

— Nathan D. Mitchell
University of Notre Dame

"These essays demonstrate the pastoral relevance of careful historical investigation of liturgy while avoiding the romantic approach to history that characterized liturgical renewal in the twentieth century. Both academic specialists and working pastors will find much here to consider. The collection demonstrates the cutting edge of liturgical studies in the twenty-first century, and it is a fitting tribute to a scholar who himself has left an indelible mark on the field."

— L. Edward Phillips
Associate Professor of Worship and Liturgical Theology
Candler School of Theology
Emory University

A Living Tradition

On the Intersection of Liturgical History and Pastoral Practice

Essays in Honor of Maxwell E. Johnson

Edited by
David A. Pitt   Stefanos Alexopoulos   Christian McConnell

A PUEBLO BOOK

Liturgical Press   Collegeville, Minnesota
www.litpress.org

A Pueblo Book published by Liturgical Press

Cover design by David Manahan, OSB. Illustration by Frank Kacmarcik, OblSB.

Library of Congress Control Number: 2012943813

Contents

Introduction

Whether through study with Maxwell Johnson or through reading his *The Rites of Christian Initiation: Their Evolution and Interpretation*, one encounters a particularly helpful observation concerning the French term, *Pastorale Liturgique*. Johnson is quite fond of noting that this term, frequently rendered in English as "pastoral liturgy," has shaped the Liturgical Movement in the United States in an immeasurable way. The term has been incorporated into the names of publications, institutions, and academic degrees. Johnson is quick to point out, however, that the proper translation of the term is not "pastoral liturgy" but rather "liturgical pastoring."[1] This, he insists, represents a fundamentally different understanding of liturgy's role in the lives of Christians. Consequently, Johnson embraces the theological vocation of the historian.[2] Not merely one immersing himself or herself in ancient texts, assembling data from the past, the historian is instead called upon to narrate the present story of the community—its living tradition—pointing out those events and themes that have contributed to its current shape and experience: "It is, then, not so much our *experience* of the rites that must be primary . . . but the evolution and interpretation of those rites themselves that are to shape, challenge, and critique

[1] Dennis Smolarski, *Sacred Mysteries: Sacramental Principles and Liturgical Practice* (Mahwah, NJ: Paulist Press, 1995), 165, quoted in Maxwell E. Johnson, "Introduction," in *The Rites of Christian Initiation: Their Evolution and Interpretation* (Collegeville, MN: Liturgical Press, 1999), xx (2nd ed., 2007, xxi).

[2] The value of history for liturgical pastoring/pastoral liturgy is evidenced in the translation of Josef A. Jungmann's book, *Pastoral Liturgy* (New York: Herder and Herder, 1962). The original German title, *Liturgisches Erbe und Pastorale Gegenwart*, is thoroughly historical, indicating that it is the received liturgical inheritance that precedes present pastoring. The first essay in Jungmann's book, "The Defeat of Teutonic Arianism and the Revolution in Religious Culture in the Early Middle Ages," was named by Balthasar Fischer as the single most important of Jungmann's articles. See "Foreword," in *Source and Summit: Commemorating Josef A. Jungmann, S.J.*, ed. Joanne M. Pierce and Michael Downey (Collegeville, MN: Liturgical Press, 1999), ix. See also Kathleen Hughes, "Jungmann's Influence on Vatican II: Meticulous Scholarship at the Service of a Living Liturgy" in *Source and Summit*, 21–32.

our experience. In other words, here it is the Christian liturgical tradition as known from the texts of that tradition that is primary, and our 'experience' of the contemporary use or misuse of that tradition that is secondary."[3] These two themes, of an inherently formative function of liturgy that has historically shaped the present incarnation of the church, are woven throughout the breadth of Johnson's work.

This volume of essays, dedicated to the Rev. Dr. Maxwell E. Johnson on the occasion of his sixtieth birthday, pays tribute to Johnson's scholarship by addressing some of the ways in which the historical study of the liturgy contributes to the liturgical pastoring of the church. Such a venture is necessary in the face of a liturgical culture that appears beset by two conflicting approaches. On one hand, Johnson has argued that the evidence gleaned from liturgical history provides the necessary foundation for avoiding liturgical relativism: "there is still a case to be made for some kind of 'normativity' based on the inherited traditions . . . centered in Sunday, assembly, baptism, word, meal, year, and some kind of ministerial ordering, together with the orthodox doctrinal heritage of the church of the first millennium, [and that] there should be plenty of room for a diversity of practices and interpretations, past and present, in which the gifts of several differing Christian churches might find a welcome place."[4] He insists that the normativity of the liturgical tradition is not simply a matter of preference: "Recent developments in Christian worship around the world—for example, the increasing phenomenon of megachurches, the church growth movement, the development of 'seeker services,' and the increasing notion across ecclesial lines that the church's liturgy is but 'one' of several options for 'worship'—challenge the historic priority of sacramental worship. What appears to be at stake in this, I would submit, is a particular theological understanding of how God is believed to act in the world and church."[5]

On the other hand, Johnson has insisted that liturgical history and liturgical antiquarianism are decisively different projects:

[3] Johnson, "Introduction," in *The Rites of Christian Initiation*, xix (xxi).

[4] Maxwell E. Johnson, "Can We Avoid Relativism in Worship? Liturgical Norms in the Light of Contemporary Scholarship," in *Worship: Rites, Feasts, and Reflections* (Portland, OR: Pastoral Press, 2004), 347.

[5] Maxwell E. Johnson, "Introduction," in *Sacraments and Worship: The Sources of Christian Theology*, ed. Maxwell E. Johnson (Louisville, KY: Westminster/John Knox Press, 2012), xiii.

> Archaeologists do not dig beneath the surface of sites where very many generations of peoples have lived and expose the different layers of habitation in order to persuade modern humans to return to the conditions of prehistoric dwellings, nor are liturgical historians bent on excavating the various strata of the past in order to restore some sort of imaginary primitive purity. . . . It is only when we have a clearer picture of the stages of that evolution that we are in a position to make any judgments about which of these trends were of genuine and lasting value and which represented a loss of something significant from earlier times. Indeed, it is not up to liturgical historians to reform liturgy; all the historian can do is to unpack as carefully and clearly as possible the richness and diversity of the liturgical traditions as they actually appear in history. What legitimate liturgical authorities in the various churches do with the results of liturgical history in service to liturgical reform and renewal is something altogether distinct.[6]

The navigation between these two polar alternatives provides the lens for each of the essays in this collection, which are organized according to three liturgical categories: liturgical year, Christian initiation, and Eucharist. Further, each author has addressed the pastoral role of liturgical history in varying combinations of three different approaches. First, several essays consider ways in which figures from liturgical history were, themselves, liturgical pastors. Second, several essays investigate ways in which liturgical history has been used in the shaping of contemporary liturgical rites and prayers. And third, several essays consider the ways in which liturgical history informs contemporary understandings and beliefs. In all, this collection is an attempt to rise to the task that Johnson sees for liturgical history and the historian, who "must attend to the great variety that actually exists—liturgically and theologically—in the sources of the various Christian traditions, as that variety is revealed to us by study of those documents themselves."[7]

The collection begins with two introductory essays that help to establish the framework for this project. Paul F. Bradshaw, Johnson's former dissertation director and now colleague and frequent coauthor,[8]

[6] Maxwell E. Johnson, "Introduction," in *Issues in Eucharistic Praying in East and West: Essays in Liturgical and Theological Analysis*, ed. Maxwell E. Johnson (Collegeville, MN: Liturgical Press, 2010), xv.

[7] Johnson, "Introduction," in *Sacraments and Worship*, ix.

[8] Paul F. Bradshaw and Maxwell E. Johnson, *The Eucharistic Liturgies: Their Evolution and Interpretation* (Collegeville, MN: Pueblo Books, 2012); Paul F. Bradshaw

introduces this anthology. In his essay, "The Relationship between Historical Research and Modern Liturgical Practice," Bradshaw identifies some of the historical perspectives and assumptions affecting the shape of late twentieth-century Western liturgical revision and reform and indicates how many of these scholarly positions have changed since then. Articulating potential difficulties associated with such a shift, he investigates some of the ways in which the historical study of the liturgy might impact how the liturgy is celebrated and understood. This focus is somewhat narrowed in the second introductory essay, Robert F. Taft's "Between Progress and Nostalgia: Liturgical Reform and the Western Romance with the Christian East; Strategies and Realities." Here, Taft examines the valuation of Eastern liturgy in the reforms of the Second Vatican Council, arguing that what Westerners saw in Eastern liturgy may well be best understood as an indication of what they perceived themselves to be lacking. After proposing alternatives to some of these (mis)perceptions, Taft offers suggestions for the renewal of Western liturgy and spirituality.

The trajectory established by the introductory essays is continued in the first essay of the section treating the liturgical year. Ruth Langer's contribution, "The Liturgical Parting(s) of the Ways: A Preliminary Foray," investigates points of seeming connection, yet ultimately divergence, between Jewish and Christian liturgical years. She not only asks the significant question as to why the connections between the two were so unexpectedly superficial but also points to the value that these differences have for interfaith relations. Michael Daniel Findikyan's article, "Saints Nicholas in Armenia," shifts the comparative focus to the Armenian Church, investigating the unusual problem of two feasts within the span of three weeks venerating the same Saint Nicholas. Findikyan explores reasons for the doubling of the feast and offers the possibility that these past reasons for Nicholas's significance might still resonate today. The final essay of the liturgical year section is Nicholas V. Russo's "The Distribution of Cyril's *Baptismal Catecheses* and the Shape of the Catechumenate in Mid-Fourth-Century Jerusalem," which presents an image of Cyril the liturgical pastor. Russo offers an arrangement of Cyril's pre-baptismal instructions that may

and Maxwell E. Johnson, *The Origins of Feasts, Fasts and Seasons in Early Christianity*, Alcuin Club Collections 86 (London: SPCK; Collegeville, MN: Liturgical Press, 2011); Paul F. Bradshaw, Maxwell E. Johnson, and L. Edward Phillips, *The Apostolic Tradition: A Commentary*, Hermeneia (Minneapolis, MN: Fortress Press, 2002).

well correspond to the expansion of the pre-baptismal period from three weeks to six weeks, resulting from the emergence of a forty-day Lenten season at Jerusalem.

The third section of this collection, which treats initiation, begins with Christian McConnell's essay, "The Meanings of Paschal Baptism in the Non-Roman West." Examining liturgical sources from Spain and Gaul, McConnell assesses the range of baptismal images that illuminate Easter baptism beyond that of death and resurrection with Christ. He argues that the clear preeminence of a Romans 6 baptismal theology in contemporary Western baptismal rites need not result in an exclusive interpretation of contemporary paschal baptism. Walter D. Ray's article, "Baptismal Images, Baptismal Narratives," expands upon the multiplicity of received baptismal images by suggesting two interrelated claims. First, Ray argues that Paul utilizes a narrative pattern associated with baptism in order to foster both the faithful's entry into salvation history through Christ and their living it out in their own experience. Ray continues by suggesting that an image of baptism that highlights such a dynamic is marriage—enacted ritually, baptism marries the Christian to Christ the bridegroom both in his death and in his life. The connection between the baptismal event and a baptismal life are further developed in Jeffrey A. Truscott's essay, "Luther's Pastoral Approach to Baptism." Truscott provides a look back at another liturgical pastor, tracing Martin Luther's baptismal theology from 1519 to 1529. He identifies ways in which Luther's treatment of baptism developed in response to both pressing theological issues of the day and a heightened awareness of the implications of baptism for the faithful. Luther's method of baptismal theology thus emerges as a formative model for contemporary pastors. The theme of baptismal living is continued in David A. Pitt's essay, "*Lex Exorcismi, Lex Vivendi*: The Minor Exorcisms of Adult Initiation and Baptismal Identity." He narrates the development of the minor exorcisms during the revision of the rite of adult initiation following the Second Vatican Council, arguing that these exorcisms are central to the period of the catechumenate. Their celebration would help establish a baptismal spirituality better equipped to combat contemporary semi-Pelagian trends. The issue of semi-Pelagian tendencies related to baptism is also taken up in Lizette Larson-Miller's essay, "'That You May Be a Christian': Baptism, Identity, and Naming." Larson-Miller explores the increased centrality given to naming those about to be baptized (particularly infants) and argues that a more traditional practice—direct reliance upon the names of the Triune God—might contribute greatly to a deeper understanding of being named as Christian.

The concluding section of this collection treats the Eucharist. In "Revisiting Egyptian Anaphoral Development," Bryan D. Spinks considers the difficulties associated with geographically based descriptions of liturgical units. Spinks examines the structure of Egyptian Basil, the Barcelona anaphora, and the anaphora of St. Thomas the Apostle. Ultimately, Spinks concludes that speaking of Egyptian eucharistic praying may require recognizing variety in anaphoral construction, proposing that the union of "Egyptian" and "West Syrian" elements found in Sarapion may actually reflect a consciously pastoral and genuinely Egyptian effort to serve a local community. The discussion on anaphoral construction is continued in the next contribution, which treats the epiclesis and institution narrative in the anaphora of Basil: "*Attempto*: Rethinking the Question of Summaries," by Gabriele Winkler. Whereas previous articles more directly concern the pastoring of the faithful, Winkler does so indirectly by pastoring scholars. Her thorough summary of her own recent German-language scholarship not only provides a clear model for what summaries ought to be but will clearly benefit a good many English-speaking scholars by minimizing the potential for interpretative errors. Anne McGowan's essay, "The Epiclesis in Eucharistic Praying Reconsidered: Early Evidence and Recent Western Reforms," builds upon the work of both Spinks and Winkler by examining the use of the epiclesis in current Roman Catholic, Lutheran, Presbyterian, Anglican, and United Methodist eucharistic prayers. She engages questions pertaining to structure and theology of ancient epicleses, leading to a survey of epicletic diversity in the contemporary Christian West. The section and collection concludes with Stefanos Alexopoulos's contribution, "'Ὅλοι μαζί': Liturgical Practice and Liturgical History." Alexopoulos engages in a case study of the use of historical sources for contemporary liturgy by examining the theological motivation and liturgical practice of an added admonition for participation in the context of Byzantine worship. Beyond the issue of this particular addition, he helps set out a method for engaging in sound tradition-based liturgical practice.

All the essays collected here demonstrate a variety of pastoral implications for the present celebrations and understandings of liturgy arising from its historical study; nevertheless, they are unified by a common thematic thread. Similarly, the authorship reflects a great diversity of persons. Gathered here is the work of Max's mentors, his former students, and his colleagues, members and (to varying degree) nonmembers of *Das Institut*, who emerge from a variety of liturgical traditions. Despite these differences, all are unified in being honored to be numbered among Max's friends. We, the editors, very much appreciate their ready willingness to give their time and energy to this project. We are, similarly, most grateful to Hans Christoffersen and Liturgical Press for so willingly publishing an honorific collection of essays in that same spirit of commitment. The eagerness with which all involved in this book have undertaken to celebrate the service that Max has rendered to the life of the church through his academic ministry is a testament to the respect that he enjoys as a scholar and as a friend.

David A. Pitt, Stefanos Alexopoulos, and Christian McConnell
March 21, 2012
The Passing of Our Holy Father Benedict
Anniversary of the Death of Sarapion of Thmuis

Part I

Introductory Essays

Paul F. Bradshaw

Chapter 1

The Relationship between Historical Research and Modern Liturgical Practice

One of Maxwell Johnson's major concerns has been whether and how we might view historical liturgical sources as being not merely descriptive but also in some way normative for Christian worship today.[1] This is also an area in which I have dabbled in the past and to which I now return. There can be little doubt that those who were engaged in the process of liturgical revision in a number of churches in the second half of the twentieth century did regard what they knew of early Christian worship practices as models on which to draw when composing their own texts. What is also clear from a vantage point some thirty years after most of these revisions took place is that historical scholarship has moved on considerably from that earlier time and that a good number of the conclusions reached by the scholars on whom the revisers then relied would now be seriously questioned as a result of the research that has been pursued in the last two or three decades.

Among the views of early Christian worship that were widely held by liturgical historians of the mid-twentieth century were the following:

- That the Easter Vigil was the principal occasion when new converts were admitted to the church in a rite that included baptism, confirmation, and First Communion; consequently, many modern rites have "restored" this pattern as normative for Christian initiation.

[1] See, for example, Maxwell E. Johnson, "Can We Avoid Relativism in Worship? Liturgical Norms in the Light of Contemporary Liturgical Scholarship," *Worship* 74, no. 2 (2000): 135–55.

- That eucharistic rites conformed almost without exception to a standard fourfold shape—taking bread and wine, giving thanks over them, breaking the bread, and distributing both to all those present—a pattern which itself was an early modification of the sevenfold shape of the Last Supper;[2] consequently, modern revisions generally either emphasize that structure as already existing in their rites or have "restored" it where it was lacking.
- That the ancient church order known as the *Apostolic Tradition* had been composed by Hippolytus of Rome and gave an accurate picture of liturgical practice in Rome in the early third century; consequently, many revised rites adopted elements from this work as the basis for modern practice, not least adaptations of its eucharistic prayer and in some cases its ordination prayer for a bishop too.

As the result of more recent research, however—research in which Maxwell Johnson has played a significant part—this former scholarly consensus no longer exists. On the contrary:

- It is now generally recognized that prior to the fourth century only in North Africa and possibly at Rome was there a preference for baptism at Easter and that during this earlier period the dominant theological motif for baptism was that of new birth (as in John 3) rather than dying and rising with Christ (as is Romans 6). In other parts of the Christian world baptisms might have taken place at any time in the year, after a final period of preparation that lasted for three weeks instead of the later forty days of the Lenten season.[3]
- The existence of anything that might be said to resemble "confirmation" is not universally attested in these early centuries. Our first- and second-century sources (the *Didache* and Justin Martyr) witness to no other ritual than immersion in water. Third-century

[2] The principal proponent of this theory was Gregory Dix, *The Shape of the Liturgy* (London: Dacre, 1945), a book that continues to be reissued. The latest edition, with an introduction by Simon Jones, was published by Continuum in 2005.

[3] See Maxwell E. Johnson, *The Rites of Christian Initiation: Their Evolution and Interpretation* (Collegeville, MN: Liturgical Press, 1999; 2nd ed., 2007), esp. 201–18; Paul F. Bradshaw and Maxwell E. Johnson, *The Origins of Feasts, Fasts and Seasons in Early Christianity*, Alcuin Club Collections 86 (London: SPCK; Collegeville, MN: Liturgical Press, 2011), 75–86.

Syrian sources are aware of an anointing with oil, but occurring before the immersion rather than after it, and apparently in two different forms: one in which the head alone was anointed and related to the gift of the Holy Spirit, and another in which the whole body was anointed as a symbolic protection or healing and the Spirit was associated instead with the water. Only Roman and North African sources reveal the existence of a post-baptismal anointing, but here it was not that action but the laying on of hands with prayer that followed it that was understood as bestowing the Spirit on the newly baptized.[4]

- A growing body of scholars now argue that the roots of Christian eucharistic practice lie not in the Last Supper alone but in the habitual meals that Jesus shared with his disciples and that the first Christians continued on a regular (apparently weekly) basis. Nor was the Eucharist at first a rite within a meal: it *was* the meal and hence took the form that was customary within the particular local cultural environment in which groups of Christians found themselves. In some cases, prayer over the cup apparently preceded prayer over bread at the beginning of the meal; in some cases wine was avoided and water drunk instead; and in some cases what was consumed was related to the remembrance of Jesus' sayings about bread being his body (and wine his blood?), while in other communities this association was not made. It was only much later, in some cases not until well into the third century, that the evening meal as such was abandoned and emphasis put instead on the holy food, which was both distributed and consumed within a communal gathering in a morning and also taken home by participants or sent to those not present for individual consumption later.[5]

- Although the liturgical provisions of the *Apostolic Tradition* were formerly treated as nearly the only solid rock in otherwise shifting sands of early evidence, the authenticity of this church order has now come to be questioned by a number of scholars. Rather

[4] See Johnson, *The Rites of Christian Initiation*, 41–114; Paul F. Bradshaw, *Reconstructing Early Christian Worship* (London: SPCK, 2009; Collegeville, MN: Liturgical Press, 2010), 85–97.

[5] See, in particular, Andrew McGowan, *Ascetic Eucharists* (New York: Oxford University Press, 1999); Paul F. Bradshaw, *Eucharistic Origins* (New York: Oxford University Press, 2004).

> than its being the official handbook of the church at Rome in the third century, these scholars argue that it is an artificial amalgam of traditions from various parts of the ancient Christian world, some elements dating back to very primitive times and other additions not being made until the fourth century. It therefore does not represent the actual practice of any single Christian community, and its eucharistic prayer in particular appears to belong to Eastern Christianity, to West Syria, rather than to Rome.[6]

In the light of the above, what, then, should be the reaction of those responsible for the process of liturgical revision in churches today? Should modern forms of worship be revised again in order to conform more closely to what we now know were the patterns adopted by early Christians? It is important to note that the aims of the twentieth-century liturgical reforms were never to reproduce exactly the earliest known forms of Christian worship or to eliminate all later developments as a departure from the ideal. It was certainly necessary, in the interests of reform and renewal, to get behind some of the accretions and distortions of the tradition that had been introduced, both in the course of the Middle Ages and during and after the sixteenth-century Reformation, in order to get a clearer perspective on the longer-term developments of liturgical practice. Rather than seeking the oldest forms, however, the modern revisers generally settled on the late fourth century as their preferred baseline but willingly included in their new texts features that they knew were introduced only in later periods. One may certainly criticize their choice of the late fourth century as their "golden age" for liturgy, when it seems on the contrary to have been a time when the church was struggling to come to terms with an influx of more "nominal" Christians and seeking to adapt the liturgy to this changed pastoral situation.[7] One may also criticize an occasional tendency to preserve archaisms that are either misleading or completely unintelligible to modern ears rather than to find more suitable

[6] See Paul F. Bradshaw, Maxwell E. Johnson, and L. Edward Phillips, *The Apostolic Tradition: A Commentary* (Minneapolis: Fortress Press, 2002); Matthieu Smyth, "The Anaphora of the So-called 'Apostolic Tradition' and the Roman Eucharistic Prayer," in *Issues in Eucharistic Praying in East and West: Essays in Liturgical and Theological Analysis*, ed. Maxwell E. Johnson (Collegeville, MN: Liturgical Press, 2010), 71–97.

[7] See, for example, Paul F. Bradshaw, "The Fourth Century: A Golden Age for Liturgy?," in *Liturgie und Ritual in der Alten Kirche*, ed. Wolfram Kinzig, Ulrich Volp, and Jochen Schmidt, Patristic Studies 11 (Leuven: Peeters, 2011), 99–115.

alternatives, as, for example, in the Roman Catholic Rite of Christian Initiation of Adults, where the retention of "Rite of Election" carries unfounded connotations of democracy in contemporary minds and the use of the term "mystagogy," if it communicates anything at all to most people, suggests that it is a mystery in a completely unintended sense! But it is surely not fair to accuse the various revisers of wholesale "liturgical fundamentalism."

The aim of these reformers was certainly not, as has sometimes been alleged, to restore what is discovered from the past as normative for the present and to eliminate from modern practice all later developments as inauthentic. As Maxwell Johnson himself has observed: "Archaeologists do not dig beneath the surface of sites where very many generations of peoples have lived and expose the different layers of habitation in order to persuade modern humans to return to the conditions of prehistoric dwellings, nor are liturgical historians bent on excavating the various strata of the past in order to restore some sort of imaginary primitive purity! The gradual development of liturgical practice involved the positive refinement and enrichment of earlier ways of thinking, speaking, and acting, even if it also tended to bring along with it elements of impoverishment and distortion."[8]

As a very obvious example of the desire not to put the clock back to the fourth century absolutely but to include what appeared to be appropriate later developments, we may point out that the text of the eucharistic prayer of the *Apostolic Tradition* has in no instance been adopted verbatim in any church today. On the contrary, various additions and amendments were made to it, as, for example, the near universal insertion of the *Sanctus*. All modern revisers have similarly believed it to be important to include a penitential unit within their eucharistic rites, in spite of the fact that such a thing is never found in the oldest texts that we possess.[9] Because there was no patristic model to follow, there has not been unanimity as to where it should be placed in today's orders—at the beginning in preparation for the whole rite, after the intercessions as part of the response to the proclamation of the Word, or immediately before the reception of Communion?

Of course, even when they have attempted to incorporate elements from early Christian practice, revisers have sometimes failed to capture the essence of their meaning. A clear instance of this is found in what

[8] Maxwell E. Johnson, "Introduction," in *Issues in Eucharistic Praying in East and West*, xv.

[9] On this, see further Bradshaw, *Reconstructing Early Christian Worship*, 132–44.

is often termed in modern rites "the exchange of the peace." Because in all ancient eucharistic sources something like this—although generally described there as "the kiss of peace"—occurs between the end of the intercessions and the presentation of the bread and wine (except at Rome, where it came to occupy a place immediately before communion[10]), it has usually been interpreted by modern revisers as intended to fulfill the injunction of Jesus: "If you are offering your gift on the altar, and there remember that your brother has something against you, leave your gift there before the altar and go, first be reconciled to your brother then come and offer your gift" (Matt 5:23-24).[11] It is true that some ancient texts do understand it as just such a gesture of reconciliation and so the emphasis falls on the word "peace," but this is not how it is interpreted in the oldest sources we possess. There, its connection is seen as being with what precedes rather than what follows. It is said to be "the seal of prayer,"[12] and a proper knowledge of the social conventions surrounding the practice of kissing in Greco-Roman culture helps to illuminate its true significance in those rites. In those days people normally only exchanged kisses with members of their immediate family or very close friends. Thus, for Christians to kiss those with whom they were not so related was in effect to proclaim that these were their true brothers and sisters in the household of faith. Indeed, there is evidence that some Christians took this so seriously that after their conversion they refused to exchange kisses any more with members of their biological family who were not baptized.[13] Thus, the real emphasis was on the act of kissing as a powerful countercultural symbol: it was "the KISS of peace," not "the kiss of PEACE." Modern practice not only interprets the meaning of the gesture differently but usually employs a quite different ritual action—the handshake—which at least in American society is generally reserved as a greeting for those with whom we are not closely connected, not for those in our intimate circle, and so tends to symbolize the opposite of what the earliest Christians were doing. There is no reason why churches should not continue this present practice if they

[10] For a possible reason for this exception, see John F. Baldovin, "The *Fermentum* at Rome in the Fifth Century: A Reconsideration," *Worship* 79, no. 1 (2005): 38–53.

[11] All translations of Scripture in this essay are by the author.

[12] See, e.g., Tertullian, *De oratione* 18.

[13] See further Michael Philip Penn, *Kissing Christians: Ritual and Community in the Late Ancient Church* (Philadelphia: University of Pennsylvania Press, 2005).

judge it to be pastorally valuable, but they should not be labeling it as "doing what the early church did."

Another example of a common symbolic action based on ancient practice but generally failing to communicate its original significance is the offertory procession or presentation of the eucharistic bread and wine. In most churches this simply involves two people carrying these elements from a small table placed near the back of the church down to the front to hand over to the presiding minister or his or her assistants to place on the altar or holy table. The twentieth-century Liturgical Movement, which introduced this custom as one of its principal expressions (along with moving the holy table away from the wall, about which more later), informed people that they were thus "doing what the early church did" and that the action symbolized the offering to God of themselves, their souls and bodies, their work and life, through the ministry of their representatives. Unfortunately, many members of congregations have failed to visualize those carrying the gifts as being their representatives because they themselves did not elect or appoint them to this task, and in most cases every member of a congregation does not eventually get to take a turn at doing this, but it tends instead to be restricted to a relatively small number of people who can be relied upon to be present when needed and to be willing to do it without too much persuasion. Moreover, what was usually omitted in the description of "what the early church did" was that in those distant days people did not simply carry things from one place to another in the building. Just as they had formerly done when the Eucharist was a complete meal, they continued to bring their contributions of bread and wine from home themselves. What they presented was truly their own offering, not something thrust into their hands by others. And in some places, including Rome, they did not actually carry it to the altar themselves, but it was collected from them. Once again, modern revisers, in their enthusiasm to replicate the past, have got hold of the wrong part of the action as being of the greatest significance. Those congregations that today have some of their members actually baking the bread to be used in the service come closer to ancient practice, though such a custom is not without its risks with regard to the quality of what is produced, and those risks are greatly magnified if wine is included in this process as well.

What, then, should be the relationship between research into the earliest known Christian worship practices and the composition or revision of modern liturgical texts? Should historical study be viewed as "pure" scholarship, without any connection to what may be going on in today's church? To some extent yes, because past research has sometimes suffered unfortunate consequences from too close an association with the issues current in the world of the researcher. Investigation into the history and origin of particular liturgical practices has rarely been completely divorced from a desire either to legitimate that practice in the present or to find grounds for changing or removing it from current use. This inevitably affected, however unconsciously, the way in which scholars evaluated the evidence they were examining. So, for example, those who have concluded that the meal ritual in chapters 9 and 10 of the early church order known as the *Didache*, which lack any reference to the Last Supper or to the bread and wine being the Body and Blood of Christ, cannot have been a Eucharist have generally been those who come from one of the ecclesiastical traditions that believe consecration to be effected by the recitation of the words of Jesus at the Supper.[14] Similarly, those who claim to discern some apostolic roots for the practice of confirmation, whether located before or after the baptismal immersion and whether by anointing or the laying on of hands, have again generally been those coming from ecclesiastical traditions in which the rite of confirmation continues to be practiced.[15] Gerard Rouwhorst has also pointed out that the conclusions reached in three major dissertations on the subject of the Sabbath and the early Christian Sunday strikingly match the practices of the particular ecclesial denomination to which each of the authors belongs.[16]

On the other hand, there are numerous historical areas that would probably never have been examined at all had it not been for related questions having arisen in today's church. The most obvious example of this is the study of the place of women in worship and ministry.[17] What is needed is not to allow the modern agenda to dictate the con-

[14] For example, Dix, *The Shape of the Liturgy*, 48 (note 2), 90ff.; Kurt Niederwimmer, *The Didache: A Commentary*, Hermeneia (Minneapolis: Fortress Press, 1998), 142–43.

[15] See, for example, J. D. C. Fisher, *Confirmation Then and Now*, Alcuin Club Collections 60 (London: SPCK, 1978; Chicago: Liturgy Training Publications, 2005).

[16] Gerard Rouwhorst, "The Reception of the Jewish Sabbath in Early Christianity," in *Christian Feast and Festival*, ed. Paul Post and others (Leuven: Peeters, 2001), 223–66, here at 226–36. The three authors were Samuele Bacchiocchi, Corrada Mosna, and Willy Rordorf.

[17] See, for example, Carolyn Osiek, Margaret Y. MacDonald, with Janet H. Tulloch, *A Woman's Place: House Churches in Earliest Christianity* (Minneapolis: Fortress

clusions that are reached but to strive to achieve a triumph of scholarship over churchmanship.

If, then, we are not to try to imitate slavishly the findings of recent research but to learn from them judiciously, in what ways may the changes of historical perspective outlined earlier in this essay help to illuminate our approach to worship today?

Baptism at Easter

The discovery that not all early Christian baptisms took place at Easter does not mean that an emphasis on Easter baptism is *wrong*, just that it is not the only "right answer." Nor should we tell people without qualification that we should do it "because that is what the early church did." In any case, we need a *theological* and not just a historical reason to do something. Easter baptism can be defended as a particularly appropriate expression of the theology of dying and rising with Christ articulated in chapter 6 of the letter to the Romans—but that is not the only interpretation of baptism in the New Testament, nor even the dominant one among Christians of the first few centuries. We need to ensure, therefore, that our explanation of the meaning of baptism draws on the full riches of the images and metaphors used for it in the Scriptures, and above all the theme of being born anew that is so fully set out in John 3; that our rites themselves reflect this same richness; and that we recognize that other times of year may be equally appropriate as Easter. Maxwell Johnson himself has suggested the possibility that Pentecost may have been the oldest regular occasion for baptism and not just an "overflow" from Easter.[18]

The Place of Confirmation

Although valiant efforts have been made to defend the apostolic origin of the rite of confirmation, it becomes increasingly difficult to do so as historical research proceeds. Whatever may have been the

---

Press, 2006); Teresa Berger, *Gender Differences and the Making of Liturgical History: Lifting a Veil on Liturgy's Past* (Burlington, VT: Ashgate, 2011).

[18] Maxwell E. Johnson, "Tertullian's '*Diem baptismo sollemniorem*' Revisited: A Tentative Hypothesis on Baptism at Pentecost," in *Studia Liturgica Diversa: Essays in Honor of Paul F. Bradshaw*, ed. Maxwell E. Johnson and L. Edward Phillips (Portland, OR: Pastoral Press, 2004), 31–44.

significance of the post-baptismal imposition of hands recorded in the book of Acts (8:14-17; 19:1-7), it is clear that the great majority of early Christian churches throughout the ancient world did not perpetuate that practice in their initiation rituals. Only North Africa and Rome retained something resembling it and understood it to be invoking the Holy Spirit. It is true that some, but not all, early Eastern rites had a pre-baptismal anointing of the head that was understood as conferring the Holy Spirit and that later all Eastern rites adopted a post-baptismal anointing that signified sealing with the Spirit. But to say that either of these is the exact equivalent of the Western post-baptismal laying on of hands is to stretch a line to breaking point.

Although all Christian traditions have believed that the Holy Spirit is received when a person becomes a Christian, there is no one universally espoused symbol of that gift, and therefore to insist that any baptismal rite that lacks a particular form of its expression is somehow deficient is to fly in the face of the historical evidence. In any case, while various ancillary rites—anointings, imposition of hands, giving of lighted candles, and so on—may *explicate* the central act of the profession of faith and immersion in water and help to draw out aspects of its meaning, baptism is always full initiation into Christ and his church even without any of these being present. One is either a Christian or one is not. Expressions such as the forgiveness of sins, new birth, dying and rising with Christ, being illuminated, and being sealed with the Spirit are different ways of speaking about the one reality, not different things that may or may not happen to someone being initiated and certainly not things that must occur in a particular temporal sequence. There may still be a place for a pastoral rite by which a person who was baptized in infancy, and especially any who have been alienated from the church in the intervening period, may make a personal profession of faith, even though there is no ancient precedent for such a rite, but that is quite a different matter.

Eucharist as Meal

The twentieth-century Liturgical Movement had been well aware of the meal character of early eucharistic practice, and this insight had been part of its desire to encourage what is often called "celebration facing the people." This way of describing it is not very helpful because it implies that this is the most important purpose of moving the altar or holy table away from the wall of the church so that the presiding minister can stand behind it. In reality, its true aim was that its nature as table might be more clearly seen and that the presider and people might gather around it. Sadly, as is well known, this objective has not always been achieved. Altars that looked fine when against the wall have often turned out to be inappropriately shaped for the new position, resembling a shop counter rather than a table as such and constituting more of a barrier between minister and people than an enabler of corporate celebration. And only in a few places has any real gathering around it been achieved: frequently the people are still placed on only one side of it rather than on three sides and, in any case, still at a considerable distance from it.

The Liturgical Movement also encouraged the idea of associating some form of socializing over food and drink with a celebration of the Eucharist, ideally a "parish breakfast" following it. But because of the problematic logistics of such an undertaking, this is often simply a "coffee hour" in the church porch or parish hall, for which only a proportion of the congregation generally stay—and thus a case of good intentions that have been only partially successful. For those who do participate in this social activity, relationships between worshipers have been greatly enhanced over against the situation where the only human contact was a handshake from the minister at the door after the service, and sometimes not even that if an introverted communicant left promptly and was able to make it out of the church before the minister reached the door. But it has mostly not succeeded in drawing all who attend the Eucharist into this circle, remaining as an optional extra and, in any case, resulting in Eucharist and social event still being seen as two separate activities rather than helping a congregation to experience Eucharist as meal.

Now that scholarly research has enabled us to appreciate better the importance of the meal character of the earliest forms of Eucharist, however, in which both the building up of the Body of Christ through interaction between participants and the practical care for the needy were as essential elements as the reception of bread and wine, is there anything that can be done to enhance these aspects for today's congregations? To set the Eucharist within a full meal is clearly impractical in all but the smallest of gatherings and, in any case, would present difficulties of comprehension in a culture where, unlike that of the first Jewish Christians, everyday meals are not generally thought of as having a sacred character. But more might be done in other ways to give the rite a greater sense of being a meal. Even where a major and potentially very expensive reordering of the building to make possible a true gathering around the altar/holy table is not a practical possibility, a relatively small congregation might be persuaded to leave their seats and stand close to it in a circle during the eucharistic action itself and to receive Communion there.

At the very least, consideration might be given to the way in which Communion is distributed. Standing in long lines to receive the bread and wine one by one from ministers may have a long history behind it, but it does nothing to enhance the sense of feeding together at the Lord's table. It is more reminiscent for some people of standing in line to receive charitable handouts. There may be no real alternative to the use of "communion stations" when there are very large numbers of communicants, but in other situations it might be possible for them to be arranged around three sides of the altar/holy table and to receive Communion together "as tables" before returning to their places in a group together rather than simply receiving as individuals.

For the first few generations of Christians, however, their regular shared meals were more than occasions for building up the body of Christ. They were a practical and not just a symbolic expression of the sacrificial love for one another that was meant to characterize the new movement. Many believers lived in such poverty that the food provided on these occasions by wealthier members of the community and also given to them to take home afterward to consume during the week was vital to their physical well-being. It is no wonder therefore that one of the names given to these meals was not Eucharist but *agape*—the Greek word for "love."[19] The confession of God's love for all in sending Jesus Christ summoned them to show their love for one another. This intrinsic link between being fed at the Eucharist and sharing food with the needy has been eroded over the centuries, first by the substitution of money for actual foodstuffs brought from home and then by the tendency to take a collection of money at every kind of religious service rather than at the Eucharist alone. Those churches that do encourage members of the congregation to bring items of food and drink to church with them on occasions and to have them brought up along with the bread and wine during the service for later distribution to those in need are obviously trying to do something to restore

[19] See Andrew B. McGowan, "Naming the Feast: *Agape* and the Diversity of Early Christian Meals," *Studia Patristica* 30 (1997): 314–18.

that connection, and those that have the members prepare and cook a meal to share with the disadvantaged of the neighborhood immediately after the Eucharist is over are taking a further step. But it is also important to try to think of ways of making the connection between the rite and those in other parts of the world who lack not only food but very often a supply of clean water also. As St. Paul warned the church at Corinth, when some indulge their appetites to excess while others go hungry, "it is not the Lord's Supper that you are eating" (1 Cor 11:20).

The So-Called *Apostolic Tradition*

The primary reason why a version of the eucharistic prayer from this church order was adopted in modern times by the Roman Catholic Church was that the original was thought to be authentically Roman in origin, but significantly different from the later Roman Canon of the Mass, especially because it included an invocation of the Holy Spirit otherwise absent from the Roman tradition but characteristic of the prayers from Eastern churches. Other churches followed suit not so much because of the alleged Roman origin but on the grounds of its apparent early date of composition—the beginning of the third century—and thus seemingly far older than any other eucharistic prayers that were known, except for the meal prayers in the *Didache*, about which there was uncertainty whether they had been intended for a Eucharist as such or not. Now that serious doubts have been raised about both the date and place of composition of the *Apostolic Tradition*, should not its use be discontinued?

This verdict does not necessarily follow, but we may certainly question the primacy that it often seems to be given in some places of worship. Even in those denominations that provide quite a wide range of alternative texts, this particular prayer appears to be used more often than the others, although one suspects that sometimes this may be because of its relative brevity in comparison with other authorized texts rather than because of its antiquity. This is a pity, because one prayer alone cannot convey the fullness of the theology of the Eucharist, and consequently congregations are being deprived of experiences that would broaden their understanding and deepen their spirituality. For example, the eucharistic prayer produced by the Consultation on Common Texts in the United States and based on the classic anaphora of St. Basil from the East that forms the basis of Prayer IV of the

Roman Catholic Church and Prayer D of the Episcopal Church, among others, offers a much richer alternative. Thus, when the time comes for different churches to contemplate a further revision of their eucharistic texts, the question of whether or not to retain the prayer derived from that in the *Apostolic Tradition* should be decided purely upon the theological and linguistic merits of the composition and not upon its alleged superior antiquity, still less upon its relative brevity. It can claim no privileged place in the repertoire over other ancient prayers.

Conclusion

The findings of historical research, therefore, should not be able to claim normative status in the sense that modern liturgical practice should be forced to follow slavishly some presumed original pattern that was handed down by the apostles as a norm to be observed throughout all ages. Indeed, the very findings of modern historical research reject the idea that there ever was such a thing as *the* apostolic liturgy and on the contrary see diversity over many aspects of Christian practice as having existed from the first. Variety tended to decrease rather than increase as time went by, especially in the fourth century onward. On the other hand, as the above examples have sought to illustrate, the results of research into Christian origins can rightly claim some sort of *illuminative* status—not models to be copied but the basis of insights that may be adapted to contemporary culture and used to bring out deeper significance in the rites that are celebrated. This includes recognizing that the tradition does not present us with just one right answer—that there can be a variety of expression. For example, Easter is not the only appropriate time for Christian initiation; the gift of the Spirit in baptism can be expressed in different ways; the fourfold shape of the Eucharist does not have to be the only pattern of eucharistic celebration thought to be legitimate; and the West Syrian shape is not the only form that modern eucharistic prayers should take. But illumination should go way beyond acknowledging this primitive diversity and recover other aspects of liturgical theology that have been lost or diminished in the course of history, among them the richness of baptismal imagery and the significance of the Eucharist as meal.

What is needed for this endeavor is a proper understanding of inculturation, both of the ancient culture in which the original practice emerged and of the modern culture on which it is desired to shed illumination. Otherwise, one ends up with either a shallow imitation of the superficial features of the liturgical act that fails to capture its true significance, as in the case of the offertory procession discussed earlier in this essay, or else a mistaken attempt to embody the alleged inner meaning in a quite different ritual form that results in sending a quite different message, as in the case of the exchange of the peace. In both instances, a lack of sufficient understanding of the historical and cultural background of the original and an insufficient grasp of its equivalent in the culture of today has caused these well-meaning efforts at "ritual translation" to miss their mark. The same is usually true of attempts to "translate" Jesus' washing of the feet of the disciples at the Last Supper into modern dress, such as the clergy polishing the shoes of members of the congregation, certainly an act of human kindness but not a true equivalent of the task of a slave in first-century Palestine toward his master and the master's aristocratic friends. Nor is the version of the ceremony adopted by kings and queens of England since the eighteenth century, in which they have handed out gifts to the poor in place of the actual washing of feet, even though their attendants continue to be vested in the towels needed for the original ritual gesture. In the first attempt, the parish clergy are not the social superiors of the congregation stooping to an act of great humility; in the second, the monarch is distributing the largesse of the economically and socially superior without any shade of humility.

Moreover, a little greater knowledge of the true history of this liturgical rite would show that even its traditional form had undergone a significant modification from its original context and meaning. It is first known to us clearly as a fourth-century ancillary in some baptismal rites, especially those of North Italy, although Martin Connell has plausibly suggested that its true root may be not as a supplement to full-body immersion but as an alternative initiation practice in some very early Christian communities.[20] In this baptismal context, the spotlight falls more on the need for those being baptized to humble themselves to accept the ministrations of another than on the show of humility of the person performing the act of service—exactly the opposite of its meaning when transferred to Holy Thursday! Most of

[20] Martin F. Connell, "*Nisi pedes*, Except for the Feet: Footwashing in the Community of St. John's Gospel," *Worship* 70, no. 6 (1996): 517–31. See also Johnson, *The Rites of Christian Initiation*, 21–23.

us are happier performing services for others than allowing others to perform acts of service to us—and especially ones that involve considerable intimacy. To replace ritual gestures that require intimate physical contact with those that put some distance between giver and receiver and so depersonalize the actions, such as substituting an outstretched arm in blessing for the laying of the hand on the head, the antiseptic dab of oil on the forehead for its being poured over and rubbed into the skin, the kissing of a wooden board for actual contact with another human being (as happened to the peace in the Middle Ages[21]), or self-administered Communion for the intimacy of being fed by another that otherwise normally only happens to the very young and very old in society—all such modifications destroy the potency of the symbolic act. Having one's shoes cleaned is not the equivalent of having one's bare feet gently massaged in warm water. Nor is a footwashing performed tentatively by the parish priest on twelve embarrassed-looking "volunteers" sitting on a bench at the front while the rest of the congregation simply watch from a safe distance the same as inviting everyone to take part, from the youngest child to the oldest senior citizen. Insisting that each one must first have his or her feet washed by someone else before he or she may wash the feet of another comes closer to capturing the essence of the early ritual and of the sacramental act of Jesus in the Fourth Gospel: "Unless I wash you, you have no part with me" (John 13:8). We cannot serve until we have discovered what it is to be served.

As in so much else of life, good intentions on their own are not enough when it comes to liturgical revision or innovation. If we are not to miss the point more often than we need to do, we must combine the finest historical research with a deep sensitivity to the nature of symbolism, to contemporary culture and to the psychology of worship. Anything less weakens our ability to communicate the depth of the treasures of our Christian past to the hunger for spirituality that is so evident in people today and can leave them with little more than the froth on the surface for their liturgical diet.

[21] See Miri Rubin, *Corpus Christi: The Eucharist in Late Medieval Culture* (Cambridge: Cambridge University Press, 1991), 74–76.

Robert F. Taft, SJ, FBA

Chapter 2

Between Progress and Nostalgia: Liturgical Reform and the Western Romance with the Christian East; Strategies and Realities*

1. No Liturgical Reform in the Orthodox East?

During the period of the pre–Vatican II "Liturgical Movement" in the West, it was thought that the very idea of "liturgical reform" was totally foreign to the mentality and history of the Eastern Christian churches. Authoritative protagonists and historians of the Liturgical Movement like Dom Olivier Rousseau, erudite Benedictine of the Monastery of Amay-Chevetogne, wrote, "There can be no question of a 'liturgical movement' in the Orthodox Church," because "the Orthodox Church has preserved the liturgical spirit of the Early Church, and continues to live by this spirit, to drink from it as from its purest source. . . . This Church has never departed in its piety and its offices from the liturgical spirit of the Early Church, to which it has always remained faithful."[1]

* A much shorter version of this paper was given as a lecture at the Lehrstuhl für Liturgiewissenschaft in the Faculty of Catholic Theology of the University of Vienna on June 1, 2009. An earlier Italian redaction of that talk, "Rinnovamento liturgico e Oriente cristiano prima, durante e dopo il Concilio Vaticano II," delivered at the Pontificio Istituto Liturgico Sant'Anselmo, Rome, during the symposium *Sacrosanctum Concilium 40 anni dopo. Giornata di Studio per commemorare la Costituzione sulla Liturgia, 11 dicembre 2003*, appeared in *Oecumenica Civitas* (Livorno, 2009), 17–29. Parts of the paper are dependent on some of my other writings, esp. "'Eastern Presuppositions' and Western Liturgical Renewal," *Antiphon* 5, no. 1 (2000): 10–22, and others cited in the footnotes. I am indebted to my former student and graduate assistant, Sr. Dr. Vassa Larin, presently teaching at the Lehrstuhl für Liturgiewissenschaft in the Faculty of Catholic Theology of the University of Vienna, for proofreading an earlier draft of this paper, correcting typographical errors, and suggesting clarifications and improvements.

[1] "C'est un truisme dans le monde catholique que l'Église orthodoxe a conservé l'esprit liturgique de l'ancienne Église, et qu'elle continue d'en vivre, de s'y

So we must ask ourselves, then, if the very idea of a liturgical reform is not an exclusively Western phenomenon. That seems to be what those like Dom Rousseau would say, continuing to believe that the oriental liturgies go back unchanged to the time of the apostles and have remained unchanged until today. That's the myth. Let us take a look now at the reality.

2. The Dynamics of Liturgical Reform: *Historia—Theoria*

In their mystagogical commentaries on the liturgy, Byzantine fathers and commentators use a method similar to the scriptural exegetes, first telling what actually happens—the *historia*—then proposing the *theoria* or contemplation of the spiritual meaning underlying this *historia*. I shall follow this same method here, first the *historia*, then the *theoria*, which is far more important: for what interests me is not the history but the underlying ideology that controlled it.

Historia: Several years ago the periodical *Peiraïki Ekklesia*, official organ of the Greek Orthodox Eparchy of Piraeus, published in the March 1997 issue a photograph of a Greek Orthodox priest celebrating the Orthodox Eucharist *versus populum* at an altar placed on the floor of the nave in front of the traditional iconostasis of the enclosed Byzantine sanctuary.

Theoria: More important than the story is the argumentation: the blurb accompanying the photo says, "The liturgy was celebrated in the center of the church in the ancient way" (p. 74). A startling liturgical innovation, unheard of in any Eastern rite, is justified by appeal to ancient tradition—just as was done in the Western liturgical movement to support the *versus populum* position. That the facts may not justify this appeal to the past is irrelevant, just as is totally irrelevant the appeal to the past among those in the Catholic West today who controvert the *versus populum* position by trying to show it was not, in fact, as traditional in antiquity as its promoters would claim. In either case, the facts are beside the point. The dynamics involved have nothing to do with conclusions from liturgical history. Rather, it is a question of

---

aboucher comme à sa source la plus pure. . . . Il ne saurait question de «mouvement liturgique» dans l'Église orthodoxe. Cette Église ne s'est jamais écartée, dans sa piété de celle de ses offices, et elle y est toujours restée également fidèle" (Olivier Rousseau, *Histoire du mouvement liturgique*, Lex orandi 3 [Paris: Éditions du Cerf, 1945], 188).

seeking precedents in earlier or Eastern tradition for what one has already decided to do. We are dealing, in short, with the strategies reformers employ to claim authority for their views.

3. Eastern Liturgy through Western Eyes

The first thing to note is that the Vatican II "preferential option" for the East was by no means something one could have automatically anticipated. A prime mover of the modern Catholic liturgical movement, Abbot Dom Prosper Guéranger of Solesmes (1805–75), treated Eastern liturgy with derision and contempt. Chapter 9 of his monumental *Institutions liturgiques* is full of outrageous statements like "one must note in the Greek liturgy a particular quality which admirably denotes the degradation of the Church that employs it. This quality . . . is a crude immobilism that renders it impervious to any progress. . . . The Greek Church has become impotent at renewal in its own core, since schism and heresy have paralyzed it at the heart."[2] In brief, the Eastern rites are the liturgical "families of a degenerate Christianity."[3] Guéranger's tirade, of course, had nothing to do with the East: he chose to slander the Orthodox East in order to firm up his plaidoyer for liturgical uniformity in France.

With all this anti-Eastern negativity at the very origins of the liturgical movement, what could have induced the council fathers of Vatican II (1962–65) to turn eastward for positive paradigms to imitate? The answer, I think, is what I would call "the myth of Eastern liturgy." The philosopher Karl Popper said the world as we know it is our interpretation of observable facts in the light of theories of our own invention. In other words, we invent our world even while we think we are just observing it and reporting on it. Of nothing is this truer than of the Western study of Eastern liturgy, which from the start has taken as its point of departure not anything in Eastern liturgy but the felt needs of

[2] *Institutions liturgiques*, 2nd ed., 4 vols. (Paris/Brussels: Sociéte générale de librairie catholique, 1878), 1:226–27: "on doit remarquer dans la Liturgie grecque un caractère particulier qui dénote admirablement la dégradation de l'Église qui l'emploie. Ce caractère . . . est une immobilité brute qui la rend inaccessible à tout progrès. . . . L'Église grecque est devenue comme impuissisante à en proclamer de nouveaux, dans son propre sein, du moment que le schisme et l'hérésie l'ont paralysée au cœur." The first edition of this famous work was published in 3 volumes at Paris in 1840–52.

[3] Ibid., 1:229: "familles d'un christianisme dégénéré."

the Western viewer. The process began in the sixteenth century, when the first serious studies and translations of Eastern liturgies were apologetic in intent, done mostly by German Catholics actively engaged in defending Catholic theological positions during the Reformation upheaval.[4] And so it remained until the more objective and disinterested scholarship of the twentieth century.[5]

By the middle of the eighteenth century things had begun to sour when the presumed superiority of Latin liturgical usages, famously formulated in the "praestantia ritus latini," attributed (mistakenly) to Benedict XIV's Brief *Etsi pastoralis* of May 26, 1742, was actively fostered by some Catholics of those pre–Vatican II days.[6] We have

[4] Cf. Anselm Strittmatter, "Missa Treverensis seu Sancti Simeonis Syracusani," *Studia Gratiana* 14 (1967): 495–518, esp. 508 note 39; Angelus Walz, "Pelargus," in *Lexikon für Theologie und Kirche*, 2nd ed. (Freiburg: Herder, 1963), 8:251–52; idem, "Ambrogio Pelargo a Trento," in *Il Concilio di Trento e la riforma tridentina. Atti del Convengo storico internazionale (Trento 2–6 settembre 1963)*, vol. 2 (Rome: Herder, 1965), 749–66. In this same context we should place the 1563 *editio princeps* of the *Apostolic Constitutions* (Venice: Ex officina Jordani Zilati, 1563) by the Spaniard Francesco Torres (d. 1584). Torres, whose name is usually Latinized as Franciscus Turrianus or Torrens, was born at Herrera in the Diocese of Valencia ca. 1509, assisted at the Council of Trent as papal theologian, entered the Jesuits in 1566, and died at Rome in 1584. Cf. Marcel Metzger, ed., *Les Constitutions apostoliques*, vol. 1, Sources chrétiennes 320 (Paris: Éditions du Cerf, 1985), 75; Giovanni Mercati, "Note on the Manuscripts of the Apostolic Constitutions Used in the *editio princeps*," *The Journal of Theological Studies* 15 (1914): 453–54. Torres later published the first Latin translation of the same invaluable document (Antwerp: Ex officina Christophori Plantini, 1578). Cf. Carlos Sommervogel, *Bibliothèque de la Compagnie de Jésus*, 11 vols. (Brussels: O. Schepens; Paris: A. Picard, 1830–1932), 8:115 no. 3.

[5] For more on this, see Robert F. Taft, "'Eastern Presuppositions' and Western Liturgical Renewal"; and esp. idem, "From Polemicists to Promoters: The Jesuits and the Liturgical Traditions of the Christian East," forthcoming from *Orientalia Christiana Periodica*.

[6] Giuseppe M. Croce, *La Badia Greca di Grottaferrata e la rivista "Roma e l'Oriente,"* 2 vols. (Vatican City: Libreria Editrice Vaticana, 1990), 1:13–15 note 60. Contrary to popular opinion, Benedict XIV did not, in fact, use the expression "praestantia ritus latini," universally attributed to him, nor did he assert *the liturgical superiority* of the Roman Rite. What he does affirm is its *canonical preeminence* in Italy as the rite of the primatial see: "Since it is the rite of the Holy Roman Church, mother and teacher of all Churches, it is above the Greek rite and prevails especially in the Italian regions where the Greeks are subject to the Latin bishops [eo quod sit ritus sanctae Romanae Ecclesiae omnium Ecclesiarum matris et magistrae, sit supra graecum ritum praevalet maxime in italibus regionibus, ubi latinis Episcopis Graeci subiecti sunt]" (Benedicti PP. XIV, *Bulla "Etsi pastoralis" de dogmatibus et*

already seen how this was exploited a century later by Guéranger, who disparaged Eastern liturgy as a means of promoting Roman usage.

Less than two generations after Guéranger, however, in the debacle following World War I, the Benedictine-fueled Catholic liturgical movement will turn Guéranger's equally Benedictine-revival romanticism on its head, and Catholic enthusiasts like the Benedictines of Amay/Chevetogne, among them Dom Olivier Rousseau, OSB, one of the early historians of the Liturgical Movement, will produce an equally romantic lyrical vision of Eastern liturgy that has lasted more or less until our own day.[7]

This is the intellectual context in which I would like to consider the role of early and Eastern liturgy in the Roman Rite liturgical reforms carried out under the mandate of Vatican II.

4. *Ecclesia Semper Reformanda*

That context goes far beyond liturgical renewal. For what we are dealing with is not just the liturgical life of the church, which the Vatican II Constitution on the Sacred Liturgy, *Sacrosanctum Concilium*, defined as its source and supreme expression (SC 2). For that life, according to the same council, must always find itself engaged in the process of renewal in Christ through the working of the Holy Spirit: whence the constantly repeated Vatican II maxim, *Ecclesia semper reformanda—a Church always needing reform*, i.e., always challenging

---

ritibus ab Italo-Graecis tenendis atque servandis [Rome: Typographia Polyglotta Sacrae Congregationis de Propaganda fide, 1889], 8).

[7] In postwar Germany, however, where the Baumstark school of comparative liturgy began to use texts rather than rose-colored glasses as the lens through which to view Eastern liturgy, things began to acquire a more realistic perspective. On Baumstark and his œuvre, see Frederick Sommers West, *Anton Baumstark's Comparative Liturgy in Its Intellectual Context* (Ann Arbor, MI: University Microfilms International, 1988); idem. *The Comparative Liturgy of Anton Baumstark*, Alcuin Club & GROW Liturgical Studies 31 (Bramcote: Grove Books, 1995); Robert F. Taft and Gabriele Winkler, eds., *Acts of the International Congress Comparative Liturgy Fifty Years after Anton Baumstark (1872–1948), Rome, 25–29 September 1998*, Orientalia Christiana Analecta 265 (Rome: Pontificio Istituto Orientale, 2001); Robert F. Taft, "Anton Baumstark's Comparative Liturgy Revisited," in ibid., 191–232; Robert F. Taft, "Comparative Liturgy Fifty Years after Anton Baumstark (d. 1948): A Reply to Recent Critics," *Worship* 73, no. 6 (1999): 521–40. As West has shown, Baumstark too had his ideological presuppositions, and his work, like the work of everyone, must be viewed in the context of the intellectual history of his day.

itself by the Word and Will of God to be ever more fully, more truly, the Church as God wants it to be.

The liturgical movements of modern times did not exist in a vacuum. They were but one aspect of the ongoing renewal of God's churches that must always characterize their life. Without this broader context, the striving for liturgical renewal runs the risk of degenerating into a concern for liturgical haberdashery and paraphernalia, as in a press release I caught online that breathtakingly recounted how on his October 19, 2008, pilgrimage to the sanctuary of Our Lady of Pompei Pope Benedict XVI changed his pontifical footwear three times!

So modern liturgical renewal, both Catholic and Orthodox, was of a piece with a concomitant return to the fathers of the church. Long before anyone ever heard of Georges Florovsky (1893–1979) and his plea at the First Congress of Orthodox Theology in Athens, November 29 to December 6, 1936, that Orthodox theology free itself from its Western captivity and return to the fathers of the church,[8] movements

[8] See Georges Florovsky, *Collected Works*, vol. 4: *Aspects of Church History* (Belmont, MA: Nordland Publishing Co., 1975), 177–82, esp. 163, where he first uses the term "pseudo-morphosis," a term not original to him, for what he considered the Western captivity of Orthodox theology of the day. On the term's origins, and for further references to where Florovsky repeats and develops his thesis, see Dorothea Wendebourg, "'Pseudomorphosis'—ein theologisches Urteil als Axiom der kirchen- und theologiegeschichtlichen Forschung," in Robert Taft, ed., *The Christian East: Its Institutions and Its Thought; A Critical Reflection; Papers of the International Scholarly Congress for the 75th Anniversary of the Pontifical Oriental Institute, Rome, 30 May–5 June 1993*, Orientalia Christiana Analecta 251 (Rome: Pontificio Istituto Orientale, 1996), 565–89, here 565 note 2; English trans. "'Pseudomorphosis': A Theological Judgement as an Axiom for Research in the History of Church and Theology," *The Greek Orthodox Theological Review* 42, nos. 3–4 (1997): 321–42, here 334 note 2; also Gerhard Podskalsky, "Ostkirchliche theologie in der Westkirche: Alternative (Antithese), Annex oder Allheilmittel?," in Taft, *The Christian East*, 531–54. On the same topic, see most recently Johannes Oeldemann, "Pseudomorphose oder Komplementarität? Historische Entwicklung und heutige Bewertung gegenseitige Einflüsse der Theologie in Ost und West," in *Ost- un Westerweiterung in Theologie: 20 Jahre Orthodoxe Theologie in München*, ed. Th. Nikolaou with K. Nikolakopoulos and A. Anapliotis (Münchener Universitäts Schriften, Reihe: Veröffentlichungen des Instituts für Orthodoxe Theologie, Bd. 9 Erzabtei St. Ottilien, 2006), 51–60. For more objective evaluations of Western influence on Orthodox theology, see Paul Meyendorff, "The Liturgical Reforms of Peter Moghila: A New Look," *St. Vladimir's Theological Quarterly* 29, no. 2 (1985): 101–14; and, more recently, Max J. Okenfuss, *The Rise and Fall of Latin Humanism in Early-Modern Russia: Pagan Authors, Ukrainians, and the Resiliency of Muscovy*, Brill's Studies in Intellectual History, vol. 64 (Leiden: E.J. Brill, 1995).

toward patristic and scriptural renewal in East and West were nurturing the concomitant impulse toward liturgical renewal.[9]

For there have been numerous "returns to the fathers" in the history of Christian theology since the beginnings of "patrology," or the science of the study of the fathers, a term first used by the Lutheran theologian Johannes Gerhard (d. 1637) in his work *Patrologia*, published in 1653, though the science itself can be said to go back to St. Jerome's inaccurate and tendentious *De viris illustribus* in AD 392,[10] and in the ninth-century Byzantine East to St. Photios's *Myriobiblia* or *Bibliotheca*. After Photios there is a gap when little valuable or new was written on the fathers until the Reformation upheaval stimulated a first Catholic "return to the fathers" by writers such as Jesuit St. Robert Bellarmine, *De scriptoribus ecclesiasticis liber unus* (1613).

In the Orthodox East a similar "return" originates a century later with St. Paisij Velichkovskij (1722–94). Born in what is now Ukraine in a frontier area of ever-shifting borders, Paisij is claimed as their own by Ukrainians, Romanians, and Russians. His influence on the *startsy* of the Optina Pustyn, especially his translation of the *Philokalia*, helped stimulate the enormous enterprise of nineteenth-century Russian translations of the fathers and the broad movement of Orthodox theological and spiritual renewal still felt today.[11] Meanwhile, in the West the nineteenth century saw the beginnings of the great patristic

[9] For summary histories of patristics or patrology, see Berthold Altaner, *Patrology* (New York: Herder & Herder, 1961), 1–12; and esp. Johannes Quasten, *Patrology*, vol. 1: *The Beginnings of Christian Literature* (Utrecht/Brussels: Spectrum, 1975), 1–22.The final "return," still reverberating today, began with the Paris- and Lyon-Fourvière-centered Catholic revival following the debacle of France's ignominious defeat in World War II, with its *ressourcement* and *retour aux Pères* movement of theological and liturgical renewal via a return to the sources and the fathers that were the slogans and program of the day, with its incomparable Jesuit Sources chrétiennes series (Paris: Éditions du Cerf, 1941–) that Jesuits Henri de Lubac and Jean Danièlou founded at Lyon-Fourvière in 1940. This movement would influence Orthodoxy of the Russian diaspora via the works of Alexander Schmemann and others: see John Meyendorff, "A Life Worth Living," *St. Vladimir's Theological Quarterly* 28, no. 1 (1984): 3–10; reprinted in *Liturgy and Tradition: Theological Reflections of Alexander Schmemann*, ed. Thomas Fisch (Crestwood, NY: St. Vladimir's Seminary Press, 1990), 145–54, and as the afterword to *The Journals of Father Alexander Schmemann 1973–1983*, trans. Juliana Schmemann (Crestwood, NY: St. Vladimir's Seminary Press, 2000), 343–51.

[10] *Patrologia Latina* 23:601–720.

[11] I am indebted to my colleague Sr. Dr. Vassa Larin for the information on St. Paisij and the patristic movement in Russia.

collections such as Jacques-Paul Migne's *Patrologia Graeca* and *Patrologia Latina*, still indispensable today.[12]

Beyond the Catholic-Orthodox world, by the end of the nineteenth century the Anglicans enter the field. The Oxford school of Eastern liturgy develops as a spinoff of the Oxford Movement for re-catholicizing the Church of England, in which a return to the fathers fostered by Newman and others was seminal, as was the concomitant interest in Eastern liturgy reflected in the writings of the Oxford school of Hammond, Swainson, Brightman, and Conybeare, to which one must add the name of the Catholic autodidact Edmund Bishop of the Cambridge school.[13]

More important for us here, the great Russian Orthodox school of liturgiology is born, the first serious and systematic study of liturgy in the Orthodox world since the seventeenth-century reforms of St. Peter Mohyla (1596–1646), metropolitan of Kiev (1632–46), and Nikon (1605–81), patriarch of Moscow (1652–58). The litany of first-class Russian Orthodox liturgiologists like Almazov, Diakovskij, Dmitrievskij, Golubtsov, Karabinov, Krasnosel'tsev, Mansvetov, Muretov, Orlov, Petrovskij, Skaballanovich, Turaev, Porforij Uspenskij—to mention some of the names that automatically spring to mind—has rendered it hazardous to undertake any serious scientific study of Byzantine liturgy without knowing Russian.[14]

[12] On which, see André Mandouze and Joël Fouilheron, eds., *Migne et le renouveau des études patristiques. Actes du Colloque de Saint-Flour, 7–8 juillet 1975*, Théologie historique 66 (Paris: Beauchesne, 1985); Adalbert-Gauthier Hamman, *Jacques-Paul Migne: Le retour aux Pères de l'Église*, Le Point théologique 16 (Paris: Beauchesne, 1975).

[13] See the superb intellectual biography of Bishop, also detailing the history of this movement, by Nigel Abercrombie, *The Life and Work of Edmund Bishop* (London: Longmans, Green & Co., 1959).

[14] On this school, see the excellent new study of Peter Galadza, "Liturgy and Life: The Appropriation of the 'Personalization of Cult' in East-Slavic Orthodox Liturgiology, 1869–1996," *Studia Liturgica* 28 (1988): 210–31. The Russian Orthodox school was not without limitations, determined by ideological aprioris. Elements in Italo-Greek manuscripts that departed from Orthodox usage were sometimes viewed as "latinizations," when, in fact, as we know from more recent modern studies of the history of the Byzantine Rite, periphery manuscripts far from the center simply preserve older usages. I detail all this in Robert Taft, *The Byzantine Rite: A Short History*, American Essays in Liturgy (Collegeville, MN: Liturgical Press, 1993); also available in French: *Le rite byzantin. Bref historique* (Paris: Éditions du Cerf, 1996), and Italian: *Storia sintetica del rito bizantino*, Collana di pastorale liturgica 20 (Vatican City: Libreria Editrice Vaticana, 1999).

Meanwhile, back in (nominally) Catholic France two patristic serials or collections, either founded by Jesuits or later placed under Jesuit direction, were of major importance for the post–World War II patristic and liturgical renewal, as well as for oriental liturgiology. For in the Christian East, allergic to Western categorizing and compartmentalizing, theology, spirituality, and liturgy still form an integrated whole. Sources chrétiennes, founded in 1940, helped fuel the paradigm shift in French Catholic theological thinking in the striking theological revival following France's ignominious defeat in World War II. This true renaissance found expression especially in the writings of Jesuits Henri de Lubac (1896–1991) and Jean Daniélou (1905–74), and Dominicans Marie-Dominique Chenu (1895–1990) and Yves-Marie Congar (1904–95), all subjected to Roman sanctions for their views, only to be eventually rehabilitated and, except for Chenu, created cardinals.[15] Stigmatized by its critics as *la nouvelle théologie*, an intentionally pejorative designation,[16] the irony of that was lost on its coiners: they were, in fact, the real practitioners of a "new theology" of arid, decadent scholasticism with respect to the return to tradition proposed by those they were denigrating. The watchword of the *nouvelle théologie* was *ressourcement*, a return to the sources as the point of departure for measuring the theology of today, rather than taking the present as the measure by which to validate (or not) the past.

All this, in turn, would have its echo in Orthodoxy of the diaspora through its influence on such Orthodox liturgy greats as protopresbyter Alexander Schmemann (1921–83).[17] A charter member of the ecumenical movement from his student days when he was vice chairman of the Youth Department of the World Council of Churches (WCC) and later member of the WCC Faith and Order Commission and Orthodox observer at the Second Vatican Council, the young Alexander was open

[15] See the account of this *ressourcement* movement in John W. O'Malley, *What Happened at Vatican II* (Cambridge, MA; London: Harvard University Press, 2008), 36–43, 75ff, 86ff. For brief biographies of the *dramatis personae* of this ferment, see ibid., 321–28.

[16] See ibid., 75, for the origins of this name.

[17] See Robert F. Taft, "The Liturgical Enterprise Twenty-Five Years after Alexander Schmemann (1921–1983): The Man and His Heritage," Twenty-Fifth Anniversary Annual Fr. Alexander Schmemann Memorial Lecture, Keynote Address at the Symposium "What Is Liturgical Theology? A Twenty-Five Year Retrospective and Prospective," January 30, 2009, at St. Vladimir's Orthodox Theological Seminary, Crestwood, NY, in *Celebrating the Memory: Fr. Alexander Schmemann 1921–1983 = St. Vladimir's Theological Quarterly* 53, nos. 2–3 (2009): 139–77.

to others from the start,[18] unlike those closed religious minds incapable of admitting that they do not inhabit this earth alone. Georges Florovsky's "pseudo-morphosis" indictment of the "Western captivity" of Orthodox theology,[19] still eagerly espoused by representatives of the "neo-orthodox" line of contemporary Greek theology[20] though rejected by other, more objective Greek theologians,[21] remains the classic expression of this cliché: whatever seems awry in Orthodoxy must be someone else's fault. But this was not the road Alexander chose to follow. In what seems to be a veiled rebuttal of this anti-Westernism, Fr. Alexander, in the original Russian edition of his landmark *Introduction to Liturgical Theology*, rejects out of hand the notion that Western influence is just "a new Western captivity [*novyi zapadnyi plen*]."[22]

Open to the postwar religious ferment going on around him, Schmemann was drawn into the liturgical renewal and return to the fathers of such greats as Anglican monk Dom Gregory Dix; Belgian Benedictines Dom Lambert Beauduin and Dom Bernard Botte; French Catholic theologians like Louis Bouyer, the Dominicans Yves Congar, Marie-Dominique Chenu, and Irenée-Henri Dalmais, and the Jesuits Jean Daniélou and Henri de Lubac; and the great new French theological serials of those heady times, like the seventy-six volumes of the series Unam Sanctam (Paris: Éditions du Cerf, 1937–70) from the Dominican Theological Faculty of Saulchoir, or the eighty volumes of Théologie (Paris: Aubier, 1944–71) from the Jesuit Theological Faculty of Lyon-Fourvière, and above all the incomparable Jesuit Sources chrétiennes series (Paris: Éditions du Cerf, 1941–) that de Lubac and Danièlou founded at Lyon-Fourvière in 1940.

Meanwhile, things have begun to move on even in Greece, as some young Greek-Orthodox theologians are beginning to perceive the

[18] See Meyendorff, "A Life Worth Living," 3–10.

[19] Florovsky first formulated this, it seems, in his remarks at the First Congress of Orthodox Theology in Athens, November 29–December 6, 1936; see note 8 above.

[20] See the views cited in Yannis Spiteris, *La teologia ortodossa neo-greca* (Bologna: EDB, 1992), chap. 7: "La corrente dei 'neo-ortodossi' "; idem, "Attuali tendenze della teologia greca," *Orientalia Christiana Periodica* 71, no. 2 (2005): 299–314, esp. 303–7.

[21] See Spiteris, "Attuali tendenze nella teologia greca," 308–10.

[22] *Vvedenie v liturgicheskoe bogoslovie* (Paris: YMCA Press, 1961), 23. The English translation, *Introduction to Liturgical Theology*, Library of Orthodox Theology 4 (London: Faith Press, 1966), 13, waters down Schmemann's strong phrase in the original Russian, translating it as "not something foreign." Sr. Dr. Vassa Larin's unpublished paper, "Die liturgische Theologie Alexander Schmemanns" (2003): 3–4, drew my attention to this.

sterility of the "neo-patristic" current in Greek theology and are turning toward a broader "post-patristic" theology, to use the expression of Professor Pantelis Kalaïtzidis of Volos,[23] one of the most important voices in Greek Orthodoxy today.[24]

My point in all this is not to write a history of Catholic-Orthodox religious culture in the modern era but simply to show that *context is everything*. Nothing, and especially no liturgical change or renewal, exists in a vacuum. The liturgical reforms that emanated from Vatican II did not evolve in isolation and were not some shocking novelty, as some constituents of today's Catholic neoconservative ascendancy seem to imagine. The Vatican II–mandated reforms were but part of a long-standing, wide-ranging movement of renewal and *ressourcement* that spread far beyond the borders of Catholicism, included far more than liturgy, and began not with a coterie of liturgical specialists who foisted it on an unwitting church at Vatican II. They began with St. Pius X's (1903–14) December 20, 1905, decree *Sacra Tridentina Synodus* on the frequency of communion and his lowering of the age of First Holy Communion from adolescence to the age of reason in *Quam Singulari* on August 8, 1910, one of the most stunningly successful liturgical reforms in Christian history. And the process was forcefully furthered by the equally successful, massive liturgical œuvre of Pius XII (1939–58),[25] most notably by his renewal of Catholic liturgical theology in his great encyclical *Mediator Dei* of November 20, 1947, a major source of the Vatican II Constitution on the Sacred Liturgy, and by its still visible results in Pius XII's restoration of the Roman Rite Easter Vigil (1951) and the services of Holy Week (1955).

5. Vatican II, Liturgical Reform, and the Christian East

Only in this context can one understand what happened at Vatican II. The historic point of reference for the role of the Catholic East at Vatican II will always remain the great figure of Melkite Catholic Patriarch

[23] See Hervé Legrand, OP, "Vers un nouvel âge de la théologie orthodoxe?," *Service orthodox de presse* 351 (septembre–octobre 2010): 35–37.

[24] See his "L'Église orthodoxe face au défi du renouveau et de la réforme," *Contacts. Revue française de l'Orthodoxie* 60 = no. 223 (juillet–septembre 2008): 212–55.

[25] On Pius XII's liturgical œuvre, see the enormous number of liturgical initiatives of his pontificate in the official documents listed in Herman A. P. Schmidt, *Introductio in liturgiam occidentalem* (Rome: Herder, 1960), 17–32; idem, *Hebdomama Sancta*, 2. vols. (Rome: Herder, 1956–57), 2:211–953.

Maximos IV Sayegh and the role he played in his own and the broader church during the twenty critical years of his historic patriarchate from October 30, 1947, to November 5, 1967. Anyone old enough to remember those heady days knows of the role played by the Melkite Catholic bishops at Vatican II, one patriarch and a mere sixteen bishops awash in a Latin sea. The list of important items on the Vatican II post-conciliar liturgical agenda that the Melkite bishops were the first to propose is simply astonishing: liturgy in the vernacular, eucharistic concelebration and Communion under both species in the Latin liturgy; and the permanent diaconate.[26] The rest is, of course, history.

But it would not have been history had the council fathers, overwhelmingly Roman, not Eastern Catholic bishops, not been receptive to these proposals. How they became so is the result of a long process of maturation, comprising two fundamental phases: (1) a perceived need and (2) the search for solutions consonant with tradition. What interests me here is the second point, the strategies the reformers used as they went about their work, and especially the role Eastern liturgy played in this process.

6. Eastern Liturgy—Western Needs

In his last article in *Worship*, the late Msgr. Frederick R. McManus (1923–2005), one of the "greats" of the Catholic Liturgical Movement in the United States, describes the Vatican II liturgical renewal's "fresh breadth and flexibility" as flowing "from a genuine return to evangelical and patristic sources."[27] The Vatican II reform, according to Msgr. McManus, was not just an updating or *aggiornamento* but a return to the "venerable traditions of the early post-biblical centuries."[28] That is what made the reform an organic and traditional development out of the existing tradition and not a modernist revolution, as some of the contemporary ignorant try to portray it. The mandate of

[26] See Robert F. Taft, "Eastern Catholic Churches (*Orientalium Ecclesiarum*)," in *Modern Catholicism: Vatican II and After*, ed. Adrian Hastings (London: SPCK; New York: Oxford University Press, 1991), 135–40, esp. 135–36.

[27] "Back to the Future: The Early Christian Roots of Liturgical Renewal," *Worship* 72, no. 5 (1998): 386–403, here 386.

[28] Ibid., 387.

Sacrosanctum Concilium was that the rites "be restored to the vigor they had in the tradition of the Fathers" (SC 50).[29]

Therein lies not only the solution but also the problem. As Msgr. McManus goes on to show, Pope St. Pius V (1566–72) used the same language in the liturgical restoration following the Council of Trent, when he wrote in his bull *Quo primum*, of July 14, 1570, about restoring the *Missale Romanum* "to the pristine norm of the holy Fathers."[30] For Pius V as for Vatican II, the issue was not, of course, a sort of conservative archaeologism, seeking to return to an irrecoverable past. Rather, as Msgr. McManus so well formulates it, "there is no commitment to one century or other, but only a search for the best sources and the best Christian thought, especially in the first few centuries. . . . [I]t is regularly a matter of restoration and recovery, scrutinizing the past precedents for what can be pastorally sound liturgy in the present."[31]

It is in this context that we must understand the modern Western Catholic romance with the Christian East and its liturgies. I believe the West has tended to define Eastern liturgy in terms of what it perceives itself as lacking. It would be easy to make a list of things in the pre– and post–Vatican II Roman Catholic liturgical renewal that were directly inspired by the East: the restoration of Holy Week and the Easter Vigil under Pius XII, liturgy in the vernacular, the Spirit-Epiclesis in the new post–Vatican II Roman Rite anaphoras, eucharistic concelebration, Communion under both species, the permanent (and married) diaconate, the recomposition of the ancient unity of Christian initiation in the justly famous RCIA or Rite of Christian Initiation of Adults,[32] revisions in the ordination and confirmation rites, and the (in my view largely unsuccessful[33]) attempts to restore the Liturgy of the Hours.

[29] *Documents on the Liturgy 1963–1979: Conciliar, Papal, and Curial Texts* (Collegeville, MN: Liturgical Press, 1982), 14.

[30] Pius V, *Quo primum*, July 14, 1570, cited ibid., 390.

[31] McManus, "Back to the Future," 400.

[32] For an enthralling account of how the RCIA can renew the life of an entire parish community, see Raymond B. Kemp, "The Rite of Christian Initiation of Adults at Ten Years," *Worship* 56, no. 4 (1982): 309–26, and the responses that follow in the same issue.

[33] See Robert F. Taft, "The Divine Office: Monastic Choir, Prayer Book, or Liturgy of the People of God? An Evaluation of the New Liturgy of the Hours in Its Historical Context," in *Vatican II: Assessment and Perspectives Twenty-Five Years After (1962–1987)*, 3 vols., ed. René Latourelle (New York and Mahwah, NJ: Paulist Press,

It would be equally easy to show that what was being done was not so much an imitation of existing Eastern liturgical usage but rather a question of deciding what should be done on the basis of several factors, above all perceived pastoral need, and then finding justification and support in patristic and Eastern precedents as interpreted—even reinterpreted—in the light of those perceived present needs.

There is, of course, nothing whatever remarkable about such a process. What the Latin West did with the East is what historians do with the past: they interpret it in the light of present aims and needs. In other words, I believe the Western Catholics' view of Eastern liturgy, the commonplaces of its virtues, is simply a mirror of their own deepest longings. The qualities they identify in Eastern liturgy are those they think the West has lost, as in the statement I cited above from Dom Olivier Rousseau, OSB. Rousseau was writing in 1944, toward the end of World War II, when the Liturgical Movement among Francophone Catholics drew inspiration from contacts with Orthodoxy of the Russian emigration that had found refuge in France in the aftermath of the Bolshevik Revolution of 1918.

This wave of Catholic romanticism for the East so impressed one ingenuous Greek Orthodox author that Zoe in Athens published his book titled *Nostalgia for Orthodoxy*, anthologizing citations from Western authors in praise of Orthodox liturgy and spirituality.[34] But of course this book missed the whole point. Catholics then and now who have become entranced by Eastern liturgy were not seeking a "return" to an Orthodoxy to which they had never belonged. That is the same mistake Catholics used to make before the birth of Catholic ecumenism, when they thought the Orthodox had to "return" to Rome, as if they had ever "belonged" to Rome in the first place. Present-day Orthodoxy in no way represents "the past" of Western Christianity, whose roots are as equally apostolic and autonomous as those of any Eastern Church.

Rather, what these Western Christians were engaged in was "imagining" an Orthodoxy, just as Prof. Edward W. Said showed, apropos of

---

1989), 2:27–46, reprinted as chapter 14 of Robert F. Taft, *Beyond East and West: Problems in Liturgical Understanding*, 2nd rev. ed. (Rome: Edizioni Orientalia Christiana, 2001). In this case the lack of success was—as I explain in that study—due in part to the reformers' refusal to accept recommendations based on Eastern precedents.

[34] Elias Mastrogiannopoulos, *Nostalgia for Orthodoxy* (Athens: Zoe, 1956; English trans., Athens: Zoe, 1959).

the Middle East, that nineteenth-century Western orientalists "imagined" an Orient that is not a place but an idea, an idea that is wholly an invention of the European orientalists.[35] All this is nothing more than the movement known as romanticism, part of humanity's ongoing attempt to re-create for itself a better present out of an imagined ideal past, out of fear that having lost yesterday, we have no today.

This romantic vision of Eastern liturgy is based on several presuppositions, the essentials of which are an idealization of "the golden age of the Fathers" and the spirit of its liturgy, the suspicion that the West has lost this spirit, and the supposition that the East has preserved it intact.[36] But, in fact, the "golden age of patristic liturgy" is itself a creation of the same romanticism. When one reads what the fathers have to say about liturgy in their day,[37] one sees that there was no "golden age of patristic liturgy" except in our daydreams. And even if there had been, present-day Eastern liturgical usage certainly has not preserved it—indeed, it has preserved some of the very abuses the fathers of that supposed "golden age" railed against with force, such as the decline in frequent Communion.

But all that is beside the point. For we are dealing here not with past facts but with present perceptions. And these perceptions tell us not about the past, nor about the East, but about ourselves. So the only relevant question is: Why has the Western Liturgical Movement, itself part of the movement of nineteenth-century romanticism like the Solesmes Benedictine revival, the Oxford Movement, and so many other aspects of Western religious culture of the day—why has it had an ongoing romance with the Christian East? In other words, what do the liturgies of the East tell Western Catholics about themselves?

Let me note but a few of those qualities I think Western Catholics perceive Eastern liturgy as possessing in ways that the West lacks. Since they have been expressed before, they may appear commonplace, but repetition does not make them any less true.

[35] Edward W. Said, *Orientalism* (London: Routlege & Kegan Paul, 1978).

[36] An idealization of which I too have been guilty. See, for example, Taft, *Beyond East and West*, 145.

[37] Numerous examples in Robert F. Taft, "Women at Church in Byzantium: Where, When—and Why?," *Dumbarton Oaks Papers* 52 (1998): 27–87; idem, *Through Their Own Eyes: Liturgy as the Byzantines Saw It* (Berkeley, CA: InterOrthodox Press, 2006), 38–39, 89–100, 119.

1. *Eastern liturgy balances a high Christology with a tender devotion for the eminently knowable, human, kenotic Christ.* East and West have different images of Christ. The liturgies of the Christian East remain indelibly marked by the trinitarian and christological controversies of the period of the first seven councils, and certain liturgical attitudes current in the contemporary West remain totally alien to the Eastern liturgical spirit. For the Christian East, Christ remains the awesome *Pantokrator*, before whose sacred mysteries the worshiper bows down in reverential awe. But Christ is also the *philanthropos / chelovekolyubets*, the one who loves humankind, loved us, indeed, unto the death on the cross. He is the kenotic Jesus of Russian piety, the Jesus of Philippians 2:6-11, "who, though his state was divine, did not cling to his equality with God but emptied himself [*ekenosen*] to assume the condition of a slave."[38] The exquisite dialectic of this Philippians text, moving back and forth between Jesus' divine glory *ab aeterno*, his self-abasement, and his glorification by the Father, mirrors perfectly the tension in the Byzantine liturgy between Christ as both *Pantokrator* and *Philanthropos-Theos*.[39]

Though there is nothing here to which Latin Catholic Christians would not subscribe, I do not think contemporary Western christological piety is as successful in holding these realities together in dynamic tension. The West tends toward christological schizophrenia, a sort of postmodern Nestorianism. Its piety ricochets from an excessive familiarity to an excessive neo-Chalcedonianism, from Christology-from-above to Christology-from-below. That is just a roundabout way of saying that Western piety tends to be historicizing, and its familiarity with the human Jesus leaves the God-man receding into the divinity,

[38] This text is emblematic of Slavic Orthodox piety, a piety both distinct from and—in my view—more balanced than that of the Greeks, who reserve their emotional devotionalism for the Mother of God and the saints. On the whole question, see Robert Taft, "Russian Liturgy, a Mirror of the Russian Soul," in *Studi albanologici, balcanici, bizantini e orientali in onore di Giuseppe Valentini, S.J.*, Studi albanesi, Studi e testi VI (Florence: Leo S. Olschki Editore, 1986), 413–35.

[39] Among the Slavs, this awesome Byzantine vision of Christ-*Pantokrator* is strikingly balanced by the Slavonic "Canon to the Most-Sweet Jesus (*Sladchaishchemu Gospodu nashemu Iisusu Khristu*)" in the Slavonic Book of Hours or *Ierejskij Molitvoslov*, a devotional text that cedes nothing to the intimate love for Jesus expressed in Western devotion to the Sacred Heart, as Joseph Ledit, SJ, showed clearly enough in his little book on the Byzantine liturgical theme of the wound in Christ's side: *La plaie du coté* (Rome: Pontificio Istituto Orientale, 1970).

as Josef A. Jungmann described in his famous essay on Teutonic Arianism.[40]

2. *Eastern liturgy is radically trinitarian.* This Western Christology runs the danger of disturbing the trinitarian structure of Christian piety. Recent attempts to enrich the pneumatological and epicletic structure of Western eucharistic prayers have not fully remedied this problem, which is one not of texts but of mentality. Eastern prayer is explicitly and consciously trinitarian in ways that Western liturgical prayer is not. I am not talking about phrases, the repetition of trinitarian formulae like doxologies, but about the *liturgie profonde,* which in the East simply cannot be regularly prayed without the attentive worshiper becoming imbued with a piety that remains trinitarian through and through. That, in my view, is simply not true of the West, where the Holy Spirit, though professed, is just not a consciously operative factor in a radically christological liturgical piety.

3. *Eastern liturgy retains a sense of the absolute and awesome holiness, transcendence, and unknowability of God, who is to be worshiped for that reason alone.* Nothing is so foreign to the Western mentality as the ancient prayers of the Assyro-Chaldean tradition, which simply pray without asking God for anything, as in the beautiful collect of the Lakumara Hymn: "For all your benefits and graces to us past recompense, Lord, we confess and glorify you without ceasing in your triumphant Church full of all helps and all blessings: for you are the Lord and creator of all, Father, Son and Holy Spirit, forever."[41]

Such "liturgical indifference" is refreshing in the face of the incessant Western mania to thematize and instrumentalize liturgy for its own ends, so that one can "get something out of it." For the Christian East, the church's liturgy is not something we appropriate to our needs by reducing it to the level of our own banality. Rather, it is the church's ideal of prayer to which we must rise. We are not the measure of the liturgy; the church's liturgy is the yardstick that measures us.

[40] Joseph A. Jungmann, "The Defeat of Teutonic Arianism and the Revolution in Religious Culture in the Early Middle Ages," in *Pastoral Liturgy* (New York: Herder & Herder, 1962), 1–101. More recently and at greater length on the same cultural shift, see James C. Russell, *The Germanization of Early Medieval Christianity* (New York/Oxford: Oxford University Press, 1994).

[41] *Missel chaldéen* (Paris: Église catholique chaldéenne, 1982), 50; F. E. Brightman, *Liturgies Eastern and Western* (Oxford: Clarendon Press, 1896), 254.

4. *Eastern liturgy is holistic.* Finally, Eastern liturgy has created and retained a synthesis of ritual, art, church design, and symbolic structure that may at times seem inflexible but that permits it to do what liturgy is supposed to do without the self-consciousness of present-day liturgy in the West. For liturgy serves no purpose outside itself. Like a living language, it cannot be reduced to sociology or anthropology; it cannot be invented or created; it simply is. And although it has a history, as I am well aware, having spent my life retracing it, that history cannot be accelerated and overridden. In the West, the Protestant Reformation tried to do so, with results that are available for all to see.

Here too, if the West would learn something pastoral from the East, it must stop getting tripped up in its own clichés. Liturgy should avoid repetitions? Repetition is of the essence of ritual behavior. Liturgy should offer variety? Too much variety is the enemy of popular participation. Liturgy should be creative? Indeed—but whose creativity? Most contemporary Western liturgical creativity is just one more cover for a neoclericalism. The liturgical "creators" do not mean the creativity of the people of God but of the celebrant and of the liturgical-establishment professionals. Furthermore, it is presumptuous for those who have never manifested the least creativity in any other aspect of their human existence to think they suddenly become Mozart and Shakespeare when it comes to liturgy. There is a sameness and a familiarity and a repetitiveness that is at the very basis of day-to-day human culture. And men and women who wish to gather to praise God must learn a similar regularity and consistency, or their prayer will not survive. Our people are sick to death of professional coteries constantly reinventing the wheel.

7. The Catholic Liturgical Reform and the Christian East after Vatican II

Historia: On April 26, 2003 (Holy Saturday for the Orthodox, that year), I was with friends in Mezzojuzo, Sicily, watching Greek television broadcasting from Athens the Holy Saturday Liturgy of St. Basil, celebrated in the cathedral there by the late Archbishop Christodoulos (d. January 28, 2008), then primate of the Orthodox Church of Greece. The Eucharist was celebrated *versus populum* on a table set up in front of the central doors of the iconostasis. The traditionally "secret prayers" were recited aloud. The deacon proclaimed the litanies from a microphone facing the people. And those who watched on television

Pope John Paul II's historic visit to Romania will not have failed to notice that the Orthodox Patriarchal Divine Liturgy in the public square on Sunday, May 9, 1999, was also celebrated *versus populum*. The so-called Innovators or *Obnovlentsy* tried to introduce the same practice into the Russian Orthodox Church in the 1920s, but the radical stance of that Soviet-controlled lapdog splinter movement led to its rejection by the Russian Orthodox despite the fact that, as can be the case with self-proclaimed reformers, some of its ideas were not without merit.

So the desire for liturgical renewal has certainly had its impact in the East, and not only in recent times, as has been demonstrated in more than one doctoral dissertation written under my direction at the Pontifical Oriental Institute,[42] showing that there has been more than one reform of the Byzantine Liturgy throughout its history. Soon thereafter, the topic of Byzantine liturgical reform achieved instant popularity: one year later two books on the topic, this time by Orthodox priests, one Russian, one Serbian, were dedicated to the topic.

Must all this be judged the result of the influence of the Catholic East on the reform of the Western liturgy that Vatican II initiated? Or was it rather the influence of the Latin reform on the East? Neither, in my view. I believe the process was a much more complex Hegelian one of thesis-antithesis-synthesis, a fruitful influence in which both East and West influenced and enriched each other mutually, as we saw above in section 4. And the process continues, as churches both Eastern Catholic and Orthodox move toward liturgical renewal, but at different rhythms from the Catholic West because of the very different history of the Christian East in our times.

8. Conclusion

But I do not intend to review that recent history. I prefer instead to conclude with some personal reflections. Though I have played no small part in Western scholarship on Eastern liturgy over the past generation, I am not one of those romantics who considers the East—

[42] Thomas Pott, *La réforme liturgique byzantine. Étude du phénomène de l'évolution non-spontanée de la liturgie byzantine*, Bibliotheca *Ephemerides liturgicae*, Subsidia 104 (Rome: CLV – Edizione liturgiche, 2000); Marcel Mojzeš, *Il movimento liturgico nelle chiese bizantine. Analisi di alcune tendenze di riforma nel XX secolo*, Bibliotheca *Ephemerides liturgicae*, Subsidia 132 (Rome: CLV – Edizione liturgiche, 2005).

for heaven only knows what imagined reasons—to possess some sort of traditional superiority over the Latin West, a deeper spirituality, a more ancient and traditional monasticism, a more faithfully apostolic liturgy. Those are nothing but clichés, most of them long discredited among those who have some real historical knowledge and practical experience of the Christian East and West.

For Christians, the only "ideal period of liturgy" is the one Divine Providence has them living in. Why, then, this renewed Western nostalgia for a presumable better liturgical past, this idealization of Trent or the East? I think that Latin Catholics, largely ignorant of the riches of their own living tradition, make the mistake of looking elsewhere for what they already have in their own closet. I am dismayed at how utterly incapable contemporary Western Catholics are of understanding and marketing the riches of their own tradition. Stuck in the late Middle Ages and stymied by this medieval captivity, the Catholic West has stalled the great movement of patristic *ressourcement* initiated in postwar France by authors like Congar and Daniélou and de Lubac, the heroes of my youth.

How many of my Latin-rite Catholic readers ever dip into a volume of the great collection Sources chrétiennes for your *lectio divina*? Turn again to the fathers and mystics at the root of your unparalleled Latin tradition. Meditate on the Rule of St. Benedict and the writings of the great St. Bernard of Clairvaux. Read or reread some of the great Catholic works on the church, its theology, its spirituality, its liturgy that led to or issued from the Vatican II renewal. Read John W. O'Malley's bracing account of *What Happened at Vatican II*[43] to find out why those who reject Vatican II are livid while Vatican II loyalists like myself are enthralled. Rediscover where you came from before it's too late. The Latin Catholic West does not need to return nostalgically to a dead and gone-forever medieval or Tridentine past. It needs to return to its roots. Latin Christianity is just as apostolic, ancient, traditional, patristic, spiritual, and monastic as that of the East.[44] I am not really convinced all Catholics know and believe that.

[43] See note 15 above.

[44] On Latin Christianity, see the seminal study of Olivier Rousseau, "Qu'est-ce qu'un latin?," *Irénikon* 15 (1938): 321–41, 436–49; 16 (1939): 521–44; also the (from my perspective) somewhat bizarre views of Ioannes S. Romanides, *Franks, Romans, Feudalism and Doctrine: An Interplay between Theology and Society* (Brookline, MA: Holy Cross Orthodox Press, 1982); and the detailed review of Romanides's thought

So what the West needs to do is not turn to the East for solutions to its own problems but to penetrate once again into the riches of its own storehouse, to bring out from it things both old and new. The Christian culture that produced Chartres and Mont Saint-Michel; Cyprian and Augustine and Cassian; Benedictine monasticism and Cîteaux; Francis of Assisi and Dominic; Ignatius of Loyola, John of the Cross, and Charles de Foucauld; the two St. T(h)eresas and Mother Teresa; and the great Vatican II popes, Blessed John XXIII and Paul VI—to mention only a few of my recent heroes already gone to their eternal reward—does not have to apologize to or imitate anybody except Jesus Christ.

---

by André de Halleux, "Une vision orthodoxe grecque de la romanité," *Revue théologique de Louvain* 15 (1984): 54–66.

Part II

Liturgical Year

Ruth Langer

Chapter 3

The Liturgical Parting(s) of the Ways: A Preliminary Foray

In 2005, Bruce Morill, SJ, and I team-taught a comparative course at Boston College on the Jewish and Christian liturgical years. Our premise in constructing the course was as follows: given that Christianity and hence Christian liturgy had its roots in Judaism and Jewish liturgy, and given that the two subsequently developed parallel to one another chronologically and often even geographically, the comparison itself should lead to deeper insights into the histories and meanings of both traditions. Much to our surprise, and in spite of many of the claims made in the Christian readings we assigned, we decided at the end of the course that the parallels and the resultant insights were superficial. The question that I would like to explore here, only in a preliminary way and only from the Jewish perspective,[1] is why.

First, a few words about the course itself. It was offered in a multi-layered pedagogical context. While Fr. Morrill was then a member of the systematics area of our theology department,[2] I sit in its comparative theology area as the department's professor of Jewish studies. My own approach to liturgy, like that of the majority of Jewish scholars of the field, has been primarily historical. Indeed, there exists relatively little specifically theological reflection on any element of Jewish liturgy and even less that applied directly to the topic of this course. Further,

[1] While I am aware of some of the discussion of Christian liturgists on this matter, I am not an expert on them and leave that discussion to others. To my knowledge, the Christian liturgist who approaches these questions with the fullest understanding of Jewish liturgical scholarship is Paul F. Bradshaw in his *The Search for the Origins of Christian Worship: Sources and Methods for the Study of Early Liturgy* (Oxford: Oxford University Press, 1992; 2nd ed., 2002), particularly his more extended discussion of Jewish liturgical scholarship in the second edition; see 23–46.

[2] He has since left to sit on the Edward A. Malloy Chair of Catholic Studies at Vanderbilt University.

the amount of applicable scholarship in English on the Jewish liturgical year, even historical in emphasis, remains sparse.[3] Thus, we were challenging each other (and our students) to apply methods outside our "comfort zones" while at the same time seeking to enrich both our understandings of each other and of ourselves.

I also serve as the associate director of Boston College's Center for Christian-Jewish Learning, one of whose goals is to foster interreligious learning. Such learning creates settings that are by definition comparative and encourages everyone participating in the course, students and professors, to engage deeply with the self-understanding of the other in order to raise new questions, to generate new insights and understandings, and to challenge and perhaps even to transform one's self-understanding.[4] Thus, one of the goals of even the historical comparisons of this course was (appropriate) transformation of today's world—specifically by contributing to building and bettering the relationships between Christians and Jews.

The students in the course were mostly students studying at the master's level, most of them preparing for ministerial degrees of one sort or another, either at Boston College or at another of the schools in the consortium of the Boston Theological Institute. They included Catholic, Orthodox, and Protestant Christians, counting several students from Korea among the last, but unfortunately no Jews. For almost all, this was their first exposure to Judaism. For a number, this was their first exposure to academic and historical study of Christian liturgy as well.

Because this was a fall course, we began with the Sabbath but turned quickly to the Jewish penitential season, pairing it with a study of Lent. We then spent a class on *Sukkot* (Feast of Booths/Tabernacles—and the class met that week at my house in our *sukkah*) before moving to a comparison of Passover and Easter, then the Easter Season and Pente-

[3] I excluded as inappropriate to our setting books like Theodor Herzl Gaster, *Festivals of the Jewish Year: A Modern Interpretation and Guide* (New York: Sloane, 1953) whose interpretation draws heavily on imaginative reconstruction of origins and who pays minimal attention to ongoing Jewish meanings, and books written as more popular guides, like Arthur Waskow, *Seasons of Our Joy: A Handbook of Jewish Festivals* (Toronto/New York: Bantam Books, 1982; New York: Summit Books, 1986), although these do include some implicit theological discussion.

[4] For a discussion of interreligious learning, see the introduction to "Courses" at http://www.bc.edu/content/bc/research/cjl/centerscholarship/courses.html (accessed November 2, 2011).

cost paired with their Jewish equivalents, ending in December with a return to the timely with a discussion of Advent and Christmas. More minor festivals like Hanukkah and Purim did not appear on the syllabus but were discussed briefly in class; similarly, we did not address the modern observances of Yom HaShoah (Holocaust Memorial Day) or the various celebrations of modern Israeli history. Our primary texts for Christian liturgy were articles drawn from Maxwell Johnson's collection, *Between Memory and Hope*,[5] and Thomas Talley's *The Origins of the Liturgical Year*.[6] We also drew heavily on Paul Bradshaw and Lawrence Hoffman's two edited comparative volumes on Passover and Easter.[7] For the complete syllabus, see the appendix to this article.

It would seem that the Jewish and Christian liturgical years have much in common, and at the level of large structural elements, there is truth in this assumption. Both communities tell their stories through the liturgical reading of Scripture, always (or frequently) in a cyclical fashion with interruptions to these cycles to read the passages relevant to particular holy days. Both celebrate one day a week that is distinct from the others, understanding it to be grounded in the Sabbath commandment at Sinai and the imagery of the first creation narrative. Both celebrate a major festival in early spring and another fifty days later. With the exception of the cyclical reading of Scripture (*lectio continua*), which probably emerged a bit later,[8] the similarity derives

[5] Maxwell E. Johnson, ed., *Between Memory and Hope: Readings on the Liturgical Year* (Collegeville, MN: Liturgical Press, 2000).

[6] Thomas J. Talley, *The Origins of the Liturgical Year*, 2nd ed. (Collegeville, MN: Liturgical Press, 1986).

[7] Volumes 5 and 6, respectively, in their Two Liturgical Traditions series: Paul F. Bradshaw and Lawrence A. Hoffman, *Passover and Easter: Origin and History to Modern Times* (Notre Dame, IN: University of Notre Dame Press, 1999); *Passover and Easter: The Symbolic Structuring of Sacred Season* (Notre Dame, IN: University of Notre Dame Press, 1999).

[8] Various rabbinic sources suggest a system still in some flux. It is clear from innumerable Second Temple sources, ranging from archaeological evidence to Philo to the New Testament to the Dead Sea Scrolls, that the reading of Scripture was a feature of late Second Temple Jewish synagogue practice. These do not, however, demonstrate a continuous reading (although the practical reality of reading Scripture from scrolls suggests that this would have been the simplest method). The tannaitic (earliest rabbinic) sources prescribe a continuous reading of the Pentateuch and give rules for the minimum number of verses to be read at a time. These rabbis disagree, however, as to whether the three midweek readings of at least ten verses each begin where the last ended or repeat each other, meaning

from the shared roots of these two traditions in the biblical calendar of Second Temple Judaism, that by which Jesus, his disciples, and the earliest Christians lived.

But does this similarity go beyond these points? Does it extend to other details, and even in these details, does it transcend being simply points of historical curiosity to shape the ways that Christians (and perhaps even Jews) can think about their holidays today? Our presumption in offering this course was that the answer would be yes or that it would, in any case, yield challenging comparative insights. The many scholars of early Christian liturgy who look to Jewish practice to explain the origins of Christian customs have obviously shared this presumption of a positive answer. On the pastoral level, many have also shared this presumption and used it to explain the events of the Last Supper and the development of the Eucharist. Particularly among liturgical historians, however, there are those who are increasingly problematizing these assumptions. This obviously has consequences for the understanding and meaning of the liturgy itself.

A significant element of this contemporary search for roots and parallels grows from the contemporary acceptance of the historical Jesus' own Jewishness and the search to unpack the implications of this for Christian self-understanding. In the atmosphere of disputation and diatribe that characterized much of official Christian-Jewish relations for most of the history of Christianity, this had been forgotten or ignored as insignificant. Jews were the villains of the gospel narratives, the foils of Pauline theology, so it was impossible to see Christianity as

that the minimum number of verses read each week could be either twenty-one or fifty-one, and the total could go much higher (M. Megillah 4:1-4, T. Megillah 3:10). Eventually two discrete cycles emerged, the annual cycle championed in Babylonia and the so-called triennial cycle of the rite of the Land of Israel in which the entire Pentateuch was completed in about three and a half years. The evidence from midrash and liturgical poetry suggests that the divisions between the weekly readings may not have been fixed at all in the triennial cycle as many divisions or selections come fast on one another's heels, referring to readings that could not have been part of the same cycle. The earliest preserved evidence for a possible *lectio continua* among Christians comes from the sermons of Origen on Genesis. See Hughes Oliphant Old, *The Reading and Preaching of the Scriptures in the Worship of the Christian Church*, vol. 1: *The Biblical Period* (Grand Rapids, MI/Cambridge, UK: Eerdmans, 1998), 342–45, and then the references to *lectio continua* in subsequent volumes. It is, of course, possible that the scriptural choices in Origen's church were influenced by the larger Jewish context in which it was operating.

anything other than an overthrow of all that was inherent to Judaism itself. The gradual and imperfect modern recognition of the humanity of contemporary Jews, the acceptance of Jews as citizens in Western societies in the past two centuries, paved the way for the gradual and still partial rectification of this understanding. As in so much else, the shock of the Holocaust was another catalyst, opening the eyes of theologians and historians to the factual and moral error of these teachings.

It thus became possible for Christian scholars, including liturgists, to begin to study Judaism seriously, sometimes as pure orientalists and at other times with the express purpose of understanding Christian origins. The complicated question, though, as Bradshaw demonstrates clearly,[9] is to discern what Judaism was in the first century in which Jesus, the apostles, and those early leaders of the church who remained in a Jewish context participated. To what extent were eventual church practices influenced by what became rabbinic Judaism, or were they closer to some, now significantly unknown, form of Hellenistic Judaism or even other religious elements of the Greco-Roman society in which the church was formed? Simply a turn to looking for the historical roots of Christianity and Christian liturgy in known forms of Judaism is insufficient, something that is well recognized by scholars today.

Scholars today also heed the warning that the rich literature of rabbinic Judaism, that which forms the authoritative textual grounding for subsequent Jewish culture, is itself a product of later generations. The redaction of the Mishnah, its earliest text, dates only from c. 200 CE, i.e., from a period when Christianity is already significantly a Gentile and not a Jewish religious community and when most or many Jews and Christians already acknowledge significant aspects of the "partings of the ways." Thus, rabbinic literature and the liturgical life it describes is not a good source for understanding early Christian liturgy. While it is possible that Christians drew significantly from the liturgical exemplars set by Hellenistic, Greek-speaking Jews, very few traces of their liturgical life remain.[10]

[9] Bradshaw, *The Search*, 23–46.

[10] For examinations of this, see David Fiensy, *Prayers Alleged to Be Jewish: An Examination of the* Constitutiones Apostolorum, Brown Judaic Studies 65 (Chico, CA: Scholars Press, 1985); Pieter van der Horst and Judith Newman, *Early Jewish Prayers in Greek* (Berlin/New York: Walter de Gruyter, 2008).

Increasingly in the past two decades, and particularly as the texts of the Dead Sea Scrolls have been deciphered and published, scholars have been turning to them and other Second Temple–period literature to develop a more appropriate understanding of the liturgical world(s) of the Judaisms of the period. This complex task, far from complete as of this writing, is helping us to understand more accurately the precursors to both rabbinic and Christian liturgies.[11] Nevertheless, the question of the nature of first-century Jewish worship life outside of the Jerusalem temple is still largely unanswerable. Retrojections from rabbinic depictions and projections from the Second Temple–era texts, which are mostly earlier, do not meet neatly in the middle to provide more than vague hints.

Thus, one problem with our course, as conceived, was its reliance on historical scholarship. We chose this route, on the one hand, because of the dominance of this method in Jewish liturgical studies and, on the other hand, because of presumptions that common origins would add meaning to the points of intersection. The liturgical years that both communities celebrate, however, although they have some roots in the first century reality, were both still evolving and emerging through subsequent centuries. Obvious examples of this include the church's abolition of the Quartodeciman celebration of Passover with its reliance on the Jewish dating of the festival or its eventual transfer of Sabbath themes to its Sunday Lord's Day observances. Thus, the forms that we have received and that shape our liturgical experiences today arise from the time when Judaism and Christianity, where they were still in contact, were actively defining the boundaries dividing one from another.

The context of lived contact was not always the case. The leaderships defining these liturgical expressions were increasingly not operating in the same geographical and cultural realms. Christians inevitably had a scriptural Jewish other (in both the Old Testament and in the references to Jews in the New) and frequently knew the presence of a living Jewish other as well. These Jews, however, were not necessarily the *rabbinic* Jewish other, those whose legacy was pre-

[11] For one of the most recent publications of this endeavor, see the three-volume set of studies on penitential prayer: Mark Boda, Daniel Falk, and Rodney Werline, eds., *Seeking the Favor of God*, Early Judaism and Its Literature 21–23 (Atlanta: Society of Biblical Literature, 2006–2008).

served and who defined today's Jewish practice.[12] Thus, one must be careful not to give too much credit to the influence of Jews on Christianity as it emerges in its first several centuries either. It is also necessary to preserve a consciousness of the complexity of the Christian map in the early centuries and not to impose a false uniformity on the practices of that era.

Whether the living presence (as opposed to a scriptural presence) of Christians influenced rabbinic Judaism is a more complex matter. Rabbinic Jews almost certainly did not understand Gentile Christians to have a claim on Judaism; thus, any competition that their Christianity represented was, to them, that of another essentially unrelated religion, albeit one that was using the Jewish Bible to attract converts. In contrast, Jewish-Christians, those whom the church through its first several centuries increasingly deemed heretical, were probably among those whom the early rabbis also deemed as heretics (*minim*) and ritually cursed.[13] Because Jewish communities were more ethnically than theologically defined, these Jewish-Christians retained places within the Jewish communities among whom they lived and competed with other Jewish groups for influence. The number of clear references to Christians in rabbinic literature, however, is actually very small and not always of historical value.[14] The Judaism that eventually became

[12] For instance, however carefully one reads John Chrysostom's famous homilies (or diatribes) against Judaizing Christians, one fails to recognize elements of rabbinic liturgical practice in his descriptions of the synagogues attracting the attention of his flock. The entertainment value of the synagogue services in Greek-speaking Antioch (Homily 1, II:7; Homily 4, VII:3-4), for example, suggests a Greek service with musical accompaniments, neither of which the rabbis would have countenanced. The extent of rabbinic influence outside of their own immediate communities is not yet well understood. There is limited evidence for rabbis actually dwelling for substantial periods of time outside of the Land of Israel and Babylonia until rather late in the first millennium CE (with some geographical variation in the earliest evidence).

[13] See my *Cursing the Christians? A History of the Birkat HaMinim* (Oxford: Oxford University Press, 2012), 59 and chap. 1, *passim*. While the term may have initially applied to inner-Jewish heretics, by the medieval period, its meaning had been extended to apply to Gentile Christians.

[14] For some important studies of this, see, among others, Daniel Boyarin, *Dying for God: Martyrdom and the Making of Christianity and Judaism* (Stanford, CA: Stanford University Press, 1999); Richard Kalmin, "Christians and Heretics in Rabbinic Literature of Late Antiquity," *Harvard Theological Review* 87, no. 2 (1994): 155–69; or Peter Schäfer, *Jesus in the Talmud* (Princeton, NJ / Oxford: Princeton University

dominant and defined normative practice for subsequent generations developed primarily in Babylonia. While Christians were present there, they were a religious minority often more oppressed because of their real or perceived relationship with the Christian empires to the West. Babylonian rabbinic Judaism was shaped more by its interchanges with Zoroastrian Sassanian society[15] and, from the seventh century, with Islam. Thus, it is difficult to see Christian influences on Jewish liturgy except as it developed in the Land of Israel.

Some, most notably Israel Jacob Yuval, argue, however, that the Jewish liturgical practices that did develop in the Land of Israel were shaped by the rabbinic need to differentiate themselves from Christianity, whether Jewish or Gentile. This found its strongest (though not exclusive) expression around Passover observances because of their transformation in Christian teaching.[16] While Yuval's questions are important ones, many do not accept his conclusions.[17] In many cases, the same sources that he cites may be read to suggest that established rabbinic (or Jewish) practice generated a Christian act of self-

Press, 2007). Travers Herford, *Christianity in Talmud and Midrash* (London: Williams & Norgate, 1903; rpt. New York: Ktav, 1975), grossly overreads the evidence. One challenge in evaluating the presence of Christianity in rabbinic literature is the censorship of the texts in Christian Europe, both by Jews themselves in the face of Christian critiques and, from the mid-sixteenth century, by official church decree. On the processes of censorship, see especially Amnon Raz-Krakotzkin, *The Censor, the Editor, and the Text: The Catholic Church and the Shaping of the Jewish Canon in the Sixteenth Century*, trans. Jackie Feldman (Philadelphia: University of Pennsylvania Press, 2007 [2005 Hebrew]).

[15] This dynamic is just beginning to be studied in detail. See, for instance, Yaakov Elman, "Middle Persian Culture and Babylonian Sages: Accommodation and Resistance in the Shaping of Rabbinic Legal Tradition," in *The Cambridge Companion to the Talmud and Rabbinic Literature*, ed. Charlotte Elisheva Fonrobert and Martin S. Jaffee (Cambridge: Cambridge University Press, 2007), 165-197; or the articles in *The Talmud in Its Iranian Context*, ed. Carol Bakhos and Rahim Shayegan (Tübingen: Mohr Siebeck, 2010). None of these deal directly with liturgical issues.

[16] For brief statements of this, see Yuval's articles in *Passover and Easter*, vol. 1. For his more extended discussion, see his *Two Nations in Your Womb: Perceptions of Jews and Christians in Late Antiquity and the Middle Ages*, trans. Barbara Harshav and Jonathan Chipman (Berkeley: University of California Press, 2006), esp. 56–92, 123–30, 205–56.

[17] *Zion* 59, nos. 2–3 (1994) [Hebrew] is entirely devoted to critical responses to Yuval's theory, first expressed in the article "Vengeance and Damnation, Blood and Defamation: From Jewish Martyrdom to Blood Libel Accusations" [Hebrew], *Zion* 58, no. 1 (1993): 33–90.

differentiation (the reigning understanding among scholars of Jewish liturgy) rather than the reverse, as Yuval posits. Therefore, the historical questions of early common roots and subsequent cross influence is extraordinarily complex on both sides and needs to be approached with a sensitivity to the gaps in our knowledge regarding critical questions.

Examples of failure to do this abound. One example of note is Lawrence Hoffman's suggestion that one origin of Lent may be the preparatory period before Passover, documented already in the Mishnah as a series of four special Sabbaths with lectionaries that, as if they were holidays, break the *lectio continua* of the Pentateuch.[18] Mishnah Megillah 3:4 defines this period as beginning approximately six weeks before Passover with a reading (called *Sheqalim*, Exod 30:11-16) that functions to remind Jews of their obligation to pay their annual half-sheqel temple tax so that it arrives in Jerusalem before Passover. This tax funded their vicarious participation in the daily temple sacrifices offered by the priests, not only on the festival, but also throughout the following year.[19]

Hoffman simply does not discuss this reading, even though its relationship to Passover is no less significant than where he does begin. In his search for a three-week period to match an apparently documented three-week Lenten fast, he presents the Jewish pre-Passover season as commencing with the third reading of the four (*Parah*, Num 19:1-22), which describes the preparation of the ashes from the red heifer needed to purify people from corpse uncleanness (and, he claims, from more general forms of ritual uncleanness, but this is questionable) so that they could take part in the sacrifices.[20] Thus, purely from an inner-Jewish perspective, one might readily dispute Hoffman's reading of the evidence. From his Christian perspective, however,

[18] In subsequent Jewish practice, these readings are additions to the regular weekly reading. In the so-called triennial cycle of the Land of Israel, well documented in midrash and liturgical poetry, these readings were the sole readings on these weeks. For Hoffman's discussion, see his "The Great Sabbath and Lent: Jewish Origins?," in *Passover and Easter: The Symbolic Structuring*, 23–27.

[19] According to M. Rosh Hashanah 1:1, Nisan is the first month of the year and when the festival cycle begins.

[20] The second reading, *Zakhor* (Deut 25:17-19), is indeed relevant only to the intervening celebration of Purim, the holiday celebrating the events of the book of Esther. It commands that later Jews remember to blot out the evil deeds of Amalek, understood as the ancestor of Haman.

Maxwell Johnson also critiques Hoffman's search for the three-week period, indicating that the Christian parallel of a three-week Lent is itself known only from other places and times, both on chronological and calendrical grounds. He also hints gently but correctly that Hoffman has failed to demonstrate that what he posits was actually known at the time among Jews.[21] Nevertheless, we should note that the nature and paucity of surviving evidence makes it exceedingly difficult to go beyond conjecture about the motivations behind any rabbinic decisions of that era.

The historical basis for our comparison of liturgical years had its share of pitfalls, but I would argue that the theological comparisons were the fundamental problem of the course. Functionally, there were simply almost no points of theological contact between the two cycles. The rabbinic Jewish liturgical year becomes rooted in the Exodus experience. Passover remains a memorial of the Exodus itself, now, like all other observances, without its sacrificial component. Its seventh day, however, now commemorates the crossing of the Sea of Reeds, the conclusion of the Israelites' escape from Egypt. The rabbis understand the Feast of Shavuot (Weeks, Pentecost) to commemorate the anniversary of the Sinai revelation, and the feast of Sukkot (Booths, Tabernacles) became for them a memorial of the fragility of Israelite life while wandering in the wilderness for forty years. Even the Sabbath has its Exodus overtones. As the prayer sanctifying the day states, it is a "memorial of the Exodus from Egypt"—pointing both to the Sabbath commandment at Sinai and the prior teaching about the Sabbath embedded in the provision of a double portion of manna on Friday.

Perhaps the lectionary focus on the pentateuchal narrative can be understood to serve the same purpose. While some prophetic readings (*haftarot*) provide additional elements of Israel's history, they appear only in fragmentary fashion and inevitably serve either the Torah reading or the liturgical season. The most marked of these liturgical seasons, the three weeks preceding and the seven weeks following the fast of the Ninth of Av, mourning for the destructions of the Jerusalem temples, does not develop the Exodus narrative, but it is a similar re-

[21] "Lent in Perspective: A Summary Dialogue," in *Passover and Easter: A Symbolic Structuring*, 63–64. Johnson also includes this discussion in his "Preparation for Pascha? Lent in Christian Antiquity," in *Between Memory and Hope*, 213–14, and Paul F. Bradshaw and Maxwell E. Johnson, *The Origins of Feasts, Fasts and Seasons in Early Christianity* (Collegeville, MN: Liturgical Press, 2011), 95–97.

demptive drama. God punished Israel by destroying the temple and causing Jews to go into exile, but God also promises a future messianic redemption, a renewed version of the Exodus.

There is hardly a hint of these Jewish foci in the Christian liturgical year, which is exclusively christological.[22] Its major festivals and observances revolve around the events and insights of the New Testament, even when the day itself has its roots in biblical Judaism. Where, as with Passover, the language itself carries over (less so in English and Germanic languages than in Romance languages), it is Jesus who is now the paschal sacrifice, and even that term becomes understood frequently through its Greek homophone *paschein*, to suffer, rather than its original Hebrew meaning. Pentecost may have a parallel element of revelation and preserve the same connection to its preceding holiday,[23] but it is the gift of the Holy Spirit to the disciples, not a celebration of the wheat harvest or a recollection of Sinai. The eighth day Lord's Day celebrating Jesus' resurrection triumphs over the seventh day Sabbath and takes on many of its characteristics, including, often, its name.

What follows here is not an insight that was apparent to me in 2005, though I do, in retrospect, think that it is important; perhaps it does not require an entire semester's study to evoke it. The course demonstrated the degree to which the memorial foci of Jewish and Christian liturgical years apparently differ completely. Consciousness of this points us to the recognition that this difference in message holds true for our daily and weekly liturgies as well. In Jewish daily liturgies, this same redemptive focus is more subtle, but it is nonetheless very present once one becomes alert to it.[24] There is a point of convergence that we missed, however, perhaps because it was too obvious. While understood differently, in both cases, the overarching concern of the

[22] As demonstrated in great detail by Fritz West, *Scripture and Memory: The Ecumenical Hermeneutic of the Three-Year Lectionaries* (Collegeville, MN: Liturgical Press, 1997).

[23] Leviticus 23:15-16 dictates that one shall count seven weeks from the day after the Sabbath of Passover. Different understandings of what this meant led to different actual datings of this festival in Second Temple Judaism. Rabbinic Jews understand this "Sabbath" to refer to the first holy day of the festival, meaning that the actual day of the week of the holiday varies depending on the cycles of the moon. Jubilees and the Dead Sea Scrolls point to the existence of alternative calendars in late Second Temple Judaism, and Christianity may draw from these.

[24] As has been well demonstrated by Reuven Kimelman, "The Daily Amidah and the Rhetoric of Redemption," *Jewish Quarterly Review* 79, nos. 2–3 (1989): 165–97.

liturgy is the past, present, and future redemptive or salvific[25] action of God. Jewish liturgy, however, very carefully distinguishes the nature of the redemption it commemorates and yearns for from Christian understandings of salvation. This extends to minimizing the role of the human person of the Messiah, especially in the redemptive drama described in the daily prayers[26] but also in the virtual absence of the historical Moses from the Passover haggadah. Methods could probably be developed by which to evoke a more nuanced and productive comparison that focuses on the means of expressing what in Christian terms would be called the anamnesis of salvation history in our two traditions.

To what extent this differentiation was deliberate and to what extent this happened in the isolated development of these two communities' ways of celebrating their stories require scholarly investigation and probably more early texts than have been preserved from the Jewish world.[27] What we can say definitively is that the "ways" did "part," with both Jews and Christians ensuring that the liturgical experiences that would shape the theologies of their communities clearly delineate their differing understandings of the state of human history and God's past, present, and future involvement in it.

What are the implications of this for our time of renewed understanding between Jews and Christians? First, I think it suggests that the search for the origins of Christian liturgy within Judaism ought to be undertaken with great caution and with recognition of the really fundamental and substantial transformation that occurred within the Christian community of any Jewish roots that it might have had. Second, as is reasonably well recognized, these roots are probably not to be found in rabbinic Jewish practice, as that practice underwent its own set of transformations before reaching forms known to us today, and some of those forms were Jewish moves to differentiate Jewish life from that of Christians. This means that visits to synagogues or Pass-

[25] Christianity is obviously comfortable with the language of "salvation," but precisely because the word has such Christian overtones in English, Jews tend to avoid the term and use the word "redemption" instead. Ultimately, I would argue, the difference is insignificant except as language choice serves as an identity marker.

[26] On this, see Kimelman, "The Daily Amidah," 165–97.

[27] There are essentially no Jewish liturgical manuscripts preserved that can be securely dated to the first Christian millennium. Even compositions that originated then have been copied by scribes who we know often "corrected" prayer texts, making them unreliable as witnesses.

over Seders be recognized as not bringing Christians closer to the experience of Jesus, for in his world, neither Christianity nor rabbinic Judaism had found its later modes of expression, if indeed they can be said to have existed at all.[28] Visits to each other's liturgies serve other dialogic purposes though, purposes of education about the other in its own integrity as living traditions today. This recognition of difference itself can lead to reflection on one's own home tradition that is enlightening—as this essay itself demonstrates from my Jewish perspective.

* * * *

Appendix

Syllabus of Boston College Course TH403.01, co-taught with Bruce T. Morrill, SJ, in Fall 2005

The Jewish and Christian liturgical years dance around each other, interpreting the seasons and their biblical celebrations in ways that are both overlapping and oppositional. Beginning with the common Sabbath and a timely exploration of the Jewish High Holy Day season and its thematic Christian parallels, this course will compare Jewish and Christian understandings and celebrations of the liturgical calendar. In the course of this comparison, we will explore the development of the celebrations, the ways that they form and inform their practitioners. Because Christianity grew out of Judaism and because Jews and Christians have constantly lived in each other's presence, we will also explore how this interaction itself shaped these liturgies.

This course is sponsored by the Boston College's Center for Christian-Jewish Learning.

Course Requirements

- Attendance, preparation for, and participation in class and in the synagogue visit.
- Posting questions and brief reflections about the readings on the WebCT discussion page before class. You may receive written or oral responses to these reflections and questions, but they will not be graded (20% of grade, along with class participation).

[28] As is discussed by Frank Senn, "Should Christians Celebrate the Passover?," in Bradshaw and Hoffman, *Passover and Easter*, 183–205.

- *Undergraduates, IREPM, and ministry students*: a reflection paper of 1,500–2,000 words comparing the penitential themes in Catholic and Jewish liturgies, due October 20 (25%) and a second paper of similar length, on a topic of your choice, due December 8 (25%).
- OR: *Theology MA and PhD students*: a substantive research paper, on a topic to be determined in consultation with the instructor. Due December 8 (50%).
- Take-home comprehensive, open-book final exam, due on the date of the scheduled exam (30%).

Texts

Available at the BC Bookstore.

A Different Night: The Family Participation Haggadah

Between Memory and Hope, Maxwell Johnson, ed.

Passover and Easter: Origin and History to Modern Times, Paul Bradshaw and Lawrence Hoffman, eds.

Passover and Easter: The Symbolic Structuring of Sacred Seasons, Paul Bradshaw and Lawrence Hoffman, eds.

The Origins of the Liturgical Year, Thomas Talley

The Sabbath, Abraham Heschel

All other readings available to registered students through the course's WebCT site on the "Readings" page.

Syllabus

Date	*Topic and Assignment*
9/8	Our Calendars.
9/15	The Sabbath I: *The Sabbath*; and pages on the Sabbath at http://www.myjewishlearning.com/daily_life/Shabbat.htm.
9/16–17	Synagogue Visit: either Friday evening or Saturday morning; information to be provided.
9/22	The Sabbath II (RL away): *Dies Domini* (Apostolic Letter of Pope John Paul II, 1998); *Between Memory and Hope*, 49–96 (Mark Searle, "Sunday: The Heart of the Liturgical Year"; H. Boone Porter, "Day of the Lord: Day of Mystery"; and Robert F. Taft, SJ, "The Frequency of the Celebration of the Eucharist throughout History"); and Pierre Jounel, "Sunday and the Week" in *The Liturgy and Time* (ed., A.G. Martimort), 9–29.
9/29	Penitential Liturgies I: Lent: *The Origins of the Liturgical Year*, 163–230; *Passover and Easter*, vol. 6, 1–68 (Paul F. Bradshaw and Lawrence

A. Hoffman, "Passover and Easter: The Symbolic Shaping of Time and Meaning"; Lawrence A. Hoffman, "The Great Sabbath and Lent: Jewish Origins?"; Maxwell E. Johnson, "Preparation for Pascha? Lent in Christian Antiquity"; and Lawrence A. Hoffman and Maxwell E. Johnson, "Lent in Perspective: A Summary Dialogue"); and *Between Memory and Hope*, 125–41 (Patrick Regan, OSB, "The Three Days and the Forty Days").

10/6 Penitential Liturgies II: High Holy Days: Selections from Sh. Agnon, *Days of Awe*; and pages on Rosh Hashanah, Yom Kippur at http://myjewishlearning.com.

10/13 *Yom Kippur—No Class—Reflection Paper due next week.*

10/20 Sukkot/Feast of Booths—*Class will meet outside in Prof. Langer's Sukkah*: Lawrence A. Hoffman, "Does God Remember: A Liturgical Theology of Memory," 41–72, and Paul F. Bradshaw, "Anamnesis in Modern Eucharistic Debate," 73–84, in Michael A. Signer, ed., *Memory and History in Christianity and Judaism* (Notre Dame, 2001); and explore the pages at http://www.myjewishlearning.com/holidays/Sukkot.htm.

10/27 Passover and Easter I: History: *Passover and Easter*, vol. 5, 1–124 (Paul F. Bradshaw, "Easter in Christian Tradition"; Lawrence A. Hoffman, "The Passover Meal in Jewish Tradition"; Blake Leyerle, "Meal Customs in the Greco-Roman World"; Joseph Tabory, "Towards a History of the Paschal Meal"; Paul F. Bradshaw, "The Origins of Easter"; and Israel J. Yuval, "Easter and Passover as Early Jewish-Christian Dialogue"); and *The Origins of the Liturgical Year*, 1–33.

11/3 Passover and Easter II: The Seder: *A Different Night*; and *Passover and Easter*, vol. 5, 127–60, 189–213 (Israel J. Yuval, "Passover in the Middle Ages"; and Carole B. Balin, "The Modern Transformation of the Ancient Passover Haggadah"); outline of the Seder (handout via WebCT). Recommended video, "Passover: Festival of Freedom" (O'Neill Media Center).

11/10 Passover and Easter III: The Triduum: *The Origins of the Liturgical Year*, 33–54; *Passover and Easter*, vol. 5, 161–85, 214–35 (Joanne M. Pierce, "Holy Week and Easter in the Middle Ages"; and John Allyn Melloh, "Revising Holy Week and Easter Rites"); *Between Memory and Hope*, 143–53 (Patrick Regan, OSB, "Veneration of the Cross"); and "Triduum Liturgies" in *Catholic Rites Today* (ed. Bouley), 313–41, 119–33.

11/17 I. Pentecost and II. The Calendar of Saints (RL away): *The Origins of the Liturgical Year*, 54–77; *Passover and Easter*, vol. 6, 94–106 (Martin F. Connell, "From Easter to Pentecost"); and *Between Memory and Hope*, 223–46, 375–83, 429–44 (Patrick Regan, OSB, "The Fifty Days and the

Fiftieth Day"; John F. Baldovin, SJ, "On Feasting the Saints" and "The Liturgical Year: Calendar for a Just Community").

12/1 Minor Jewish Feasts and Fasts (and Shavuot/Pentecost): Celebrating History: *Passover and Easter*, vol. 6, 71–93 (Efrat Zarren Zohar, "From Passover to Shavuot"); and pages on Tisha B'av, Purim, Hanukkah, Modern Holidays (those beginning with "Yom") at http://www.myjewishlearning.com/.

12/8 Advent-Christmas-Epiphany: *The Origins of the Liturgical Year*, 79–162; and *Between Memory and Hope*, 273–90, 349–71 (Susan K. Roll, "The Origins of Christmas: The State of the Question"; and Martin J. Connell, "The Origins and Evolution of Advent in the West").

Michael Daniel Findikyan

Chapter 4

Saints Nicholas in Armenia

The *Directory of Feasts* of the Armenian Church, the liturgical calendar known as the *Tōnac'oyc'*, registers two feasts for saints named "Nicholas." The First Saturday of Advent[1] is dedicated to the commemoration "of Saints Gregory the Wonderworker [*Grigori Sk'anč'elagorcin*], Nicholas the Patriarch [*Nikołayosi hayrapetin*] and Bishop Myron [*Miwṙonay episcoposin*]."[2] The second commemoration falls just two

[1] Advent (*Yisnak*) begins on the Monday nearest November 18. The calendar of the Armenian Church, one of the more complex in the Christian world, is characterized by its transparent hagiopolite pedigree, on the one hand, and by its overwhelming variability from year to year owing to its septenary structure, on the other hand. Charles Renoux's manifold studies on aspects of the Armenian liturgical year are to be consulted. Cesare Tondini de Quarenghi, *Étude sur le calendrier liturgique de la nation arménienne avec le calendrier arménien de 1907* (Rome: Pustet, 1906) remains helpful. Archbishop Khajag Barsamian provides a convenient survey in English based on Tondini de Quarenghi: idem, *The Calendar of the Armenian Church* (New York: St. Vartan Press, 1995). For an English translation of the *Tōnac'oyc'* with generous and helpful annotations (though many are in need of updating in light of recent scholarship), see *Domar: A Compendium of the Directorium and Calendar of the Armenian Apostolic Orthodox Church According to the Traditions of the Apostolic See of Jerusalem*, ed. Ghevont Samoorian (n.p.: Armenian Orthodox Theological Research Institute, 2006). The best study of the topic in Armenian is Ṙ.H. Vardanyan, Հայոց Տոնացոյցը [The Directory of Feasts of the Armenians] (Erevan: Gitut'yun Press, 1999). Apropos of the Armenian sanctoral, see especially Nicholas Adontz, "Les fêtes et les saints de l'église arménienne," *Revue de l'Orient Chretien* 26 (1927): 74–104, 225–78; Charles Renoux, "Les fêtes et les saints de l'église arménienne de N. Adontz," *Revue des Etudes Arméniennes* 14 (1980): 287–305; and idem, "Les premières manifestations liturgiques du culte des saints en Arménie," in *Saints et sainteté dans la liturgie*, Conférences Saint-Serge, Collectio Subsidia 40 (Rome: Bibliotheca Ephemerides Liturgicae, 1987), 291–303.

[2] Տօնացոյց հատոր առաջին յորում նշանակին տօնք, պահք, ընթերցուածք, արարողութիւնք հայաստանեայց սուրբ եկեղեցւոյ [Directory of Feasts Volume One in which are Designated Feasts, Fasts, Lections, Ceremonies of the Holy

weeks later, on the Third Saturday of Advent, and is reserved for "Saint Nicholas the Wonderworking 'Smyrnian' Patriarch [*Srboyn Nikołayosi Zmiwṙnac'woy sk'anč'elagorc hayrapetin*]."[3] Who are these two saints named Nicholas, if indeed they refer to different persons? And if not, why do the Armenians commemorate the same saint twice, just two weeks apart, during the season of Advent?

In homage to my good friend and colleague, Reverend Professor Maxwell E. Johnson, whose numerous scholarly contributions on the origins of the liturgical year, and whose abiding affection for the saints handily merit him the exalted Armenian honorific, *Tōnasēr* (Lover of Feasts),[4] I offer this modest investigation into a curious anomaly in the liturgical calendar of the Armenian Church: an essay that illustrates once again, I hope, the urgent requisite for continued historical study of the ancient Armenian Rite, among other reasons, for the purpose of effectively pastoring God's people in this remote corner of the Lord's vineyard, a summons relentlessly voiced by Professor Johnson throughout his distinguished teaching and writing ministry.

Hṙač'ea Ačaṙyan's exhaustive Armenian prosopographical dictionary lists forty-six individuals named Nicholas (Nikołos, Nikawlayos, Niwkowłayos, Nikołayos, Nikełos, Nikol, Nikawl) who are known to the Armenians.[5] They include five Roman popes, two Russian czars, an Armenian patriarch of Constantinople (1477–89),[6] a fifteen-year-old martyr from Tigranakert (d. 1642)[7] and another from Bursa (d. 1694),[8] and the notorious Armenian Bishop Nikol T'orosovič' of Lviv (1662–90), who became Catholic and whom Armenian historians accuse of having turned the Armenian people of Poland away from their ancestral church.[9] The rest of the Nicholases in Ačaṙyan's inventory are

Church of the Armenians], (Jerusalem: Press of the Apostolic See of Saint James, 1915), 265; henceforth, *Tōnac'oyc'*.

[3] Ibid., 271.

[4] Detailed explanations and annotations scattered throughout the *Tōnac'oyc'* that assist the user in navigating the calendar's complicated structure are often quaintly addressed to the intrepid user: "O Lover of feasts . . ." [Ով տօնասէր . . .]. The editor of the modern *Directory of Feasts* was Catholicos Simēon Erewanc'i (1710–80). *Tōnac'oyc'*, 215 *et infra*.

[5] Hṙač'ea Ačaṙyan, Հայոց անձնանունների բառարան [Dictionary of Armenian Personal Names], 5 vols. (Yerevan: State University Publisher, 1942), 4:75–80. N.B. numbers 19 and 20 in Ačaṙyan's list are duplicates; ibid., 77.

[6] Ibid., 4:78.

[7] Ibid., 4:78–79.

[8] Ibid., 4:79.

[9] Ibid.

scribes, clergymen, and patrons of letters whose names are mentioned in passing in sundry manuscript colophons but who are otherwise unknown. All but a few date from the thirteenth century, when, according to Ačaṙyan, the name "Nicholas" becomes more common in Armenian circles. Only one Nicholas in Ačaṙyan's inventory is identified as a saint of the Armenian Church: "Nikołayos, the great patriarch of Miwṙon of the Lycians [*Miwṙonay Likēac'woc'*], whom the Armenian Church commemorates; he has odes [*ganjer*], anthems [*tałer*], prayers and a hymn [*šarakan*]."[10] This great Nicholas, the bishop and wonderworker much loved throughout Christendom, is doubtless to be identified with the second of the two Armenian Nicholas commemorations, that on the third Saturday of Advent, which falls close to December 6, the traditional and unanimous date of Nicholas' death and of his commemoration in the Byzantine East[11] and Roman West.[12] Moreover, the same saintly thaumaturge must also be identified with "Nicholas the Patriarch," subject of the preceding feast,[13] since the Armenians seem to know no other Nicholas worthy of veneration.

The existence of two commemorations for St. Nicholas in the Armenian sanctoral is problematic not only because of their close occurrence but because the distinctive structure of the Armenian liturgical year only allows saints' commemorations on Mondays, Tuesdays, Thursdays, and Saturdays, and that only outside of fasting periods and "dominical" feasts and seasons (the octave of Theophany, Holy Week, the fifty days of Eastertide, the seven days of Pentecost, the three days of Transfiguration, the nine days of the Assumption of the Mother of God, and the septenary of the Feast of the Cross,[14] and all dominical feast days).[15] In sum, only around one-third of the days of the year are eligible for saints' commemorations. This restriction

[10] Ibid., 4:75.

[11] Alexander Kazhdan, "Nicholas of Myra," in *The Oxford Dictionary of Byzantium*, ed. Alexander P. Kazhdan, 3 vols. (New York/Oxford: Oxford University Press, 1991), 2:1469.

[12] *Butler's Lives of the Saints, New Full Edition*, 12 vols. (Collegeville, MN: Liturgical Press, 1999), 12:59.

[13] Tondini de Quarenghi asserts this unequivocally by designating the subject of the earlier commemoration as "St. Nicolas, éveque de Myre." Tondini de Quarenghi, *Étude sur le calendrier liturgique*, 60.

[14] Which is actually the ancient octave of *Encaenia*. See Michael Daniel Findikyan, "Armenian Hymns of the Holy Cross and the Jerusalem *Encaenia*," *Revue des Études Arméniennes* 32 (2010): 25–58.

[15] Tondini de Quarenghi, *Étude sur le calendrier liturgique*, v, 2–4 et *infra*.

ultimately serves to reserve Sunday as the *dies dominica*, when all devotion may be focused on the divine economy of the Lord. Few, consequently, are the days in the Armenian liturgical year entirely devoted to a single saint,[16] and highly privileged are those few saints who have been assigned more than one annual commemoration.[17] In the case of multiple annual commemorations of a particular saint, they tend to be separated by intervals of several months. Thus the two-week span separating the two feast days for St. Nicholas is highly unusual. Before turning to this circumstance, however, we need to consider yet another anomaly that should strike the eye of any devotee of St. Nicholas.

What are we to make of the curious attribute *Zmiwṙnac'woy*, "the Smyrnian," attributed to Nicholas on the Third Saturday of Advent? According to the testimony of the various *vitae*, Nicholas was born in the town of Patara in the Province of Lycia in southwestern Asia Minor.[18] He later became the bishop not of "Smyrna" but of Myra. As far as I can tell, Nicholas does not seem ever to have set foot in Smyrna, some six hundred miles to the west. Without patently acknowledging any incongruity in the place of St. Nicholas' ministry, Patriarch T'orgom Gušakean seems to have sought to reconcile the inconsistency in his famous handbook, *Saints and Feasts*. He notes this about Nicholas' episcopal see: "*Miwṙay* [Myra] . . . a city in *Likia* [Lycia], is near *Zmiwṙin* [Smyrna]."[19]

[16] In addition to the second commemoration of St. Nicholas in Advent, the saints who merit their own exclusive commemorations are: Saints John the Baptist, Anthony of the Desert, Vahan of Gołtn, Athanasius, Gregory the Theologian, Theodore the General, Gregory the Illuminator, Prophet Zecheriah, Prophet Elisha, Prophet Isaiah, Prophet Jeremiah, John Chrysostom, King Abgar, Asduacatur (a.k.a. Adeodat, Hiztibuzd) the Martyr, Stephen the First Martyr. Feasts of the Mother of God fall under the category of "dominical" [*tērunakan*] days.

[17] In addition to St. Nicholas, they are: Saints Athanasius, Cyril of Alexandria, Cyril of Jerusalem, (Ps-)Dionysius the Areopagite, Epiphanius of Cyprus, Gregory the Illuminator, Gregory of Nazianzus, Apostle James (the Minor), John Chrysostom, John the Baptist, Lucien of Antioch, Bishop Meletius of Persia, Mesrob, Apostle Philip, Sahak Part'ew the Patriarch, Sahak the Prince and Martyr.

[18] Patriarch T'orgom [Gušakean], Սուրբք եւ տօնք հայաստանեայց եկեղեցւոյ [Saints and Feasts of the Church of the Armenians], 2nd printing (Jerusalem: Saint James Press, 1957), 90; henceforth, *Saints and Feasts*.

[19] Ibid. Gušakean's popular but comprehensive guide lists only this entry for a saint named "Nicholas." The author mentions nothing about a double commemoration for the wonderworking bishop.

As a matter of fact, medieval Armenian manuscript lectionaries, synaxaria, and other liturgical texts give a number of variant designations for Nicholas' provenance. We find several apparent variations of "Myra" in the sources: *Miwřon / Miwřonay*,[20] *Miwřia / Miwřioy*,[21] *Miwřis*,[22] or *Miwřay*.[23] Equally well represented are references to the Wonderworker's place of origin as *Zmiwřin / Zmiwřnoy*[24] or, according to a late fourteenth-century manuscript, *Zmiřn / Zmřna*.[25] Just as frequently, however, the manuscripts designate the saint as merely "Nicholas the Patriarch."

Alas, the disparate bynames that appear to allude to the city of "Smyrna" are actually alternative appellations for one and the same "Myra," deriving from an alternate reading of Acts 27:5 in the Armenian version. Long before the birth of the Wonderworker, St. Paul transited at Μύρα τῆς Λυκίας at the outset of his fateful journey toward

[20] Ms. synaxarion Erevan 1339 (sixteenth century), Մայր ցուցակ հայերէն ձեռագրաց Մաշտոցի անուան մատենադարանի [Main Catalogue of Armenian Manuscripts in the Maštoc' Matenadaran], ed. A. K'eōškerean, K. Suk'easean, and Y. K'ēōsēean, vol. 4 (Erevan: Nairi Press, 2008), 4:798; henceforth, *Mayr C'uc'ak* 4. Ačaṙyan too uses this appellation. Idem, 4:75.

[21] Ms. lectionary Venice 612 (thirteenth to fourteenth century), Մայր ցուցակ հայերէն ձեռագրաց մատենադարանին Մխիթարեանց ի Վենետիկ [Main Catalogue of Armenian Manuscripts in the Library of the Mxit'areans in Venice], ed. Sahak Jemjemian, vol. 4 (Venice: St. Łazar, 1993), 4:798; henceforth, *Venetik* 4.

[22] From the *vita* in the so-called Armenian Synaxarion of Tēr-Israel, which was actually compiled by one Kirakos of the East [*Arewelc'i*], who is probably to be identified with the famous historiographer, Kirakos Ganjakec'i (d. 1271). This concise *vita* is attributed to Gregory of Nyssa. G. Bayan, *Le Synaxaire arménien de Ter-Israel*, Patrologia Orientalis, vol. 16, bk. 1 (Brepols, 1922), 168, 170. See also Patricia Boisson-Chenorhokian, "Notes sur Kirakos Ganjakec'i," *Revue des Études Arméniennes* 30 (2005–2007), 237–46, for a convincing argument supporting this attribution.

[23] Gušakean, *Saints and Feasts*, 90.

[24] Ms. Hymnal Vienna 38 (nineteenth century) f. 30v., Ցուցակ հայերէն ձեռագրաց մատենադարանին Մխիթարեանց ի Վիեննա [Catalogue of Armenian Manuscripts in the Library of the Mxit'areans in Vienna], ed. Jacobus Dashian [Tašean] (Vienna, 1895), 196; henceforth, Dashian. Ms. Homiliary Vienna 224 (olim 8, AD 1428), f. 31v. Ibid., 573. Ms. Homiliary Erevan 941 (AD 1689), Մայր ցուցակ հայերէն ձեռագրաց Մաշտոցի անուան մատենադարանի [Main Catalogue of Armenian Manuscripts in the Maštoc' Matenadaran], ed. O. Eganyan, et al., vol. 3 (Erevan: Magałat', 2007), 3:1334–35; henceforth, *Mayr C'uc'ak* 3. Ms. Erevan 941 (AD 1689), ibid., 1325. Ms. Erevan 938 (seventeenth century) has *Nikołayosi zmiwřonac'oy*, f. 250rv, ibid ,1308.

[25] Ms. lectionary Venice 602 (AD 1349), *Venetik* 4:672.

Rome. The Armenian text in the Zohrapean Bible has *smiwṙa likiac'woc'* (Smyra/Myra of the Lycians).[26] An annotation indicates this significant variant: *zmiwṙnia likac'woc'* or *lwkiac'woc'* (Myra/Smyrna of the Lycians), which even more closely resembles the various bynames for St. Nicholas in the manuscripts. Whatever the original etymological rationale for the odd Armenian rendering of the Lycian seaport town mentioned in Acts 27:5, it is evident that medieval Armenian scribes assimilated the place of Nicholas' episcopal see to the biblical phrase that was no doubt well known to them.

The multiplicity of variations for the name of Nicholas seen in the manuscript tradition was likely compounded by a characteristic of Classical Armenian grammar, whereby the letter z (զ) is prefixed to words in the accusative case to indicate the definite article. This invariably causes confusion in distinguishing whether unusual proper nouns that begin with the letter z (զ) are just that or are simply in the accusative case.

Worth noting as well in this regard is the remarkable coincidence that on the First Saturday of Advent (mentioned above), a certain Bishop *Miwṙon* is commemorated alongside "Nicholas the Patriarch," who hails from *Miwṙon* according to one of the common Armenian designations of Nicholas' episcopal see, as we have seen. Is the concurrence on this day of the proper noun *Miwṙon* as *both* a prosoponym *and* a toponym sheer serendipity? Or did the common name somehow factor into the eventual shared commemoration of these two saints? I have found no evidence to support the latter conjecture.

One thing is certain. In faraway Armenia, the people's love and admiration for the Wonderworker evidently did not translate into precision regarding their memory of his place of ministry.

The Armenian commemoration of St. Nicholas in early December dates only to the very end of the thirteenth century. There is no feast of anyone named "Nicholas" in *Čašoc'* manuscripts copied before that time, including, notably, in the Armenian Lectionary of Jerusalem[27]

[26] Աստուածաշունչ մատեան հին եւ նոր կտակարանաց [Divinely Inspired Scripture of the Old and New Testaments], ed. Yovhan Zōhrapean, reprint of the Venice 1805 edition (Delmar, NY: Caravan Books, 1984), 747.

[27] Charles A. Renoux, *Le codex arménien Jérusalem 121. Édition comparée du texte et de deux autres manuscrits. Introduction, textes, traduction et notes*, Patrologia Orientalis, vol. 36, bk. 2 (Turnhout: Brepols, 1971), 188–92; henceforth, *Čašoc' II*. Curiously, the Georgian version of the Lectionary of Jerusalem, representing liturgical prac-

and the oldest "Cilician" Lectionary [*Čašoc'*] (Erevan 832), whose *terminus ante quem* is AD 1105, when the physiognomy of the Armenian Lectionary changes notably due, among other factors, to the multiplication of saints' commemorations.[28] That sudden burgeoning cannot be unrelated to the prolific career of Catholicos Grigor II Pahlawuni (d. AD 1105), known as *Vkayasēr* (Martyrophile), who devoted much of his life to studying and translating the lives of saints.[29] The inclusion of Nicholas' commemoration may well be connected with the Martyrophile's work, although the precise number, identity, and origin of the *vitae* translated or edited by Gregory remains unknown.[30] Nor is there any mention of St. Nicholas in the famous Armenian Homeliary of Muš, compiled in AD 747.[31]

It should also be recalled that the earliest formal account of St. Nicholas' life was written some five hundred years after his death, by an "incompletely-identified Michael the Archimandrite" between 814 and 842.[32] While no texts concerning the Wonderworker exist from

---

tices between the fifth and eighth centuries, has a commemoration, *Patris Sabbae et sancti Nicolai*, on December 5. Michel Tarchnischvili, trans., *Le grand lectionnaire de l'église de Jerusalem II*, Corpus Scriptorum Christianorum Orientalium 205, Scriptores Iberici 14 (Louvain: Peeters, 1960), 55.

[28] Charles A. Renoux, *Le Lectionnaire de Jérusalem en arménie. Le Čašoc' I: Introduction et liste des manuscripts*, Patrologia Orientalis, vol. 44, bk. 4 (Turnhout/Belgique: Brepols, 1989), 451ff.; henceforth, *Lectionnaire I*.

[29] Charles A. Renoux, *Le codex arménien Jérusalem 121. Introduction aux origines de la liturgie hierosolymitaine. Lumières nouvelles*, Patrologia Orientalis, vol. 35, bk. 1 (Turnhout: Brepols, 1969), 452–60; henceforth, *Čašoc' I*. See M. Avdalbegyan, Յայսմաւուրք ժողովածուները եւ նրանց պատմագրական արժէքը [The *Yaysmavurk'* Collections and Their Historiographical Value] (Erevan, 1982), 29–37. A. Kapoïan-Kouyoujian, "Le Catholicos Grégoire II le Martyrophile (Vkayasēr) et ses peregrinations," *Bazmavēp* 132 (1975): 306–25. Małak'ea Ōrmanean (Ormanian), Ազգապատում [*Azgapatum*. History of a People: Passages of the Armenian Orthodox Church from the Beginning to Our Times, Narrated in the Context of National Circumstances], 3 vols., 2nd ed. (Beirut: Sevan, 1960), 1:1282, 1285–86; henceforth, *Azgapatum*.

[30] Renoux, *Čašoc' I*, 452; *Azgaptaum* 1:1283.

[31] Michel Van Esbroeck, "Description du répertoire de l'Homéliaire de Muš," *Revue des Études Arméniennes* 18 (1984): 237–80.

[32] Charles William Jones, *Saint Nicholas of Myra, Bari and Manhattan: Biography of a Legend* (Chicago, IL: University of Chicago Press, 1978), 45. I resume the early history of Nicholas' *vita* in this paragraph from Jones's study. Jones's erudite "biography" concerns not the historical Nicholas *per se*, but the so-called *N.*, the St. Nicholas *legenda* or mythical figure that developed in the devotional imagination

before this time, the Life of St. Nicholas of Sion, a sixth-century monk named after the Wonderworker and hailing from the same town, testifies, in that era, to a well-established cult of the Wonderworking bishop, including a church dedicated to him in Myra, an annual commemoration, and many contemporary figures named Nicholas. Scholars have determined that the Life of Nicholas of Sion became an important model for the Life of the fourth-century Wonderworker.[33] Shortly after Michael the Archimandrite's *vita* of Nicholas, another Life by a certain Methodios becomes the source for the Latin Life written by John the Deacon of Naples about the year 880. This Methodius, who has been plausibly identified as the iconodule Patriarch of Constantinople (843–47), is to be distinguished from a homonymous hagiographer, who, sometime after 860, pens an independent *vita* known as the *Encomium Methodii* that is twice as long as the work of the Patriarch and proves very popular. This longer version was translated into several eastern languages, including Armenian.[34]

The earliest Armenian commemoration of St. Nicholas is found in the richly illuminated manuscript lectionary Erevan 979 dated AD 1286.[35] It designates "the life and repose of the wonder-working Patriarch Nikołayos" on the twenty-eighth of the Armenian month of *Trē*, which corresponds to December 6.[36] Several other early manuscript

---

of worshiping Christian communities. The definitive study of all the textual evidence is Gustav Anrich, *Hagios Nikolaos: Der heilige Nikolaos in der griechischen Kirche. Texte und Untersuchungen*, 2 vols. (Leipzig/Berlin: Teubner, 1913, 1917). Unavailable to me, this work is said to contain all the Greek texts of any interest, better edited than in Migne, and with a full introduction and notes. See also N. Del Re and M. C. Celletti, "Nicolas, vescovo di Mira," in *Bibliotheca Sanctorum* 9 (Rome: Instituto Giovanni XXIII della Pontificia Universita Lateranense, 1967), cols. 923–48. Philipp Niewöhner, "Neues zum Grab des hl. Nikolaus von Myra," *Jahrbuch für Antike und Christentum* 46 (2004): 119–33, provides an archaeological study of Nicholas' tomb in Kale/Demre, Turkey, where a church still stands. For the history of Nicholas' cult in the West, see Karl Meisen, *Nikolauskult und Nikolausbrauch im Abendlande*, Forschungen und Volkskunde 9–12 (Düsseldorf: Schwann, 1931).

[33] Ihor Ševčenko and Nancy Patterson Ševčenko, *The Life of St. Nicholas of Sion* (Brookline, MA: Hellenic College Press, 1985).

[34] A philological analysis of the various Armenian *vitae* of St. Nicholas has yet to be undertaken.

[35] *Mayr C'uc'ak* 3:1571, cf. 1561. The manuscript includes an illumination of Nicholas on f. 417v.

[36] Similar to the ancient Egyptian year, the calendar in use at the dawn of Armenia's Christianization consisted of twelve thirty-day months followed a five-

lectionaries appoint the commemoration of the wonderworking patriarch either on this specific date according to its Julian designation[37] or, according to its liturgical designation, the "Saturday of the third week of Advent," which remains today one of the two St. Nicholas observations in the Armenian Church's calendar.[38] Other manuscript lectionaries designate the commemoration on the "*Monday* of the third week of Advent"[39] or, in a manuscript synaxary copied in the city of Van in AD 1441, on *K'ałoc'* 3 / December 11.[40] The latter date for the commemoration will spread to a series of seventeenth-century ms. synaxaria copied in Persia in the seventeenth century.[41] The variability in the dating of the feast is a sign that it was an innovation, yet to take root in the Armenian sanctoral calendar. In any case, in the thirteenth and fourteenth centuries we see the seeds of the second of today's two Nicholas feasts.

As for the first one, long before becoming a feast of three wonderworking saints, this day seems originally to have been dedicated

---

or six-day intercalary period. In AD 1116, Yovhannēs the Deacon aligned it with the Julian calendar such that the first day of the Armenian year, *Nawasard* 1, corresponded with August 11. A. G. Abrahamyan, Հայոց գիր եւ գրչութիւն [Armenian Script and (Paleo)graphy] (Erevan: Erevan State University, 1973), 100, 107, 118–19; Edouard Dulaurier, *Recherches sur la chronologie arménienne: Technique et historique*, unabridged facsimile of the Paris 1859 edition (np: Elibron Classics, 2006), 111–15.

37 Among the older ones, ms. Erevan 940 (thirteenth to fourteenth century), *Mayr C'uc'ak* 3:1327; ms. Venice 612 (thirteenth to fourteenth century), *Venetik* 4:798.

38 Ms. Venice 602 (AD 1349), *Venetik* 4:672; ms. Venice 606 (AD 1425), ibid., 747.

39 Among the older ones are Venice 603 (AD 1356), *Venetik* 4:710; Erevan 982 (AD 1460), *Mayr C'uc'ak* 3:1602 with an illumination on 508v.

40 Ms. Venice 729, Մայր ցուցակ հայերէն ձեռագրաց մատենադարանին Մխիթարեանց ի Վենետիկ [Main Catalogue of Armenian Manuscripts in the Library of the Mxit'areans in Venice], ed. Sahak Jemjemian, vol. 5 (Venice: St. Łazar, 1995), 108; henceforth, *Venetik* 5. A colophon from the year 1615 mentions that ms. Erevan 24 was completed on Saturday, December 9, which was the feast of St. Nicholas the Patriarch. Մայր ցուցակ հայերէն ձեռագրաց Մաշտոցի անուան մատենադարանի [Main Catalogue of Armenian Manuscripts in the Maštoc' Matenadaran], ed. O. Eganyan et al., vol. 1 (Erevan: Armenian S.S.R. Academy of Sciences, 1984), 82; henceforth, *Mayr C'uc'ak* 1.

41 For example, mss. New Julfa 241 (AD 1630), 249 (AD 1658); 252 (AD 1694); 256 and 257 (seventeenth century), Smbat Tēr-Awetisean, ed., Ցուցակ հայերէն ձեռագրաց Նոր Ջուղայի Ամենափրկիչ Վանքի [Catalogue of Armenian Manuscripts in the All Savior's Monastery of New Julfa], vol. 1 (Vienna: Mkhitarian Press, 1970), 375, 392, 410, 441, 456.

exclusively to the third-century St. Gregory the Wonderworker. The oldest *Thaumaturge* to be commemorated as such by the Armenians, Gregory is mentioned for the first time in second-generation Armenian lectionaries. Manuscripts of this class contain the first indigenous Armenian additions and adaptations to the structure of the liturgical year vis-à-vis that adumbrated in the ancient Armenian Lectionary of Jerusalem. Their prototypes date from the fifth to the eighth centuries.[42] St. Gregory the Wonderworker, unknown to the Armenian Lectionary of Jerusalem, appears on the Saturday before Great Lent in two medieval Armenian lectionaries from this period in the company of a number of prominent church fathers: Athanasius, Basil, Gregory the Theologian, Gregory of Nyssa, John (Chrysostom), Cyril (of Alexandria), Proclus (of Constantinople), Irenaeus, Epiphanius of Cyprus, Ephrem, and Meletius of Antioch.[43] Eventually, via historical pathways that have yet to be traced, St. Gregory will migrate from the threshold of Great Lent to the cusp of Advent. The ms. lectionary Erevan 979 (AD 1289), in which we also found the oldest commemoration of St. Nicholas, assigns St. Gregory alone to November 17.[44] As late as AD 1425, ms. Venice 606 still has Gregory alone on the First Saturday of Advent, with Nicholas feted two weeks later.[45] We find Gregory and Nicholas celebrated together for the first time in ms. Venice 602, a lectionary dated AD 1349.[46] What is more remarkable is that the same manuscript also appoints the second commemoration for Nicholas two weeks later. Here, therefore, at least according to the

[42] Charles Renoux, "Un bilan provisoire sur l'héritage grec du rite arménien," *Le Museon* 116, no. 1 (2003): 56–57.

[43] Ms. Venice 596 (olim 169, tenth to eleventh century), *Venetik* 4:571; ms. Tübingen MA XIII 21 (twelfth century?), cited in Charles A. Renoux, *Le lectionnaire de Jérusalem en arménie. Le Čašoc' II: Édition synoptique des plus anciens témoins*, Patrologia Orientalis, vol. 48, bk. 2 (Rome: Pontificio Istituto Orientale, 1999), 103–59; henceforth, *Lectionnaire II*.

[44] *Mayr C'uc'ak* 3:1570. Cf. ms. Venice 612 (olim 920), dated to the thirteenth and fourteenth centuries. *Venetik* 4:797; Erevan 940 (thirteenth to fourteenth centuries). *Mayr C'uc'ak* 3:1326. About a century later, another manuscript lectionary appoints his feast day on Saturday of the tenth week following the feast of the Exaltation of the Cross (the Sunday nearest September 14 by Armenian Church reckoning), thus, in late November or early December. Ms. Erevan 982 (AD 1460), *Mayr C'uc'ak* 3:1601.

[45] *Venetik* 4:747.

[46] *Venetik* 4:672.

data available in the catalogues,[47] is the earliest manuscript containing the double commemoration of the Wonderworker from Myra.

St. Miwṙon the Thaumaturge, a fourth-century bishop of Crete,[48] not to be confused with two other saintly Miwṙons known to the Armenians,[49] joins Gregory and Nicholas, only much later. His earliest commemoration is found in a thirteenth- to fourteenth-century ms. Lectionary, Erevan 940, where he is commemorated alone, on *Aweleac'* 4 /August 9.[50] This will become a fairly stable date for Miwṙon's feast in the manuscript tradition. While some early sources devote that day exclusively to Miwṙon,[51] many others from the sixteenth century on place him together with St. Antoninos, a third-century martyr of Alexandria.[52] Yet, as late as the eighteenth century, numerous other manuscript synaxaries and lectionaries omit Miwṙon of Crete entirely,

[47] I have surveyed the catalogues of the most important repositories of Armenian manuscripts except for the collection of the Monastery of Saints James in Jerusalem; Archbishop Bogharian's otherwise magisterial catalogue does not provide detailed information on the contents of manuscript lectionaries or synaxaria. Մայր ցուցակ ձեռագրաց սրբոց Յակոբեանց [Main Catalogue of the Manuscripts of Saints James], ed. Norayr Połarean (Bogharian), 11 vols. (Jerusalem: Saint James Press, 1966–1991).

[48] Gušakean, *Saints and Feasts*, 90–92.

[49] The first is a certain Miwṙon the Priest, a martyr of the Decian persecutions. His martyrology is found in several Armenian ms. synaxaria, usually early in the Armenian month of Nawasard (mid-August). G. Bayan, Max de Saxe, *Le Synaxaire arménien de Ter Israel I. Mois de Navasard*, Patrologia Orientalis, vol. 5, bk. 3 (1910), 395–97. Cf. Renoux, "Les premières manifestations," 293, 296–97. The second is an obscure figure known as Meṙinos or Miwṙonos, who is associated with St. John the Evangelist in various ms. synaxaria. Ms. Miscellany Erevan 5 (AD 1783), *Mayr C'uc'ak* 1:16. Cf. ms. Homiliary Erevan 941 (AD 1689), *Mayr C'uc'ak* 3:1334; ms. Miscellany Erevan 995 (AD 1278), ibid., 1733.

[50] *Mayr C'uc'ak* 3:1322. In this manuscript, the other wonderworkers, Gregory and Nicholas, each have their own commemoration, on November 17 and December 6, respectively. Cf. ms. synaxary Vienna 1048 (AD 1302). Hamazasp Oskean, Ցուցակ հայերէն ձեռագրաց Մխիթարեան մատենադարանին ի Վիեննա Բ [Catalogue of Armenian Manuscripts of the Mxit'arean Library in Vienna Volume 2], Calouste Gulbenkian Foundation Armenian Library (Vienna: Mxit'arean Press, 1963), 710.

[51] For example, ms. Venice 727 (AD 1427), *Venetik* 5:55; and Vienna 7 (olim 4, AD 1439), Dashian, 46. As late as the sixteenth century, a ms. synaxary, Vienna 10, still devotes the day exclusively to Miwṙon. Dashian, 93.

[52] The earliest one I have uncovered is the ms. synaxary Vienna 1035, dated AD 1584. Oskean, 632. Today St. Antoninos is commemorated on the Monday of the fifth week of Pentecost. *Saints and Feasts*, 42.

securing August 9 for St. Antoninos alone.[53] This suggests that Miwṙon's devotion was not yet universal at the dawn of Catholicos Simēon Erewanc'i's reform of the calendar. The triple commemoration of Gregory, Nicholas, and Myron and their commemoration on the First Saturday of Advent are both phenomena unknown in any manuscript sources to my knowledge,[54] suggesting strongly that today's Armenian commemoration of the three wonderworkers on the First Saturday of Advent is an eighteenth-century innovation of Catholicos Simēon.

Conclusion

The double commemoration of St. Nicholas in Armenia is hardly a modern lapse but goes back over six hundred years, almost to the time of the emergence of Nicholas' veneration in the Armenian calendar in the late thirteenth century. Why just a generation later, in the mid-fourteenth century, would the manuscript lectionary Venice 602 designate two commemorations for Nicholas during Advent, just two weeks apart? The evidence suggests that the decades about the turn of the fourteenth century were a period of transformation in the Armenian sanctoral calendar. St. Gregory the Wonderworker is transferred to the beginning of Advent from his ancient position before Great Lent, and St. Nicholas is introduced into the Armenian calendar. By the arrangement of some unknown authority, a local church appointed St. Nicholas on the First Saturday of Advent in order to bring together the two Wonderworkers. Whether this was the original place for St. Nicholas in that community or whether the intent was to transfer

[53] For example, the ms. synaxaries Nor Julfa 252 (AD 1694) and Nor Julfa 256 (seventeenth century), Ter-Awetisean, 419, 450.

[54] An early edition of the *Tōnac'oyc'* printed in Venice in 1782 has the Wonderworkers Gregory and Miwṙon on the First Saturday of Advent, but not Nicholas. Տօնացոյց եւ աւետարանացոյց եւ կարգաւորութիւն եւ հրահանգ տէրունական տօնից [Tōnac'oyc' and Directory of Gospel Readings and Arrangement and Instruction on the Dominical Feasts] (Venice, 1782), 298. The addition of St. Miwṙon to the older commemoration of St. Gregory on that date could be under the influence of Simēon Erewanc'i's reform, since the Venice *Tōnac'oyc'* seems to contain some, though not all, of his reforms. In this case, the absence of Nicholas on that date would be the result of subsequent editing, presumably to eliminate the duplication of Nicholas' veneration. Yet lacking any supporting documentation, it is impossible to confirm this hypothesis.

him there from the Third Saturday of Advent we do not know. What is certain is that both dates stuck, resulting in the double commemoration that survives to this day. The Cretan bishop's incorporation with his wonderworking saintly colleagues, likely in the context of Catholicos Simēon's reforms, was the result of the same inclination to unite saints of the same generic category. As the register of venerable saints grows, such generic conglomeration will become a necessary and essential force driving the shape of the Armenian sanctoral calendar, the grouping of saints of a common genus on one day, one of its most distinctive features.

Furthermore, we must conclude that a "duplication" that seems exceptional today must have been anything but redundant to those communities that, especially early on, feted Nicholas twice within three weeks. The circumstance testifies to a heady time, perhaps concomitant with the appearance of his *vita* in Armenian, when St. Nicholas' devotion among the Armenians was much more fervent than it is today. The surge in Armenians named Nicholas from the thirteenth century surely attests to this,[55] as does the growing body of Armenian ecclesiastical poetry that emerges during this era.[56] A manuscript hymnal (*Šarakan*) dated AD 1295, one of the earliest surviving manuscript compendia of Armenian hymnography,[57] contains a *šarakan* in

[55] See above. Another curious indicator of the Wonderworker's popularity is found in the marginalia of many manuscripts. Scribes often invoke Nicholas in the scribbles that they inevitably scratch into the base or margins of manuscript folia as pen tests, called *grč'ap'orj* in Armenian. A certain priest-scribe Łazar invokes the protective eye of the Illuminator, the Catholicos, Parsuma the Hermit, and the Patriarch Nicholas "*Zmřnoy*" in a graffito at the beginning of the ms. Miscellany Erevan 1196 (seventeenth century). *Mayr C'uc'ak* 4:606.

[56] To these hymns I hope to return in a future study.

[57] The oldest ms. *Šarakans* are Bzommar 64 (AD 1187), Erevan 9838 (AD 1193), and Bzommar 59 and 60 (thirteenth to fourteenth centuries). Charles A. Renoux, "Le *Iadgari* géorgien et le *Šaraknoc'* arménien," *Revue des Études Arméniennes* 24 (1993): 91. See also Renoux's assessment of the evidence in idem, "Un bilan provisoire sur l'héritage grec du rite arménien," *Le Museon* 116, nos. 1–2 (2003): 61, esp. n.41. M. Keschischian, *Katalog der armenischen Handschriften in der Bibliothek des Klosters Bzommar* (Vienna: Mechitharisten-Buchdruckerei, 1964), 103–4. Ցուցակ ձեռագրաց Մաշտոցի անվան մատենադարանի [Manuscript Catalogue of the Maštoc' Matenadaran], ed. O. Eganyan, A. Zeyt'unyan, and P'. Ant'abyan, 2 vols. (Erevan: Academy of Sciences of the Armenian S.S.R., 1970), 1:1001. The *editio princeps* was published in Amsterdam in 1664, two years before the first printed edition of the Armenian Bible.

honor of St. Nicholas, a hymn that is sung to this day on the Third Saturday of Advent.[58]

> The bodiless ones were amazed when they saw blessed Nicholas, whose conduct in the body was without compare to those possessing a body.[59] By his prayers, entreat forgiveness of sins.
>
> Rejoice, Mother Sion, and ineffably adorn your bridal chamber, for blessed Nicholas in his body has triumphed over bodiless Beliar. By his prayers, entreat forgiveness of sins.
>
> Imploring, we sinners entreat you, Most Holy Trinity, to forgive our sins by the supplications of Nicholas. By his prayers, entreat forgiveness of sins.
>
> Holy lady, Mary, golden urn and ark of the covenants, who gave the gift of the Bread of life from heaven to our starving natures. Intercede always with him for the expiation of our sins.[60]

Additional monuments to the erstwhile popularity of St. Nicholas in Armenia are the scattered Armenian churches named after the Wonderworker of Myra: four in Constantinople[61] (active churches in the Beykoz [AD 1776][62] and Topkapi [AD 1630] districts,[63] and two his-

[58] *Hiac'an anmarmink'n tesanelov.* The hymn appears under the designation, "*Mankunk'* [Hymn for Psalm 112] for Nikołayos the Patriarch." Venice 458 (olim 154) AD 1295. f. 312v. *Venetik* 4:42. Cf. ms. Vienna 212 of AD 1305, f. 317r. Dashian, 535. Cf. Մատենագիրք հայոց [Armenian Classical Authors], ed. Zaven Yagavian, 14 vols. (Antelias, Lebanon: Armenian Library of the Calouste Gulbenkian Foundation, 2001–2008), 8:350.

[59] Possible allusion to the famous legend of St. Nicholas' mysterious translocation from his see in Myra to Constantinople, where he appeared to Emperor Constantine, adjuring him to spare the lives of three accused soldiers. As Jeanne Ancelet-Hustache wrote, "Certainly there are cases of bilocation in the history of the saints, but they are rare, and the greatest theologians disagree about them." Jeanne Ancelet-Hustache, *Saint Nicholas*, trans. Rosemary Sheed (New York: Macmillan Company, 1962), 12.

[60] My translation of the text in Ձայնքաղ շարական [*Šarakan*-Hymnal Arranged by Tone] (Jerusalem: Saint James Press, 1914), 415.

[61] Cf. Dashian, 657, 912.

[62] For a brief history of the church, as well as others in Istanbul, see Ronald T. Marchese and Marlene R. Breu, *Splendor and Pageantry: Textile Treasures from the Armenian Churches of Istanbul* (Istanbul: Armenian Patriarchate of Istanbul, 2010), 191, 297 *et infra.*

[63] Ibid., 186, 297 *et infra.*

toric churches that are no longer in service or existence, in the districts of Edirnekapi [AD 1475] and Yenikapi [first half seventeenth century]);[64] at least two in Crimea[65] (in Kafa [Feodosiya] in the East[66] and Yevpatoriya on the west coast); Amasya, Turkey;[67] Kamieniec, Poland (a.k.a. Kamenic'; Kamenets-Podolskly);[68] Chernivtsi, Ukraine; and Jaffa, Israel,[69] among others.

The Armenians' veneration of Nicholas, complete with its inconsistencies, anomalies, and, in more recent times, decline, nevertheless represents a salient chapter in the history of this holy man's universal—or rather, *ecumenical*—appeal. Yet it reflects at least as much about the devotional heart of the Armenian people and their ancient church. At a time when the exemplary Christian witness, human virtues, and intercessory power of the communion of saints is overlooked in the dust of this tiny, ancient church's desperate efforts to engage its people despite their increasingly postmodern, global, materialistic, and neo-nationalist proclivities, a fresh look at the saints themselves, and in particular the history of their veneration by Armenian Christians throughout the ages, may uncover surprising treasures most pertinent

[64] Ibid., 298.

[65] Kafa alone was said to have "dozens" of Armenian churches. Martijn Theodoor Houtsma, ed., *E.J. Brill's First Encyclopedia of Islam* 1913–1936 (Leiden: E. J. Brill, 1913–38), 617.

[66] This church seems to have been an active scriptorium. The final colophon in a ms. philosophical compendium dated 1375 states that the manuscript was completed "in the capital city of Kafa under the roof of St. Nikōlas the Wonderworking Patriarch." Dashian, 721. The final colophon in ms. Erevan 1182, Vardan Arewelc'i's *Commentary on the Psalms*, states that the manuscript was completed on Tuesday, July 21, 1610, "at Hadrian's Gate in the eparchy of St. Nikołos *Zmiwṙnac'oy* ['the Smyrnian'] Patriarch" in Kafa, Crimea. *Mayr C'uc'ak* 4:569–70.

[67] The ms. Vienna 312 (olim 60, AD 1367) contains this note in the final colophon: "This book of sermons was completed in the city of Amasia at the gate of St. Nikołayos Church by the hand of the pseudonymous Bishop Vasil for my delight." Dashian, 744. Cf. Ačaṙyan, 4:77.

[68] The colophon of ms. Miscellany Vienna 140 states: "This *History of the Seven Philosophers* was completed on October 6 in the year 1616 in the capital city of Kamenic' at the gate of Holy Annunciation to the Holy Mother of God and at St. Nikōlayosi." Dashian, 439, cf. 692. On the Armenian community there, see Robert H. Hewsen, *Armenia: A Historical Atlas* (Chicago, IL/London: The University of Chicago Press, 2001), 161.

[69] Ուղեցոյց սրբազան տեղեաց [Directory of Holy Places] (Jerusalem: St. James, 1910), 12.

to our trying times and circumstances. May the eternal memory of the just be blessed. Amen! Amen! Amen![70]

[70] Յաւիտենական յիշատակն արդարոցն օրհնութեամբ եղիցի. Եղիցի. եղիցի: The refrain chanted at the end of the litany of the saints during the Morning Office (*Aṙawōtean žam*) of the Armenian Church.

Nicholas V. Russo

Chapter 5

The Distribution of Cyril's *Baptismal Catecheses* and the Shape of the Catechumenate in Mid-Fourth-Century Jerusalem

Though he cut his scholarly teeth in the liturgical sands of fourth-century Egypt with his pioneering work on the *Euchologion* of Sarapion of Thmuis,[1] Maxwell Johnson has proven equally influential in the study of Hagiopolite worship. Through doctoral seminars,[2] his extensive research on the origins and development of the rites of Christian initiation,[3] narrower studies on St. Cyril of Jerusalem and Egeria,[4] and his tireless collaborative efforts on behalf of Das Institut für eklektische Liturgiewissenschaft, Professor Johnson has contributed much to our understanding of Jerusalem's liturgy. To this indefatigable scholar, teacher, mentor, bluesman, and friend, on the occasion of his sixtieth birthday, the following is dedicated.

[1] *The Prayers of Sarapion of Thmuis: A Literary, Liturgical, and Theological Analysis*, Orientalia Christiana Analecta 249 (Rome: Pontifical Oriental Institute, 1995); *Liturgy in Early Christian Egypt*, Alcuin/GROW Liturgical Study 33 (Bramcote/Nottingham: Grove Books, 1995); "The Baptismal Rite and Anaphora in the Prayers of Sarapion of Thmuis: An Assessment of a Recent 'Judicious Reassessment,'" *Worship* 73 (1999): 140–68.

[2] Most recently, "Liturgy in Ancient Jerusalem," University of Notre Dame, Fall 2009.

[3] Ed., *Living Water, Sealing Spirit: Readings on Christian Initiation* (Collegeville, MN: Liturgical Press, 1995); *The Rites of Christian Initiation: Their Evolution and Interpretation* (Collegeville, MN: Liturgical Press, 1999; 2nd ed., 2007); E. C. Whitaker, *Documents of the Baptismal Liturgy*, rev. and exp. by Maxwell E. Johnson, 3rd ed. (Collegeville, MN: Liturgical Press, 2003).

[4] "Reconciling Cyril and Egeria on the Catechetical Process in Fourth-Century Jerusalem," in *Essays in Early Eastern Initiation*, Alcuin/GROW Liturgical Study 8, ed. Paul F. Bradshaw (Bramcote/Nottingham: Grove Books, 1988), 18–30.

1. Introduction

Several sources allow us to trace the early evolution of the baptismal program in fourth-century Jerusalem. In chronological order, the *Letter of Macarius to the Armenians*, Cyril of Jerusalem's *Baptismal Catecheses*, Egeria's travel diary, Cyril/John II's *Mystagogical Catecheses*, and the Armenian and Georgian lectionaries provide a surfeit of data with which to reconstruct Jerusalem's initiatory practices. The *Letter of Macarius* (AD 335), for instance, reveals that the feasts of Epiphany, Pascha, and Pentecost were the preferred occasions for celebrating baptisms.[5] The *Baptismal Catecheses*, "the only extant complete set of Lenten catechetical lectures in the early church,"[6] record the content of pre-baptismal instruction. Egeria provides a precious eyewitness account of the services of Lent and Great Week as well as a lengthy description of the catechumenate. The *Mystagogical Catecheses* recount the rites of initiation and their symbolic meaning for the newly baptized. And the Armenian and Georgian lectionaries furnish an annual cycle of liturgical readings and rubrics especially rich in detail for Lent.

With such an abundance of source material, one would expect that the task of reconstructing Jerusalem's catechumenate and baptismal liturgy would be a relatively simple process of connecting dots.[7] Unfortunately, as soon as one attempts to align the data, it becomes painfully apparent that the sources corroborate one another only in the broadest outline. Rather than providing a greater level of certainty and clarity to our understanding, each document complicates the picture further. One especially irksome problem has been the effort to coordinate the data from the *Baptismal Catecheses* with the other roughly contemporaneous hagiopolite sources.

[5] Abraham Terian, *Macarius of Jerusalem: Letter to the Armenians, AD 335*, Avant 4 (Crestwood, NY: St. Vladimir's Seminary Press and St. Nersess Armenian Seminary, 2008), 83, 121–22.

[6] John F. Baldovin, *Liturgy in Ancient Jerusalem*, Alcuin/GROW Liturgical Study 9 (Bramcote/ Nottingham: Grove Books, 1989), 11.

[7] To borrow a metaphor from Paul F. Bradshaw, *Search for the Origins of Christian Worship: Sources and Methods for the Study of Early Liturgy* (Oxford: Oxford University Press, 1992; 2nd ed., 2002), 20.

2. When Was the Last Lecture Delivered?

The famous collection of *Baptismal Catecheses* attributed to Cyril of Jerusalem dates to the late 340s, or perhaps 350.[8] The collection is comprised of eighteen lectures plus one introductory lecture (*Procatechesis*) delivered to the *photizomenoi* during Lent in preparation for receiving the sacrament at Pascha. The Armenian Lectionary verifies Cyril's catechetical curriculum with its list of nineteen readings for those "preparing to receive baptism," but it provides that list *en bloc* at the head of the Lent cycle, without indicating on what days they were employed.[9] Consequently, there has been much dispute over how this syllabus was distributed throughout a period that lasted, at least nominally, forty days.

Fortunately, there are clues within individual lectures that may hint at when they were delivered in relation to one another and to Pascha. One of the most important passages is an apparent reference to the fast and vigil of Good Friday in the final instruction: "And with respect to these instances we might say much, rehearsing in detail the marvelous circumstances of each event: *but as you have been already wearied both by the superposed [extended] fast of the Preparation, and by the watchings [vigil]*, let what has been cursorily spoken concerning them suffice for a while; these words having been as it were sown thinly, that you, receiving the seed like richest ground, may in bearing fruit increase them."[10] If "fast of the Preparation" and "watchings" refer to

[8] Cyril's episcopate was interrupted twice by exile (the dates he held office are given variously as 348 or 350–57, 359–60, 378–86 and 348/9–57, 361–66, 378–86). For issues of dating and authorship, see *Cyrille de Jérusalem, Catéchèses mystagogiques*, introduction and commentary by Auguste Piédangel, trans. Pierre Paris, Sources Chrétiennes (=SC) 126bis (Paris: Éditions du Cerf, 1971), 177–87. While the dating and attribution of the *Baptismal Catecheses* has been generally accepted, several scholars have argued that Cyril's *Mystagogical Catecheses* are the work of his successor, John II (386–417); for the most recent and sustained exponent of this position, see Juliette Day, *The Baptismal Liturgy of Jerusalem: Fourth- and Fifth-Century Evidence from Palestine, Syria, and Egypt* (Aldershot: Ashgate, 2007), 11–25, 138–40.

[9] Athanase Renoux, *Le codex arménien Jérusalem 121*, Patrologia Orientalis, vol. 35, bk. 1, and vol. 36, bk. 2 (Turnhout: Brepols, 1969–71), here at vol. 36, bk. 2, heading 17, 232–37.

[10] BC 18.17; J. P. Migne, ed., *Patrologiae Cursus Completus, Series Graeca Tomus 33: Cyrillus Hierosolymitanus, Petrus II, Timotheus Alexandrini, alii* (= PG 33), (Paris: Garnier, 1857–68), 1037b; English translation (= ET) in Philip Schaff and Henry

Good Friday, as some commentators understood them to have,[11] then it would appear that the catechetical program concluded on Holy Saturday.[12]

Though the chronology inherent in the passage seems clear enough, it has often been thought to be irreconcilable with our second bit of evidence: the testimony of Egeria. According to her travel diary, catechetical instruction (1) was delivered by the bishop, (2) occurred daily during Lent (3) for a period of seven weeks, (4) included a literal and spiritual exegesis of the whole Bible as well as an exposition of the Creed, and (5) came to a close before the eighth and final week of Lent—"Great Week"—because during that week "there is no time for them to have their teaching if they are to carry out all the services."[13] To square the two schemas, some have argued that Cyril's final lecture must have been given on Palm Sunday or even earlier.[14] Others have attributed the inconsistency to Egeria's ignorance of Greek and her need to rely on an interpreter whom she must have misunderstood.[15]

Wace, eds., *Nicene and Post Nicene Fathers* (= NPNF), ser. 2, vol. 7: *Cyril of Jerusalem, Gregory Nazianzen* (Edinburgh: T & T Clark, 1893), 138; emphasis added.

[11] A. A. Stephenson, "The Lenten Catechetical Syllabus in Fourth-Century Jerusalem," *Theological Studies* 15 (1954): 103–16. It is for this reason that Stephenson rejects the schema of Ferdinand Cabrol who placed lecture 18 on Palm Sunday. Cf. Ferdinand Cabrol, *Les Églises de Jérusalem: La discipline et la liturgie au IVe siècle* (Paris: H. Oudin,1895), 143–59.

[12] In addition, we can be sure that, in the years since Macarius's *Letter*, Lazarus Saturday initiation (a later Byzantine custom) was not yet introduced in the Holy City, lest we assume that Cyril continued to instruct the *photizomenoi* on the Creed *after* their baptism. Lecture 18 is an exposition of the final strophes of the Creed; Cyril charges his audience to repeat the Creed and to commit it to memory (18.21). And a passage toward the end of the lecture proves beyond cavil that baptisms had not yet been conferred: "But now the holy day of the Passover is at hand, and ye, beloved in Christ, *are to be enlightened by the Laver of regeneration*" (ἐνεστώσης δὲ λοιπὸν τῆς ἁγίας τοῦ Πάσχα ἡμέρας, καὶ τῆς ὑμετέρας ἐν Χριστῷ, διὰ λουτροῦ παλιγγενεσίας, ἀγάπης φωτιζομένης·), BC 18.32; PG 33:1053b; NPNF, ser. 2, vol. 7, 142; emphasis added.

[13] *Peregrinatio* 46.1-5. Hèléne Pétrè, *Ethérie: Journal de voyage*, SC 21 (Paris: Éditions du Cerf, 1971), 256–59; ET in John Wilkinson, *Egeria's Travels* (Warminster: Aris and Phillips, 1999), 162–63. Octaua enim septimana quadragesimarum, id est quae appellatur septimana maior, iam non uacat eos doceri, ut impleantur ea, quae superius <dicta> sunt.

[14] E.g., Cabrol; see above, note 11.

[15] Stephenson, "The Lenten Catechetical Syllabus," 116.

Taking Cyril and Egeria at their word, Johnson proposed a far less byzantine solution. He attributed the discrepancy to the liturgical development of hagiopolite Great Week / Holy Week and the lengthening of Lent (from six to eight weeks), which had occurred in the interim between the two testimonies.[16] Simply put, ca. 350, instruction ended on Holy Saturday; by the time of Egeria's pilgrimage (381–84), it came to a close a week earlier because the liturgical schedule of Great Week had become fuller. Aside from being the most reasonable explanation, Johnson's is noteworthy because it reveals the culmination of catechesis on/before Lazarus Saturday in Egeria to be a *later* evolution rather than remnants of what some believe may have been a more ancient custom of conferring baptisms in connection with that commemoration in other Christian centers.[17]

In the most recent contribution to the debate, however, Sebastià Janeras has claimed again that the eighteenth catechesis was delivered by Cyril prior to Great Week.[18] According to his analysis, the final lecture had to have fallen on the Friday before Lazarus Saturday. First, Egeria says unequivocally that there was no pre-baptismal instruction during Holy Week. Second, as we have seen, Cyril speaks in his final catechesis of the fatigue of the faithful as a result of their Friday fast and vigil.[19] Egeria describes a vigil at Sion on the Friday of the seventh week of Lent, i.e., the Friday *before* Holy Week, but there is no official vigil on Good Friday. Third, there would have been no time for a lecture on Good Friday, given the hectic schedule of services for that day

[16] Johnson, "Reconciling Cyril and Egeria," 28.

[17] Thomas J. Talley, *The Origins of the Liturgical Year* (New York: Pueblo, 1986; 2nd ed., Collegeville, MN: Liturgical Press, 1991), 176–214. Talley posits that connection for Alexandria and Constantinople.

[18] Sebastià Janeras, "En quels jours furent prononcées les Catéchèses 14–18 de Cyrille de Jérusalem?," *Orientalia Christiana Periodica* 74 (2008): 195–207; reiterating his position already articulated in idem, "Sobre el cicle de predicació de les antigues catequesis baptismals," *Revista Catalana de Teologia* 1 (1976): 159–82; "À propos de la catéchèse XIVe de Cyrille de Jérusalem," *Ecclesia Orans* 3 (1986): 307–18; "Novament sobre la Catequesi XIV de Ciril de Jerusalem," *Revista Catalana de Teologia* 21 (1996): 333–41; "Le vendredi avant le Dimanche des Palmes dans la tradition liturgiques de Jérusalem," *Studi sull'Oriente Cristiano* 4 (2000): 59–86; Ciril de Jérusalem, *Catequesis baptismals*, Clàssics del Cristianisme 67 (Barcelone: Edicions Proa, 1997).

[19] Cyril of Jerusalem, *Baptismal Catechesis* (= BC), 18.17; PG 33:1037b: Διὰ δὲ τὸν κάματον τὸν προγενόμενον ὑμῖν, ἔκ τε τῆς ὑπερθέσεως τῆς νηστείας τῆς Παρασκευῆς, καὶ τῆς ἀγρυπνίας, ἐκεῖνα μὲν τέως ἐν παραδρωμῇ λελέχθω.

according to Egeria's description. And finally, the word ὑπέρθεσις (ἕκ τε τῆς ὑπερθέσεως), which Cyril uses to denote the "extension" of the fast, is found in several later liturgical manuscripts and monastic *vitae* to refer explicitly to the Friday before Palm Sunday.[20]

Janeras's first three arguments can be addressed with little difficulty. Most scholars agree in assigning the *Baptismal Catecheses* to the mid-fourth century, usually between 348 and 351 depending on how one interprets the various internal dating clues.[21] As such, the *Catecheses* were delivered over thirty years prior to Egeria's pilgrimage. There is no doubt that the fourth century was a period of intense liturgical development, and while few would speak in terms of revolution—i.e., completely abandoning earlier patterns of worship in favor of entirely new ones—it is highly unlikely that the liturgy of Jerusalem remained unchanged in the thirty-plus-year interim between the *Baptismal Catecheses* and the *Itinerarium*.[22] Consequently, as Johnson has already argued, pre-baptismal catechesis may have ended before Palm Sunday in Egeria's day precisely because the interim between Cyril and Egeria saw the further liturgical development of Great Week.[23]

Similarly, the packed schedule of Egeria's Good Friday might have been somewhat freer in the mid-fourth century. But this is quite beside the point since A. A. Stephenson and Johnson argued that this lecture was originally delivered on Holy *Saturday*;[24] the Good Friday schedule is unimportant. As for the "official" nature of the Good Friday vigil, there are several examples in Egeria's own testimony where the more devout remain for services long after the rest of the faithful have retired to their homes. And, in point of fact, Egeria does describe a vigil

[20] Janeras, "Les Catéchèses 14–18?," 195–202.

[21] On this issue, see NPNF ser. 2, vol. 7, chap. 9, §1, li–lii.

[22] One only has to consider the development of modern Roman Catholic worship in the same thirty-year span of the twentieth century to accept the plausibility of such rapid evolution.

While scholars have often criticized Dom Gregory Dix for crediting the liturgical evolution of Holy Week solely to the initiative of Cyril, the exaggeration is certainly rooted in the fact that Cyril was a force of liturgical innovation. See Dom Gregory Dix, *The Shape of the Liturgy*, 2nd ed. (New York: Seabury Press, 1982), 350ff.

[23] Johnson, "Reconciling Cyril and Egeria," 28. We do not mean to suggest that there were no Holy Week synaxes when Cyril ascended the episcopal throne. We are simply suggesting that Holy Week continued to develop in the interim prior to Egeria's arrival.

[24] Stephenson, "The Lenten Catechetical Syllabus."

for Good Friday, and she does so in some detail.[25] Thus, Egeria's testimony is an insufficient basis for excluding Good Friday/Holy Saturday as the day on which Cyril's final catechetical lecture was delivered.

The same cannot be said, however, for Janeras's fourth argument. The consistent use of ὑπέρθεσις to refer to the Friday before Palm Sunday is strong evidence indeed and, at first glance, the case for that Friday could rest on this point alone. On closer inspection, however, even this datum can be interpreted otherwise. According to G. W. H. Lampe, the first use of the word as a liturgical *terminus technicus* occurs in the *Canonical Letter* of Dionysius of Alexandria (+ 264).[26]

Evidently, a certain Basilides, bishop of the churches in the Pentapolis (Cyrenaica, the eastern coastal region of modern-day Libya), had written to Dionysius over the matter of the proper time to break the paschal fast. It appears that some of Basilides's flock *extended* (ὑπέρθεσις) the fast until cockcrow on Easter morning, in accordance with Roman custom, while the more common practice was to end the fast somewhat earlier in the night.

Always the exegete, Dionysius insists that a firm ruling on the matter would have to be grounded in Scripture. But after examining the accounts in the gospels, he points out that the precise hour of Christ's resurrection cannot be ascertained. Matthew and John indicate that the women who visited the tomb at some late hour in the night found the Lord already risen, while in Mark and Luke the women arrived a bit later, at dawn. The most that can be said is that Christ rose at some very early hour on Easter morning. Nevertheless, Dionysius continues, the rigor with which the faithful have kept the fast must also be taken into account. The passage is worth quoting at length:

> These facts being as stated, we venture to express our opinion of the matter to precisionists as follows: As for the question respecting the

[25] *Peregrinatio Egeriae* 37.9: "On this day there is no announcement that people are to keep vigil in the Anastasis. Obviously they are tired. But none the less it is the custom to watch there, and all who wish—I should have said, all who can—keep vigil there. Some cannot watch till morning, and they do not stay, but the vigil is kept by the clergy, or at any rate by the ones young enough to have the energy. All the night through they sing hymns and antiphons till morning comes. Most of the people watch, but some only come later on, and some at midnight, doing whatever they can manage." Pétrè, *Ethérie*, 238–39; ET in Wilkinson, *Egeria's Travels*, 157; cf. Renoux, *Le Codex Arménien Jérusalem* 121, heading 44, 294–95.

[26] G. W. H. Lampe, *A Patristic Greek Lexicon* (Oxford: Clarendon, 1961), 1439b: ἡ ὑπέρθεσις, 1442b: ὑπερτίθημι.

precise hour, or half hour, or quarter of an hour, it would be fitting to commence rejoicing over the resurrection of our Lord from the dead, we are inclined to find fault with those who accelerate the time too fast, and want to have it allowed to start even before midnight, on the ground that they are heedless of the hour and impetuous, as nearly having stopped the race, whereof a wise man has said: "The least is not a little in life." On the other hand we espouse those who procrastinate and advance the hour as much as possible, and show fortitude in waiting till even the fourth watch, in which our Savior appeared walking upon the sea to those in the ship, as we consider them brave and assiduous. But let us not quarrel with those who take the middle course, as they have been actuated or have been able to do, since not all men can endure even the six days of fastings equally, nor in the same manner; but, on the contrary, some of them *pass* [ὑπερτιθέασιν] all of those days without any food, while others [pass] only two, and others only three, and others only four, and some none at all. Accordingly, to those who have striven to the utmost *in passing* [ὑπερθέσεσιν] through all the days of fastings, and have afterwards become exhausted, having all but expired, it is pardonable for them to taste of food so much the sooner. But if some men, *not as having passed* [ὑπερτιθέμενοι] through all those days fasting, but not having even fasted or having even spent the first four days in luxuriating, and afterwards coming to the last two remaining days, namely, Friday and Saturday, *confine* [ὑπερτιθέντες] their fasting to these alone, we do not deem them to be doing anything great and splendid; if they stick it out till dawn, I am not of the opinion that they are entitled to equal credit for their exploit with those who have fasted a greater number of days. These things I have written by way of advice as what I think.[27]

[27] ET in Denver Cummings, *The Rudder (Pedalion) of the Metaphorical Ship of the One Holy Catholic and Apostolic Church* (Chicago, IL: The Orthodox Christian Educational Society, 1957), 716. Original in Charles Lett Feltoe, ed. and trans., *The Letters and Other Remains of Dionysius of Alexandria* (Cambridge: Cambridge University Press, 1904), 100–102: Τούτων οὕτως ἐχόντων, τοῦτο τοῖς ἀκριβολογουμένοις ἀποφαινόμεθα κατὰ ποίαν ὥραν, ἢ καὶ ποῖον ἡμιώριον, ἢ ὥρας τέταρτον, ἄρχεσθαι προσῆκε τῆς ἐπὶ τῇ τοῦ κυρίου ἡμῶν ἐκ νεκρῶν ἀναστάσει χαρᾶς· τοὺς μὲν λίαν ἐπιταχύναντας καὶ πρὸ νυκτὸς ἐγγὺς ἤδη μεσούσης ἀνιέντας ὡς ὀλιγώρους καὶ ἀκρατεῖς μεμφόμεθα, παρ᾽ ὀλίγον προκαταλύοντες, τὸν δρόμον, λέγοντος ἀνδρὸς σοφοῦ· οὐ μικρὸν ἐν βίῳ τὸ παρὰ μικρόν. τοὺς δὲ ἐφυστερίζοντας καὶ διακροῦντας ἐπὶ πλεῖστον καὶ μέχρι τετάρτης φυλακῆς ἐγκαρτεροῦντας, καθ᾽ ἣν καὶ τοῖς πλέουσιν ὁ σωτὴρ ἡμῶν περιπατῶν ἐπὶ τῆς θαλάσσης ἐπεφάνη, ὡς γενναίους καὶ φιλοπόνους ἀποδεξόμεθα. τοῖς δὲ μεταξὺ ὡς ἐκινήθησαν ἢ ὡς ἠδυνήθησαν ἀναπαυσαμένοις μὴ πάνυ διοχλῶμεν· ἐπεὶ μηδὲ τὰς ἓξ νηστειῶν ἡμέρας ἴσως μηδὲ ὁμοίως πάντες διαμένουσιν· ἀλλ᾽ οἱ μὲν καὶ πάσας *ὑπερτιθέασιν* ἄσιτοι διατελοῦντες, οἱ δὲ δύο, οἱ δὲ τρεῖς, οἱ δὲ τέσσαρας, οἱ δὲ οὐδεμίαν. καὶ τοῖς μὲν πάνυ

Several things are worthy of note. First, in a footnote to this passage, Feltoe indicates that ὑπερτιθέναι/ὑπερτίθημι and its derivatives, meaning "to exceed," "to extend," or "to delay," "is the technical term for continuing the fast until cockcrow, whereas the ordinary fast ended at 6 p.m. and that of the station days (Wednesdays and Fridays) at 3 p.m."[28] This meaning is commensurate with Janeras's interpretation, namely, a fast *extended* throughout the night on the occasion of a vigil—a vigil, according to his reading, that was observed on the Friday before Lazarus Saturday. There is nothing in Dionysius's response, however, that indicates that the more athletic abstainers fasted within the context of a vigil, though such may have been understood.

Second, it is noteworthy that ὑπερτιθέναι is used cumulatively, i.e., not merely with respect to one night. Dionysius remarks that "some pass [ὑπερτιθέασιν] all [of those days][29] without any food, while others [pass] only two, and others only three, and others only four, and some none at all." So it seems that ὑπερτιθέασιν could refer both to the extension of the fast throughout the night *and* to the extension of the fast across several days.[30]

Third, and perhaps most significant, the word is employed to describe fasting regimens during the six days prior to Pascha.[31] Whether

---

διαπονηθεῖσιν ἐν ταῖς *ὑπερθέσεσιν*, εἶτα ἀποκάμνουσι καὶ μόνον οὐκ ἐκλείπουσι, συγγνώμη τῆς ταχυτέρας γεύσεως. εἰ δέ τινες, οὐχ ὅπως οὐχ *ὑπερτιθέμενοι* ἀλλὰ μηδὲ νηστεύοντες ἀλλὰ καὶ τρυφήσαντες τὰς προαγούσας τέσσαρας, εἶτα ἐλθόντας ἐπὶ τὰς τελευταίας δύο καὶ μόνας αὐτὰς *ὑπερτιθέντες*, τὴν τὲ παρασκευὴν καὶ τὸ σάββατον, μέγα τι καὶ λαμπρὸν ποιεῖν νομίζουσιν, ἂν μέχρι τῆς ἕω διαμείνωσιν, οὐκ οἶμαι τὴν ἴσην ἄθλησιν αὐτοὺς πεποιῆσθαι τοῖς τὰς πλείονας ἡμέρας προησκηκόσι. ταῦτα μὲν οὖν, ὡς φρονῶ, συμβουλεύων περὶ τούτων ἔγραψα.

[28] Feltoe, *The Letters of Dionysius*, 102, n. to line 1.

[29] πάσας accusative plural whose antecedent is ἡμέρας ["days"], also in the accusative plural.

[30] See also NPNF ser. 2, vol. 7, 138, note 2284: "The ecclesiastical term τῆς ὑπερθέσεως we have rendered, according to the interpretation received among the Latins, by the word 'superpositio.' The ancients meant by it a fast continued for two or three days without food. Moreover, since the great week was observed with severer fastings, there were many who passed either the whole week or four, three, or two days, namely, the Preparation and the Holy Sabbath (Easter Eve), entirely fasting as is testified by S. Irenaeus (Euseb. *Hist.* V. 24) and others. The continuance of the fast throughout the Friday and Saturday was highly approved, as may be seen from the *Apostolical Constitutions*, V. 18."

[31] Following the corrective of Harald Buchinger, it would be anachronistic to refer to these six days as Holy or Great Week properly so called. See his "On the Early History of Lent: A New Look at an Old Problem and Some Proposed Solutions,"

the faithful are commended or upbraided depends not on the fast of the Easter vigil alone but on their ascesis throughout the six days leading up to Pascha. And, it is not inconsequential that the bare minimum of extended fasting was undertaken on the Friday and Saturday before Pascha.[32] The fact that Dionysius takes pains to chastise Pentapolitans who fast only those two days is proof positive that at least some of the faithful considered the Friday/Saturday fast to be the indispensable core of pre-paschal ascesis. Thus, it seems that ὑπερτιθέναι was, in fact, a *terminus technicus*, but it did not originally refer to the Friday before Palm Sunday.

Admittedly, the evidence adduced emerges from Egypt, not Jerusalem, and from a period a century prior to Cyril, and so it is possible that ὑπέρθεσις had, in fact, acquired the new technical meaning Janeras claims it to have had.[33] There are, however, other indicators in the *Catecheses* themselves that would prevent one from assigning the final lecture to the Friday before Lazarus Saturday/Palm Sunday.

In the passage cited above, Cyril refers to the fatigue the faithful have endured "from the extension of the fast of Friday, and from the vigil" (ἔκ τε τῆς ὑπερθέσεως τῆς νηστείας τῆς παρασκευῆς, καὶ τῆς

in *Liturgies in East and West: Ecumenical Relevance of Early Liturgical Development? First International Symposium Vindobonense, Vienna, November 17–20, 2007*, ed. Hans-Jürgen Feulner (Münster: LIT-Verlag, forthcoming). See also *Didascalia Apostolorum* 21:14–17; ET in Sebastian Brock and Michael Vasey, eds., *The Liturgical Portions of the* Didascalia, Grove Liturgical Study 29 (Bramcote/Nottingham: Grove Books, 1982), 26–27.

[32] From note 30 above, cf. *Apostolic Constitutions* 5.18.1-2. Ἐν ταῖς ἡμέραις οὖν τοῦ πάσχα νηστεύετε, . . . Τὴν μέντοι παρασκευὴν καὶ τὸ σάββατον ὁλόκληρον νηστεύσατε, οἷς δύναμις πρόσεστιν τοιαύτη, μηδενὸς γευόμενοι μέχρις ἀλεκτοροφωνίας νυκτός· "Fast during the days of Pascha [i.e., Holy/Great Week]. . . . Fast the Friday and the Saturday completely, those who are able, tasting nothing up until the night cockcrow." Marcel Metzger, *Les Constitutions Apostoliques, Tome II: Livres III–VI*, SC 329 (Paris: Les Éditions du Cerf, 1986), 268–71.

[33] A case can be made for this view. According to Egeria (*Peregrinatio* 29.2; Pétré, *Éthérie*, 216–17; ET in Wilkinson, *Egeria's Travels*, 150), all of the Friday vigils throughout Lent are held in the Anastasis except one: the vigil of the Friday of the seventh week, i.e., the Friday before Lazarus Saturday and Palm Sunday. This vigil is held on Sion and "since Sion was the ancient center of the Jerusalem church," Bradshaw has argued, "we may conjecture that the services held there were of long standing" (Paul F. Bradshaw, *Daily Prayer in the Early Church* [London: SPCK, 1981], 91). Thus, while the order of this vigil is the same as that of the first six Friday vigils, its celebration on Sion may suggest that it is older than the others.

ἀγρυπνίας).[34] And, accordingly, several scholars have concluded that this catechesis must belong to a Saturday, though they do not agree on which Saturday.[35] Since Janeras believes that there is no official Good Friday vigil in Egeria, however, he speculates that Cyril must be referring "to a fast and a vigil yet to come."[36] If this is correct, he continues, "then Cyril could be speaking of a fatigue already borne during all of Lent which had reached the end . . . and of a prolonged fast and of a vigil which will commence the evening of the same day, of the same Friday.[37]

There are two problems with this interpretation. First, it is now generally accepted that Lent in the mid-fourth century lasted six weeks, Holy Week included.[38] Consequently, if we are to accept Janeras's reading, then we must conclude that Lent came to a close on the Friday of the fifth week; this was simply never the case in any Christian community. The distinction between Lent and Holy Week, observable by the end of the fourth century and predicated on a total fast of at least seven weeks,[39] is not yet evident in Cyril's *Catecheses*. Second, the syntax of the Greek seems clear: the "fatigue having already come about on account of the fast of Friday and . . ." (Διὰ δὲ τὸν κάματον τὸν προγενόμενον ὑμῖν, ἔκ τε τῆς ὑπερθέσεως τῆς νηστείας τῆς παρασκευῆς, καὶ τῆς ἀγρυπνίας). The word προγενόμενον is an aorist middle participle (masculine accusative singular, from προγίγνομαι)[40] and it means "having already come about"; its antecedent is τὸν κάματον (masculine

[34] See above, note 19.

[35] Johnson, "Reconciling Cyril and Egeria," 27; Stephenson, "The Lenten Catechetical Syllabus," 106.

[36] Janeras, "Les Catéchèses 14–18 de Cyrille de Jérusalem," 197.

[37] Ibid., 197–98.

[38] Talley, *Origins of the Liturgical Year*, 168–74, esp. 173, following Alfred Rahlfs, "Die alttestamentlichen Lektionen der griechischen Kirche," *Mitteilungen des Septuaginta-Unternehmens der K. Gessellschaft der Wissenschaften zu Göttingen*, Band 1 (Berlin, 1909–15), 176; Johnson, "Reconciling Cyril and Egeria," 21. Talley, following Rahlfs, argues that it was six weeks total (Holy Week included) on the basis of the lectionaries that have liturgical provisions for every day of the second week of Lent and Holy Week, indicating that originally these must have been the first and the last week of hagiopolite Lent. This, in turn, would corroborate Sozomen's claim that Lent was six weeks long in Palestine (*Historia ecclesiastica* 7.19).

[39] E.g., *Apostolic Constitutions* 5.13.3-4. Metzger, *Les Constitutions Apostoliques*, 246–47.

[40] Or προγίνομαι as patristic Greek often omits the second gamma in γί(γ)νομαι and its prefix-compound forms.

accusative singular), "the labor" or "fatigue." And the mood and tense/aspect of the participle apply by extension to the following clause. That is, "the fatigue you have already endured" is "from the extension of the fast of Friday and from the vigil."[41] If Cyril intended to refer to *additional* fatigue from a fast and vigil yet to come, we should expect him to use another verb, perhaps γίγνομαι[42] in the future tense, especially when doing so would have created rhetorical symmetry.

Lazarus Saturday may be more convincingly excluded as the day of the final lecture on the basis of Egeria and the Armenian Lectionary. According to Egeria, pre-baptismal instruction took place in the Great Church, the Martyrium, from six to nine in the morning.[43] According to the Armenian Lectionary, there was only one synaxis on Lazarus Saturday—that at the Lazarium at the tenth hour[44]—but Egeria also adds that "the usual Offering of a Saturday morning" (i.e., the eucharistic liturgy) was made on that day as well. At the dismissal of the Offering the archdeacon announces, "At one o'clock today let us all be ready at the Lazarium."[45] There is no mention of baptismal instruction.

While silence alone is not enough to preclude the possibility, there are other markers that suggest that catechesis did not occur on this or any other Lenten Saturday. According to Egeria, catechesis ended at nine o'clock whereupon the bishop is led to the Anastasis for Terce, a cathedral hour that was done only in Lent.[46] Earlier in her diary, when she describes the weekly services for Lent, Egeria mentions only one synaxis on Saturdays—the eucharistic liturgy celebrated before sunrise; there is no office of Terce. The Offering is made at this early hour

[41] The enclitic τε might mistakenly cause one to read the passage as follows: "On account of the fatigue you have already endured, *and* from the extension." In other words, one might suppose that the extension and vigil are *in addition* (τε) to the fatigue already endured, as Janeras argued, but this reading is incorrect. The enclitic τε need not be translated; it refers forward to the καὶ clause, that is, τε . . . καὶ ([both] . . . and); the entire unit is governed by ἔκ which in turn modifies the preceding participle. See Henry George Liddell and Robert Scott, *A Greek-English Lexicon with a Supplement* (Oxford: Clarendon Press, 1968), 1763b.

[42] See above, footnote 40.

[43] *Peregrinatio* 46.3: id est ab hora prima usque ad horam tertiam; Pétré, *Éthérie*, 258–59; ET in Wilkinson, *Egeria's Travels*, 162.

[44] Armenian Lectionary §33.

[45] *Peregrinatio* 29.3; Pétré, *Éthérie*, 216–17; ET in Wilkinson, *Egeria's Travels*, 150.

[46] Robert F. Taft, *The Liturgy of the Hours in East and West: The Origins of the Divine Office and Its Meaning for Today* (Collegeville, MN: Liturgical Press, 1986), 51.

so that the "hebdomadaries," those who had been fasting all week, might break their fast as soon as possible on Saturday morning;[47] Saturdays, except Holy Saturday, and Sundays are non-fast days in hagiopolite Lent.[48] When we couple Egeria's testimony with the numerous references to fasting in Cyril's lectures, we may argue that catechesis took place on fast days only—Monday through Friday—and that the lessons concluded with the office of Terce. The notable exception to this pattern, of course, would be Holy Saturday and it may be no accident that Egeria says that "they have the normal services at *nine o'clock* [i.e., Terce] and midday" on this day.[49] Accordingly, while Egeria indicates that catechesis came to a close before Great Week,[50] the presence of Terce on Holy Saturday may suggest that a lecture was once delivered on this day in the past. If this analysis is correct and if Cyril's final lecture was delivered on a Saturday, then it could have only been delivered on Holy Saturday—the only Saturday fasted during hagiopolite Lent and the only Saturday on which the office of Terce was prayed.

Though this may seem coincidental on its own, there are further clues in *Baptismal Catechesis* (hereafter BC) 18 pointing to its proximity to Pascha. The first is a series of references to the liturgical reading just heard by the *photizomenoi*. In the course of his proofs of the resurrection of the dead on the last strophe of the Creed, Cyril says the following:

> Turn now to the Samaritans, who, receiving the Law only, allow not the Prophets. To them *the text just now read from Ezekiel* appears of no force, for, as I said, they admit no Prophets; whence then shall we persuade the Samaritans also?[51]

A little further on, he quotes a passage from the prophecy directly: "And the Prophet Ezekiel now before us, says most plainly, '*Behold I*

[47] *Peregrinatio* 27.8-9; Pétré, *Éthérie*, 212–15; ET in Wilkinson, *Egeria's Travels*, 149.

[48] See *Peregrinatio* 27.1; Pétré, *Éthérie*, 208–9; ET in Wilkinson, *Egeria's Travels*, 148.

[49] *Peregrinatio* 38.1: Sabbato autem alia die iuxta consuetudinem fit ad tertia, item fit ad sexta; Pétré, *Éthérie*, 233–39; ET in Wilkinson, *Egeria's Travels*, 157; emphasis added.

[50] *Peregrinatio* 46.4; Pétré, *Éthérie*, 258–59; ET in Wilkinson, *Egeria's Travels*, 162.

[51] BC 18.11; PG 33:1029a; ET in NPNF ser. 2, vol. 7, 136; emphasis added: τὸ παρὸν ἀνάγνωσμα τοῦ Ἰεζεκιὴλ, lit., "the passage of Ezekiel now at hand."

will open your graves, and bring you up out of your graves' (Ez 37:12)."[52] The Armenian Lectionary prescribes readings from Ezekiel on only three occasions: Ezekiel 18:20b-23 is listed as the second of nineteen readings for catechetical instruction; Ezekiel 37:1-14 appears once as the eighteenth of the nineteen readings and again on Holy Saturday as the eleventh of twelve readings for the Paschal Vigil. Because of its vivid resurrection imagery, the Valley of the Dry Bones pericope is a stock reading for Pascha. Since a separate provision is made for its reading in the Armenian Lectionary, however, can we be entirely sure that Cyril's *photizomenoi* heard it within the context of the paschal liturgies?

I believe that we can. Toward the end of the lecture, Cyril indicates more than once that baptism and Pascha are imminent.

> And now, brethren beloved, the word of instruction exhorts you all, to prepare your souls for the reception of the heavenly gifts. As regards the Holy and Apostolic Faith delivered to you to profess, we have spoken through the grace of the Lord as many Lectures, as was possible, in these past days of Lent; not that this is all we ought to have said, for many are the points omitted; and these perchance are thought out better by more excellent teachers. *But now the holy day of the Passover is at hand*, and ye, beloved in Christ, *are to be enlightened by the Laver of regeneration*.[53]

A little further on, he exhorts again: "'Finally, my brethren, rejoice in the Lord always; again I will say, Rejoice (Phil 3:1, 4:4): *for your redemption hath drawn nigh* (Lk 21:28),' and the heavenly host of the Angels is waiting for your salvation."[54] And after a series of quotes from Isaiah alluding to baptism and Eucharist, Cyril states that "*within a little while ye shall hear* that excellent lesson which says, 'Shine, shine, O thou new

[52] BC 18.15; PG 33:1036a; ET in NPNF ser. 2, vol. 7, 138; σαφέστατα δὲ ὁ παρὼν προφήτης Ἰεζεκιὴλ λέγει· Ἰδοὺ ἐγὼ ἀνοίγω τὰ μνήματα ὑμῶν, καὶ ἀνάξω ὑμᾶς ἐκ τῶν μνημάτων ὑμῶν·

[53] BC 18.32; PG 33:1053a-b; ET in NPNF ser. 2, vol. 7, 141–42; emphasis added: ἐνεστώσης δὲ λοιπὸν τῆς ἁγίας τοῦ Πάσχα ἡμέρας, lit., "the holy day of Pascha is already/finally/now upon [us]."

[54] BC 18.34; PG 33:1056b; ET in NPNF ser. 2, vol. 7, 142; emphasis added: ἤγγικε γὰρ ἡ ἀπολύτρωσις ὑμῶν.

Jerusalem; for thy light is come' (Is 60:1 LXX)."[55] The *photizomenoi* are about to hear another classic paschal text; the Armenian Lectionary confirms the passage from Third Isaiah as the sixth of the twelve vigil readings and it is read on *no* other occasion.[56]

The mention of the fatigue of fasting *already* endured, the repeated references to the nearness of Pascha and the imminent conferral of baptism, together with the citation of biblical passages read within the context of the paschal liturgies, prove beyond reasonable doubt that Cyril's eighteenth lecture was delivered on Good Friday/Holy Saturday. The conclusion of pre-baptismal instruction prior to Great/Holy Week witnessed by Egeria represents a later shift likely undertaken to accommodate the fuller schedule of services that had developed in the interim.

3. The Distribution of the Lectures throughout Lent

Related to the issue above is the broader question of the manner in which the *Baptismal Catecheses* were distributed throughout Lent. The problem of determining the syllabus stems, as we have seen, from the difficulty of having to align the clues from the *Baptismal Catecheses* themselves with the other hagiopolite data. One of the more successful attempts at solving this puzzle was presented by Johnson in 1988.[57] According to Johnson's schema (shown below), the lectures would have been delivered daily, from Monday to Saturday, for three weeks at the end of Lent. In the mid-fourth century, they would have come to

[55] BC 18.34; PG 33:1057a; ET in NPNF ser. 2, vol. 7, 142; καὶ μετ' οὐ πολύ, τῆς ἀγαθῆς ἀναγνώσεως ἀκούσεσθε λεγούσης· Φωτίζου, φωτίζου, ἡ νέα Ἱερουσαλήμ· ἥκει γὰρ σου τὸ φῶς. It may be of some significance that the word νέα does not appear in the received LXX text. It does however make its way into the Byzantine and Armenian hymns for Pascha that trope this passage. I am grateful to the Very Rev. Dr. Daniel Findikyan for drawing my attention to the Armenian paschal hymns.

[56] The Georgian Lectionary assigns Isaiah 60:1-22 here also and as the second reading for the Epiphany vigil after the Blessing of the Waters.

[57] Johnson, "Reconciling Cyril and Egeria"; see also the sources cited by Janeras, "Les Catéchèses 14–18 de Cyrille de Jérusalem," 195 note 1, especially John F. Baldovin, *The Urban Character of Christian Worship: The Origins, Development, and Meaning of Stational Liturgy*, Orientalia Christiana Analecta 228 (Rome: Pontifical Oriental Institute, 1987), 90–93; idem, *Liturgy in Ancient Jerusalem*, 11–15.

an end on Holy Saturday, but by the time of Egeria's visit, the three-week course would have been shifted back one week due to the liturgical development of Great Week.

Johnson's Distribution of the Baptismal Catecheses according to Cyril and Egeria

Cyril (ca. 350)		
Week One	No Catechetical Lectures	
Week Two	No Catechetical Lectures	
Week Three	No Catechetical Lectures	
Week Four	Mon	BC 1
	Tues	BC 2
	Wed	BC 3
	Thurs	BC 4
	Fri	BC 5
	Sat	BC 6
	Sun	No lecture
Week Five	Mon	BC 7
	Tues	BC 8
	Wed	BC 9
	Thurs	BC 10
	Fri	BC 11
	Sat	BC 12
	Sun	No lecture
Week Six	Mon	BC 13
	Tues	BC 14
	Wed	BC 15
	Thurs	BC 16
	Fri	BC 17
	Sat	BC 18
	Pascha	Baptism @ Vigil

Egeria (ca. 381–83)		
Week One	No Catechetical Lectures	
Week Two	No Catechetical Lectures	
Week Three	No Catechetical Lectures	
Week Four	No Catechetical Lectures	
Week Five	Mon	BC 1
	Tues	BC 2
	Wed	BC 3
	Thurs	BC 4
	Fri	BC 5
	Sat	BC 6
	Sun	No lecture
Week Six	Mon	BC 7
	Tues	BC 8
	Wed	BC 9
	Thurs	BC 10
	Fri	BC 11
	Sat	BC 12
	Sun	No lecture
Week Seven	Mon	BC 13
	Tues	BC 14
	Wed	BC 15
	Thurs	BC 16
	Fri	BC 17
	Sat	BC 18
	Sun	No lecture
Great Week	Mon	
	Tues	
	Wed	
	Thurs	
	Fri	
	Sat	
	Pascha	Baptism @ Vigil

Johnson's proposed distribution is significant because (1) it reconciles Cyril's lectures with Egeria's claim that catechesis occurred daily[58] and (2) it hearkens to a primitive core of three weeks that Mario Lages, and Antoine Chavasse before him, proposed may have been the length of pre-paschal preparation (at least at Jerusalem and Rome) prior to the emergence of a forty-day Lent after Nicaea.[59] Johnson took these insights a step further and argued that this three-week pattern was originally an ancient free-floating period, not necessarily prepended to Pascha, observed whenever baptisms were to be administered.[60]

If this was, in fact, the original shape of pre-baptismal instruction, there is evidence that Jerusalem had begun to depart from it somewhat by 350. In BC 4 on the Ten Dogmas, there are two data which may suggest that instruction, at least at that time, did not occur daily. Cyril introduces the lecture as follows: "However, before our presentation concerning the Creed, it seems to me a good idea now to provide a concise summary of the necessary dogmas, in case the length of my instructions and the intervening days of holy Lent[61] should lead the simpler-minded among you to forget them. Nevertheless, while we sow the seed thinly in a summary fashion now, we must not lose sight of these teachings when we cultivate them more widely later."[62]

Cyril provides a summary at this point, lest the length of his lectures "and the interval between of the days *of the whole* of holy Lent"[63] (καὶ τὸ μεταξὺ διάστημα τῶν ἡμερῶν τῆς ἁγίας Τεσσαρακοστῆς ἁπάσης) cause some to forget his teaching; he goes on to admonish his hearers to remember well, for this summary will be fleshed out later in due

[58] *Peregrinatio* 46.4; Pétré, *Éthérie*, 258–59; ET in Wilkinson, *Egeria's Travels*, 162.

[59] Antoine Chavasse, "La préparation de la Pâque, à Rome, avant le Ve siècle. Jeûne et organization liturgique," in *Memorial J. Chaine*, Bibl. de la Fac. Cath. de Theol. de Lyon, vol. 5 (Lyon, 1950), 61–80; "Temps de préparation à la Pâque, d'après quelques livres liturgiques romains," *Rech. de Sciences religieuses* 37 (1950): 125–45; "La structure du Carême et les lectures des messes quadragesimales dans la liturgie romaine," *La Maison-Dieu* 31 (1952): 76–119; Mario Lages, "Étapes de l'evolution de carême à Jérusalem avant le Ve siècle. Essai d'analyse structurale," *Revue des Études Armeniénnes* 6 (1969): 67–102; but against Lages and Chavasse, see the significant critiques of Buchinger, "On the Early History of Lent."

[60] Johnson, "Reconciling Cyril and Egeria."

[61] Yarnold leaves the Greek word ἁπάσης (fem. gen. sing. of ἅπας, "of the whole" or "quite all") untranslated; see below.

[62] BC 4.3; PG 33:457a; ET in Edward Yarnold, *Cyril of Jerusalem* (London: Routledge, 2000), 98.

[63] Or "the interval between erstwhile of the days of *all* of holy Lent."

course. The passage seems to indicate that this lecture was delivered at the beginning of Lent and that there was a lengthy interval between this lecture and BC 5 wherein Cyril begins his presentation of the articles of the Creed. It may be that the *Procatechesis* and the first four lectures were delivered at the beginning of Lent or just prior.[64]

A little later in BC 4, Cyril mentions baptism in passing only, for "we said enough about baptism *the day before yesterday*" (i.e., in BC 3 whose topic was indeed baptism).[65] "If Cyril's 'day before yesterday' (*proēn*) is to be taken literally," Yarnold writes, then "we have confirmation that the catechetical meetings did not take place every day."[66] It is possible that BC 4 was delivered on a Monday and, since no instruction took place on Sunday, BC 3 would have been given on Saturday, i.e., "on the day before yesterday." But no one, to my knowledge, has suggested such a distribution.

Similarly, Edwin Gifford has suggested that there may also have been an interval of several days between BC 14–15 and BC 16–18. In BC 14, Cyril capitalizes on the happy coincidence between the topic of his lecture and the liturgical reading from the previous day: "The grace of God so ordered it, that thou heardest most fully concerning it, so far as our weakness allowed, *yesterday on the Lord's day*,[67] since by the providence of divine grace the course of the Readings in Church included the account of our Saviour's going up into the heavens."[68] Commenting on the clause of the Creed on the resurrection, ascension, and session at the right hand, Cyril refers to an account from "the course of readings"[69] heard in church. Gifford believed the passage may have been Hebrews 9:11-14 (Christ's "ascension" to the heavenly tabernacle),[70] which he finds attested as the *Apostlos* for the Fifth

[64] We can be certain that the *Procatechesis* was given then because Cyril counsels the *photizomenoi*: "You have *forty days* for repentance; you have plenty of time to take your clothes off and wash them and come back properly dressed." *Procatechesis* 4; PG 33:341a; ET in Yarnold, *Cyril of Jerusalem*, 80; emphasis added.

[65] Ἀλλὰ περὶ τοῦ λουτροῦ πρώην αὐτάρκως εἰρηκότες; BC 4.32; PG 33:493b; ET in Yarnold, *Cyril of Jerusalem*, 108; emphasis added.

[66] Yarnold, *Cyril of Jerusalem*, 197 note 16.

[67] τῇ χθὲς ἡμέρᾳ κατὰ τὴν Κυριακήν; PG 33:856b-c.

[68] BC 14.24; PG 33:856b-c; ET in NPNF ser. 2, vol. 7, 100; emphasis added.

[69] Gifford indicates that ἀναγνωσμάτων is "a term including the portions of Scripture (περικοπαί) appointed for the Epistle and Gospel as well as the daily lessons from the Old and New Testaments." See NPNF ser. 2, vol. 7, 101 note 1774.

[70] NPNF ser. 2, vol. 7, chapter 9, §2, liii.

Sunday of Lent, according to Frederick Scrivener's lectionary table of "the Greek Church."[71] Accordingly, Gifford concluded that BC 14 was delivered on the Monday of Passion Week, two weeks before Pascha.[72] And in BC 15, Cyril speaks as though there will be a break in instruction: "If the grace of God should permit us, the remaining Articles also of the Faith shall be *in good time* declared to you."[73]

By contrast, the last three lectures appear to have been given just before Easter. BC 16 and 17, both on the Holy Spirit, were delivered in

[71] NPNF ser. 2, vol. 7, 101 note 1775; Scrivener, "Lectionary," in William Smith and Samuel Cheetham, eds., *A Dictionary of Christian Antiquities*, vol. 2 (London: William Clowes and Sons, 1880), 958b.

[72] NPNF ser. 2, vol. 7, chapter 9, §2, liii.There are many problems with the contention that Hebrews 9 was, in fact, the reading to which Cyril referred. First, Gifford assumed that Scrivener's lectionary table for "the Greek Church" (i.e., the Byzantine lectionary) also reflects the usage of mid-fourth-century Jerusalem. Second, Gifford himself recognized that the reference may be to another reading entirely: Luke 24:36-53 (on the ascension), the sixth of the repeating cycle of eleven resurrectional gospels (*Eothina*) for Orthros in the Byzantine Lectionary; here again, however, citing Scrivener, *Dictionary of Christian Antiquities*, 959a; see NPNF ser. 2, vol. 7, 101 note 1775. Finally, Hebrews 9 is only loosely related to the theme of the ascension; the passage from Luke actually recounts the event. Nevertheless, the indication in BC 15.33 (see below) that catechesis will be interrupted for some time is sufficient to suggest a break between BC 14–15 and BC 16–18.

A surer indication of the date of BC 14 may be gleaned from a reference to the equinox just passed: "And now, as thou seest, already every herb is yielding seed. And as at that time God made the sun and moon and gave them courses of equal day (and night), so also *a few days since was the season of the equinox*." BC 14.10: καὶ πρὸ ὀλίγων ἡμερῶν ἰσημερίας ἦν ὁ κόσμος (lit., "and a few days before was the time of the equinox"); PG 33:836b–524a; ET in NPNF ser. 2, vol. 7, 96.

If the lectures were given in the Lent of 350, as some have argued, Pascha would have fallen on April 8 and BC 14 would have been delivered on Monday, March 26: two days after the beginning of the month of Xanthicus (to which Cyril also refers in BC 14.10), four days after the equinox, and in the penultimate week of Lent. Jan Willem Drijvers, following Doval, assigns the *Baptismal Catecheses* to 351 and argues that BC 14 was given on March 25; in 351, Pascha fell on March 31 and March 25 would have been the Monday of Holy Week. Jan Willem Drijvers, *Cyril of Jerusalem: Bishop and City* (Leiden: Brill, 2004), 56–58; Alexis J. Doval, "The Date of Cyril of Jerusalem's Catecheses," *Journal of Theological Studies* 48 (1997): 129–32. In favor of dating to the year 350, see W. Telfer, *Cyril of Jerusalem and Nemesius of Emesa*, Library of Christian Classics 4 (London: Westminster Press, 1955), 36–38; and Sebastià Janeras, "A propos de la catechese XIV° de Cyrille de Jerusalem," *Ecclesia Orans* 3 (1986): 307–18.

[73] BC 15.33; PG 33:916a; ET in NPNF ser. 2, vol. 7, 114; emphasis added, "in good time," κατὰ καιρόν.

sequence. Gifford draws attention to Cyril's distinction between "these present lectures" (i.e., BC 16–17) and "our previous discourses":[74] "and by this time, both from *these present Lectures*, and from *what has before been told you*, hold more steadfastly the Faith in 'One God the Father Almighty; and in our Lord Jesus Christ, His Only-Begotten Son; and in the Holy Ghost the Comforter.'"[75] And in BC 16–18, Cyril refers often to the shortness of time and nearness of Pascha: "But the time is short; and we must be careful of the proper length of the lecture";[76] "*For as the Holy Festival of Easter is now at hand* we have this day lengthened our discourse and yet we had not room to bring before you all the testimonies from the New Testament which we ought";[77] and, "But now the holy day of the Passover is at hand, and ye, beloved in Christ, are to be enlightened *by the Laver of regeneration*."[78] The final three lectures, Gifford concluded, must have been delivered in the week leading up to Pascha, and BC 18, as we have seen, just before the feast itself. Evidently, Cyril's syllabus was not delivered in an uninterrupted course of daily instruction.

If catechesis did not occur every day and if there were hiatuses between the formal lectures, then what exactly were the *photizomenoi* doing during Lent? Toward the end of the *Procatechesis*, Cyril gives the following instruction:

> When the exorcism takes place, while you are waiting for the others to arrive for their exorcism, the men and the women are kept apart. . . . So let the men sit together and have a good book [βιβλίον χρήσιμον];[79] one man can read and the rest listen. If there isn't a book available, one man might pray, and another speak a few helpful words. The unmarried women should be kept together in the same way, either singing or reading silently, so that their lips move inaudibly. . . . Married women should observe the same practice, praying and moving their lips silently.[80]

[74] NPNF ser. 2, vol. 7, chapter 9, §2, liii.

[75] BC 17.34; PG 33:1008b-c; ET in NPNF ser. 2, vol. 7, 132.

[76] BC 16.32; PG 33:964a; ET in NPNF ser. 2, vol. 7, 123; BC 17.34; PG 33:1008b-c; ET in NPNF ser. 2, vol. 7, 132.

[77] BC 17.20; PG 33:992c; ET in NPNF ser. 2, vol. 7, 129.

[78] BC 18.32; PG 33:1053b; ET in NPNF ser. 2, vol. 7, 141.

[79] While the phrase does not appear in reference to the Bible (the word normally used is ἡ γραφή), the noun ἡ χρῆσις is found in other roughly contemporary writers to mean "a saying" of a passage from Scripture; see Lampe, *A Patristic Greek Lexicon*, 1528a.

[80] *Procatechesis* 14; PG 33:353c–356a; ET in Yarnold, *Cyril of Jerusalem*, 84.

It seems that, on occasion at least, there were times that the *photizomenoi* were gathered when no formal lecture was being delivered to them. At such times, Cyril instructs his students not to remain idle but to read or, lacking a book, to pray. The catechetical meetings, then, may have involved reading, meditation, and prayer in smaller groups, in addition to formal instruction. Edward Yarnold reaches a similar conclusion based on the time allotted to catechesis by Egeria. He surmises that "since the extant *Catecheses* would not take anything like three hours to deliver,[81] the time was presumably taken up with repeating the talks in Syriac, in explanations and discussions in small groups, and in exorcisms and prayers."[82]

There is also evidence to suggest that Cyril envisioned independent biblical study as an integral complement to his formal lectures. First, the contents of Cyril's lectures suppose a very high level of biblical literacy. When he begins his instruction on the articles of the Creed in BC 5, Cyril ranges over a myriad of proof texts, (1) all of which could not possibly have been proclaimed liturgically and (2) to which he often refers only in the most cursory fashion. When discoursing on the resurrection of the dead, for example, Cyril says:

> And many Scriptures there are which testify of the Resurrection of the dead; for there are many other sayings on this matter. But now, *by way of remembrance only, we will make a passing mention of* the raising of Lazarus on the fourth day [Jn 11:39-44]; *and just allude, because of the shortness of the time,* to the widow's son also who was raised [Lk 7:15-16], *and merely for the sake of reminding you,* let me mention the ruler of the synagogue's daughter [Mt 9:25], and the rending of the rocks, and how there arose many bodies of the saints which slept, their graves having been opened [Mt 27:51-53]. But specially *be it remembered* that Christ has been raised from the dead [1 Cor 15:20]. *I speak but in passing* of Elias, and the widow's son whom he raised [1 Kgs 17:19ff.]; of Elisseus also, who raised the dead twice; once in his lifetime, and once after his death. For when alive he wrought the resurrection by means of his own soul [2 Kgs 4:34]; but that not the souls only of the just might be honoured, but that it might be believed that in the bodies also of the just there lies a power, the corpse which was cast into the sepulchre of Elisseus, when it touched the dead body of the prophet, was quickened [2 Kgs 13:21], and the dead body of the prophet did the

[81] Cf. Egeria, *Peregrinatio* 46.4: id est ab hora prima usque ad horam tertiam, quoniam per tres horas fit cathecisin; Pétré, *Éthérie*, 258–59.

[82] Yarnold, *Cyril of Jerusalem*, 37.

> work of the soul, and that which was dead and buried gave life to the dead, and though it gave life, yet continued itself among the dead.[83]

And likewise in his treatment of the power of the Holy Spirit, Cyril simply drops a series of names and a word or two as an *aide de memoire*:

> In the might of this Spirit, as we have it in the Book of Judges, Othniel judged [Judg 3:10]; Gideon waxed strong [Judg 6:34]; Jephtha conquered [Judg 11:29]; Deborah, a woman, waged war [Judg 4:4]; and Samson, so long as he did righteously, and grieved Him not, wrought deeds above man's power [Judg 13:25; 14:6, 9]. And as for Samuel and David, we have it plainly in the Books of the Kingdoms, how by the Holy Ghost they prophesied themselves, and were rulers of the prophets;—and Samuel was called *the Seer* [1 Sam 9:9].[84]

In many other instances, the string of biblical allusions is far more esoteric, and yet he routinely passes quickly over them, quoting only the briefest snippets to elicit what is already familiar to his audience. The presumption is that his hearers know these passages well.

It may indeed be the case that the *photizomenoi*, especially those who had had long stints in the catechumenate, or were themselves the children of Christian parents, were scripturally literate. Cyril often refers to members of his audience, however, who have only very recently come from paganism[85] or some heretical sect[86] and commends Scripture reading as a necessary component of his syllabus. In his explanation of the last of the Ten Dogmas in BC 4, Cyril enjoins the following:

> *Read* the holy Scriptures [Ἀναγινώσκετε τὰς θείας Γραφάς], the twenty-two books of the Old Testament which were translated by the seventy-

[83] BC 18.16; PG 33:1036a-c; ET in NPNF ser. 2, vol. 7, 138.

[84] BC 16.28; PG 33:957a–960a; ET in NPNF ser. 2, vol. 7, 122.

[85] E.g.: "*If then there is present among you any from among the Heathen* (ἐξ ἐθνῶν) who has ever spoken evil against Christians, or in times of persecution plotted against the Holy Churches, let him take Nabuchodonsor as an example of salvation: let him confess in like manner, that he may also find the like forgiveness"; BC 2.19; PG 33:424b (variant in Roe and Casaubon); ET in NPNF ser. 2, vol. 7, 12 note 564; emphasis added.

[86] E.g., "*Here let converts from the Manichees gain instruction, and no longer make those lights their gods*; nor impiously think, that this sun which shall be darkened is Christ"; BC 15.3; PG 33:873b-c; ET in NPNF ser. 2, vol. 7, 105; emphasis added.

two translators. . . . *Read* the twenty-two books of these Scriptures, and have nothing to do with the apocrypha. *Give careful study* to these books and to these only; these are the ones in which we have confidence for reading in church. . . . *Study* the twenty-two books of the Old Testament. . . . In the New Testament there are four gospels, and only four. . . . You should also accept the Acts of the twelve apostles, and in addition the seven catholic epistles of James, Peter, John and Jude; and finally, to set the seal on them all, the fourteen epistles of Paul, which form the last work of the disciples. Treat any other books as secondary. Those which are not read in churches you should not *read privately* either, as you have already been told. . . . Take every means to safeguard your soul by *fasting, prayer, almsgiving* and *the reading of Scripture,* so that after living the rest of your earthly lives in temperance and holy beliefs, you may enjoy the one salvation which comes through baptism.[87]

Here, Cyril exhorts the *photizomenoi* five times to read and study the Scriptures and continues encouraging them to do so throughout the remaining lectures.

Second, Cyril commends independent Scripture study to fill what is lacking in his discourses. The lectures on the articles of the Creed (BCs 5–18), for instance, are largely exercises in proof-texting, and Cyril often complains that, because of the tried patience of his audience or the lack of time, he is forced to give short shrift to many topics. In these instances, he encourages the more diligent to continue mining the Scriptures on their own for further proof:

> But, as I said before, it has been proved possible for Him [Christ] to be made man: and *the rest of the proofs may be left for the studious to collect* [from Scripture].[88]
>
> But do thou, I pray, receive the testimonies, and seal them in thine heart. And, since they are many, and the rest of our time is narrowed into a short space, listen now to a few of the more important as time permits; and having received these beginnings, *be diligent and seek out the remainder*. Let not thine hand be only stretched out to receive, but let it be also ready to work.[89]

[87] BC 4.33-37; PG 33:496b–504a; ET in Yarnold, *Cyril of Jerusalem*, 109–11; emphasis added.

[88] BC 12.16; PG 33:744b; ET in NPNF ser. 2, vol. 7, 76; emphasis added.

[89] BC 13.8; PG 33:784b; ET in NPNF ser. 2, vol. 7, 84; emphasis added.

> And to the power of the Holy Ghost Himself it must belong, to grant to us forgiveness for what we have omitted because the days are few, and upon you the hearers to impress more perfectly the knowledge of what yet remains; *while from the frequent reading of the sacred Scriptures those of you who are diligent come to understand these things*, and by this time, both from these present Lectures, and from what has before been told you, hold more steadfastly the Faith in "One God the Father Almighty; and in our Lord Jesus Christ, His Only-Begotten Son; and in the Holy Ghost the Comforter."[90]

> And when we desire to gain this eternal life, the sacred Scriptures suggest to us the ways of gaining it; of which, because of the length of our discourse, *the texts we now set before you shall be but few, the rest being left to the search of the diligent.*[91]

Third, since every tenet of the faith is established by biblical testimony, not persuasive philosophical argument, Cyril commends the study of the orthodox canon, and to avoid heretical texts, as the surest guarantee of the truth of the doctrines which the *photizomenoi* are now called to preserve.

> So keep always in your mind the seal of which we have now spoken to you summarily, touching on the most important points. *However, if the Lord allows it, I shall speak about this later as best I can and give scriptural proof.* For where the divine and holy mysteries of the Creed are concerned, *one must not teach even minor points without reference to the sacred Scriptures*, or be led astray lightly by persuasive and elaborate arguments. Do not simply take my word when I tell you these things, unless you are given proof for my teaching from holy Scripture. *For this is the guarantee of our Creed, not clever argument, but proof based on Scripture.*[92]

> *Nourish thy soul with sacred readings*; for the Lord hath prepared for thee a spiritual table.[93]

> This man [Manes] has had three disciples, Thomas, and Baddas, and Hermas. *Let none read the Gospel according to Thomas* for it is the work not of one of the twelve Apostles, but of one of the three wicked disciples of Manes.[94]

[90] BC 17.34; PG 33:1008b-c; ET in NPNF ser. 2, vol. 7, 132; emphasis added.

[91] BC 18.30; PG 33:1052a; ET in NPNF ser. 2, vol. 7, 141; emphasis added.

[92] BC 4.17; PG 33:476b–477a; ET in Yarnold, *Cyril of Jerusalem*, 103; emphasis added.

[93] BC 1.6; PG 33:377b; ET in NPNF ser. 2, vol. 7, 7; emphasis added.

[94] BC 6.31; PG 33:593a; ET in NPNF ser. 2, vol. 7, 42; emphasis added.

Scripture reading is an essential propaedeutic to catechesis, nourishment for the soul as it prepares for baptism, a source of sound doctrine, a bulwark against heresy, and a repository of revealed truth for continued study. From his repeated admonitions to read Scripture, it seems evident that Cyril envisioned biblical reading as a necessary component of the catechetical process and that he crafted his lectures with the presumption that the *photizomenoi* were engaged in additional study on their own or in groups.

If this was, in fact, the pattern in the period when the *Baptismal Catecheses* were delivered, how can it be squared, on the one hand, with the contentions that three weeks constituted the original core of hagiopolite Lent (Lages) and that it was the length of final preparation for baptism (Johnson) and, on the other, with Egeria's testimony that catechetical instruction occurred daily during the first seven weeks of an eight-week Lent by the time of her pilgrimage.[95] The fact that there are eighteen (or nineteen) lectures, roughly three-weeks' worth, may hearken to a time when that interval was indeed the core of prebaptismal preparation. The hiatuses between the catecheses may have been a secondary development, arising from the need to graft the original three-week pattern onto the new forty-day Lent that, after Nicaea, recalibrated the bounds of pre-baptismal instruction and marked Pascha as the preferred occasion for initiations.[96] The extension of this period, moreover, may have been the impetus for Cyril to incorporate a biblical component to the catechetical course, a measure

[95] *Peregrinatio* 46.4-6; Pétré, *Éthérie*, 258–59: "ac sic tribus horis docentur ad die per septimanas septem. Octaua enim septimana quadragesimarum, id est quae appellatur septimana maior, iam non uacat eos doceri, ut impleantur ea, quae superius <dicta> sunt. . . . Per istas septem septimanas legem omnem edocti estis scripturarum nec non etiam de fide audistis."

[96] The short-lived preference for paschal baptism seems to have been nothing more than that—a *preference*—that lasted for less than a century, for that feast as one among several auspicious occasions for conferring baptisms. See Paul F. Bradshaw, "'*Diem baptismo sollemniorum*': Initiation and Easter in Christian Antiquity," in *ΕΥΛΟΓΗΜΑ: Studies in Honor of Robert Taft, S.J.*, Studia Anselmiana 110, Analecta Liturgica 17, ed. Ephrem Carr, Stefano Parenti, Abraham-Andreas Thiermeyer, and Elena Velkovska, 137–47 (Rome: Pontificio Ateneo S. Anselmo, 1993), 41–51, reprinted in Maxwell E. Johnson, ed., *Living Water, Sealing Spirit: Readings on Christian Initiation* (Collegeville, MN: Liturgical Press, 1995); and Maxwell E. Johnson, "'*Diem baptismo sollemniorum*' Revisited: A Tentative Hypothesis on Baptism at Pentecost," in *Studia Liturgica Diversa: Essays in Honor of Paul F. Bradshaw*, ed. Maxwell E. Johnson and L. Edward Phillips (Portland, OR: Pastoral Press, 2004), 31–44.

especially necessary as a stopgap for the scripturally ignorant pagan converts now thronging to the font amid a sea of heresy.

It is quite possible that, prior to Cyril, the final stages of preparation lasted three weeks. The organization and the content of the lectures as they have come down to us, however, reflect a departure from this primitive pattern. As they stand, the three-week core of instruction has been expanded to cover six weeks by the intercalation of a biblical component.[97] And it may be that this syllabus emerged precisely because the recently adopted forty-day pre-paschal fast provided the framework within which lengthier preparation might take place. If Lent had only recently emerged in the Holy City, then it was a season in search of a *raison d'être*, and Cyril knew just how to make good use of it: he simply adapted the primitive three-week pattern to the newly adopted forty-day Lent. What is enshrined in the *Baptismal Catecheses*, therefore, may represent a midpoint in the development of a catechetical process and a Lenten season still in flux.

[97] Even if she is speaking in hyperbole when Egeria claims that the first five weeks of Lent were devoted to exegesis of the entire Bible, by 381 to 383 biblical reading appears to have coalesced into a more formal component of the catechetical structure; *Peregrinatio* 27.1, 46.3; Pétré, *Éthérie*, 206–9, 256–59; ET in Wilkinson, *Egeria's Travels*, 148, 162.

Part III

Christian Initiation

Christian McConnell

Chapter 6

The Meanings of Paschal Baptism in the Non-Roman West

In the liturgical renewal of the twentieth century, the recovery of the practice of paschal baptism has been accompanied by a recovery of a richer interpretation of the sacrament. Rather than an operative theology focused heavily on a clinical washing away of original sin, liturgical reforms have emphasized both the ecclesial nature of baptism, as initiation into the church, and a strong sense of baptism as participation in the death and resurrection of Christ, as in Romans 6. This can be most clearly seen, of course, in the restored catechumenate in various Western liturgical churches, such as the Roman Catholic Rite of Christian Initiation of Adults, in which baptism at the Easter Vigil is normative and Romans 6 language, while not entirely exclusive, is predominant.

The important work of Gabriele Winkler since the 1970s, along with the work of Sebastian Brock,[1] has highlighted that, contrary to previous perceptions, neither paschal baptism nor a Romans 6 theology of baptism were universal in early Christianity. Armenian, early Syrian, and later specifically East Syrian practice gave very little attention to death and resurrection imagery, focusing instead on the baptism of Jesus in the Jordan and rebirth or regeneration imagery derived from John 3:5,

[1] See, for example, Gabriele Winkler, "Original Meaning of the Prebaptismal Anointing and Its Implications," *Worship* 52, no. 1 (1978): 24–45, reprinted in Maxwell E. Johnson, ed., *Living Water, Sealing Spirit* (Collegeville, MN: Liturgical Press, 1995), 58–81; Sebastian P. Brock, "Studies in the Early History of the Syrian Orthodox Baptismal Liturgy," *Journal of Theological Studies* 23, no. 1 (1972): 16–64; Sebastian P. Brock, "Syrian Baptismal Ordines (with Special Reference to the Anointings)," *Studia Liturgica* 12, no. 4 (1977): 177–83.

in which those reborn of water and the Spirit enter the kingdom of God. This emphasis may also have been strong in pre-Nicene Egypt.[2]

The emergence of the awareness of this Eastern model has left the West as the home of the paschal/Romans 6 model, based especially on the full range of North African sources and the *Apostolic Tradition*, with its stratum of apparently Roman baptismal practice in chapter 21. This is by no means, however, a broadly accurate or comprehensive portrayal of Western baptismal imagery in late antiquity. Pushing further the recovery of the full range of baptismal images, Maxwell Johnson has argued that one can see the rebirth image rather extensively in the West as well, and the Jordan image is by no means foreign to the West.[3]

Nonetheless, in the non-Roman West in particular, the *practice* of paschal baptism does seem to linger longer than elsewhere. Continuing Johnson's work in recovering a richer array of baptismal images,[4] this essay will provide an examination of Gallican and Hispanic (pre-Mozarabic) sources and a demonstration that while a practice of paschal baptism existed in the non-Roman West, its interpretation drew upon burial with Christ very little. As Johnson observed, "Outside Rome, in that Western medieval Spanish tradition known as 'Mozarabic,' extant liturgical and other texts *do* make some reference to this image, though it is by no means the dominant or central one."[5] This is not simply a non-paschal tradition, as seen in some early Eastern practice, but a tradition of paschal baptism, with a wide range of images, *including* a variety of paschal ones. Romans 6 does occasionally appear among them, but much less frequently and less prominently than others. It is hoped here that in addition to the broader, non-paschal interpretation of baptism that has been available for some time now, specifically paschal baptism might be enriched further today.

[2] Maxwell E. Johnson, *The Rites of Christian Initiation: Their Evolution and Interpretation* (Collegeville, MN: Liturgical Press, 1999; 2nd ed., 2007), chap. 2.

[3] Maxwell E. Johnson, "Baptism as 'New Birth Ex Aqua Et Spiritu': A Preliminary Investigation of Western Liturgical Sources," in *Comparative Liturgy Fifty Years after Anton Baumstark (1872–1948)*, ed. Robert F. Taft (Rome: Pontificio Istituto Orientale, 2001), 787–807. See also Killian McDonnell, *The Baptism of Jesus in the Jordan: The Trinitarian and Cosmic Order of Salvation* (Collegeville, MN: Liturgical Press, 1996).

[4] Johnson, *The Rites of Christian Initiation;* Maxwell E. Johnson, *Images of Baptism*, Forum Essays No. 6 (Chicago, IL: Liturgy Training Publications, 2001).

[5] Johnson, *Images of Baptism*, 12.

The Practice of Paschal Baptism in the Non-Roman West

In Gaul and Spain, the transition between adult paschal baptism and infant baptism occurs in the sixth and seventh centuries, respectively. In the liturgical books, the practice is (however inaccurately) taken for granted much later.

In her *Itinerarium*, Egeria describes her observation of Pascha in Jerusalem, while slightly revealing something about practice at her home, whether that be in Gaul or Spain:

> They keep their paschal vigil like us, but there is one addition. As soon as the "infants" have been baptized and clothed, and left the font, they are led with the bishop straight to the Anastasis. The bishop goes inside the screen and after one hymn says a prayer for them. Then he returns with them to the church, where all the people are keeping the vigil in the usual way. They do all the things to which we are accustomed, and, when the Offering has been made, they have the dismissal. After their dismissal in the Great Church they at once go with singing to the Anastasis, where the resurrection Gospel is read, and once more the bishop makes the Offering. They waste no time during these services, so as not to detain the people too long; in fact they are dismissed from their vigil at the same time as us.[6]

The "one addition" that makes the hagiopolite vigil differ from "at home" is the procession to the Anastasis, with the hymn and prayer, after the "infants" have already been baptized and clothed. It appears that Egeria knows a paschal vigil at home and that the mere fact of baptizing on that occasion seems to be a part of it. Her comparison of Lent and the Easter octave with these times "at home" similarly suggests paschal baptism at home as well.

Conciliar sources from Gaul illustrate the late sixth-century shift away from Easter, as infant baptism becomes more common. Taking note of Paul Bradshaw's principle that liturgical legislation is evidence for what it seeks to forbid,[7] it should be noted that sometimes prescriptive texts provide evidence *for* practices by merely assuming

[6] Egeria, *Itinerarium*, 38, 1-2. Translation from John Wilkinson, *Egeria's Travels*, rev. 3rd ed. (Warminster: Aris & Phillips, 1999).

[7] Paul F. Bradshaw, *The Search for the Origins of Christian Worship: Sources and Methods for the Study of Early Liturgy*, 2nd ed. (New York/Oxford: Oxford University Press, 2002), 18.

them while prescribing something else, or prescribing how the assumed practice is to be done in detail. At the beginning of the century, the Council of Agde (506) calls for the presentation of the Creed in preparation for what appears to be actual paschal baptism: "It was agreed by all the churches that upon the one day, that is, the eighth before the day of the Lord's resurrection, the Creed should be delivered to the *competentes* publicly in church."[8]

Later in the century, Gallican councils attempt to maintain paschal baptism and resist the move away from Easter to *quamprimum* baptism. From the Council of Auxerre (578): "It is forbidden to baptize at any time except the Easter service, except in the case of those who are near to death and those whom they call bedridden. And if anyone living in another district shall after this interdict stubbornly bring his children to be baptized in our churches, let them not be received, and any presbyter who shall presume to receive them shall be banned from the communion of the Church for three months."[9] And from the Second Council of Macon (585):

> We learn from our brothers that Christian people, not observing the appointed day for baptism, baptize their children on other days, and on the festivals of martyrs, so that at the holy Pascha only two or three can be found to be regenerated by water and the Holy Spirit. And therefore it is our decision that none shall hereafter be permitted to do such things, except if they are compelled by serious illness or approaching death to have their children baptized: and therefore we require all people, being recalled by this present admonition from their errors or ignorance, to attend church with their children from the first Sunday of Lent, that having received the imposition of hands on certain days, and being anointed with the holy oil, they may rejoice in the festivities of the appointed day, and be regenerated by holy baptism.[10]

These prescriptions, of course, are not merely attempts to impose an ideal but a vain attempt to *maintain* one. While the move away from paschal baptism in Gaul was well underway at the end of the sixth century, it is clear that it had been a normal practice before then.

[8] E. C. Whitaker, *Documents of the Baptismal Liturgy* (DBL), rev. and exp. by Maxwell E. Johnson (Collegeville, MN: Liturgical Press, 2003), 256.

[9] Ibid., 257.

[10] Ibid.

In Spain, the transition seems to occur a little later. Both infant and adult baptism exist side-by-side for some time, with the weight shifting toward infant baptism in the seventh century, between the commentaries of Isidore of Seville and Ildefonse of Toledo. It may be that the actual practice of adult baptism was maintained longer in Spain than elsewhere, with debates continuing in the seventh century and later over Sisebut's policy of the forced conversion of Jews.[11]

The rise of infant baptism can be seen in the Second Council of Braga (572), as it forbids the common problem of simony:

> It was agreed that every bishop is to instruct throughout his church concerning those who present their children for baptism, that if they voluntarily offer any gift for it, it is to be received from them. Yet if by the need of poverty anyone has nothing to offer, no pledge is to be violently taken from them by clergy; for many poor people, fearing this, hold back their children from baptism. If they leave this life without the grace of baptism while deferring it, their perdition must be required of the ones whose theft they feared when they withdrew from the grace of baptism.[12]

Still, this practice of infant baptism may not yet be *quamprimum*, and thus divorced from Easter, since the same council requires "infants" to be brought for a pre-baptismal exorcism in mid-Lent.[13]

In the seventh century, in his *De Ecclesiasticis Officiis*, Isidore of Seville still seems to see a need to justify infant baptism to his readers, in terms of both its "profitability" and its legitimacy for one who can't make a profession of faith: "We believe baptism to profit at full age, whether for the purgation of the original crime, or for the abolition of actual sins; even to children, that they may be cleansed of original sin, which they received from Adam through their first birth . . . and which children themselves are baptized with another making the profession, because thus far they do not know how to speak or believe, just as also with the sick, the mute and the deaf, in whose turn another

[11] For fuller treatment of Spanish evidence, see Christian McConnell, *Baptism in Visigothic Spain: Origins, Development and Interpretation* (PhD dissertation, University of Notre Dame, 2005).

[12] Second Council of Braga, canon 7. Latin text in José Vives, et al., eds., *Concilios Visigoticos e Hispano-Romanos* (Barcelona-Madrid: Consejo Superior de Investigationes Científicas, Instituto Enrique Flórez, 1963), 83.

[13] Second Council of Braga, canon 9. See Vives, *Concilios*, 84.

professes, so that they may respond for them while they are baptized."[14] There's nothing surprising in the rationale offered here, but it does appear that infant baptism, while clearly common, seems to warrant an explanation. It also appears that adult baptism is still happening, as Isidore mentions a washing of the heads of catechumens on Palm Sunday: "The people call that day the *capitilavium*, because then there is a custom of washing the heads of the infants who are to be anointed, lest by chance they approach the anointing dirty from the observance of Lent."[15] He does refer to the catechumens as *infantes*, but the common use of this term for (adult) catechumens does appear elsewhere in his work, and it seems that adults would be more likely to have been undertaking penitential practices, observing Lent in a way that might leave them dirty. In short, infant baptism is increasingly common, but adult baptism certainly lingers. Isidore seems to be right in the middle of the transition.

Later in the seventh century, Ildefonse of Toledo, on the other hand, seems to take infant baptism as more normal throughout his *De Cognitione Baptismi*, and a little later, in 666, the Council of Mérida forbids simony with explicit mention of infants and parents: "presbyters, who hand on the holy baptism of God to infants, are not to presume to carry off anything from the parents for such a grace."[16]

More directly related to our purpose here, Ildefonse provides strong evidence for a practice of *quamprimum* baptism in his grudging acknowledgment of it, along with a continuing ideal of baptism at Pascha:

> Apostolic and paternal antiquity have sanctioned that this celebration of baptism be held only at Easter and Pentecost and in the Sees of legitimate bishops and in their presence. In the neighboring churches of suffragan bishops this ought not be done; lest firstly where the congregation is scattered about in different places there be no one to whom the grace of doctrine can be conferred; and secondly because it detracts from the venerable dignity of the bishop. In distant parochial churches, however, it is rightly permitted lest the length of the journey defer the desirable grace which should be received as soon as possible. Outside

[14] Isidore of Seville, *De Ecclesiasticis Officiis* 2.25.7; my translation. Christopher M. Lawson, ed., *Sancti Isidori Episcopi Hispalensis*, Corpus Christianorum, Series Latina, 113 (Turnhout: Brepols, 1989).

[15] Ibid., 1.28.2.

[16] Council of Mérida, canon 9. Vives, *Concilios*, 332.

of these two times the right to baptize is freely granted where there is danger of death.[17]

While the *practical* normativity of paschal baptism has thus declined by the middle of the seventh century, this same *ideal* of paschal baptism, along with at least some continuing practice of adult baptism, would continue into the Mozarabic tradition, and baptism would be included in the Paschal Vigil with the emergence of the Mozarabic *Liber Ordinum*. In both the Mozarabic and Gallican traditions, while *quamprimum* baptism would decrease the frequency of paschal baptism, the theological interpretation of baptism would be informed by at least an ideal association of baptism with Pascha.

Theological Images of Paschal Baptism in Gallican Sources

This is not to say, however, that baptism was ever strongly associated with Romans 6 in either of these traditions. Sources in both Gaul and Spain provide a wide range of images for baptism, among which the image of burial with Christ appears very infrequently. In terms of the earlier models in East and West, both of these traditions draw heavily on the language of rebirth and regeneration (which is not always equated with rebirth). John 3:5 appears often, and the association of Gallican baptism with Epiphany is well known. Besides this "Eastern" imagery, sometimes associated with non-paschal baptism, there is a wide range of images that *are* paschal, but not Romans 6 burial language. The narratives of Pascha, of course, are rich, and these traditions draw heavily on that richness.

Gabriele Winkler has noted both the absence of Romans 6 and the dominance of John 3:5 and the Jordan in key Gallican sources:

> The blessing of the font with the reference to being born of water and the Spirit (John 3:5), as well as the allusion to Jesus' baptism in the river Jordan in all three of these Gallican documents, mirrors the earliest Syrian tradition. It is also important to note in this context that neither the *Missale Gothicum* nor the *Bobbio Missal* ever cite Romans 6.

[17] Ildefonse of Toledo, *De Cognitione Baptismi*, 108. For the text of the *De Cognitione Baptismi*, see *Patrologia Latina* 96. The translation here is from Method C. Billy, *Liber de cognitione baptismi* (Washington, DC: Catholic University of America Press, 1951).

In other words, Paul's baptismal theology, with its christocentric "death-mysticism," is quite absent here, as it is in the earliest Syrian (and Armenian) tradition. The key New Testament text here is John 3:5, with the result that being born again of water and the Spirit provides the fundamental *leitmotiv* for initiation.[18]

That dominance of rebirth in water and the Spirit is indeed apparent in Gallican sources. In the above-cited Second Council of Macon, the insistence on paschal baptism in the face of *quamprimum* baptism involves the complaint that "only two or three can be found to be regenerated by water and the Holy Spirit."[19] Likely much later,[20] the homily of Pseudo-Faustus of Riez, in supplying what would be one of the theologies later applied to confirmation, repeatedly refers to baptism as rebirth:

> What the imposition of the hand bestows in confirming individual neophytes, the descent of the Holy Spirit gave people then in the world of believers. . . . [T]he Holy Spirit, who descends upon the waters of baptism by a salvific falling, bestows on the font a fullness toward innocence, and presents in confirmation an increase for grace. And because in this world we who will be prevailing must walk in every age between invisible enemies and dangers, we are reborn in baptism for life, and we are confirmed after baptism for the strife. In baptism we are washed; after baptism we are strengthened. And although the benefits of rebirth suffice immediately for those about to die, nevertheless the helps of confirmation are necessary for those who will prevail. Rebirth in itself immediately saves those needing to be received in the peace of the blessed age. Confirmation arms and supplies those needing to be preserved for the struggles and battles of this world. But the one who arrives at death after baptism, unstained with acquired innocence, is confirmed by death because one can no longer sin after death.[21]

The pneumatic emphasis, with the Spirit coming upon the water, is also worth noting.

[18] Gabriele Winkler, "Confirmation or Chrismation: A Study in Comparative Liturgy," *Worship* 58, no. 1 (January 1984): 6.

[19] Second Council of Macon, in DBL, 257.

[20] See Winkler, "Confirmation or Chrismation"; and Johnson, *Rites of Christian Initiation*, 184–85.

[21] Pseudo-Faustus of Riez, *Homily 29 on Pentecost*, in DBL, 257–58.

In the *Missale Gothicum*, the frequent references to rebirth, the Jordan, and the Holy Spirit appear in several different texts. In a collect for the Sunday before Easter, when the Creed is handed on, the catechumens are "being prepared to receive the fullness of your grace by the gift of your Spirit . . . [that] they may be reborn in the fount of the holy laver which they have longed for."[22] In the order "for the making of a Christian," the font is blessed as a "laver of rebirth unto the remission of all their sins," followed by a collect that speaks of a "new birth."[23]

The *contestatio* that follows maintains the strongly pneumatic emphasis throughout, as well as another reference to rebirth and *two* references to the Jordan. These images are enhanced with others. The prayer also alludes to creation in addressing God "who before the beginning of the world bestowed your Holy Spirit upon the waters which supported him." The font is healing water like the waters of Bethsaida, the water "washes away the stains of the former life," and the baptized "receive the pardon of their sins." The exorcism of the water and further collects continually repeat the John 3:5 language.[24]

Death and resurrection imagery (though *not* Romans 6 imagery) is not entirely absent. Besides the placement of the whole baptismal rite in the Easter Vigil, the pouring of chrism into the font is cruciform, as is common in Western sources, and the blessing of the font intriguingly names it as the place from which the baptized are "voyagers [who] embark and ply their trade upon a new sea. They set sail with the cross for their mast, with heavenly desire to guide them, with no staff but the sacrament."[25]

In the formulary for the first Mass of Easter, the paschal language is predictably more overt. The preface has gentle echoes of the Exodus, with the gathered church as "freed from the darkness of this world, and chosen unto the promised grace of righteousness and heavenly light." The church is made up of those "which he sought by the Passion and most glorious Blood of his most loving Son."[26] The *immolatio* (post-*Sanctus*) strings together no fewer than seven different biblical quotations naming God as Creator, in rapid succession, followed by a rich description of the salvific meaning of Pascha:

[22] *Missale Gothicum*, in DBL, 259.
[23] Ibid., 260.
[24] Ibid., 260–62.
[25] Ibid., 259–60.
[26] Ibid., 262.

> It is meet and right, fitting and right, that here and in all places we should thank you, should sing your praises and offer sacrifices and confess your mercies, O Lord holy, Father Almighty, everlasting God, *for you are great and do wondrous things, you are God alone, you in your wisdom made the heavens*, you formed the earth above the waters, you made *great lights, the sun to rule the day, the moon* and stars *to rule the night; it is you that made us and not we ourselves; disregard not the work of your own hands. The day is yours and the night is yours, you have granted your lovingkindness in the daytime and the nightseason*, you have declared what we celebrate in today's vigil, in the festival of this light. For this is the night which has knowledge of the saving sacraments, the night in which you offer pardon to sinners, make new men from old, from worn out old men restore full-grown infants, whom you bring from the sacred font renewed unto a new creature. On this night your people are new born and brought forth unto eternal day, the halls of the kingdom of heaven are thrown open, by your blessed ordinance human conversation is changed to divine. For this is the night which was made in joy, in which you *made us glad through your works*, the night in which hell opened its gates, the night in which Adam was set free, the night in which the piece of *silver which had been lost was found*, the night in which the *lost sheep was carried upon the shoulders of the good shepherd*, the night in which the devil slept and Christ the *sun of righteousness* arose, when the bonds of hell were burst and its bars broken, and *many bodies of the saints broke out from their tombs and entered the holy city*.[27]

In this text, it is worth noting that the expected mention of rebirth in baptism is surrounded with references to creation: God is repeatedly named as Creator, the newly reborn are a "new creature," and the night of Pascha is when "Adam was set free." Spanish sources will be more explicit about the place of creation in the interpretation of baptism, including an idea that Pascha, at the beginning of the year, was the time of year of creation itself, and regeneration becomes *both* rebirth and re-creation.

In the letter of Pseudo-Germanus of Paris, the rebirth-Jordan-pneumatic emphases again show themselves. The chrism is that by which Christ was anointed, oil indicates the grace of the Holy Spirit, and an extensive explanation of the delivery of the Creed at the Vigil makes constant comparisons of the catechumens with infants. Cush-

[27] Ibid., 262–63; italics in DBL signify quotations from Scripture. I have removed the Scripture citations found in DBL.

ions and towels laid out in the rite signify the delicate faith of the catechumen. To push the metaphor of infants, chrism is even strangely compared to milk.

Baptism is interpreted in more directly paschal terms, however, as the author proceeds to explain the red cover on the book of the gospel, signifying Christ's blood, and "the vessels of chrism are brought in chalices because all the sacraments of baptism are founded in the Passion of Christ." The balsam in the chrism comes from the *lentiscus*, "and there is a tradition that the part of the Lord's Cross to which the wicked man nailed the Lord's hands was made from the *lentiscus*."[28] Going to creative lengths, this part of the text associates baptism very strongly with the passion, but again without *any* reference to Romans 6.

In the order of baptism in the *Bobbio Missal*, as Winkler notes, regeneration, rebirth, adoption, and the Jordan appear repeatedly and extensively, among a range of other images. The second of the prayers for the exorcism of water speaks of the "creation of a new people" and later grounds the "sanctifying power" of water in "God, whose spirit at the beginning of the world was borne upon the waters, so that even the nature of water should be endowed with sanctifying power." As paschal blessings of water often do, the collect after it refers to numerous biblical images of water: the waters of the flood, the waters of creation, the water from the rock in Exodus, the water at Cana, the water on which Jesus walked, the water of the Jordan, and the water that flowed from the side of Christ.[29]

In short, it is true that a Johannine rebirth and Jordan theology of baptism is most certainly dominant in the Gallican sources, but the (at least ideally) paschal occasion for baptism makes a mark as well. Baptism is a means by which those baptized are re-created as a new people and washed (or born) in the blood and water of Christ's side. While not extensive or overt, the exodus is subtly part of the context of baptism's interpretation as well. One paschal image that never appears (except, as Winkler notes, in the *Gallicanum Vetus*[30]) is burial with Christ.

[28] Ibid., 264.
[29] Ibid., 270–71.
[30] Winkler, "Confirmation or Chrismation," 6.

Theological Images of Paschal Baptism in Hispanic Sources

Pre-Mozarabic sources for baptismal practice and theology come from two periods: some evidence in the fourth century and then the councils and commentaries of the sixth and seventh centuries, with a relative lack of evidence in the fifth. While the commentaries of Isidore and Ildefonse present increasingly highly developed theologies of baptism, many of the key motifs are already present in the fourth century. Pacian of Barcelona, in his third letter in a debate with a rigorist named Sympronian, accepts his interlocutor's use of John 3:5 as a commonsense baptismal image: "But these descriptions of ours will come later. For the present, let us consider those of yours. 'The Church is a people born again of the water and the Holy Spirit.' Well now, who has closed off the fountain of God to me? Who has snatched away the Spirit? In fact, with us is 'the living water,' the very water which gushes from Christ."[31]

With this noteworthy allusion to the blood and water of John 19:25, Pacian relates baptism directly to the passion and then goes on to anticipate and accept a similarly commonsense connection with Romans 6:

> "In baptism," you will say, "we die once and no more according to the Apostle, 'Do you not know that whoever of you have been baptized in Jesus Christ have been baptized in his death? Therefore you have been buried with him by baptism into death so that just as Christ arose again from the dead, so you, too, may walk in the newness of life.'" What is so extraordinary here? The Apostle was teaching that we were renewed so that no one might sin. And yet it followed that he who had sinned should repent. The one is to live unimpaired, the other one, cured. The one should receive a reward; the other, a remedy.[32]

In his *De Baptismo*, Pacian directly applies rebirth language to his discussion of original sin. He anticipates a rhetorical objection to the idea of the fallen as "born of Adam," and an attempt at an *ad absurdum* argument that would make the redeemed "born of Christ," by arguing that, in fact, the baptized *are* "born of Christ":

[31] Pacian of Barcelona, *Letter 3*, 3.1. *PL* 13. Translation from C. Hanson, *Iberian Fathers*, vol. 3, The Fathers of the Church, vol. 99 (Washington, DC: Catholic University of America Press, 1999).

[32] Ibid., 9.3.

> Do not think of these things in a carnal manner and then you will see how we are born of Christ, our parent. . . . [The incarnation] represents the marriage of the Lord, joined together in one flesh, so that according to "that great mystery" they might become "two in one flesh, Christ and the Church." From this marriage is born the Christian people, with the Spirit of the Lord coming from above. And at once, with the heavenly seed being spread upon and mingled with the substance of our souls, we develop in the womb of our [spiritual] mother, and once we come forth from her womb, we are made alive in Christ.[33]

He goes on to equate rebirth with resurrection, in terms of both Romans 6 and John 11:25: "And so it is that the whole man is born again and renewed in Christ, 'so that just as Christ was resurrected from the dead, so we, too, may walk in the newness of life.' . . . If we act in this manner, dearly beloved, we shall die no more. For even if we die in this body, we shall live in Christ, as he himself says, 'He who believes in me, although he were dead, shall live.'"[34]

For Pacian, then, John 3:5 is the primary motif for baptism, but he fully integrates the image of rebirth into a paschal context of death and resurrection and, in this case, Romans 6.

The other important fourth-century source for Iberian interpretation of baptism is the poet Prudentius, who makes several references to baptism in his hymns.[35] Typically, he sees baptism as cleansing from sin, and the images of the Jordan and baptism as illumination are very common. He supplements this Jordan paradigm with two paschal images, neither of which is Romans 6. Throughout a hymn that served as an inscription, "On a Spot in Calahorra Where Martyrs Suffered and Where Is Now a Baptistery," he compares the blood of martyrdom with the font of baptism, at the same site, yielding the same hope of heavenly glory. Cleansing is again a prominent image when he says of the spot, "This is a spot chosen of Christ for raising tried souls to heaven through blood, and for cleansing them with water." Further, he says that "here too mercy flows in the limpid fount / and washes

[33] Pacian of Barcelona, *De Baptismo*, 6.1. *PL* 13. Translation from Hanson, *Iberian Fathers*.

[34] Ibid., 6.2.

[35] For the texts of Prudentius, see H. J. Thomson, *Prudentius*, 2 vols., Loeb Classical Library (Cambridge, MA: Harvard University Press, 1953). The translation here is from Sr. M. Clement Eagan, *The Poems of Prudentius*, Fathers of the Church, vol. 43. (Washington, DC: Catholic University Press, 1962).

away old stains in its new stream." This connection with martyrdom is enhanced with another mention of John 19: "The Lord of this place is He from whose two wounded sides / flowed here discharge of blood, there of water."[36] One more Johannine image appears, where the font is compared to the spittle in the healing of the blind man in John 9.[37]

By the time of the later commentaries, Isidore and Ildefonse pick up on the full range of themes found in the fourth-century sources, include several other themes, and, perhaps most important, develop as fully as possible the relationship between Pascha (and thus baptism) and the exodus.

The key text from Isidore is in the *De Ecclesiasiticis Officiis* 2.25, where he largely interprets Christian baptism in terms of two types: the Red Sea and John the Baptizer, although he carefully delineates the theological distinction between Christian baptism and the baptism of John. He starts with 1 Corinthians 10, saying, "Moses baptized in the sea and in the cloud, both in type and in figure, . . . Therefore, the sea had the form of water, the clouds truly that of the Holy Spirit, the manna that of the bread of life. . . . [T]he people of God arose renewed by the Holy Spirit, who thus passed through the Red Sea with unhindered steps."[38]

He explains that there are three baptisms, including those of blood and of tears, in which the first one is explicitly called the "laver of regeneration," and then he turns to John 19: "Baptism is the water which at the time of the passion flowed forth from the side of Christ. There is no other element which in this world cleanses all, vivifies all, and for that reason as we are baptized in Christ, through him we are reborn, and purified, we are brought to life."[39] Again in this passage, one sees the full integration of rebirth into paschal language. Without any attempt at separating birth and death language, we are reborn in the water which flowed from Christ's side.

Isidore employs other biblical passages, as well. In terms of Daniel 3 and Colossians 1, he describes the seven steps of the font, the middle of which is the bottom of the font itself, as "like the Son of Man, extinguishing the furnace of fire, the steadiness of the foot, the foundation

[36] Prudentius, *Peristephanon*, 8, lines 1-16.

[37] Prudentius, *Apotheosis*, lines 692-703.

[38] Isidore of Seville, *De Ecclesiasiticis Officiis* 2.25.1.

[39] Ibid., 2.25.2-3.

of the water, in whom the fullness of divinity dwells bodily." Arguing against rebaptism, he uses both Ephesians 4 and Romans 6: "For if there is one God, and there is one faith, it is necessary that there be one baptism, because there is one death of Christ for us, in whose image we are submerged through the mystery of the sacred font, that we may be buried with Christ, dying to this world, and from these waters in the form of his resurrection we might emerge."[40] Addressing the growing normativity of infant baptism and the problem of profession of faith, he quotes John 3:5 directly, contrasting rebirth with the "first birth" from Adam.[41]

For Isidore, then, the traditional centrality of rebirth and Jordan language is being complemented by a wider range of biblical references. Among these, the use of John 19 complements Romans 6 as a particularly important paschal motif.

This trend, of widening the range of biblical images, reaches full fruition in Ildefonse's *De Cognitione Baptismi*. Most notably, Ildefonse also uses language of regeneration extensively, but in addition to frequent citations of John 3:5, he explicitly relates regeneration to re-*creation*: "Whence, because the sacrament of this regeneration consisted in water and the spirit, the perfect institution of causes emulated the form of that operation, as is said: 'and the spirit of God is moved over the waters', that in the beginnings of those same causes the restoration is shown to be prefigured in these things."[42] Interpreting catechumenal rites, he combines paschal language with regeneration language: "The power of God, through the victory of the Cross, took the prey of the human race from the power of the devil and made it a chosen race through the gift of regeneration. . . . What was once effected generally in the human race through the death of Christ is specifically repeated each day by the washing of those regenerated."[43] Later, he relates the Holy Spirit to both water and oil, and explicitly joins Christ's anointing in the waters of the Jordan to the waters of creation: "as oil naturally floats on every liquid so in the beginning the Holy Spirit moved on the waters. Whence we read that the Lord was anointed with the oil of exultation, that is, with the Holy Spirit."[44]

[40] Ibid., 2.25.6.

[41] Ibid., 2.5.7.

[42] Ildefonse of Toledo, *De Cognitione Baptismi*, 13.

[43] Ibid., 24–25.

[44] Ibid., 70–71.

A comparison of the font to the Red Sea leads to an extended allegorical exegesis of the exodus narrative. The bricks of the Israelite slaves are the sin and allurement of the world, the pillar and cloud are the grace of God, Moses is a type of Christ, the waters of the Red Sea are a type of the baptismal waters, Egypt is the world that Christ left behind, and the Egyptians and Pharaoh are sin and the devil. The opening of the baptistery, which had been sealed throughout Lent, is compared to the parting of the Red Sea waters.[45] In the rite itself, Exodus 15 is sung immediately after the water bath.[46]

The important feature of Ildefonse's interpretation, seeing regeneration not only as rebirth but as re-creation, he also sees as paschal, since creation occurred at the beginning of the year: "The font begins to signify the effect of the new regeneration at the time when the world begins to have its origin; so that the creation of things and the regeneration of souls are intimately connected with each other, all the more so since both occurred in the Spring of the year."[47]

Romans 6 is not commonly used, but it does come into play at precisely the point where Ildefonse describes the water bath. After a defense of single immersion, however, Ildefonse turns right back to rebirth language when he addresses the unrepeatability of baptism, adding: "Whence just as one already born of Adam cannot again be generated from Adam, so one born of Christ cannot again be generated by Christ; because as the womb of the mother cannot be repeated so neither can the baptism of the Church."[48]

In summary, then, while paschal baptism remains normal in Spain into the seventh century, Spanish interpretation of baptism employs several main themes that, elsewhere, were not associated with paschal baptism: it is intensely pneumatic, very much a rebirth as in John 3:5, and the Jordan is brought into play (for the catechumenate if not for the font). In addition, Romans 6 is complemented by a wide range of other paschal images: the water from the side of Christ in John 19, the promises of resurrection in John 6 and John 11, the re-creation of the world at Pascha, and martyrdom. Most important in the seventh century, the exodus becomes the dominant paschal image, not simply in

[45] Ibid., 101, 109.

[46] This detail seems not to be merely metaphorical in Ildefonse, as Isidore seems to correlate it in his commentary on Exodus. Isidore, *Commentary on Exodus*, 20.

[47] Ildefonse, *De Cognitione Baptismi*, 104.

[48] Ibid., 104.

terms of the Red Sea, but in more and more parallels between the exodus narrative and the baptismal rite. Finally, among the variety of other biblical texts that are used, there is a tendency to use John when possible.

Implications for Baptismal Theology and Catechesis

Today, the recovery of the rebirth-Jordan paradigm has been extremely important for taking us beyond a narrow appropriation of the paschal–Romans 6 paradigm in contemporary liturgical renewal. Rather than a binary appeal to both "paschal" and "non-paschal" models, Gallican and Spanish sources provide a rich tradition of a third way, in which rebirth and the Jordan event are applied to, even integrated into, baptism during the celebration of Christ's (and our) death and resurrection. Additionally, the Spanish tradition especially emphasizes a rich range of images, well beyond Romans 6, that *are* paschal in themselves, such as the waters of creation, the crossing of the Red Sea, the blood and water flowing from Christ's side, and drinking the cup that Christ had to drink (even to a sharing in martyrdom). Baptism becomes not simply a burial with Christ, but a participation in the full range of everything that Pascha itself means.

Of course, taken by themselves, none of these images are unique to these sources. It is becoming clear that Western traditions in general were *never* reducible to a Romans 6 emphasis. Even today, one text in our restored Roman Catholic rites of paschal baptism continues to retain a wide range of images, namely, the blessing of water. These sources, however, model the approach our theologizing on baptism can take, creatively integrating a rich array of motifs into our theology, catechesis, and mystagogical preaching; taking what is presently a brief mention of several images in one prayer; and breaking them open more widely in our discourse. Our restored practice of paschal baptism can only be enhanced by more careful attention to *all* of these images in our operative theology.

Walter D. Ray

Chapter 7

Baptismal Images, Baptismal Narratives

What happens in liturgy? What are we doing when we go to church? Such questions are not easily answered. One of the values of studying liturgical history is that we can see how Christians of the past might have answered these questions, helping us to understand what we ourselves are doing and perhaps how to do it better. Maxwell Johnson always has this end in view in his studies of liturgical history. Among his many contributions to the history of the rites of initiation is a small book devoted exclusively to this purpose, *Images of Baptism*.[1] This book will serve as a springboard for my reflections in this brief contribution to a book honoring Johnson's achievements. First, I want to widen the perspective on these baptismal images somewhat to include the idea of narrative. It is the narratives within which the images are found that give them their meaning, make them "come to life," so to speak, and bring them into relationship with each other. Then, I want to add another image to Johnson's list, that of marriage. Though it has been little studied, there is evidence that the image of marriage was operative in early Christian baptismal liturgies and continues to be operative, at least in the East. Though probably not ritualized in the earliest baptismal rites, the image does witness to a New Testament narrative of salvation that has baptismal implications. I think it brings a needed complement to the images of new birth and death that have historically dominated understandings of baptism.

I first became interested in liturgical narratives while writing my dissertation on the early Jerusalem calendar under Johnson and Paul Bradshaw.[2] I noticed a correlation of certain dates and narrative themes

[1] Maxwell E. Johnson, *Images of Baptism*, Forum Essays no. 6 (Chicago, IL: Liturgy Training Publications, 2001).

[2] "August 15 and the Development of the Jerusalem Calendar" (PhD dissertation, University of Notre Dame, 2000).

between this calendar and the calendar of the pre-Christian Jewish *Book of Jubilees*: August 15/IV 16 (conception of Jesus/conception of Isaac); May 15/III 15 (birth of Christ/birth of Isaac); and Pascha/Passover (crucifixion of Jesus/binding of Isaac). Underlying the Jubilees narrative themes is a repeated narrative pattern in which one person's faithful act liberates the people of God from evil powers in order that they might receive the fulfillment of the promises made to Abraham. Jubilees anticipates a final iteration of this pattern in which the evil powers will be definitively defeated and, as God promises the people through Moses, "I will create a holy spirit for them. . . . I will become their Father and they will become my children" (Jub 1:24-25). In the Jubilees narrative world the faithful persons in the pattern are Abraham and Moses and, in a later development represented in the Dead Sea Scrolls, Isaac, who participates in his own sacrifice (cf. 4Q225, "Psuedo-Jubilees"). I find that Paul presupposes this same narrative pattern in his argument in Galatians and Romans. In Paul's treatment of the narrative, Jesus is *the* (singular) offspring of Abraham and heir to the promises (Gal 3:16),[3] and the faithful person whose sacrifice on the cross defeats the anti-God powers (Gal 3:13, 23-24; 4:3-4; cf. Rom 5:17, 19-21) and ushers in the eschatological age in which all who share in Jesus' faithfulness receive the Holy Spirit (Gal 3:14; 4:6) and are adopted as God's children (Gal 3:26; 4:5; cf. Rom 8:9-17).

In his argument Paul appeals not only to this narrative but also to the ritual of baptism. The experience of baptism, he tells the Galatians, shows you that you have obtained the promises of the Spirit and adoption as God's children and therefore have no need of circumcision. They are already children of God because they can already call God "Abba! Father!" In my dissertation and a later article,[4] I assumed that Paul was making use of a traditional image of baptism as "being born of water and Spirit" (John 3:5). The image is not explicit, however, and I am no longer certain that Paul had it in mind. Baptism for Paul certainly means the reception or the "seal" of the Holy Spirit (1 Cor 12:12; 2 Cor 1:22). And he calls the Holy Spirit the "spirit of adoption" (Rom 8:15). His notion of adoption as children of God appears to come from

[3] Paul does not make this argument in Romans but simply presents Abraham as a model of the kind of faithfulness that inherits the promises; Rom 4:13-25.

[4] "Toward a Narrative-Critical Approach to the Study of Early Liturgy," in *Studia Liturgica Diversa: Essays in Honor of Paul F. Bradshaw*, ed. Maxwell E. Johnson and L. Edward Phillips (Portland, OR: Pastoral Press, 2004), 21.

tradition; adoption belongs to the Jews (Rom 9:4). He also knows baptism as washing for sanctification (cf. 1 Cor 6:11). Yet he does not call baptism the "water of rebirth" (Titus 3:5) as one might expect, especially in Galatians. Had he known this as a traditional or liturgical name for baptism, he could have argued simply that the Galatians are children of God because they have experienced the new birth in water and the Spirit. Instead, his argument is more convoluted: You are baptized into Christ, therefore united to the Son of God, who is also the offspring of Abraham, the heir to the promises; therefore, in Christ you are also heirs of Abraham and have received the promised adoption and Spirit, as your prayer to "Abba! Father!" proves. "Washing of new birth" and related formulae must have developed later, perhaps based on Paul's argument or, more likely, simply on the force of the underlying narrative. In Romans, of course, the image Paul uses is different. He says explicitly that baptism is being united with Christ in death (Rom 6:2-5). But this image is also not traditional; Christians will not use it to understand baptism for another three centuries, and then they will use it on Paul's authority.

In its narrative context in both Galatians and Romans, baptism marks the transition from the reign of anti-God forces to eschatological fulfillment. But this narrative pattern is found on different levels. For the person being baptized the movement is from being subject to hostile powers, sin, or death to receiving the promise of the Holy Spirit and a filial relationship with God. At this level the transition marked by baptism is appropriately imaged as new birth. But at the cosmological or historical level, the moment of transition from the reign of anti-God powers to fulfillment is the defeat of the hostile powers through the faithful act of Christ on the cross. We might also call this the christological narrative since this moment is also the point of transition in Christ's life. For Paul, baptism means above all being united to Christ. The specifically liturgical formula he cites is being baptized "into Christ" (Gal 3:27) or "into Christ Jesus" (Rom 6:3), which is probably shorthand for or an interpretation of "into the name of Christ/Jesus" (cf. 1 Cor 1:13; 10:2; Acts 2:38; 8:16; 19:5). He also cites more than once a possible baptismal hymn about the unity of the baptized in Christ, there being neither Jew nor Greek, slave nor free (see Gal 3:28; 1 Cor 12:13; cf. Col 3:11; I'll return later to the "male and female" of Gal 3:28). This understanding of baptism permits Paul to juxtapose the narrative levels, the personal and the christological. In the personal narrative the moment of transition is baptism; in the christological narrative, to which the baptized is being joined, this moment is death on the cross. Being united with Christ in baptism means being identified with Christ and therefore sharing in Christ's destiny: "I have been crucified with Christ; and it is no longer I who live, but Christ who lives in me" (Gal 2:19-20).

It is important to note that the narrative pattern is the same at each level, or rather becomes the same. Put another way, the ritual of baptism aligns a person's own story with that of Christ and the church, which is the world saved in Christ. By joining the church through baptism, a person enters into the world brought into being through Christ's death. One answer to the question of what we do in church, then, is that we align our personal stories with God's story of salvation, through participation in the church's rituals. We are able to realize ourselves as part of something bigger than ourselves, to which the rituals connect us as we enter into the narratives they access. The rituals provide us a way of understanding our history and destiny. They also provide a rhythm and pattern for our lives. We learn the story and become part of the story so that we can live out the story.

Whether we think of baptism as birth or death, we are still operating in the same narrative world. The giving of the Spirit can also be understood as part of that narrative. In the remainder of this essay I would like to examine, briefly and in a preliminary fashion, another image with a different narrative. This is the image of marriage. For purposes of this essay, I will not make a distinction between baptism understood as marriage to Christ and baptism understood as betrothal to Christ for a marriage to be consummated in the Eucharist or in the eschatological age. This image, I will argue, accesses a different narrative, which makes possible other ways of understanding our relationship with God. An examination of the passages referenced under the entry "marital imagery" in the index of Everett Ferguson's magisterial *Baptism in the Early Church* reveals the use of this image in connection with baptism across a broad spectrum of early Christian writings. Some of these are from Gnostic sources, e.g., Irenaeus's description of certain Valentinian rites in which a bridal chamber is prepared for those being initiated,[5] or the *Gospel of Philip*'s listing of "mysteries" as "baptism, chrism eucharist, ransom [redemption], and bridal

[5] Irenaeus, *Against Heresies* 1.21.3, cited in Everett Ferguson, *Baptism in the Early Church: History, Theology, and Liturgy in the First Five Centuries* (Grand Rapids, MI: Eerdmans, 2009), 279.

chamber."[6] The value of these sources will depend on how one interprets the relationship of these groups to the main streams of Christianity. Other uses of the imagery might have an exegetical basis, such as when Origen compares the waters of baptism to "the wells and waters" at which the Old Testament patriarchs found their brides.[7] Syriac authors such as Aphrahat and Ephrem reflect a tradition of drawing on parables of the kingdom as marriage banquet (e.g., Matt 22:1-14; 25:1-13) to explain baptism as being clothed in the wedding garment.[8] Such an interpretation might be inspired by the common rite of clothing the newly baptized. But there are enough casual references to baptism as betrothal or marriage from a diversity of early sources—e.g., Tertullian's passing reference to baptism as marriage to the Holy Spirit in *On the Soul* 41[9] and a possible reference to baptism as the bridal chamber of Christ in *Odes of Solomon* 42 (see more below)[10]—that it seems there is a tradition of thinking about baptism in this way.

This impression is strengthened when one finds ritualization of this image in baptismal liturgies. In particular, in all the Eastern liturgies of baptism except the Byzantine there is a crowning of the newly baptized that recalls the crowning of the couple in these rites' wedding liturgies. In his examination of the use of crowns at both baptism and marriage, George Bebawi argues that the marriage ritual was based on the baptismal, which is earlier, and that the crowns refer to martyrdom.[11] He adduces the crowning prayer from the Syrian marriage liturgy as evidence of its prior baptismal context: "By your coming in the flesh, O Lord, you have filled your holy church with the sweet fragrance of your divine wisdom, and with the finest robes of non-fading

[6] *Gospel of Philip* II, 3, 67, 27–30, cited in Ferguson, *Baptism*, 285. On the meaning of these mysteries, see April D. DeConick, "The True Mysteries: Sacramentalism in the *Gospel of Philip*," *Vigiliae Christianae* 55 (2001): 225–61.

[7] Origen, *Homilies on Genesis* 10.5, cited in Ferguson, *Baptism*, 416.

[8] For Aphrahat, see Ferguson, *Baptism*, 497–98; for Ephrem see Ferguson, *Baptism*, 516, and also Sebastian Brock, *The Luminous Eye: The Spiritual World Vision of Saint Ephrem the Syrian*, Cistercian Studies Series 124 (Kalamazoo, MI: Cistercian Publications, 1992), 94–97, 122–26.

[9] Cited in Ferguson, *Baptism*, 346.

[10] Ferguson, *Baptism*, 224, notes the use of the imagery in *Ode* 42, but does not connect it directly with baptism.

[11] George Bebawi, "The Crown of Life: An Orthodox Perspective," *The Ecumenical Review* 34 (1982): 263–70.

glory; and with the crown of righteousness you adorned and glorified her. From Water and Spirit you made her your glorious betrothed." But this prayer rather suggests a nuptial significance for the crown even in baptism. While their use in baptism may well be earlier than their use in the ritual of Christian marriage, the association of crowns with marriage in Christian literature is much earlier than even their use in baptism.

Bebawi finds the earliest reference to crowning in baptism in the *Odes of Solomon* (second century). Whether the *Odes* are baptismal in the strict sense has been called into question recently.[12] But even if they are not baptismal, they may still be initiatory.[13] And in the *Odes* initiation appears to be associated with nuptial imagery, as does the crown. For those who acknowledge him, says *Ode* 42, Christ throws the yoke of his love over them "like the arm of the bridegroom over the bride"; he spreads out his love over them "as the bridal chamber is spread out by the bridal pairs' home" (42:7-9).[14] For those even in Sheol who run to him, Christ says, I will "place my name upon their head because they are free and they are mine" (42:20). This last verse of the *Odes* recalls

[12] Michael Lattke, *Odes of Solomon: A Commentary*, Hermeneia, trans. Marianne Ehrhardt (Minneapolis, MN: Fortress Press, 2009), tries to show at every turn that the earlier view of seeing the *Odes* as baptismal hymns cannot be sustained. See also Susan Myers, "Initiation by Anointing in Early Syriac Christianity," *Studia Liturgica* 31 (2001): 158–66, who argues that the references to water in the *Odes* are sapiential and do not have baptism in view.

[13] Since Lattke does not find baptism in the *Odes*, he also does not find initiation there. Myers, "Initiation," 160, recognizes that "the sheer volume of terms elsewhere employed in initiatory contexts, and the references to incorruption and new life, suggest that many of the terms are indeed being used to speak of Christian initiation" in the *Odes*. Since her main argument is that in some places in early Syriac Christianity initiation was by anointing alone, without a water baptism, it is not necessary to find baptism specifically in order for the *Odes* to have initiatory significance.

[14] Translations by James Hamilton Charlesworth, ed. and trans., *The Odes of Solomon* (Oxford: Clarendon Press, 1973). Lattke's comment (*Odes*, 590) that "the terms in 8a and 9a are meant literally, the first describing a universal amatory gesture and the second traditional Jewish marriage customs. 'Bride' and 'Bridegroom' are therefore not metaphors for the 'Christ' and 'the church'" defies logic. Obviously, the arm of a groom and a bridal chamber are real things, but, equally obviously, they are being used here metaphorically to refer to Christ's love, which makes Christ the bridegroom of the metaphor and the object of the amatory gesture; those who love (v. 5), acknowledge, and believe in Christ, Christ's bride.

the very first verse: "The Lord is on my head like a crown" (1:1).[15] Reflection on this "crown of truth" occupies the whole of the extant portion of the first ode. Though the second ode is missing, where the third ode picks up the context is clearly nuptial and quite possibly initiatory (3:1-8):

> I am putting on the [love of the Lord].[16] And His members are with Him, and I am dependent on them; and He loves me. For I should not have known how to love the Lord, if He had not continuously loved me. Who is able to distinguish love, except him who is loved? I love the Beloved and I myself love Him, and where His rest is, there also am I. And I shall be no stranger, because there is no jealousy with the Lord Most High and Merciful. I have been united (to Him), because the lover has found the Beloved, because I love Him that is the Son, I shall become a son. Indeed he who is joined to Him who is immortal, truly shall be immortal.

The *Odes of Solomon* are generally thought to come from the region of Syria.[17] The third-century Acts of Thomas are certainly Syrian and know both marriage imagery for baptism (or initiation[18]) and the nuptial crown. Although there is nothing overtly nuptial in the initiation rituals and formulas they record, the narrative frame of the Acts makes clear that initiation is understood as betrothal for "the incorruptible and true marriage" (Act 12) in which believers are "yoked with [the] true man" (Act 14).[19] The action begins at a wedding feast for a king's only daughter at which the apostle, as Jesus' twin, prepares himself for the true marriage with scented oil and a crown (which, the narrative says, were brought to each of the guests): "[T]he apostle anointed

[15] For the identification of God's crown with the divine name in a Judaism contemporary with the *Odes*, see Arthur Green, *Keter: The Crown of God in Early Jewish Mysticism* (Princeton, NJ: Princeton University Press, 1997), 42–48.

[16] This is Charlesworth's suggestion for a phrase missing in the manuscript.

[17] Lattke, *Odes*, 11–12, is less sanguine than the majority of scholars about our ability to identify the place of origin but favors Syria slightly.

[18] Water baptism is not always used in the *Acts of Thomas*, at least in their Greek version, which is thought to represent the older recension. See Myers, "Initiation," for the argument that water baptism might not have always been the means of Christian initiation in Syria.

[19] Translations of the Greek text are from Edgar Hennecke, *New Testament Apocrypha*, ed. Wilehm Schneemelcher and R. McL. Wilson, 2 vols. (Philadelphia, PA: Westminster Press, 1965), 2:442–531.

the crown of his head and smeared a little upon his nostrils, dropped some also into his ears, touched his teeth with it, and carefully anointed the parts about his heart; and the crown that was brought to him, woven of myrtle and other flowers, he took and set upon his head; and he took a branch of a reed in his hand and held it" (Act 5). This last element is clearly meant to recall Jesus at the crucifixion (cf. Matt 27:29),[20] which would make the nuptial crown an image of the crown of thorns. This suggests one possible route by which the marriage crown might have come to be associated with the crown of martyrs once it was incorporated into the baptismal liturgy, though only the Coptic liturgy specifically refers to the baptismal crown in this way.[21]

When and how crowns came to be a part of baptismal liturgies remains to be studied, though we can make a few observations. Ephrem of Syria in the fourth century may refer to a baptismal crown with nuptial significance in his hymns on Epiphany.[22] While Narsai in the next century does not specifically mention crowns in his commentary on the baptismal liturgy, he does say that the newly baptized person is clothed "as a bridegroom on the day of the marriage supper."[23] The earliest certain liturgical reference to the crown at baptism comes in a fifth-century Syriac liturgical commentary. There, "the crowns placed on the heads of the baptized signify the freedom they have received from Christ." The commentary also says that the entry into the church of the newly baptized "indicates their spiritual marriage."[24] It is noteworthy that an Egyptian baptismal liturgy from the sixth century does not yet have crowns.[25] Because of the early and persistent use of marriage imagery in connection with baptism in Syrian Christianity, it is

[20] The similarity between this description of Thomas and the Byzantine icon of Christ the Bridegroom, also known as Extreme Humility, is fortuitous or providential but nevertheless bears noting.

[21] See E. C. Whitaker, *Documents of the Baptismal Liturgy*, rev. and exp. by Maxwell E. Johnson (Collegeville, MN: Liturgical Press, 2003), 139.

[22] Ephrem, *Hymns on Epiphany* 12 and 13, cited in Ferguson, *Baptism*, 516. The authenticity of these hymns is questioned, however; see Myers, "Initiation," 159, and note 30.

[23] *Homily* 21 in Whitaker, *Documents*, 59.

[24] Sebastian Brock, "Some Early Syriac Baptismal Commentaries," *Orientalia Christiana Periodica* 46 (1980): 45, 47.

[25] Anton Baumstark, "Eine aegyptische Mess- und Taufliturgie vermutlich des 6 Jarhunderts," *Oriens Christianus* 1 (1901): 1–45.

likely that it was there the crowns first became part of the baptismal liturgy. It is not unreasonable to suppose that the crowns entered the baptismal rite because marriage was already an image associated with baptism, and crowns were culturally associated with the nuptial feasts in both pagan and Jewish wedding rituals.[26] The same cultural factors will have inspired the crowns in the Eastern Christian marriage liturgies, quite apart from baptism.[27]

Ferguson finds only one instance in the New Testament of marriage imagery for baptism, Ephesians 5:26, where baptism is the nuptial bath for the bride of Christ, the church, which is also his body because "the two will become one flesh" (Eph 5:29-32, citing Gen 2:24). The genuine Paul applies this Genesis verse to the relationship between the Christian and Christ: "Anyone united with the Lord becomes one spirit with him" (1 Cor 6:17). In 2 Corinthians 11:2 Paul says that he "promised" the Corinthian church "in marriage to one husband," to Christ. In Galatians Paul also appears to have marriage in mind when he speaks about being one in Christ through baptism. Not only is there no longer Jew or Greek and slave or free; there is also no longer "male and female," a citation of Genesis 1:27. The primitive fault line in humanity, which comes from creation and is partly overcome through marriage, is now overcome in the unity of Christ. In Romans, after his long discussion about baptism as a sharing in Christ's death, he inserts an awkward example from marriage law: Just as a woman

[26] See Green, *Keter*, 82–84.

[27] Whether marriage imagery had obtained any ritualization in baptism before the crowns is an open question. One area that might be explored is in the use of oil, the importance of which for Syrian baptismal liturgy is well known. Stephanie Dalley reports that ancient, pre-Christian Mesopotamian sources knew four uses of oil: when washing or dressing, when sacrificing to cult statues, in a meal context when making oaths, and in the selection of a wife or a vassal king. In the first three instances, oil is applied by rubbing, either onto the body or onto the statue or cultic object. In the last case, however, "oil is poured on the head of the chosen person by the selector" (Stephanie Dalley, "Anointing in Ancient Mesopotamia," in *The Oil of Gladness: Anointing in the Christian Tradition*, ed. Martin Dudley and Geoffrey Rowell [London: SPCK/Collegeville, MN: Liturgical Press, 1993], 19). Pouring on the head is precisely the manner of anointing in the Acts of Thomas (see Acts 27, 121, 133, 158). Might not the original meaning of this anointing have been Christ's acceptance of his chosen bride? Later interpretations of the anointing in terms of the Old Testament anointing of priests and kings or the spiritual anointing of Christ in the Jordan would have been attempts to redefine the rite in terms of canonical narratives.

may legally marry after her husband has died, so Christians have "died to the law through the body of Christ, so that [they] may belong to another, to him who has been raised from the dead, in order that we may bear fruit for God" (Rom 7:1-4).

Did Paul think of baptism in terms of marriage? Or, better, did Paul know a narrative within which baptism might be thought of in terms of marriage? In my dissertation I identify several iterations of the Jubilees narrative pattern in both Galatians and Romans. In Galatians the exposition of this narrative is compact, being limited to chapters 3 and 4. In Romans the exposition is diffuse. Interwoven with this narrative is another in which the image of marriage is prominent. The background for this narrative is the idea of Israel as the bride of God, as presented by the prophets, especially Hosea. Paul quotes Hosea 2:23 and 1:10 directly in Romans 9:25-26. I think he also relies on this prophet earlier in the epistle. The story in Hosea 2 is that Israel takes "other lovers," the Baals, whom she credits with giving her blessings: "They give me my bread and my water, my wool and my flax, my oil and my drink" (2:5). She failed to recognize that it was the Lord "who gave her the grain, the wine, and the oil, and who lavished upon her silver and gold that they used for Baal" (2:8). As a consequence, the Lord threatens to take back the grain, wine, wool, and flax and "uncover her shame in the sight of her lovers" (2:10). Israel "shall pursue her lovers, but not overtake them; and she shall seek them, but shall not find them" (2:7). But the Lord will woo Israel back: "And I will take you for my wife forever; I will take you for my wife in righteousness and in justice, in steadfast love, and in mercy. I will take you for my wife in faithfulness; and you shall know the Lord" (2:19-20). The last verses serve as a kind of template for Paul's arguments in Romans: God's sacrifice of Christ proves both God's righteousness (Rom 3:21, 25) and God's love (5:8)[28] and shows that God is faithful even when humans are unfaithful (3:3). Paul takes the Israel-specific narrative of Hosea and transposes it into a cosmological key involving all of creation.[29] In Romans too the narrative begins with human infidelity and

[28] Ἀγάπη, while the LXX of Hos 2:21 has ἔλεος and οἰκτηρμός. I would argue that ἀγάπη is equivalent to the hendiadys of the LXX. Similarly, the δικαιοσύνη Θεοῦ of Romans can stand for both the δικαιοσύνη and κρίματα of God in the Hosea text, as Paul's citation of Ps 50:4 (LXX) in Rom 3:4 shows.

[29] This transposition of the Hosea narrative is consistent with Paul's application of Hosea 2:23—"Those who were not my people I will call 'my people'; and her

failure to recognize the true source of blessings: those who knew God "did not honor him as God or give thanks to him" but instead "worshiped and served the creature rather than the Creator" (1:21, 25). The result was rupture in the relationship not only with God but among humans, exemplified by the complete breakdown in relations across the primordial human divide between male and female.[30] As with Israel chasing after her lovers, God gave humans up to their own desires (1:24). But even in the face of human perfidy, God remains faithful and finds a way to reestablish the relationship with humans in righteousness and love: the crucifixion of his Son. The result of this act is peace and reconciliation with God (5:1, 10-11), so that nothing will be able to separate us from God's love (8:38-39). Creation itself is restored, Paul tells us, again using language that recalls the epitomic breakdown in the created order, the disruption in the relationship between man and woman. Like the woman of Genesis 3:16, all of creation—along with us—groans in labor pains waiting for "the revealing of the children of God" (8:19-26).

Paul reaches back to the creation story in part because it serves his larger purpose, which is "to redefine the relationship between Jew and Gentile within the saving purpose of the one creator God."[31] The specific appeal to marriage in the creation account serves another Pauline interest, to show how the division between Jew and Gentile is overcome in the one body of Christ. In the Genesis 2 account, marriage, "the two becom[ing] one flesh" (Gen 2:24), partly restores the original unity that man and woman, male and female, had before the fall. Marriage becomes a metaphor or, better, a symbol or image of the overcoming of divisions of all kinds. Marriage is the "becoming one" relationship. Although this theme is not prominent in Romans, where

---

who was not beloved I will call 'beloved' "—to the Gentiles rather than wayward Israel; cf. Rom 9:23-25.

[30] This is how I think the problematic verses Rom 1:26-27 are to be understood. If marriage images the overcoming of this primordial divide, the rejection of male-female relations images the opposite, the irreparable dissolution of human society epitomized as "male and female" (Gen 1:27). That Paul's use of the terms "male" and "female" in these verses is meant to recall the creation account has been noted by commentators. See, e.g., James D. G. Dunn, *Romans 1–8*, Word Biblical Commentary 38A (Dallas, TX: Word, 1988), 64.

[31] James D.G. Dunn, *Romans 9–16*, Word Biblical Commentary 38B (Milton Keynes, UK: Word, 1991), 716.

Paul is concerned with the problem of the unbelieving Jews,[32] it is elsewhere in the Pauline corpus, especially in the epistle to the Ephesians: "[Christ] is our peace; in his flesh he has made both groups into one . . . that he might create in himself one new humanity in place of the two, thus making peace, and might reconcile both groups to God in one body through the cross" (Eph 2:14-16). This passage provides a necessary context for the quotation of Genesis 2:24 in Ephesians 5:31, and its interpretation in 5:32: "This is a great mystery, and I am applying it to Christ and the church." This is, of course, the passage where baptism is imaged as a nuptial bath. Similarly, Paul's use of Genesis 2:24 in 1 Corinthians 6:16-17, where he uses the expressions "one body" and "one flesh" interchangeably, sheds light on his assertion in 1 Corinthians 12:13 that "in the one Spirit we were all baptized into one body—Jews or Greeks, slave or free." I have already suggested that Paul has the creation narrative in mind in Galatians 3:28 when he adds "male and female" to this list of divisions overcome through baptism into Christ.

The marriage narrative is useful to Paul in other ways. The focus throughout is on the relationship between God and humans established at creation, broken by human sin, and restored by divine action. In contrast to the Jubilees narrative, in the marriage narrative the initiative in restoring this relationship is clearly with God. The crucifixion is no longer simply the faithful act of a human person toward God ("one man's obedience," as in Rom 5:19) but God's faithful act with respect to faithless humanity. In a twist on his presentation of the Jubilees narrative in Galatians, in Romans Paul casts God the Father in the role of Abraham, not sparing his own Son (Rom 8:32), but presenting him as a sacrifice of atonement (3:25). In Galatians it is Christ who "loved me and gave [παραδόντος] himself for me" (2:20). In Romans it is God who gave up (παρέδωκεν) his Son (8:32) and who "proves his love for us in that . . . Christ died for us" (5:8). In contrast to the parent-child relationship imaged by the Jubilees narrative, which is characterized by the ideas of command and obedience to rules (hence, "Law"),[33] the operative ideas in marriage are love, faithfulness, and

[32] But see 12:4-8 for the theme of unity in the one body, and 15:7-13 for the unity of Jews and Gentiles in praise.

[33] See Gal 3:24, 4:1-2: "The law was our disciplinarian until Christ came. . . . [H]eirs, as long as they are minors, are no better than slaves . . ., but they remain under guardians and trustees until the date set by the father."

trust, the last two terms both translating πίστης, "faith." Thus, Abraham trusted in God before the covenant was ratified by circumcision and was justified, because God justifies the one "who without works trusts him who justifies the ungodly" (Rom 4:5 and *passim*). With the image of marriage Paul moves beyond the idea of covenant and its notions of reward and punishment for meeting or not meeting certain conditions. God's love is unconditional.

The image of marriage provides a different criterion than the covenantal law for behavior in the "becoming one" community: the law of self-giving love. The model for this standard of behavior is God acting in Christ. Thus, Paul begins his instructions in Romans with an appeal to "present your bodies as a living sacrifice" in service to the one Body of Christ (Rom 12:1-8). They are to "let love be genuine," hating what is evil but "cleaving" (the word is the same as the husband cleaving to his wife in Gen 2:24 LXX) to what is good (Rom 12:9). They are to "owe no one anything, except to love one another; for the one who loves another has fulfilled the law" (Rom 13:8). Paul's letters are filled with calls for mutual care and deference toward the other. "Welcome one another . . . as Christ has welcomed you" (Rom 15:7). "Bear one another's burdens, and so fulfill the law of Christ" (Gal 6:2). "Let each of you look not to your own interests, but to the interests of others. Let the same mind be in you that was in Christ Jesus" (Phil 2:4-5). And, of course, there's the "more excellent way" of 1 Corinthians 13, which is to govern relations in the assembly, which "is patient . . . [and] kind; . . . does not insist on its own way" but "bears all things, believes all things, hopes all things, endures all things."

Given this narrative background, it is not surprising that baptism came to be seen as marriage to Christ. However else Paul might have understood baptism, he certainly thought about it as union with Christ in one body through the Holy Spirit. Insofar as he presents this union in terms of marriage, it is quite possible that marriage was among his images of baptism. It certainly was for his successors in the Pauline community.[34] Though this image found ritual expression in many Eastern rites, it was completely overshadowed by the images of birth and death in Western and to a large extent in Byzantine Christianity. Should this image be restored? Let me first dispense with two

[34] The image was not exclusive to Pauline Christianity. The idea of the community of the saved as the bride of the Lamb plays a significant role in Revelation (see Rev 19:7-9; 21:2ff, 9-27). Christ is also identified as the bridegroom in Matt 9:15 and in John 3:29, where the Baptizer is the "friend of the bridegroom."

possible objections to restoring marriage as an image. First, the image is not primarily sexual. Or, rather, the sexual is the lowest level of the image. In an age in which sex is sometimes seen as the highest form of human experience, it is useful to remind ourselves that even within marriage the fleeting sexual union is only an image and aid to the deeper, permanent union of two humans sharing a common life. Second, it might be objected that using marriage as an image of the relationship between God and humanity reinforces patriarchal notions of the subordination of women within marriage, especially in light of its use in Ephesians 5. A full recovery of the image of marriage for the divine-human relationship, however, would actually undermine such patriarchal views. In the Genesis account the subordination of the woman is presented as a consequence of sin and does not reflect God's original intention for humanity. The marriage narrative underlying the baptismal image is not about the bride but about God's unconditional love for creation. The only model for action the narrative presents is God in Christ. Ephesians' retelling of the Pauline marriage narrative begins only with 5:25: "Husbands, love your wives, just as Christ loved the church and gave himself up for her, in order to make her holy by cleansing her with the washing of water by the word, so as to present the church to himself in splendor, without a spot or wrinkle or anything of the kind—yes, so that she may be holy and without blemish. In the same way, husbands should love their wives as they do their own bodies . . . just as Christ does for the church, because we are members of his body." When the model is applied to the members of the church in general, we get "therefore be imitators of God, as beloved children, and live in love, as Christ loved us and gave himself up for us, a fragrant offering and sacrifice to God" (Eph 5:1-2); and "lead a life worthy of the calling to which you have been called, with all humility and gentleness, with patience, bearing with one another in love, making every effort to maintain the unity of the Spirit in the bond of peace" (Eph 4:1-3); and "be kind to one another, tender-hearted, forgiving one another, as God in Christ has forgiven you" (Eph 4:32); and "be subject to one another out of reverence for Christ" (Eph 5:21). "Being subject to one another," "bearing with one another," and "giving oneself up for the other" are all examples of the self-giving love required of all Christians in all their relationships but especially in the relationship that provides the image, marriage.

What is the value of this image? Besides providing criteria for living that go beyond law and covenant, the image of marriage provides a unique way of understanding the relationship between God and his creation. Of all the human relationships the Bible uses as images of the relationship between God and humans—master-slave (Matt 25:14-30; Rom 1:1; 6:22), teacher-disciple (the gospels, *passim*), parent-child (*passim*), friendship (John 15:15; Jas 2:23), and marriage—only marriage conveys the sense of totality and permanence. The first three are relationships of inequality and separation. They are built on structures of command and obedience and are governed by standards and rules. The teacher-disciple and parent-child images imply processes of development and maturation. Friendship and marriage, on the other hand, are mature relationships and suggest equality and mutuality. Indeed, in their biblical presentation, the images of friendship and marriage bear a striking resemblance. Both are grounded in self-giving love (John 15:13; Eph 5:25) that leads to bearing fruit for God (John 15:16; Rom 7:4). But marriage goes beyond friendship in its intimacy. It is the "becoming one" relationship. This image presents a different understanding of salvation than the other images. Salvation is found in the relationship itself. God in Christ espouses humanity,[35] submits himself to us, is "given over into human hands [παραδίδοται εἰς χεῖρας ἀνθρώπων]" (Mark 9:31),[36] though it costs him his life. In response, we submit ourselves to God, ceasing to "insist on our own way" but trusting ourselves to God. In Christ God fully embraces human life so that we might share in divine life. This last formulation is deliberately intended to recall the Eastern Christian concept of *theosis*, deification. There is a relationship between this concept and nuptial imagery that needs to be explored.

For each image he presents, Johnson concludes his discussion by suggesting ways it might be (re)connected with the baptismal liturgy. How might we do this for the image of marriage? I will let Western liturgiologists decide whether and how to reconnect marriage imagery with baptism in Western liturgy. Perhaps Johnson will have some ideas about this. For my own tradition, the Byzantine, simply restoring Easter as the main baptismal feast would go a long way. Christ as Bridegroom is the central figure of Holy Week and Easter. The first

[35] If in the Old Testament nuptial imagery the people of God are elevated to take the place of the divine consort in the *hieros gamos* of Canaan's pagan past, in the New Testament God in Christ descends to our level, enters into our world, to espouse his people. That is why the marriage is with Christ and not God the Father.

[36] Or "gives himself over" if one takes the verb form as middle voice, though the parallels in Mark 8:31 and 10:33 argue for the passive. Translation by author.

three days are celebrated with Bridegroom Matins, with frequent repetition of the service's main hymn—"Behold, the Bridegroom comes at midnight"—and its admonition to be ready. Then, the Easter midnight service celebrates Christ "who has come forth from the tomb like a bridegroom in procession" (Paschal Verses, Matins of Pascha). In the meantime, on Great Saturday, comes the ancient baptismal vigil with its lengthy Old Testament readings, the baptismal reading from Romans 6, and the processional from Galatians 3:27: "As many as have been baptized into Christ have put on Christ. Alleluia." Today this service is frequently understood as a celebration of Christ's Sabbath "rest" in the tomb. When baptisms are celebrated, the meaning changes. Through baptism we are "united to Christ in a death like his" (Rom 6:5), but we are also united to Christ the Bridegroom. The two images are merged together to show two aspects of the same reality. The tomb is where God in Christ fully embraces humanity and where humanity embraces God. The tomb is the nuptial chamber of Christ. In death, in the tomb, Christ enters into the full depths of human reality, embraces humanity fully in all its brokenness. Humans, giving themselves to Christ through baptism, entering into the depths of his reality, find that they embrace divinity in all its glory. They share Christ's life, but first they must share his death.

Jeffrey A. Truscott

Chapter 8

Luther's Pastoral Approach to Baptism

It is indeed an honor to contribute to a collection of essays celebrating the work of my doctoral father, Dr. Maxwell E. Johnson. I was privileged to be Johnson's first dissertationist at the University of Notre Dame, 1999–2000. I deeply appreciated his scholarly insights, ecumenism, humor, and no-nonsense approach to everything! His wide-ranging interests and voluminous scholarly output have set a high standard for students and colleagues alike. We especially owe him a debt of gratitude for challenging us to listen to history rather than blithely dismiss it. Yet Johnson has always maintained that we study history not to *copy* it but to be *instructed* by it. It is in this spirit of seeking instruction from history—being "pastored" by it—that I offer this article on the baptismal theology of Dr. Martin Luther (1483–1546), a topic treated in Johnson's magnum opus, *The Rites of Christian Initiation: Their Evolution and Interpretation*.[1]

My purpose is to describe the development of Luther's baptismal theology as expressed in several major treatises dating from the years 1519 to 1529. My thesis is that Luther's baptismal theology was essentially pastoral in nature—that is, focused on the meaning of baptism for the church and for the individual Christian. In that sense, we can say that Luther was a liturgical pastor who strove to guide and shape the people of God by means of and with reference to the sacrament of baptism.

The Holy and Blessed Sacrament of Baptism (1519)[2]

The second of three works on the sacraments from 1519, this "sermon" has a tripartite structure. In paragraphs 1–2, Luther defines baptism

[1] Revised and expanded edition (Collegeville, MN: Liturgical Press, 2007), 317–25.

[2] *Luther's Works* (LW), American edition, gen. ed. Helmut T. Lehman and Jaroslav Pelikan, vol. 35 (Philadelphia, PA: Fortress Press, 1960), 26.

and identifies its constituent parts, namely, the sign, its significance, and the faith in it. The sign, which distinguishes Christians from non-Christians, is the baptismal washing, which ought to be administered by immersion in order to portray aptly the meaning of the word baptism (*die Taufe*), which is to "dip" or plunge under water.

The significance of baptism (pars. 3–11) is understood by the reformer in terms of the Romans 6 imagery of death and resurrection, specifically, a dying to sin and a rising to new life. Although baptism is a single, once-for-all act, the dying to sin lasts throughout a person's life and is only completed at death. All of life, he says, is a spiritual baptism.[3] Likewise, the drawing out from the water effectively represents the growth in right living that occurs throughout a Christian's life and is completed at the final resurrection. For Luther, baptism has a strong eschatological flavor: the baptized person is already dead and raised, since God does not impute the guilt of sin to the one baptized. Yet, he or she is not sinless and must remain committed to subduing sinful tendencies.

Baptism is beneficial because it involves a covenant between the person who receives it and God. What this means is that a person "pledges" to resist sin and God "tests and trains [a person] with good works and sufferings in order to help [him or her] overcome sin."[4] Without this "testing and training" sin would ultimately come to rule the person's life. As long as the person undertakes an intentional struggle against sin, God does not reckon sin against him or her.[5] Although the language here seems to imply a bilateral *pactum* (covenant) theology whereby a person cooperates in salvation, Bryan Spinks argues against such an interpretation. According to Spinks, Luther equated *pactum* with *testamentum*, which refers to the saving benefits of Christ that are always a divine gift unilaterally given and never earned through one's efforts. "Thus for Luther 'covenant' is explained as God's promise in the sacraments which are signs of justification. The human response is to trust that the covenant is indeed unilateral—that it is God's work from start to finish."[6]

The final section of *The Holy and Blessed Sacrament of Baptism* (pars. 12–20) takes up the theme of faith. Here, Luther does not mean faith in

[3] Ibid., 35.

[4] Ibid., 33.

[5] Ibid., 33–34.

[6] Bryan D. Spinks, *Reformation and Modern Rituals and Theologies of Baptism: From Luther to Contemporary Practices* (Aldershot/Burlington, VT: Ashgate, 2006), 6–7.

general but rather faith that is directed toward God's baptismal promises. Specifically, the baptized person is to believe that baptism will effect what it signifies. Without this faith, the person will despair over sins.[7] Such faith gives rise to a humility that takes sin seriously and accordingly strives to subdue sin, rather than deal with sin through acts of satisfaction (e.g., pilgrimages, monastic vocation, etc.). Indeed, a lack of faith is a "hindrance" to baptism because only by believing can one take hold of the baptismal promise. Thus, the fruitfulness of baptism is entirely dependent on the faith of the recipient.[8]

Perhaps most significant about this work is the manner in which Luther relates baptism to the Christian life. Specifically, all stations of life and all vocations are the *loci* of the Christian's ongoing baptismal struggle against sin. That is to say, one lives out one's baptism by meeting the challenges of being a parent, son/daughter, laborer, government leader, or farmer. In something of a polemical swipe at medieval monasticism, he states that there is no special station of life meant for slaying sin and there is no higher vow than that of baptism.[9] Because of the rich meaning of baptism and its important spiritual implications, Luther laments that the church of his time neglected to place baptism at the center of the Christian pursuit of holiness, preferring instead to encourage Christians to justify themselves through personal works and efforts. Thus, we can see a deep pastoral concern in this first of Luther's major works on baptism.

The Babylonian Captivity of the Church (1520)[10]

One of three so-called Reformation treatises from 1520,[11] *The Babylonian Captivity of the Church* is Luther's attempt to deconstruct the medieval sacramental system. Although it discusses all the sacraments, roughly half of the work is devoted to the Lord's Supper and baptism. With respect to the latter, Luther again decries the church's neglect of baptism and the tendency of Christians to seek spiritual comfort in

[7] Luther, *The Holy and Blessed Sacrament of Baptism*, LW, vol. 35, 36.

[8] Ibid., 38.

[9] Ibid., 41.

[10] Martin Luther, *The Babylonian Captivity of the Church*, LW, vol. 36, 3–126.

[11] See *To the Christian Nobility of the German Nation Concerning the Reform of the Christian Estate* (1520), LW, vol. 44, 115–217; and *The Freedom of a Christian* (1520), LW, vol. 31, 327–77.

things other than baptism (e.g., vows, religious orders, etc.). The root of the problem is Jerome's teaching that, after the "shipwreck" of sin, penance constitutes the "second plank" that Christians can reach for in order to overcome the effects of sin.[12] This idea, Luther contends, leads people to overlook baptism.

As in *The Holy and Blessed Sacrament of Baptism*, Luther again identifies the constituent parts of baptism, but in *Babylonian Captivity* the first of these is the divine promise attached to baptism (cf. Mark 16:16), which is the basis for its being a sacrament of salvation. *Pace* Jerome, precisely because baptism involves God's promises, one can always "return" to baptism in repentance, by remembering and trusting in God's promise. Baptism is by no means useless, such that we have to turn to penance and other works. Accordingly, baptism can be a very comforting thing, since the divine promise is entirely trustworthy. Perhaps in something of an overstatement, Luther declares that it is not the sins themselves that condemn as much as a lack of faith in baptism.[13]

But neither baptism nor faith in it are "works" that humans perform in order to merit salvation. Indeed, faith is a divine gift (cf. Eph. 2:8), and it is really *God* who baptizes. Thus, we should avoid splitting baptism into an outward part performed by humans (the sacramental act) and the inward part performed by God (the saving grace). Both parts are ascribable to God, the human minister only acting as God's instrument. In an appeal to *lex orandi*, Luther states that the baptismal formula ("I baptize you in the name of the Father," etc.) points to the divine nature of the sacrament, since it shows that the actions are administered in God's name and by God's authority.[14] Indeed, regardless of how baptism is administered, it would still be a saving action if administered in God's name.

The second part of baptism is the "sign" or "sacrament," i.e., the baptismal act. Although baptism is an effective sign, Luther denies the extreme *ex opere operato* theology which holds that sacraments of the new covenant are of such surpassing value that they do not require faith. To the contrary, he argues, the sacraments of the new covenant do not differ from those of the old covenant in their effectiveness. The latter (e.g., circumcision, Noah's rainbow) involved the giving of

[12] Luther, *Babylonian Captivity*, LW, vol. 36, 58.

[13] Ibid., 60–61.

[14] Ibid., 63.

promises that required faith on the part of the recipients.[15] Both the sacraments of the new covenant and the sacramental signs of the old covenant are "signs or sacraments of justification, for they are sacraments of justifying faith and not of works."[16] Moreover, it is not the sacramental act itself that justifies (i.e., puts one into a right relationship with God), but *faith*. Thus, Luther again ties sacramental efficacy to faith.[17]

Finally, Luther discusses the significance of baptism, namely, the death and resurrection of the Christian. This reality he considers to be "full and complete justification."[18] As in the earlier treatise/sermon of 1519, the immersing (dipping, washing) of the candidate signifies the person's death, and the drawing out from the font signifies new life. This paschal reality is not merely allegorical but actual, and faith is what enables it to come about: "as soon as we begin to believe, we die to this world and live to God in the life to come so that faith is truly a death and resurrection."[19] This death and resurrection signified by baptism involves a constant struggle against sin (mortifying the flesh) that results in a "'real' and bodily passing out of this world unto the Father."[20] This struggle is completed only at one's death.

Once again exhibiting his pastoral concern, Luther concludes with an appeal for the Christian life to focus on fulfilling the meaning of baptism. In language reflecting the basic thesis of his treatise *The Freedom of a Christian* (1520),[21] the reformer states that the saving significance of baptism frees the Christian from all other works that purportedly justify. Christians should take hold of that freedom and not submit to any spiritual tyranny that forces various laws and ceremonies on them.[22]

In something of a coda, Luther turns to the question of whether infant baptism rules out the place of faith in baptism. To the contrary, God responds to the liturgical prayers of parents and sponsors who bring infants to baptism by regenerating these children and granting

[15] Luther distinguished these "signs" of the old covenant that were effective on account of faith from mere "legal symbols" in the Old Testament.

[16] Luther, *Babylonian Captivity*, LW, vol. 36, 65.

[17] Ibid., 66–67.

[18] Ibid., 67.

[19] Ibid., 68.

[20] Ibid., 69.

[21] "A Christian is a perfectly free lord of all, subject to none. A Christian is a perfectly dutiful servant of all, subject to all" (LW, vol. 34, 344).

[22] Luther, *Babylonian Captivity*, LW, vol. 36, 70–71.

them an "inpoured faith."[23] Concerning the latter phenomenon, Johnson comments that for Luther "The 'faith,' which receives and trusts the promise given in baptism, is worked by the same Holy Spirit, who is operative in and bound inseparably to that sacrament. In other words, baptism itself *is* the way in which God's salvific message of justification is proclaimed. Faith, which is worked by the Holy Spirit precisely *in* this sacrament, is nothing other than trust in what this sacrament declares to be true, that is, 'forgiveness of sins,' redemption 'from death and the devil,' and the granting of 'eternal salvation.'"[24]

The *Babylonian Captivity*'s baptismal section shows continuity and discontinuity with *The Holy and Blessed Sacrament of Baptism*. Luther still speaks of the significance of baptism in terms of a death and resurrection (Rom 6) and assumes baptismal immersion.[25] He continues to describe the sacrament as a reality that encompasses the whole of Christian life. Likewise, the ideas that baptism comforts the sin-oppressed soul and that faith receives the baptismal promise both remain. Nevertheless, gone is the language of a baptismal "covenant," and while the structural outline of the earlier work was (1) sign, (2) significance, and (3) faith, that of *Babylonian Captivity* is (1) promise/faith, (2) sign, and (3) significance. This shift of emphasis seems to be part of a greater concern to relate baptism to his doctrine of justification by faith alone, which involves a distinction between faith and works.[26] We have noted above the relationship between sacraments and justification as described in *Babylonian Captivity*.[27] Perhaps Luther avoided covenant language so that the justifying action of God in baptism was not undermined. Even with this intensified focus on justification, a pastoral focus remains, for the reformer still exhorts Christians to believe in God's baptismal promise.

[23] Ibid., 73.

[24] Johnson, *Rites of Christian Initiation*, 320. See Martin Luther, *Small Catechism*, in *The Book of Concord: The Confessions of the Evangelical Lutheran Church* (BC), ed. Robert Kolb and Timothy J. Wengert (Minneapolis, MN: Fortress Press, 2000), 359.

[25] Luther, *Babylonian Captivity*, LW, vol. 36, 64.

[26] Luther's most concise explanation of his doctrine of justification is found in the *Smalcald Articles* (1537), BC, 301.1–5.

[27] Luther, *Babylonian Captivity*, LW, vol. 36, 65.

The Order of Baptism (1523),[28] *The Order of Baptism Newly Revised* (1526)[29]

In 1523 Luther produced a German baptismal service based on the Latin *Magdeburg Agenda* (1492) and the *Agenda Communis* (1505–20).[30] In order not to give offense, he kept the customary pre-baptismal ceremonies of insufflation, signing with the cross, conferral of salt, exorcisms with the sign of the cross (though fewer in number), the Lord's Prayer, the *effeta* (opening of the ears) with the use of spittle, the threefold renunciation of Satan, profession of faith, and an anointing. Also retained were the washing rite (by immersion) with the trinitarian formula, the traditional post-baptismal anointing, and the conferrals of the baptismal garment and candle. Interestingly, between the salt ritual and the pre-baptismal exorcisms, Luther inserted the so-called Flood Prayer (*Sindflutgebet*), which may have been his own composition. Drawing on images from vigil readings and traditional font blessings, this prayer that beseeches the saving effects of baptism embodies Luther's doctrine of justification.[31]

In an epilogue to the 1523 *Order of Baptism*, Luther picks up and develops a theme previously sounded in the coda to the *Babylonian Captivity*'s baptismal section, namely, the faith-filled prayers of parents and sponsors in the baptismal liturgy. Luther states that he has translated the baptismal service precisely so that they can participate intelligently and with greater devotion. They should listen carefully and reverently to the prayers, and the presiding priest should read clearly. In line with his previous statement about the importance of liturgical prayer,[32] he reminds sponsors and parents that their role is to pray that God will help the child to persevere in the lifelong struggle against the devil. Luther suggests that many Christians have turned out poorly because the church's praying for infant baptismal candidates lacked earnestness and zeal![33] Yet with all this concern for earnest participation, neither the 1523 rite nor the later revision assumed the presence

[28] Martin Luther, *The Order of Baptism* (1523), LW, vol. 53, 95–103.

[29] Martin Luther, *The Order of Baptism Newly Revised* (1526), LW, vol. 53, 106–9.

[30] Spinks, *Reformation and Modern Rituals and Theologies of Baptism*, 10.

[31] Herman A. J. Wegman, *Christian Worship in East and West: A Study Guide to Liturgical History*, trans. Gordon W. Lathrop (New York: Pueblo, 1985), 308, quoted in Johnson, *Rites of Christian Initiation*, 323.

[32] Luther, *Babylonian Captivity*, LW, vol. 36, 73.

[33] Luther, *The Order of Baptism* (1523), LW, vol. 53, 102.

of a liturgical assembly—a testimony to the ongoing influence of *quamprimum* baptism.

The revised German baptismal rite of 1526 eliminated most of the secondary (catechumenal) rites (e.g., exorcism, anointing) but kept the traditional post-baptismal anointing formula in a slightly modified version to accompany the garment ceremony. The drastic excision of ceremonies should not be taken as proof that Luther was anticeremonial and averse to baptismal symbolism. Reflecting comments in *The Holy and Blessed Sacrament of Baptism* about the desirability of immersion, both the 1523 and 1526 rites direct the priest to "dip [the child] in the font" while saying the traditional baptismal formula.[34] Furthermore, it could be argued that Luther eliminated most of the secondary rites in the 1526 rite so that the washing itself could be more prominent. After all, for Luther the significance of baptism is tied to the action of being plunged into the water and drawn out again, acts signifying death and resurrection. Additionally, Luther might have desired to accent the washing ritual since its trinitarian formula evidenced the divine nature of the sacrament, which was the basis of its being a saving action to be received by faith. Honing the rite to its core ritual—the washing—as well as exhorting sincere participation by parents and sponsors suggests a strong pastoral focus.

Concerning Rebaptism (1528)[35]

During December 1527 to January 1528, Luther wrote a treatise on the topic of "rebaptism"[36] in response to a query from two pastors, who were apparently Roman Catholic priests. It represents a significant

[34] Ibid., 100; *The Order of Baptism Newly Revised* (1526), LW, vol. 53, 109.

[35] Martin Luther, *Concerning Rebaptism* (1528), LW, vol. 40, 225–62.

[36] After 1525, the influence of the Anabaptist movement was spreading throughout Germany and other countries. Adherents of the movement basically held that the baptism of infants was a sign of the church's compromise with the world and that only those who could confess the faith of the church for themselves and make a mature commitment to the church were appropriate candidates for baptism. In their view, baptism administered to infants was, in fact, no baptism at all, and they deemed it appropriate for themselves to be baptized a second time. Hence the designation "Anabaptists," whose prefix "ana" means "again"—although, of course, Anabaptists would not have considered it a "rebaptism," due to the illegitimacy of the previous sacramental action. See Eric W. Gritsch, *A History of Lutheranism* (Minneapolis, MN: Fortress Press, 2002), 44.

development in his thinking on the relationship between faith and baptism, serving as something of a prelude to his defense of infant baptism in the *Small Catechism*. *Concerning Rebaptism* is his attempt to answer the various arguments put forth by Anabaptists, of which he admits incomplete knowledge.[37]

To begin with, Luther rejects the argument that, since the corrupt Roman Church baptizes infants, that practice is to be rejected and believers should be (re)baptized as a sign of their break with Rome. Although the papacy may be guilty of various abuses, the reformer says, the rejection of traditional baptism is not an appropriate way to respond to ecclesiastical abuse, since it represents an attack on something that is good and true in the church. If we reject the baptism of infants, we might as well reject the Scriptures and the office of ministry.[38]

As to the Anabaptist argument that rebaptism is necessary because those baptized in infancy cannot be sure they were really baptized, Luther responds that social order would be completely overthrown if we rejected all knowledge given to us by others. If one's baptism as an infant were rejected because it involves secondhand knowledge, one could therefore refuse to recognize someone as a parent and thereby disobey the fourth commandment. Likewise, following the Anabaptist line of argumentation, one could flout the teachings of the church regarding salvation, since these too are based on events and realities not directly experienced firsthand.[39]

Probably the most significant section of *Rebaptism* is Luther's response to the Anabaptist teaching about the relationship between faith and baptism. Essentially, the Anabaptist argument, as Luther understands it, is that no one should be baptized until they believe.[40] But, the reformer counters, one can never be sure that one actually has faith, in which case, all "rebaptism" proceeds on uncertainty. If baptism is based on faith, a person could possibly have scruples about whether he or she truly believed at the time of their second baptism and consequently experience a need to be baptized again. Indeed, when baptism "requires" faith, the need for rebaptism is potentially endless. The biblical verse "He who believes and is baptized will be saved" (Mark 16:16), Luther argues, does not make faith a prerequisite for baptism

[37] Luther, *Concerning Rebaptism*, LW, vol. 40, 230.

[38] Ibid., 231.

[39] Ibid., 234–35.

[40] Ibid., 239.

but rather invites Christians to consider whether they truly are people of faith, as opposed to thinking that the mere reception of the sacrament is sufficient for authentic Christian identity.[41]

Contrary to Anabaptist assumptions about faith and children, Luther argues for the possibility of infant faith. The Scriptures would not speak of children as holy and innocent (Ps 72) if they did not have "spirit and faith." New Testament examples suggestive of infant faith include the infants murdered by Herod (insofar as they are "holy and blessed" in Luther's view), and St. John the Baptizer, who leapt in the womb at the sound of Mary's voice (Luke 1:41). Christ implied infant faith with his statement that the kingdom of God belongs to children (Matt 19:14). Christ, in fact, is present in baptism and so is able to call forth faith in children since he always speaks an effective word (cf. Isa 55:11). If Anabaptists can admit the possibility of Christ speaking a fruitful, faith-creating word through the minister of baptism, then they cannot defend rebaptism. Anabaptists therefore have the impossible task of trying to prove that children are without faith once they are baptized.[42]

Within this rather complicated and somewhat meandering section on infant faith, Luther rebuts various Anabaptist arguments against infant/child baptism and advances reasons why infants and children are suitable candidates for baptism. Contrary to Anabaptist interpretations, when Christ commanded followers to bring children to him (Matt 19:14), he was speaking not merely about the humble but about real children. Yes, the children who came to Christ were already circumcised, unlike "heathen" children and the children of Christian parents in Luther's own day. But both sexes were brought to Christ, which means that children were not brought to Christ on account of circumcision but rather so that they might be blessed by him and receive the kingdom of God through him. Indeed, child baptism is more certain because adults might come to baptism for wrong or deceptive reasons, whereas children do not deceive.[43] If God could accept children because of circumcision, then God will likewise accept children brought to baptism by Christian parents. Although there is no explicit command to bring children to baptism, neither is there an explicit command to bring adults. Rather, there is one command to "baptize

[41] Ibid., 241.
[42] Ibid., 246.
[43] Ibid., 244.

all nations," and children constitute part of this mass of people. Luther then opines that those households baptized by the apostles (cf. Acts 16:15; 18:8) undoubtedly contained children/infants. In general, he says, the Scriptures do not differentiate among people and thus envisioned the baptism of infants/children. The case is bolstered by the reference to "little children" in 1 John and by St. Augustine's contention that the baptism of infants was given to the church by the apostles.

The reformer then considers faith and its role in sacramental efficacy. Is it really sufficient to disqualify the first baptism on the basis that faith was (supposedly) not present?

> What does it matter if it is still a baptism? It was a correct baptism in itself, regardless of whether it was received rightly. For the words were spoken and everything that pertains to baptism was done as fully as when faith is present. If a thing is in itself correct you do not have to repeat it even though it was not correctly received. You correct what was wrong and do not have to do the entire thing over. Abuse does not change the nature of the substance, indeed it proves the substance. There can be no abuse unless the substance exists.[44]

In the (theoretical) case that there is no faith at the time of baptism, and faith appears ten years later, rebaptism is unnecessary since the person has done what baptism requires, "for faith doesn't exist for the sake of baptism, but baptism for the sake of faith."[45] If the person ultimately comes to faith, then the first baptism was sufficient. Regardless of whether a lack of faith occurs before or after the administration of baptism, there is no need for a repetition of the sacrament, since baptism does not proceed on human faith.[46] Even if Anabaptists could prove that children do not have faith, they would have only proved that true baptism had been improperly *received*, in which case they would have only proved the need for an abuse to be corrected. The Anabaptist position is based on a righteousness of works, because it means abandoning faith in the effective Word of God spoken in baptism and placing confidence in one's own decision to be rebaptized.

The basis of baptism in the biblical command and promise, Luther notes, also refutes the Anabaptist position that baptism *administered* by

[44] Ibid., 246.
[45] Ibid.
[46] Ibid., 248.

a person without faith is inefficacious. Like the Donatists, they base baptism on the holiness of the minister, although we can never be certain about any minister's faith. Yet there are numerous examples in Scripture where the Word was spoken through godless individuals, e.g., Balaam (Num 24:17). Indeed, Luther says, it is a blessing when that happens, since there is always the danger that people will come to rely more on the "holiness" of people rather than the holiness of the Word. If the Word of God can come through faithless and godless persons, how much more can the church baptize properly, since it is a greater thing to teach the Word of God than to baptize?[47] If baptism is dependent on the faith of the baptizer, we could never *receive* baptism from anyone, since it is impossible for any human to discern the faith of another! The certainty of baptism rests on God's (1) nature as a covenant-making God and (2) command to baptize, both of which are more certain than an individual's faith. When one bases baptism on "faith," one is basing it on something of one's own, which is a gift from God. Faith must be added to baptism, but it is still valid even without faith. If something is wrong or incorrect because it is of no value to a person, then nothing would be of value in this world. Analogously, although godless people see no value in God, that does not mean that God is not God![48]

In a concluding section, Luther advances several reasons why the baptism of "children" (infants) is good and right, which are summarized as follows:[49]

1. The baptism of children is of apostolic origins. If infant baptism were not right, then one is only guilty of administering a sacramental sign in vain; but if it is right and one did away with it, one would, in effect, be denying salvation to children.
2. If infant baptism were wrong, God would not have permitted it to continue so long nor be so universally established throughout the church. In that case, infant baptism is in the same category of things universally accepted in the church, e.g., the Bible, faith, and the Lord's Prayer.[50]

[47] Ibid., 251.
[48] Ibid., 253.
[49] Ibid., 254ff.
[50] Ibid., 255.

3. God has given spiritual gifts to those baptized as children, e.g., an understanding of Scripture. But God would not have given them to a church that was wholly disobedient. If infant baptism were wrong, there would not even be Christendom, because God would have withheld all things that make the church's existence possible (spirit, faith, etc.).[51]

4. If God's covenant is for the "heathen" and baptism is a sign of it, then children cannot be excluded from it. In an analogous way, circumcision made the children of Abraham to be people of God. Baptism, therefore, has to be even more efficacious.[52]

5. Rebaptism would not be necessary in the case of a person who sincerely believed him- or herself to be baptized but in reality was not, because "before God he has what he believes."[53] Rebaptizing in this case would have the unsalutary effect of leading the person to wonder whether faith was to no avail. If we would not rebaptize such a person, how much more would we *not* rebaptize someone who believes with certainty that he or she *is* baptized?[54] Rebaptism, in a sense, is a "gambling game," because it is based on a "faith" about which Anabaptists cannot be sure, which means committing the sin of "tempting God." It is much better to base baptism on the more certain commandment of God rather than faith, since the former is certain, sure, and immutable while the latter is changeable and uncertain.[55]

Concerning Rebaptism is a turning point for Luther in three ways. First, while his baptismal writings had previously been directed toward the Roman Church and its failure to ground Christian identity and spirituality in baptism, Luther must now address the "Enthusiasts" and their objections to the ancient and universal practice of infant baptism. Second, unlike all the previous works on baptism, this work is *not* written at his own initiative but in response to a specific query. In a sense, *Concerning Rebaptism* is pastoral care for pastors, a form of re-

[51] Ibid., 256. For Luther baptism is one of the distinguishing marks of the church that not only signifies its identity but also constitutes it as a holy people of God. See Luther, *On the Councils and the Church* (1539), LW, vol. 41, 151–52.

[52] Luther, *Concerning Rebaptism*, LW, vol. 40, 257–58.

[53] Ibid., 260.

[54] Ibid.

[55] Ibid., 261.

medial sacramental formation for ministers dealing with the challenge of the Anabaptist movement. Third, whereas extreme *ex opere operato* theologies within Roman Catholicism led Luther to emphasize God's *promise* and faith in that promise, the questioning of infant baptism's legitimacy by Anabaptists prompts Luther to emphasize God's *command*.[56]

Not all of the evidence that Luther marshals in support of infant baptism would seem convincing to modern readers. But Luther does not rely entirely on the baptism of households in the New Testament, "infant faith,"[57] analogies to circumcision, and the universality of infant baptism. Just as there is a ritual core for him—immersion in the triune name of God—so there is a theological core, namely, the command of God. For Luther, baptism is bound with God's saving mission in the world. Yes, the human response to that mission has its place. But faith, decision, and conversion cannot be exalted at the expense of God's redeeming initiative expressed in baptism, for baptism would then become a semi-Pelagian exercise that undermines the doctrine of justification. Luther's arguments against rebaptism and for infant baptism, with their emphasis on the divine command, must be judged a formidable response to Anabaptism as well as sound catechesis for his pastoral inquirers. The latter would rightly have been grateful for Luther's reply to their query.

Large Catechism (1529)[58]

This particular work was meant for the instruction of clergy with little or no training in the basic tenets of the Christian faith. It grew out of the catechetical preaching that Luther did during the second half of 1528 and was originally published in Wittenberg, Germany, in April of 1529.[59]

[56] Spinks, *Reformation and Modern Rituals and Theologies of Baptism*, 8.

[57] According to Johnson, Luther's notion of infant faith is not far from the modern Christian understanding that faith, being more than a rational assent to doctrine, involves a relationship with God that is nurtured in community (*Rites of Christian Initiation*, 318–19).

[58] Martin Luther, *Large Catechism*, BC, 377–480. In early 1529 Luther also published his *Small Catechism* (BC, 345–75), which contains what is essentially a summary of the baptismal teaching in the *Large Catechism*.

[59] Luther, *Large Catechism* ("Editor's Introduction to the Large Catechism"), BC, 377.

Luther begins the baptismal section of the *Large Catechism* with a discussion about the "nature and dignity" of baptism. Referring to Matthew 28:19 and Mark 16:16, he declares that baptism is of "divine origin" and that the divine command gives baptism its worth and value.[60] It is, in fact, God who baptizes. This then leads him to say that baptism is not mere water but "water placed in the setting of God's Word and commandment and made holy by them."[61] By way of support, he notes Augustine's famous dictum that a sacrament is a physical sign to which the divine Word is added (*Accedat verbum ad elementum et fit Sacramentum*).[62]

Next, Luther discusses the purpose of baptism, which is to *save* from sin, death, and the devil. Against the argument that external things are unnecessary since faith alone justifies, he argues that faith still needs something to "cling to."[63] In other words, baptism is necessarily an outward, perceptible thing so that humans can appropriate meaning from it. "[Baptism] must be perceived by the senses so that it can be brought to the heart."[64] Faith, however, will recognize that the outward act of baptism is not just a bath but a washing to which God's Word has been attached.

Luther's third point concerns the beneficiary of baptism, namely, whoever believes the baptismal promise ("He who believes and is baptized will be saved"). Without faith, baptism is useless. While some might ask whether baptism is a work and that believing in it per se undermines a righteousness of faith, Luther counters that baptism is not merely a human work but God's work and, as such, demands faith on the part of the recipient.[65] There is no salvific meaning to baptism unless there is faith.

Luther concludes this first section by rhapsodizing on how baptism is a great spiritual "treasure" and by urging Christians to remember it and take comfort from it in times of doubt and trial: "Now, here in baptism there is brought, free of charge, to every person's door just such a treasure and medicine that swallows up death and keeps all people alive. . . . Thus we must regard baptism and put it to use in such a way that we may draw strength and comfort from it when our

[60] Ibid., 457.
[61] Ibid., 458.14.
[62] Ibid., 458.18.
[63] Ibid., 460.29.
[64] Ibid., 460.30.
[65] Ibid., 460.35.

sins or conscience oppress us, and say 'But I am baptized! And if I have been baptized, I have the promise that I shall be saved and have eternal life, both in soul and body.' "[66]

A second section considers infant baptism,[67] beginning with the same arguments used in *Concerning Rebaptism*, namely, that the very existence of the church is proof that infant baptism is God-pleasing and that the validity of baptism rests not on faith but on the Word of God. Interestingly, the theme of the faithful intercession of the church for the baptismal candidate is taken up briefly: "We bring the child [to baptism] with the intent and hope that it may believe, and we pray God to grant it faith. But we do not baptize on this basis, but solely on the command of God. Why? Because we know that God does not lie. My neighbor and I—in short, all people—may deceive and mislead, but God's Word cannot deceive."[68] This statement contrasts with remarks in the 1523 *Baptismal Booklet* that attributed the poor spiritual and moral formation of some Christians to a lack of intercessory zeal by participants in the baptismal liturgy. Now in the *Large Catechism* Luther seems to correct himself by subordinating intercession to the dominical command, perhaps to downplay human efforts and to underscore God's saving activity, in line with his doctrine of justification.

The concluding paragraphs are more pastoral in tone, taking up the significance of baptism, with Luther again drawing on the Romans 6 imagery. The ritual action points to the killing of the old sinner (the "old Adam") and the raising up of a new person, which takes place throughout the Christian's life.[69] Interestingly, Luther is now more specific (and positive) about the meaning of baptismal death and resurrection: "Now when we enter Christ's kingdom, this corruption must daily decrease so that the longer we live the more gentle, patient, and meek we become, and the more we break away from greed, hatred, envy, and pride."[70] This transformation is not only signified by baptism but *empowered* by it when the sacrament is rightly received: "Where faith is present with its fruits, there baptism is not an empty symbol, but the effect accompanies it; but where faith is lacking, it

[66] Ibid., 462:44-45.

[67] Ibid., 462.49ff.

[68] Ibid., 463.56–464.57.

[69] Ibid., 465.65. For Luther, "old Adam" is a metaphor for the sinful human inclination, based on Paul's reference to Adam as the archetypical sinner (cf. Rom 5:18 and 1 Cor 15:22).

[70] Luther, *Large Catechism*, BC, 465.67.

remains a mere unfruitful sign."[71] Because baptism is an effective sign that brings about the slaying of the sinful self, there is no need (*pace* Jerome) to think of *penance* as the second plank of salvation; one can always return to *baptism* through repentance. Luther accordingly exhorts Christians to consider baptism as their "daily garment," in other words, to renew the struggle against sin every day, recognizing that the forgiveness of sin granted in baptism is good for all time.[72]

The section on baptism in the *Large Catechism* represents a compendium of the reformer's baptismal doctrine. If anything is new, it is the greater stress on the practical meaning of baptism in the lives of Christians. *The Holy and Blessed Sacrament of Baptism* has much to say about the significance of baptism, but there the reformer is mostly negative, stressing baptism as a "dying to sin."[73] This earlier work gives only passing mention to Christian holiness.[74] But in the *Large Catechism*, as noted above, Luther takes on a far more positive tone, speaking about a growth in virtues (patience, kindness, etc.). Additionally, the *Large Catechism* expresses a more realized eschatology of the baptismal garment: while *The Holy and Blessed Sacrament of Baptism* states that one may only put on the "true baptismal garment" at the final resurrection,[75] the *Large Catechism* exhorts one to wear the baptismal garment *daily*. Perhaps this shift reflects the pastoral purpose of the present work, namely, the theological formation of pastors and the consequent need to be more concrete and practical. In a sense, with the *Large Catechism*, Luther's teaching on baptism has come full circle in that he has returned to his notion of the ongoing significance of baptism, but with a renewed emphasis and creativity, as evidenced by his image of the "daily garment" (an allusion to one of the baptismal ceremonies).

Conclusion

Luther's baptismal writings exhibit both development and continuity. His interpretation of baptism comes to be more influenced by his all-important doctrine of justification by grace alone through faith

[71] Ibid., 465.73.
[72] Ibid., 466.84.
[73] Luther, *The Holy and Blessed Sacrament of Baptism*, LW, vol. 40, 31.
[74] Ibid., 41.
[75] Ibid., 31.

alone. This is apparent in the sparse use of covenant language after 1519 and the increased emphasis on the role of the divine Word and promise in baptism. An initial stress on the baptismal battle against sin eventually gives way to a more balanced discussion that speaks of a growth in holiness. Yet even within this steady development of thought, there is a consistent understanding that baptism is not just a *rite* but a *reality*—one that Luther always depicts in terms of the Romans 6 paschal imagery. The basing of baptism on the biblical command and promise, and the corollary of faith in this promise, is likewise seen in all of Luther's baptismal works. Because baptism is a response to the divine command and its spiritual gifts are to be received in faith, infant baptism is not only appropriate but even desirable.

But perhaps the most important of the constants in Luther's baptismal writings is his essentially pastoral approach. With the exception of the *Babylonian Captivity*, all of his major works on baptism are written in German, the language of his people.[76] Moreover, Luther is always aware that baptism is an act of the church and an integral part of Christian life. Hence, his baptismal theology is not so much for the academy as for the church and for each baptized person. The academy today is therefore reminded to reflect on baptism with an eye to the life and mission of the church so that baptism might remain tied to its essentially ecclesial moorings. If Luther's baptismal writings can inspire an ecclesial approach to baptismal scholarship, they will have served a good purpose and the reformer of Wittenberg will have proved himself a worthy shepherd of God's people, both in his own day and in ours.

[76] For this insight, I am indebted to my former colleague at Japan Lutheran Theological Seminary, Rev. Dr. Yoshikazu Tokuzen, DD.

David A. Pitt

Chapter 9

Lex Exorcismi, Lex Vivendi: The Minor Exorcisms of Adult Initiation and Baptismal Identity*

Maxwell Johnson has consistently and convincingly set forth the argument that the historical study of Christian liturgy is essential for the identity of Christianity itself. The goal of liturgical history, he argues, is "faithfulness, fidelity to the God who acts and works for human salvation through sacraments, people, and communities and to the sacramental worldview that continues to define and characterize classic Christianity."[1] That is, to discover God here and now, we must be willing to explore the ways in which God was celebrated and encountered in the past. Undertaking the study of liturgical history, by no means an easy task, demands moving beyond personal experience in order to grapple with the handed-on tradition, for it is "the evolution and interpretation of those rites themselves that are to shape, challenge, and critique our experience."[2] Studying liturgical history also demands that we move beyond what we, ourselves, have understood in order to grapple with the many and various ways in which Christians have interpreted God's offer of salvation.[3] In short, a historical methodology requires being open to new experiences *and* alternative ways of interpreting. Such a disposition is entirely consistent with Johnson's understanding of baptismal spirituality, which "calls

* I am most grateful for the comments and suggestions of Nancy Johnson, Frank Agnoli, and Bernadette Gasslein.

[1] "Can We Avoid Relativism in Worship? Liturgical Norms in the Light of Contemporary Scholarship," in *Worship: Rites, Feasts, and Reflections* (Portland, OR: Pastoral Press, 2004), 348.

[2] Maxwell E. Johnson, *The Rites of Christian Initiation: Their Evolution and Interpretation*, 2nd ed. (Collegeville, MN: Liturgical Press, 2007), xxi.

[3] See, for example, Maxwell E. Johnson, "The Study of the Rites of Christian Initiation Today," xiii–xxii, in E. C. Whitaker, *Documents of the Baptismal Liturgy* (DBL), rev. and exp. by Maxwell E. Johnson (Collegeville, MN: Liturgical Press, 2003).

us to a renewed sense of all Christian life as nothing other than a continual, day-after-day living out of our baptism. And that, of course, means a life of continual conversion and re-conversion, a life of death and resurrection, of continual claiming of that new birth and Spirit of our baptism."[4] While there are, clearly, many important points of distinction between them, in their own ways liturgical history and baptismal spirituality share the common demand that participants willingly embrace possibilities that exist beyond their own conceptions.

This essay is an attempt to approach the interrelated themes of liturgical history and baptismal spirituality by highlighting a dimension of conversion and reconversion within the Roman Catholic Rite of Christian Initiation of Adults (RCIA)—the very much underutilized minor exorcisms of the period of the catechumenate.[5] The historical process by which these prayers were located in the RCIA will shed light on their centrality to the entire process of initiation and thus their foundational relationship to baptismal spirituality, which itself is so vital within contemporary Christianity. As Johnson has proposed,

> The recovery of a baptismal spirituality as the center out of which the church lives and the center to which it constantly returns by the repeatable sacrament of initiation, the Eucharist, calls the churches, perhaps today more than ever, to a renewed stance against that sort of creeping Pelagianism which affects much of what today is generically called "spirituality" in especially an American context. God's gracious initiative, concretized and mediated as sheer *gift* in the font and in the assembly around the eucharistic table, should give the churches a firm basis from which to critique and shun so much of contemporary Gnosis and individualism that passes before our eyes constantly and influences so many in our churches. Indeed, a clear baptismal spirituality

[4] Johnson, *Rites of Christian Initiation*, 476.

[5] The argument that the minor exorcisms are rarely used within catechumenates in the United States is a difficult claim to demonstrate. It rests upon both an argument from silence as well as anecdotal evidence obtained through conversations with James Schellman, executive director of the North American Forum on the Catechumenate and various diocesan directors of worship whose diocesan policies explicitly mention the possibility of appointing lay catechists to celebrate them. The consensus opinion is that these minor exorcisms are celebrated rarely, if at all. This assessment is seemingly supported in United States Catholic Conference, *Journey to the Fullness of Life: A Report on the Implementation of the Rite of Christian Initiation of Adults in the United States* (Washington, DC: United States Catholic Conference, 2000), where the two mentions of exorcisms clearly referred to the scrutinies.

places the theological emphasis where it should be: on God, the great author and initiator of salvation.[6]

Through an examination of the history and theology pertaining to the minor exorcisms and their place within the period of the catechumenate, their contribution to the recovery of an anti-Pelagian baptismal spirituality will become clearer. The use of the minor exorcisms in pastoral catechumenal practice will better enable Christians to recognize God as "author and initiator of salvation" and thus can contribute to Christians returning to the center of their Christian vocation.

The Minor Exorcisms and the Reform of Adult Initiation

The group entrusted with the revision of the *Rituale*, *Coetus* 22 of the *Consilium ad Exsequendum Constituionem de Sacra Liturgia (Consilium)*, was comprised of ten members who were liturgical and patristic scholars, pastors, and missionaries: Balthasar Fischer (Relator); Xavier Seumois, PB (Secretary); Jacques Cellier (additional Relator for Adult Initiation); Louis Ligier, SJ (additional Secretary for Adult Initiation); Emil Lengeling; Frederick McManus; Boniface Luykx; Alois Stenzel, SJ; Joseph Lécuyer, CSSp; and Jean-Baptiste Molin, FMC.[7] Excepting Ligier, who began working with the *Coetus* in early 1965, they commenced revising the *Ordo Initiationis Christianae Adultorum* in September 1964. From their initial discussion of adult initiation through the end of their work they were convinced of the necessity of celebrating minor exorcisms within the rite, not only because of their overall approach based on liturgical catechesis, but also because of the significance of this element in the process of conversion.[8] Traces of

[6] Johnson, *Rites of Christian Initiation*, 463.

[7] A sketch of the work done by this group on adult initiation is found foremost in Annibale Bugnini, *The Reform of the Liturgy: 1948–1975*, trans. Matthew J. O'Connell (Collegeville, MN: Liturgical Press, 1990), 584–97. For a more complete treatment of this process, see David Pitt, *Revising the Rites of Adult Initiation: The Structural Reform of the* Ordo Initiationis Christianae Adultorum, *1964–1972* (PhD dissertation, University of Notre Dame, 2007).

[8] "*Coetus* XXII et XXIII: Rapport I," in *Centre Nationale de Pastorale Liturgique* Archives (CNPL), box 1, folder B, subfolder i: 24. See also Alois Stenzel, *Die Taufe: Eine genetische Erklärung der Taufliturgie* (Innsbruck: Verlag Felizian Rauch, 1957), 199–240. More recently, see Thomas Morris, "Period of the Catechumenate," in *The RCIA: Transforming the Church; A Resource for Pastoral Implementation*, 2nd ed. (New York/Mahwah, NJ: Paulist Press, 1997), 116–49.

their significance can still be detected within the structure of the current RCIA.

A brief word about the nature of the catechumenate, that period of "training them in the Christian life" (RCIA 75[9]), is essential to this discussion. The period of the catechumenate was always understood by the *Coetus* as being a time for conversion of life and spiritual growth, not for the teaching of rules and regulations. To this end, the first mention of dogmatic and moral formation within the catechumenate only appeared eighteen months after the *Coetus* began their work. Citing paragraph 14 of *Ad Gentes* in December, the *Coetus* rejected the possible perception that the catechumenate was to be equated with a classroom setting: "the catechumenate . . . is not a mere exposition of dogmatic truths and norms of morality, but a period of formation in the whole Christian life."[10] This understanding of the catechumenate is maintained in the current RCIA text, where a distinction is drawn between knowledge and practice and catechumens are to be given an "*appropriate acquiataince* with dogmas" so that they might be led to "a *profound sense* of the mystery of salvation in which they desire to participate" (RCIA 75.1, emphasis added).[11] Throughout the process of revision, the intended progression of the RCIA was that catechumens learn through participation, observation, gradual immersion in the community's method of prayer, and hearing the Word of God. Without denigrating intellectual formation, the *Coetus* argued consistently that the focus of the catechumenate was the spiritual development of the person. Yet despite the official insistence on the nature of the catechumenate, the inclusion of dogmatic and moral formation would fundamentally shape the way in which the revised rite would be received.

[9] All citations of "The Rite of Christian Initiation of Adults," approved for use in the dioceses of the United States of America, are taken from the International Commission on English in the Liturgy, *The Rites of the Catholic Church*, vol. 1 (Collegeville, MN: Liturgical Press, 1990).

[10] English translations of Vatican II documents in this essay are taken from Austin Flannery, ed., *Vatican Council II: The Conciliar and Post Conciliar Documents*, vol. 1, rev. ed. (Northport, NY: Costello Publishing Company, 1996). See *Schemata* (S) 147, *De Rituali* (DRi) 9, "Rituale Romanum, Titulus Primus, De Initiatione Christiana, Sectio I, De Initiatione Christiana Adultorum," "Adnexum I: Normae pastorals pro experimentis," 2.1.1. Official texts in the DRi series are located within the archives of the University of Notre Dame.

[11] See also RCIA 78; in this instance, the drafts of the rite make reference to *Ad Gentes* 14. This reference was omitted from the Latin *editio typica*.

Theological Foundations and the Nature of the Texts

The *Coetus* intended liturgical catechesis during the catechumenate to occur through the use of minor exorcisms. Understood as having direct pertinence to missionary work, particularly among cultures where a more vivid interaction with the realm of spirits existed, the *Coetus* thought that exorcisms would be important even in modern Western cultural contexts.[12] Here, they found Heinrich Schlier's *Principalities and Powers in the New Testament* to offer a most helpful perspective.[13] Since the apostolic church had believed unhesitatingly in demonic activity, Schlier insisted that it was incumbent upon the contemporary church to understand the relation of that belief to the present by discovering what those powers are and how they operate:

> Satan and his hordes, those manifold developments and effusions of the spirit of wickedness with their combination of intelligence and lust for power, exist by influencing the world and mankind in every sector and at all levels . . . making them instruments and bearers of their power. There is nothing on earth which is absolutely immune from their power. They can occupy the human body, the human spirit, what we call "nature," and even the forms, bearers, and situations of history. Even religions, including the Christian teaching, can become tools of their activity. Their spirit penetrates and overwhelms everything. . . . When the principalities penetrate the world and the circumstances of human life in order to exercise their power through them, they thereby conceal themselves in the world and in the everyday life of mankind. They withdraw from sight into the men, elements, and institutions through which they make their power felt.[14]

Schlier concluded that evil spirits were not simply antiquated notions of the past but entities still present and active in the world, even though named and understood differently. The *Coetus* sought to emphasize that those yet to be enlightened in baptism into Christ (not to

[12] See especially Xavier Seumois, *L'Adaptation dans le Culte III: L'Initiation Chrétienne*, C.I.P.A., 1957, no. 4 (Rome: Typografia Operaia Romana, 1957). See also Joseph Lécuyer, "Théologie de l'initiation chrétienne chez les Pères," *Le Maison-Dieu* 58 (1959): 11–12.

[13] Heinrich Schlier, *Mächte und Gewalten im Neuen Testament*, Quaestiones Disputatae 3 (Frieburg: Herder, 1958). English translation: *Principalities and Powers in the New Testament* (New York: Herder and Herder, 1961). See also Balthasar Fischer, "Baptismal Exorcism in the Catholic Baptismal Rites after Vatican II," *Studia Liturgica* 10, no. 1 (1974): 55.

[14] Schlier, *Principalities and Powers*, 28–29.

mention those already assured of victory through baptism) grappled with demonic opponents who were often "not even separate from ourselves."[15] Celebrating exorcisms within the process of adult initiation was vital for communicating this truth.

Recognizing the significance of exorcisms within the process of initiation within all cultures, the *Coetus* was faced with three significant issues. First, while the three exorcisms associated with the scrutinies were elements contained in the *Ordo baptismi adultorum* of both 1614 and 1962, other exorcisms during the period of the catechumenate could be considered to be innovations, which had been forbidden in *Sacrosanctum Concilium* "unless the good of the Church genuinely and certainly require[d] them" (SC 23). Appealing to the witness of *Apostolic Tradition* 20, the *Coetus* could point to a period in the past where exorcisms had occurred daily within the Roman tradition.[16] Nevertheless, it was pastoral necessity, not archaeologism, that was the defining principle for reform, and pastoral necessity strongly supported their inclusion. At a meeting of the subcommittee on baptism in November 1964, Fischer, Stenzel, Seumois, and Cellier unanimously affirmed the general principle that frequent celebration of the minor exorcisms during the period of the catechumenate would have the effect of forming the catechumen regarding the relationship between spiritual conflict, grace, and salvation. But perhaps even more substantially, celebrating minor exorcisms repeatedly (especially in the modern West) would reestablish a context for increasing the effect of the exorcisms at the scrutinies. Exorcisms were not foreign in antiquity. Early Christians—indeed, pre-Enlightenment Christians—possessed a worldview that embraced the engaged existence of supernatural beings besides God. This is not necessarily the case today. As Jeffrey

[15] Ibid., 60.

[16] See *Hippolyte de Rome, La Tradition apostolique*, trans. Bernard Botte, Sources Chrétiennes 11 (Paris: Éditions du Cerf, 1948), 20; and Gregory Dix, ed., *The Treatise on the Apostolic Tradition of St. Hippolytus of Rome, Bishop and Martyr*, vol. 1: *Historical Introduction, Textual Materials and Translation, with Apparatus Criticus and Some Critical Notes* (London: SPCK, 1937), xx, 3. Witnesses to the administration of exorcisms to catechumens include Cyril of Jerusalem's *Procatechesis* 9 (DBL, 28) and John the Deacon's *Letter to Senarius* 3 (DBL, 208–9). For a critique of this position, see Paul F. Bradshaw, *The Search for the Origins of Christian Worship: Sources and Methods for the Study of Early Liturgy*, 2nd ed. (Oxford/New York: Oxford University Press, 2002), 215–19. See also Paul F. Bradshaw, Maxwell E. Johnson, and L. Edward Phillips, *The Apostolic Tradition*, Hermeneia (Minneapolis, MN: Fortress Press, 2002), 108–11.

Burton Russell has chronicled, evil spirits are not easily accepted "in the materialist view that has dominated Western society for nearly three centuries."[17] Thus, the challenge faced by the *Coetus* was finding a way to foster a context in which the fundamentally important and traditionally Roman exorcisms of the scrutinies could speak more clearly. Through the incorporation of minor exorcisms into the period of the catechumenate, the major exorcisms of the rite could appear as natural and integral outgrowths of the catechetical process rather than as expressions of archaeological curiosity and formalism.[18]

A second issue, initially raised in November 1964, concerned the form of exorcisms. Some of the *Coetus* preferred the long-standing Roman practice of imperative prayers, where the minister expelled the demon. Others preferred the deprecatory form prevalent in the East, where the minister invoked God to act. Based on the research of Josef Jungmann pertaining to John Chrysostom's interpretation of the baptismal formula, the *Coetus* accepted the deprecatory form to be more ancient than the imperative form.[19] Schlier's work lent support to the latter approach: if the powers recognized as evil spirits in the New Testament were still active in the world but were named differently, then utilizing direct imperative address of evil spirits could have the appearance of being merely archaeological. Further, a deprecatory form would better enable precision in the content of the exorcism; principalities and powers manifest themselves in a variety of different ways, including not only demons, sin, and death but also pride, self-centeredness, and self-sufficiency.[20] The earliest decision, a compromise position, was to offer the clearly Roman imperative form alongside the original deprecatory forms for the exorcisms of the scrutinies and to reserve the deprecatory form for the minor exorcisms.[21]

[17] Jeffrey Burton Russell, *The Prince of Darkness: Radical Evil and the Power of Good in History* (Ithaca, NY: Cornell University Press, 1988), 274, 276.

[18] "Directives for Choice of Rite—Trier, Nov. 4, 1964," in CNPL 1.B.ii.

[19] "Protocollum junii 3–6, 1965," in CNPL 1.C.iii. Here, based on the prevailing belief that there was a common initiatory pattern that developed differently in varied locations, the *Coetus* argued that in some instances earlier versions of extant Roman texts could be available. See also Josef A. Jungmann, *The Place of Christ in Liturgical Prayer*, Classics in Liturgy, trans. A. Peeler (Collegeville, MN: Liturgical Press, 1989).

[20] See Fischer, "Baptismal Exorcism," 55.

[21] "Trier Protocollum," in CNPL 1.B.ii, 6. See also "Trier Protocollum Draft," in CNPL 1.B.ii, 6. The imperative form within the scrutinies would be suppressed based on the results of experimentation.

The third challenge, then, was in finding deprecatory texts that could effectively be used within the rite. Following upon the *Consilium*'s approval of the *Coetus*'s plans for the rite as a whole, Ligier was asked to assemble a broad range of examples from Eastern liturgical sources that might supplement the Roman texts. In response, he collected thirty-eight prayer texts from ancient and current sources. Among these were fifteen exorcism prayers arranged into three categories: five imperative, eight deprecatory, and two mixed (imperative and deprecatory). During the *Coetus*'s meeting on September 19–24, 1965, at Galloro, three minor exorcism prayer texts would be chosen and edited from Ligier's collection of deprecatory exorcism texts. Another would be chosen from Ligier's collection of pre-baptismal anointing formulae, and four others would be composed based on scriptural

RCIA	Incipit	Source
94a	God of power, who promised us the Holy Spirit . . .	East Syrian Rite: Before the Renunciation of Satan[22]
94b	Lord our God, you make known the true life . . .	*Testamentum Domini* II.7: Pre-baptismal Exorcism[23]
94c	God of power, you created us in your image . . .	Byzantine Rite: Third Exorcism for Making Catechumens[24]
94g	Lord Jesus Christ, loving Redeemer of all . . .	Coptic Rite: Before the Pre-baptismal Anointing[25]
94h	Lord Jesus Christ, sent by the Father . . .	Inspired by Isa 61:1-3, 18; Luke 4:16-30; Eph 2:2-12
94d	Lord Jesus Christ, when you climbed the mountain . . .	Inspired by Luke 6:20-26; Matt 5:1-16
94i	Lord Jesus Christ, after calming the storms . . .	Inspired by Matt 9:1-18; 8:23-24
94j	God of infinite wisdom, you chose the apostle Paul . . .	Inspired by Gal 1:15-16; Phil 3:8, 13

[22] See Henricus Denzinger, *Ritus Orientalium, Coptorum, Syrorum, et Armenorum*, vol. 1 (Würzburg: Stahel, 1863), 272: "Te invoco, Domine omnipotens . . . quae mundum a malo liberat."

[23] English translation in DBL, 116–17: "O Lord of Sabaoth, the God of Israel. . . . O Lord, you are our master. . . . Drive away from him every evil and unclean spirit . . . throughout all ages. Amen."

[24] Ibid., 75: "O Lord God, great and glorified by all creatures . . . unto eternity of eternities."

[25] Ibid., 136: "Master, our Saviour . . . to the will of your good Father and the Holy Spirit."

source texts, following SC 23. All eight utilized the deprecatory form, with four being addressed to God the Father and four to the Son. While the phrasing of the content of these texts would change, the eight original selections would become part of the final rite. The preceding chart presents the eight original minor exorcism formulae in the order they would appear until the final printer's galleys of the completed rite.[26]

Minor Exorcisms and the Shape of the Catechumenate

Throughout the process of revising the rite, the minor exorcisms would remain in place during the period of the catechumenate, but, as shown in the following chart, their priority would be obscured and eventually displaced through the addition of other elements. The earliest ritual content of the period of the catechumenate was exclusively the celebration of minor exorcisms within the context of a celebration of the Word and a ritual blessing. Catechumens would thus be formed in the Christian way of living and led to an experience of baptismal life by an initial participation in the liturgy. The *traditiones* of Creed, Lord's Prayer, and Bible were added to the core in November 1964, though all of these would quickly become optional. As single-occurrence events, these did not affect the foundational structure of the catechumenate. Far more significant for the shape of this period was the February 1965 allowance that celebrations of the Word might occur without the minor exorcisms and that these celebrations might themselves provide a sufficient basis for catechesis. Despite this allowance, the formal title of this stage—"The Second Station of Christian Initiation: Minor Exorcisms and *Traditiones*"[27]—seems to imply that the minor exorcisms were still intended to form the nucleus of the catechumenate. It is noteworthy that at this point in the *Coetus*'s work they allowed that the minor exorcisms could be separated from celebrations of the Word, occurring during catechetical sessions or even privately if necessary. As a consequence, by February 1965 the shape of the catechumenate was quite flexible: celebrations of the Word

[26] The three additional prayers found in the current rite, 94 e, f, and k, would be added in September 1969. Their provenance is undocumented.

[27] See, for example, S 77, DRi 2bis, "Relatio qua descributur futurus ritus baptismi adultorum," April 26, 1965, 23: "De statione secunda, nempe de exorcismis minoribus et de traditionibus." The use of the term "statione," implying spiritual progression, would only be employed from February to June 1965.

could (but need not) include exorcisms and/or dismissal blessings, and exorcisms could be celebrated in other contexts, as necessary.

Version/Sketch Element/Focus (RCIA reference)		1964: September	1964: November	1965: February	1965: June	1965: September	1965: October	1966: March	1969: June	1969: July	Current (USA)
Repeated	Dogmatic/Moral Formation (75, 78)							•	•	•	•
	Celebrations of the Word (81–89)			•	•	•	•	•	•	•	•
	Minor Exorcism (90–94)	•	•	•	•	•	•	•	•	•	•
	Blessing (95–97)				•	•	•	•	•	•	•
	Anointing (98–103)									○	○
Stand-alone	Giving of Salt [44]	○									
	Traditio: Gospels[28] (64)		•	○	○						
	Traditio: Creed (104–5, 157–62)		•	•	○	○	○	○	○	○	○
	Traditio: Lord's Prayer (104–5, 178–83)		•	•	○	○			○	○	○
	Redditio: Creed (193–96)									○	
	Ephphetha (104–5, 197–99)									○	○
	Pre-baptismal Anointing (33.7)								○		

• = Intended Element within the Catechumenate
○ = Optional Element within the Catechumenate

By the time that the *schema* of the rite was sent out for experimentation between 1966 and 1968, celebrations of the Word had emerged as primary settings for liturgical catechesis. Their priority would be retained throughout the rest of the revision process. The pastoral instructions sent with the experimental rite described catechetical formation as occurring, first, during these celebrations or through

[28] From November 1964 to February 1965, the Bible was to be presented. April 1965 allowed either the Bible or the gospels. By June 1965, gospels were preferred, in part because catechumens could include Jews, who did not need to be presented with the Hebrew Bible. RCIA 64 translates "Porrectio Evangeliorum" as "Presentation of a Bible," but the instructions indicate that the book should contain the gospels.

instruction and, second, through liturgical rites: minor exorcisms and blessings.[29] Despite different points of emphasis, this flexible ritual structure was maintained, unaltered, until June 1969.

The next addition to the structure of the catechumenate was the pre-baptismal anointing. In the course of reviewing the reports of experimentation, it was revealed that some experimenters found the different uses of oil in such close proximity to be potentially confusing: pre-baptismal anointing, post-baptismal anointing, and confirmation. Other experimenters argued that the multiplication of anointings disrupted the overall sense of the rite.[30] Some change was deemed pastorally necessary, and so, given the connection between the pre-baptismal anointing and exorcism found in *Apostolic Tradition* 21, the *Coetus* initially opted to move the pre-baptismal anointing to a point following the third scrutiny[31] and then later allowed its possible anticipation during the period of the catechumenate.[32] Seumois, who had overseen experimentation in five Rwandan parishes, lent experiential support to the latter decision. Arguing that the theme of strengthening did not make sense so close to the end of the journey toward baptism, he suggested that a catechumenal anointing could "give the strength necessary for conversion, spiritual combat, and perseverance to the catechumen when it was most needed."[33] But whether anticipated during the catechumenate, celebrated as a transitional rite, or occurring immediately before baptism, the pre-baptismal anointing was intended to occur only once. Only in the final *schema* prepared by the *Coetus* in September 1969 was it permitted that the pre-baptismal anointing could be celebrated multiple times. This decision, suggested by experimentation in both Rwanda and Togo, had the effect of expanding the final shape of the catechumenate as it increased the number of repeatable rites of the catechumenate. Accompanying the shift of this transitional rite to the catechumenate, allowance was also

[29] S 147, DRi 9, "Adnexum I: Normae pastorals ad usum illorum qui experimenta moderantur," March 18, 1966, 4.

[30] "Compte rendu de l'expérimentation du nouveau rituel baptismal des adultes," in CNPL 1.D.v, 4.

[31] S 147, DRi 9a, "Session du Coetus XXII (Vanves, France) sur les éxperiments du Rituel du Baptême des adultes," January, 4, 1969, 5.

[32] S 344, DRi 35, 144.

[33] Xavier Seumois, "Rapport sur les experimentations de l'Ordo Baptismi Adultorum faites dans de diocese de Butare (Rwanda)—janvier–mars, 1967," in CNPL 1.D.iii, 18.

given to celebrate three other transitional rites during the catechumenate: the *traditio* of the creed, the *traditio* of the Lord's Prayer, and the *ephphetha*. These decisions were made in light of the same pastoral concern that had motivated the anticipation of the single pre-baptismal anointing: the period between election and initiation was sufficiently dense, and particularly in mission territories, there were frequently too many catechumens for these transitional rites to be celebrated effectively.[34] With missionaries in mind, it was also in this final version that allowance was given to an officially deputed catechist to pray the minor exorcisms.[35] These were the last of the revisions made to the period of the catechumenate by the *Coetus*.

Implications Drawn from the Process of Revision

This brief historical survey reveals three factors affecting the place of the minor exorcisms within the period of the catechumenate. First, the necessary clarification that catechumenal formation was intended to move beyond dogmatic and moral instruction engendered a shifted understanding of the catechumenate. Given the history of revision, it is clear that the *Coetus* understood liturgy and catechesis, while distinctive, to be so integrally connected that doing one was doing the other. While the *Coetus* emphasized the liturgical elements as the vehicle for catechumenal catechesis, liturgical elements would be seen as catechetical supplements.[36] Consequently, the liturgical elements, including minor exorcisms, were and are exposed to the possibility of neglect in pastoral implementation of the rite. Second, the addition of other ritual elements obscured the significance of the minor exorcisms within the period of the catechumenate. During the process of revision the liturgical elements prescribed for the period of the catechumenate were expanded from a single repeatable element with a single standalone optional element to three or four repeatable elements and four

[34] S 352, DRi 36, "Relatio de christiana adultorum initiation quorum textus textus [*sic*] post experimenta recogniti et locupletati sunt," 32.

[35] The additional term, "qualified," was added between the production of the final *schema* and the printed proofs of the *editio typica*.

[36] See, for example, RCIA 75.1. The original verb in the draft *Praenotanda* of June 1969 (located in CNPL 2.D.i), *nutria*, which carries the implication of breast-feeding, raising a child, or looking after the sick, was replaced by *fulcio*, to support or to strengthen, in the next version (located in CNPL 2.E.i). Though similar, *nutria*, unlike *fulcio*, suggests a necessary reliance of catechesis upon rites.

stand-alone optional elements. Given the possibility of a minimized role for liturgy in catechumenal practice noted above, the expansion of the number of liturgical options further decreased the centrality of the minor exorcisms and their accompanying theology within the period. Third, the primacy of the minor exorcisms was given over to celebrations of the Word. Whereas these celebrations originally provided contexts for the celebration of the minor exorcisms, they now became discrete ritual celebrations, to which minor exorcisms could be added. Consequently, the past centrality of the minor exorcisms and their theological insistence on "the real nature of Christian life, the struggle between flesh and spirit, the importance of self-denial for reaching the blessedness of God's kingdom, and the unending need for God's help" (RCIA 90) has been displaced.

Nevertheless, an exorcistic framework for the catechumenate can still be detected because all the liturgical rites presently located within the catechumenate found their place within that period as a result of the minor exorcisms. First, stand-alone celebrations of the Word found their place within the catechumenate because they were separated from minor exorcisms. While the nature of the Word clearly extends well beyond the theological category of exorcism, traces of the foundational connection to minor exorcisms remain in the current rite, where the primary purpose of these celebrations is "to implant in [catechumens'] hearts the teachings they are receiving: for example, the morality characteristic of the New Testament, the forgiving of injuries and insults, *a sense of sin and repentance*, the duties Christians must carry out in the world" (RCIA 82, emphasis added). Second, blessings became independent rites of the catechumenate through the same process identified above and similarly reflect their separation from the minor exorcisms: "The blessings of the catechumens are a sign of God's love and of the Church's tender care. They are bestowed on the catechumens so that, even though they do not as yet have the grace of the sacraments, *they may still receive from the Church courage, joy, and peace as they proceed along the difficult journey they have begun*" (RCIA 95, emphasis added).[37] Third, anointings were located within the catechumenate through a different process, but one nevertheless reliant upon exorcisms. This relationship is clearly perceptible: "The anointing with

[37] Furthermore, exorcistic ideas can be clearly seen in at least four of the blessing prayer texts: RCIA 97d, e, f, and h.

oil symbolizes [*the catechumens'*] *need for God's help and strength so that, undeterred by the bonds of the past and overcoming the opposition of the devil*, they will forthrightly take the step of professing their faith and will hold fast to it unfalteringly throughout their lives" (RCIA 99, emphasis added). Finally, the optional anticipation of the *traditiones* of the Creed and Lord's Prayer as well as the *Ephphetha* during the period of the catechumenate derives clearly from the anticipation of the prebaptismal anointing during that period. Even so, the final petition of the Lord's Prayer is a petition for exorcism—"lead us not into temptation, but deliver us from evil"—and the *Ephphatha* is certainly related to exorcism, as the rite "impresses on the elect their need of grace in order that they may hear the word of God and profess it for their salvation" (RCIA 197). In sum, every rite celebrated within the period of the catechumenate is somehow derived from the intended centrality of the minor exorcisms therein; therefore, it is reasonable to insist that the theology of the rites pertaining to the catechumenate is, in some degree, inherently exorcistic.

Pastoral Applications

The catechumenate functions as "an extended period . . . aimed at training [catechumens] in the Christian life" (RCIA 75). Given this connection between catechumenal formation and baptismal living, a clear theological progression begins with the exorcistic proclamation of reliance upon God's power to save from evil in the catechumenate and leads to the recognition of our continued need for grace that extends beyond baptism into the Eucharist. Indeed, God's offer of salvation through Christ by the power of the Holy Spirit permeates the entirety of Christian life.[38] As such, the lack of attention paid to the liturgical prayers that express the theology of exorcism most clearly should be considered detrimental to fostering an understanding of the rite and to the reclaiming of a baptismal spirituality. Even where the catechumenate is treated as a process of formation rather than a period of education, these important prayers do not appear to be celebrated frequently within the United States at all.[39] Three principal obstacles may

[38] See Rita Ferrone, "Scrutiny, Exorcism, and the Construction of the Christian Self," *Catechumenate* 33, no. 1 (January 2011): 20–21, where she highlights the connection between exorcism, sacramental reconciliation, and baptism.

[39] James Schellman, telephone conversation with author, July 5, 2011.

account for this situation: understanding the nature of the minor exorcisms, the availability of ministers, and the lure of semi-Pelagianism. The intersection of liturgical history and baptismal spirituality suggest some pastoral responses to these issues.

Central to the first obstacle is perception—understanding what the minor exorcisms are and what they are not. Though the minor exorcisms of the catechumenate are connected to the better-known *Ritus exorcismi maiores* intended for the demonically possessed, they are different.[40] As Fischer argued, since this sort of rite "is performed over every baptismal candidate without distinction, this baptismal exorcism certainly cannot be interpreted as an expulsion of the devil. Rather, it springs from the fact that, according to the traditional theological understanding (itself based on the New Testament), to be baptized is to be snatched from Satan's power."[41] Unfortunately, confusion surrounding this distinction has affected the implementation and reception of the minor exorcisms even from the period of experimentation between 1966 and 1968. In response to the reports of experimentation, Cellier summarized that "the minor exorcisms were thoroughly appreciated wherever they were used. They filled a void; they permitted delineating the progression of the catechumens between their entry into the catechumenate and their election. However, it is necessary to note the embarrassment of many experimenters when faced with these rites; consequently they did not take advantage of them. Such a difficulty requires that we insist . . . on the nature and usage of these rites."[42] The places where they were used successfully were typically mission territories. Reliant upon missionary methods of evangelization, the African and Japanese experimenters were better able to move beyond "mere observance of the laws governing valid and lawful celebration" (SC 11) and demonstrated a willingness to interpretatively work with the rites in order to more effectively communicate the theology embedded within them. The Japanese use of the minor

[40] See, for example, Edward Foley, "Minor Exorcisms," in *Celebrating the Rites of Adult Initiation: Pastoral Reflections*, ed. Victoria M. Tufano (Chicago, IL: Liturgy Training Publications, 1992), 30–31. See also Daniel Van Slyke, "The Ancestry and Theology of the Rite of Major Exorcism (1999/2004)," *Antiphon* 10, no. 1 (2006): 95–100.

[41] Fischer, "Baptismal Exorcism," 48–49.

[42] "Compte Rendu de l'Expérimentation du Nouveau Rituel Baptismal des Adultes," in CNPL 1.D.v.

exorcisms was particularly successful and the experimenters seemed surprised at how well-received they were.[43] Alternatively, experimenters primarily serving multigenerational Catholics in European and North American centers were reluctant to move beyond both the rites and approaches that they had inherited. The minor exorcisms were not celebrated at all in Strasbourg, Belgium, or Canada, and the summary report for the five centers in the United States bluntly rejected them, arguing that "the exorcisms and scrutinies need to be simplified, revised, and even dropped."[44] Cellier's observation that the cause underlying their reception may have been "embarrassment" seems apt. The acceptance of supernatural involvement in a post-Enlightenment Western world seems to have been unpalatable. This issue, however, can be reframed considerably once a distinction between types of exorcisms is drawn and an enlarged understanding of the presence of demons and evil, consistent with Schlier's work, is employed.[45]

The second obstacle to the celebration of the minor exorcisms is one of authority—the availability of ministers to celebrate the minor exorcisms. RCIA 91 indicates that the proper minister for these rites is "a priest, a deacon, or a qualified catechist appointed by the bishop for this ministry." Two complementary solutions are possible here. Perhaps the most feasible is the one not requiring special episcopal deputation: priests and deacons celebrating these rites. Officially, the regular participation of clergy in the catechumenal process is normative. Priests have "the responsibility of attending to the pastoral and personal care of the catechumens. . . . With the help of deacons and catechists, they are to provide instruction for the catechumens; . . . they are to be diligent in the correct celebration and adaptation of the rites throughout

[43] See the reports from Michel Christiaens and Albert Corvaisier, both located in CNPL 1.D.v.

[44] "Report of the National Conference of Catholic Bishops, Bishops' Committee on the Liturgy, on the Experimental Rite of Christian Initiation of Adults: The Order of the Catechumenate Arranged in Stages," in CNPL 1.D.v.

[45] See, for example, Eileen D. Crowley, "Making More Visible Our Invisible Baptismal Promises," *Proceedings of the North American Academy of Liturgy* (2011): 92–109. On pages 96–97 she recounts an expansion of the renewal of baptismal promises where the evil works of Satan include war, selfishness, materialism, power, and injustice. See also Louis Cameli, *The Devil You Don't Know: Recognizing and Resisting Evil in Everyday Life* (Notre Dame, IN: Ave Maria Press, 2011); and W. Scott Poole, *Satan in America: The Devil We Know* (Lanham, MD: Rowman & Littlefield, 2009).

the entire course of Christian initiation" (RCIA 13). Here, priests are recognized as primary ministers in the initiation process as a whole, rather than simply ministers of the sacraments. This fact was clearly demonstrated in the period of experimentation. Seumois, for example, was forced to omit their celebration in the experimentation he oversaw. In a single year in Rwanda the five parishes served by him and twelve other priests served a catechumenate of nearly twenty-five thousand people, of whom 1,153 were baptized, confirmed, and communed using the experimental rite.[46] The pastoral inability to celebrate the minor exorcisms, despite their importance, led Seumois to wonder whether deputing catechists to celebrate the minor exorcisms might be possible. The fact that all the minor exorcisms were deprecatory rather than imperative was a factor in granting this permission, and his proposed solution, realized in RCIA 14, 16, and 91, certainly has merit beyond the sort of circumstances encountered by Seumois. The celebration of the minor exorcisms by catechists appointed by the bishop would contribute greatly to realizing the structure of the catechumenate intended by those responsible for revising the process of adult initiation.

The third obstacle to the celebration of the minor exorcisms is one of self-awareness—the lure of semi-Pelagianism. No doubt Cellier's naming of the "embarrassment" with the minor exorcisms among some experimenters, particularly those in Europe and North America, was due not only to discomfort with the realm of the spiritual but also a cultural discomfort with a theology of grace that stood in opposition to post-Enlightenment theories of self-sufficiency. Commenting more recently, Johnson has argued that "especially in an American context of individualism, with its focus on self-actualization, and an understanding of life based on a system of achievement and reward, even the grace-filled sacraments of Christian initiation can become interpreted in a rather Pelagian manner, that is, viewed as particular rewards to be received by individuals as a result of their so-called 'free choice,' their 'decision for Christ,' or their somehow 'earning' them through a program of required catechesis and preparation."[47] Johnson sees infant initiation as inherently instructive in combating semi-Pelagianism: "what could be more counter-cultural, more contrary to the prevailing

[46] Seumois, "Rapport."

[47] Johnson, *Rites of Christian Initiation*, 464.

tide of modern American culture, and still more anti-Pelagian and grace-filled than doing something so apparently foolish and silly as to celebrate God's salvific activity, God's choice, God's adoption of children into God's reign, as it is known and celebrated in the faith community through the initiation of infants?"[48] But that which is supplied in infant initiation by age—a context of helplessness—is paralleled in adult initiation by the minor exorcisms. How better to dispense with the notion of self-reliance in adults than by insisting on God's necessary activity in salvation? In every case of the minor exorcism prayer texts, the gathered community petitions God to act on behalf of catechumens who are presented as passive recipients. While Edward Foley's pastoral suggestion that "catechumens may be invited to mention any special difficulty or weakness that they would like exorcised from their lives" has the benefit of encouraging "them to speak and act, not simply be spoken to or acted on,"[49] the concern for combating semi-Pelagianism may well recommend encouraging the "passivity" desired in the rite.

In describing the exorcisms celebrated in fourth-century Jerusalem, Thomas Finn indicates that "their intended effect is gradual withdrawal from the power of their culture and their past—a therapeutic rite."[50] Might not individualism and self-sufficiency be demons in need of exorcism today? The *Coetus* certainly understood this to be the case in their treatment of the first scrutiny; the demon afflicting the Samaritan woman still afflicts humanity today. The devil had caused her to complacently accept her sinfulness. Ultimately, she did not recognize that she was in a state of sin until Christ expelled the demon and revealed her true condition to her.[51] In this sense, the first scrutiny, prepared for by the minor exorcisms, communicated the power of Christ to overcome the demon of ignorance and open the minds of the elect to perceive the truth of their human condition and their human need to be reoriented toward God.[52] Finn later recounts that the later renunciation of Satan in fourth-century Jerusalem marked a particular turning point for those about to be baptized: "Up to this time, the

[48] Ibid., 465.

[49] Foley, "Minor Exorcisms," 35–36.

[50] Thomas Finn, *From Death to Rebirth: Ritual and Conversion in Antiquity* (New York/Mahwah, NJ: Paulist Press, 1997), 197.

[51] See S 147, DRi 9a, Adnexum I, 20–21.

[52] See also Johnson, *Rites of Christian Initiation*, 194–96.

exorcists had acted on them as if they were passive recipients. Now they stand on their own two feet . . . and in their own voices break their ancient pact with Satan."[53] Having been broken of inherited patterns inconsistent with Christianity, the *photizomenoi* (i.e., those to be enlightened) were invited by Cyril to imitate "Christ naked on the cross, who in his darkness 'disarmed the principalities and powers' and on the wood of the cross publicly 'triumphed over them.'"[54] Is this not the same progression desired in Christian initiation and fostered through the use of the minor exorcisms?

As Johnson has argued, "If, on some levels of meaning . . . adult baptism [is] about making Pelagian choices . . . then there is no other recourse for the liturgical theologian but to the 'official' theological and doctrinal meanings themselves. Knowing and describing the various meanings even of rites which have 'survived' gets one little further than laying out the data. And, unless liturgical theologians are to be nothing other than chroniclers of history, or sociological and/or anthropological 'observers,' there must be some room for theological *prescription* as well. . . . [For] what appears to be at stake is the very identity and liturgical self-expression of classic orthodox Christianity itself."[55] The minor exorcisms have the potential to function effectively within the RCIA structure as theological prescription. The fundamental insight of the *Coetus* regarding these prayers is vital for fostering a baptismal identity that continually proclaims, through our conversion and reconversion, the victorious salvation authored and initiated by God, through Jesus Christ, in the power of the Holy Spirit.

[53] Finn, *From Death to Rebirth*, 202.

[54] *Mystagogical Catechesis* 2.2 in DBL, 32.

[55] Johnson, "Can We Avoid Relativism in Worship," 347, 348.

Lizette Larson-Miller

Chapter 10

"That You May Be a Christian":[1] Baptism, Identity, and Naming

Introduction

Tracing the history of baptismal theologies, liturgies, and texts has been an important part of the scholarly and pastoral contributions of Maxwell Johnson, but even more intriguing at times are the questions for contemporary liturgical theology and practice that Johnson invites us to draw from these trajectories of Christian tradition. Either in highlighting ritual consistencies through changed historical contexts, or tracing changes in practice that lead to altered interpretations, we are invited to see various elements of baptismal practice functioning as mirrors held up to our own contemporary baptismal practices. The study of the longer baptismal tradition challenges us to overcome the frequently perceived chasm between narrow academic obsessions and authentic pastoral practice with regard to a primary sacrament of ecumenical importance, while not presuming that our experience is the pinnacle of reflective brilliance on the shape of the liturgy.[2]

One element in Western baptismal practice that has shifted from late antiquity to the current day is the use of a personal name in baptism. Neither the interrogative creed combined with the water bath nor the early use of a declarative sentence as the form of trinitarian baptism incorporated the individual name of the one being baptized in any extant sources of the first centuries of Christian practice. Only gradually did naming the candidate come into the moment of baptism, first in

[1] "[Order] for the Making of a Christian," *The Missale Gothicum*, in E. C. Whitaker, *Documents of the Baptismal Liturgy* (DBL), rev. and exp. by Maxwell E. Johnson (Collegeville, MN: Liturgical Press, 2003), 259.

[2] See Maxwell E. Johnson, *The Rites of Christian Initiation: Their Evolution and Interpretation*, 2nd ed. (Collegeville, MN: Liturgical Press, 2007), xxi–xxii.

the *Missale Gothicum* from c. 700, and eventually into other Western rites. Through the various liturgical constructions of baptism emerging from the Protestant reformations, the centrality of naming the infant candidate in particular became more and more prominent, a "'naming ceremony' for the child ('christening'),"[3] in which baptism "was not, for much of the population, so much a religious rite as a naming ceremony . . . one that gave them their individual identity, carried in their forename."[4]

We can reconstruct many of the reasons why this shift came about, noting the changes in the order of Christian initiation, the candidates for initiation, theological priorities in baptism, and the role of baptism in the midst of multiple cultures. Those reconstructions are the fruit of historical research undertaken from the perspectives of various academic disciplines. But it is bringing contemporary questions to bear on this historical development, above all, concerns about current trends in baptismal practice, that suggests that revisiting the theological question of whose name is central in baptism might be timely. Is the focus of the naming that of the individual child or incorporation into the name of one's new identity in Jesus the Christ? Consistent with Johnson's concern that "especially in an American context of individualism, with its focus on self-actualization, and an understanding of life based on a system of achievement and reward, even the grace-filled sacraments of Christian initiation can become interpreted in a rather Pelagian manner, that is, viewed as particular rewards to be received by individuals,"[5] this Pelagian approach to sacramental engagement, when joined by the tendency to make infant baptism individualized, "special," and entertaining for those watching, results in a focus on the completion of an event and the infant as primarily "cute," rather than on a profound mystery into which not only the newly baptized but also the gathered Body of Christ are conformed and reconformed to Christ in a lifelong process. Within these overall concerns about infant baptism losing its primary foci, what might we learn from the developing history of the focus on requesting the name, stating the name, baptizing with the name, introducing the newly baptized by their name? What has been lost in sacramental participa-

[3] Ibid., 265.

[4] Will Coster, *Baptism and Spiritual Kinship in Early Modern England* (Aldershot: Ashgate, 2002), 167.

[5] Johnson, *The Rites of Christian Initiation*, 464.

tion in the name of our triune God by this focus on the name of the baptismal candidate, most often an infant?

By reviewing first the centrality of the trinitarian name, the designation "Christ/Christian," and theologies of naming and, second, by reviewing the history of this development in Western Christian baptismal rites, this essay suggests that limiting the individual name to the "threshold" rites of infant initiation may assist in recapturing a theological balance in many contemporary North American infant baptismal rites.

Baptized into "Your Holy Name"[6]

In his study, *Baptism and Change in the Early Middle Ages*, Peter Cramer returns to the New Testament focus on the power of the name of Jesus in the story of the apostle Peter's preaching at Pentecost in Acts 2:38. There, he says, "In Judaism, the name has profound significance based on the idea that it is inseparable from the person or object which bears it. Personal names have in them in varying degrees the authority, the power and the inner character or quality of the person."[7] But rather than continuing on a trajectory that many other authors have followed about the essence of a personal name in Judaism and thus in early Christianity, Cramer makes a christological turn with his assertion that "the act of naming has a precise transformative effect,"[8] so that "a person is baptized in the authority of Jesus Christ" in this passage from Acts, but in the writing of the apostle Paul, "by saying simply *eis Christon* . . . Paul makes the relationship with Christ direct and without mediation."[9] Whether focused on the anointing, the water bath, or on the whole baptismal process, this biblical and early church focus on baptismal naming was a way to speak of divine "manifestation or theophany" in initiation, in which the focus was on the reality that the person coming to baptism came "as if possessed" by *this* Name, *revealing* this name, not with an emphasis on one's own name.[10]

[6] *Missale Gothicum*, in DBL, 259.

[7] Peter Cramer, *Baptism and Change in the Early Middle Ages, c. 200–c.1150* (Cambridge: Cambridge University Press, 1993), 40.

[8] Ibid.

[9] Ibid. The reference is to Rom 6:3.

[10] Ibid., 42. Part of this is a sacramental assumption "that the recipient of a sacrament is radically altered—his or her very identity is changed—by the sacramental action" (Kimberly Hope Belcher, *Efficacious Engagement: Sacramental Participation in the Trinitarian Mystery* (Collegeville, MN: Liturgical Press, 2011), 68).

Acknowledging the difficulty of actually "naming" a trinitarian God-as-God, rather than how God-is-for-us, Gail Ramshaw writes, "A significant complication in the Christian naming of God arises because the word 'Father' functions in both categories: as language for God-for-us and also as language for God-as-God. . . . [S]ome are using the word 'Father' *subjectively*, as a metaphor of God-for-us, and others are using it *objectively*, as a historically pre-eminent theological term denoting God-as-God."[11] Recognizing this ongoing challenge of trinitarian language, however, does not change the theological primacy that the "name" in and of baptism is the name of Jesus the Christ. That primary naming, together with the source of Christ, and their Spirit, remains central because "Christians name God through and in reference to the mystery of Christ."[12] Nor does the application of modern psychoanalysis, with its focus on one's personal name and "the idea that naming is decisive in the constitution of the sacramental subject," make much sense with regard to infant baptism in Louis-Marie Chauvet's sense of changing self-perception.[13] Rather, the personal name of the baptizand used in many threshold initiation rites functions as the cultural identity bringing in tow the multiple societal belongings of every individual human, including their familial identity, to the new "Christ-name" that identifies the individual being initiated theologically and eternally at the font and in chrismation. Kimberly Hope Belcher describes this as part of the process of naming throughout the rites of initiation. Beginning with the rituals at the door in which the parents respond to the inquiry with the name of their child,

> the trajectory of naming in the rites becomes quite complex, with the celebrant "claiming" the child in the name of "the Christian community"; the assembly invoking the names of the saints; . . . the celebrant anointing the child "in the name of Christ our Savior"; and the assembly praying the Lord's Prayer "in the name of this child." The central

[11] Gail Ramshaw, "In the Name: Towards Alternative Baptismal Idioms," *Ecumenical Review* 54, no. 3 (2002): 347.

[12] Ibid., 349 (keeping in mind Ramshaw's careful caveat that "there was never a time that the "father" existed prior to the "son" [347]).

[13] Louis-Marie Chauvet, *Symbol and Sacrament*, trans. Patrick Madigan and Madeleine Beaumont (Collegeville, MN: Liturgical Press, 1995), 439. Nor does the personal forename actually factor that heavily in the initiation of adults in that very few adult catechumens in the United States change their name at baptism. The *new* identity is that of Christ, along with the changed self-perception related to that name.

"naming," of course, is that of the trinitarian formula: "N., I baptize you in the name of the Father, and of the Son, and of the Holy Spirit." These naming incidents alter the child's name from an identity marker exclusively associated with his or her family status . . . to one that identifies him or her with the Trinitarian love.[14]

This "central naming" with and of the Trinity in the actual baptism is the true "christening," the bestowal of the Christian identity by the putting on of Christ, here by means of efficacious linguistics, but understood to be embodied—water blessed with words, body transformed—marked as Christ's own forever and drawn into participation in the life of the Trinity, body, soul, and mind.

"Name This Child":[15] The Use of Personal Names in the History of Baptism

The historical development of the ritual use of an individual's own name in the Western baptismal rites is uncovered partially in shifts in liturgical structure, partially in the changing character of those presenting themselves for baptism (primarily a move from adults to infants for both theological and cultural reasons), and partially in the cultural role that baptism played in various societies. A fine overview of the question and the history has been presented by J. D. C. Fisher, in his classic book *Christian Initiation: Baptism in the Medieval West*,[16] on which this summary is partially based.

Beginning with the extant hybrid Roman-Gallican *Gelasian Sacramentary* of the eighth century (with scholarly agreement that the liturgical patterns are those of the early sixth century),[17] Fisher traces the Western initiation liturgies in which the names of those to be baptized were called out and/or written down during the scrutinies or other

[14] Belcher, *Efficacious Engagement*, 143. Belcher's references are to the Roman Catholic Rite of the Baptism for Children (RBC). While this section of Belcher's interesting work seems perfectly consistent with the historical and theological trajectory, there is an odd reversal several pages later when she says "the name of the child becomes the name of God, the Trinity." It would seem more appropriate to reverse that claim: "the name of God, the Trinity becomes the name of the child."

[15] This is the rubric instructing the priest to declare the name immediately before baptism in the 1662 *Book of Common Prayer*.

[16] J. D. C. Fisher, *Christian Initiation: Baptism in the Medieval West* (London: SPCK, 1965), appendix 2.

[17] See DBL, 212.

pre-baptismal rites in an initiation pattern that reflected a temporal process marked by a series of rituals. For the Roman tradition, starting with the commentary of John the Deacon (early sixth century), through the *Gelasian Sacramentary, Ordo Romanus XI, Ordo Romanus L,* and continuing through the twelfth-century *Roman Pontifical,* it is apparent that the actual baptism does not use the name of the individual to be baptized, even with the move from the interrogative form to the declarative formula.[18] So the pattern of the *Gelasian Sacramentary* water bath combining the interrogative creed and the water bath was:

> *Then when the font is blessed you baptize each one in order, and ask these questions:*
>
> Do you believe in God the Father Almighty? R. I believe
>
> And do you believe in Jesus Christ his only Son our Lord, who was born and suffered? R. I believe.
>
> And do you believe in the Holy Spirit: the holy Church; the remission of sins; the resurrection of the flesh? R. I believe.
>
> *Then by single turns you dip him three times in the water.*[19]

On the other hand, the *Roman Pontifical,* using the declarative trinitarian formula (based on Matt 28:18), requests the name of each candidate before the renunciation of Satan and again before the confession of faith, but not in conjunction with the baptismal formula.

> What are you called? John
>
> *And then says the officiant:*
>
> John, do you believe in God the Father almighty . . .?
>
> Do you wish to be baptized? R. I wish it.[20]
>
> I baptize you in the name of the Father, and of the Son, and of the Holy Spirit.[21]

[18] Fisher and others suggest that this shift to the declarative formula happened by the time of Pope Zachariah I (c. 744), because there is extant a letter dealing with "the question whether a presbyter who incorrectly pronounced the Latin formula had administered a valid baptism." Letter 7, *ad Bonifacium,* in Fisher, *Christian Initiation,* 17.

[19] *The Gelasian Sacramentary, XLIV,* in DBL, 235.

[20] See Fisher, *Christian Initiation,* 154.

[21] The Roman conservatism in maintaining the baptismal formula with the focus on the name of the Trinity continues through the 1487 *Rituale Romanum,* where the name of the candidate is requested a number of times at the church door and in the

In the ritual books mixing Roman and non-Roman liturgical practices, especially in those where the Roman influence was not primary, the use of the personal name is more varied. Hence, in the several liturgical books falling under the title "Gallican," we see in the *Missale Gothicum* (c. 700):

> *While you baptize him you question him and say:*
> I baptize you, *N.*, in the Name of the Father and of the Son and of the Holy Spirit, unto the remission of sins, that you may have eternal life. Amen.[22]

But in the *Gallicanum Vetus* and the *Bobbio Missal*, the name of the infant is mentioned at several points immediately prior to the baptism but is not folded into the trinitarian baptismal formula.[23]

The extant sources for the medieval Spanish baptismal liturgies are late (the *Liber Ordinum* is primarily known through an eleventh-century manuscript), and they contain an interesting instruction for the priest to give the name:

> *Sign him upon the forehead and give him his name in this exorcism:*
> *he asks his name and says to him as follows:*
> *N.*, receive the sign of the cross . . .

After coming near to the font, and after the exorcisms and blessing of the font, the renunciation, confession, and baptism take place:

> *N.*, you servant of God, do you renounce the devil and his angels. *The ministers reply:* I renounce . . .
> What is your name? R. *N.*
> *N.*, do you believe in God the Father Almighty? R. I believe . . .
> Then I baptize you in the Name of the Father and of the Son and of the Holy Spirit, that you may have life eternal.[24]

We know less of the details of the medieval Anglo-Saxon and Irish practices. The *Stowe Missal* of Irish provenance (c. 800) instructs the priest to question the baptismal candidate "through the deacon, whether he believes in the Father, the Son and the Holy Spirit":

---

pre-baptismal rituals, but not in the baptismal formula ("nor at any later point"). Fisher, *Christian Initiation*, 155.

[22] *Missale Gothicum*, in DBL, 261.

[23] Fisher, *Christian Initiation*, 151.

[24] See DBL, 166–70, especially n. 4 on p. 170, noting the alternative formulae.

Do you believe in God the Father Almighty?

Let him reply, I believe . . .

He goes down into the font and is dipped or sprinkled three times: after he has been baptized, let him be anointed with chrism on his head, on his forehead . . .[25]

The various Anglo-Saxon resources date primarily from the tenth and eleventh centuries and reveal the growing importance of the role of godparents in naming and speaking for the infant baptismal candidates. The *Red Book of Darley* includes the request for the child's name by the priest, "then the godfather says the child's name," followed by the renunciation, confession, and baptism proper.[26]

It is only with the various Reformation baptismal rites that the appearance of the individual candidate's name within the baptismal formula becomes normative, especially in the English rites.[27] This latter trend may be based in part on the *Sarum Usage*,[28] which used the proper name in the baptismal formula. Similar to a number of rites already reviewed above, *The Rite of Baptism in the Sarum Manual* asks for the name of the child several times in the pre-baptismal rites and again at the font immediately prior to the renunciation.

Let the priest place his right hand over him: and his name being asked, let those who hold him reply, N. So let the priest say:

N., dost thou renounce Satan?

Let the godfathers and godmothers reply: I renounce . . .

The pre-baptismal anointing follows (done with the name) and then the priest asks the name again before using it in the interrogative confession of faith. After asking what the candidate desires, the priest baptizes the infant, asking the name a third time in sequence.

[25] DBL, 281–82.

[26] Bryan D. Spinks, *Early and Medieval Rituals and Theologies of Baptism: From the New Testament to the Council of Trent* (Aldershot: Ashgate, 2006), 127ff. Spinks cites the primary article on the *Red Book of Darley*: Christopher Hohler, "The Red Book of Darley," *Nordiskt Kollokvium II.I. Latinsk Liturgiforskning*, Stockholm University (1972): 39–47.

[27] Although many continental Protestant rites inherit the same joining of the use of the individual name and the name of the Trinity. See Johnson, *The Rites of Christian Initiation*, especially 315–62.

[28] See appendix 3 in Fisher, *Christian Initiation*, 158–79. Fisher uses the sixteenth-century edition printed in Rouen, "the last edition to be published before the introduction of the first English Prayer Book in 1549" (158).

> N., I also baptize thee in the name of the Father (*and let him dip him once with his face turned towards the north and his head towards the east*) and of the Son (*and again let him dip him once with his face turned towards the south*) and of the Holy Ghost. Amen (*and let him dip him the third time with his face towards the water*).[29]

The *Sarum Usage* clearly had an impact on the English baptismal rites of the sixteenth century (and beyond), but those rites were also influenced by the *Consultation* of Hermann, archbishop of Cologne, "a work used by Cranmer in compiling the Prayer Book of 1549."[30] In this baptismal rite, the child's name is used in the pre-baptismal rites on the evening before baptism, and then again "just before the actual baptism the pastor is bidden to ask the names 'that they shall have,' the future tense suggesting that they have not yet formally been given; and when he baptizes each child, he says, *'I baptize thee, N., in the name of the Father,'* etc. Here there seems to be a deliberate intention to combine the giving of the name with the act of baptism."[31] The 1549 Prayer Book also used the future tense for requesting the child's name: "Here shall the priest aske what shall be the name of the childe," and that name is used for the rites at the door and then at the renunciation, confession, and baptism at the font. The rubric immediately before baptism instructs the priest to "take the childe in his handes, and aske the name. And naming the childe, shall dyppe it in the water thrice."[32] With the 1552 Prayer Book, the rites at the door were abolished, the consignation and prayer moved to after the actual baptism, which meant that "the child is now called by his name for the first and only time in this rite at the moment of baptism."[33] By the time the baptismal rite is reconstituted in the 1662 Prayer Book, the "accidental" alignment of naming and baptism in the 1552 book has become intentional, "because, right before baptizing, the priest says to the godfathers and godmothers, *'Name this child'*, and then naming it after them . . . he shall dip it in the water discreetly and warily, saying, *N., I baptize thee in the name . . .*"[34] Here is the apex of Fisher's trajectory in linking

[29] Fisher, *Christian Initiation*, 172–74.

[30] Ibid., appendix 2, 155. The work attributed to the archbishop of Cologne was most likely authored by Martin Bucer and sponsored by Hermann von Wied. See Johnson, *The Rites of Christian Initiation*, 340.

[31] Fisher, *Christian Initiation*, 155.

[32] Ibid., 156.

[33] Ibid.

[34] Ibid., 157.

baptism and naming: "it is the command to the godparents in the Book of 1662, *'Name this child'*—a command which is not found in the earlier books—which has done most to encourage among the ignorant the notion that baptism is primarily a naming ceremony, and that 'to christen' means, chiefly if not entirely, 'to name.'"[35]

Why did this linking of baptism and naming come about? Fisher, as well as other scholars,[36] point to the succession of rituals marking the process of Christian initiation that are telescoped into a single rite. Thus, the pre-baptismal rites associated with the individual name of the candidate become juxtaposed to the actual baptism so that what were once rituals separated by weeks and then days became rituals separated by minutes. And this initiatory process, now a single event, was perceived by seventeenth-century Anglican Christians (as well as others) as normative, having been the tradition of more than one hundred years. It made sense, then, to many participants, that the first public naming of an infant followed immediately by baptism meant that naming was a primary "effect" of the sacrament itself.

But this loss of the fullness of the initiatory sequence was itself a result of another change, and that had to do with *who* was being initiated. While there is evidence that infants were initiated in the early church,[37] the interrogative creed combined with baptism ritually supported the theology that personal profession of faith was integral to baptismal practice; that the "normative" candidate was, therefore, above the age of reason; and that the normative baptism was fundamentally a profound expression of the experience of conversion. The oddity of the adult form of baptism enduring long "after the habit of infant baptism had become widespread in the churches of Latin Christendom" is a puzzle that many historians have played with, including Peter Cramer, who continues this line of thought by writing, "Infant

[35] Ibid. Spinks points out that "in Old English *cristnen* meant to be made a catechumen, but as the rites themselves coalesced into one, the term *cristnen* came to mean naming in baptism" (*Early and Medieval Rituals and Theologies of Baptism*, 129).

[36] Bryan Spinks, Maxwell Johnson, and Mark Searle would be among these "other scholars."

[37] Tertullian describes infant baptism with some reservations c. 200 in *De Baptismo* 18. See also *Apostolic Tradition* 21 (Ethiopic translation): "And first the little children are to be baptized; and if he is able to speak for himself, he is to speak; and if they are not able, their parents are to speak on their behalf or one of their relatives." See Paul F. Bradshaw, Maxwell E. Johnson, and L. Edward Phillips, eds., *The Apostolic Tradition* (Minneapolis, MN: Fortress Press, 2002), 112.

baptism puts the dramatic stress of the old rite of conversion in a quite different place, and would have drawn under the umbrella of the little-changed forms the manifold associations carried by the child. Indeed, the child, and the small body of the child with its vulnerable nakedness and its suggestions of uncertainties and precariousness, perhaps replaced water as the central symbol of baptism."[38]

This shift in the subject of baptism, which occurred long before the liturgy officially adapted itself to the change of subject, raises, in turn, another question: why were adults no longer being baptized? Why were the majority of baptismal candidates infants? This question has multiple answers and is messier than the liturgical processes described above. At the heart of the answer are two responses. First, simple mathematics of ecclesial development; as more Christians were initiated within their Christian families and households, there were fewer adults to be baptized. Second, theology, particularly the trajectory of the necessity of baptism that finds inspiration in the teachings of Augustine of Hippo and gains traction in particular inculturations of Christian baptism in the medieval West. The resulting *quamprimum*[39] baptismal practice was not embraced in all places with equal conviction or timing, but it gradually became an essential popular concern, and in many locations, an official ecclesial mandate.[40]

Peter Cramer actually sees the two trajectories as more closely cause and effect than others do, drawing on Augustine's developing thinking about original sin and the integration of the oppositions of "active coming-to-truth and the passive reception" of baptismal dynamics.[41] The earlier Augustinian sense that good is active being allowed for the potential of will to triumph over sin. "For since the good is the perfection of form, and being is dependent on form, sin, which is a movement away from the good and therefore from form, is a departure from being. Evil, towards which sin moves, is not-being: it has no existence outside the acts or tendencies which cause it."[42] Later, Augustine, countering Pelagianism in particular, read from Scripture that sin was

[38] Cramer, *Baptism and Change in the Early Middle Ages*, 3.

[39] Generally translated "as soon as possible."

[40] For example, the seventh-century law imposed by Ine, king of Wessex, by which parents were fined for having unbaptized children older than thirty days. See Fisher, *Christian Initiation*, 82.

[41] Cramer, *Baptism and Change in the Early Middle Ages*, 40.

[42] Ibid., 116–17.

built into the DNA of human beings because of the sinful sexual act by which all were put into the world"[43] and that this inherited tendency meant the "movement towards not-being" was one in which humanity "is necessarily caught up" by their "very existence."[44] Thus far these theological reflections of Augustine do not, of necessity, affect baptism, but the turn to "the necessity of sin" and therefore to the inescapable passivity of the human person between the absolutes of good and evil meant that, once baptized, all evil actions by parents or self could not undo the divine effect, and vice versa; without baptism, no good could take root: "Whatever is born of this concupiscence of the flesh is as born to the world not to God. It is born to God, however, when it is reborn from water and the Holy Spirit. The guilt of this concupiscence, incurred by generation, is dismissed only by regeneration."[45] The only simple and logical deduction from this is that to die without baptism was to be damned and that baptism was something done to a passive candidate, an "exact and negative function of removing the adverse judgment incurred by 'birth in Adam.'"[46] But in spite of this literal linking, the Middle Ages were conflicted, or at least ambiguous, about the rite of baptism when applied to infants. Was it solely about the individual or was it a corporate act of the whole community? Was it a "once-for-all triumph of good over evil" or "an intense enactment of the continuously repeated ethical journey"?[47] The double theological strands of dying and rising (drawing on Romans) and rebirth modeled in part on the imitation of Jesus' own baptism, together with the tension between *quamprimum* baptism and annual paschal baptisms, meant that the opposing regulations and assumptions continued in parallel.

The additional cultural and ritual factor that tipped the balance of baptismal practice was the option for "emergency baptism." The establishing of this ritual option is generally traced to the "Gallican" elements added to the Roman *Gelasian Sacramentary* "that included a separate order for the initiation of a 'sick catechumen.'"[48] This abbre-

[43] Ibid., 121.

[44] Ibid.

[45] Augustine, *De nupt et concup* 1.19, pp. 233–34, cited in Cramer, *Baptism and Change in the Early Middle Ages*, 123.

[46] Ibid., 113.

[47] Ibid., 116.

[48] Johnson, *The Rite of Christian Initiation*, 230. He cites the "Brief Form for a Sick Catechumen" from DBL, 240–43.

viated rite, which streamlined and compressed the order of initiation rites, was applied to infant baptism at a time when the general consensus was that "infancy was itself so precarious a condition that to be newborn was ipso facto to be in a life-threatening situation."[49] Both the high infant mortality rate and the theologically inspired sense of urgency combined to encourage *quamprimum* baptism. Mark Searle points out the interesting situation of the officially sanctioned eighth-century *Hadrianum* rite of infant initiation with its order of rituals for the making of catechumens and then baptism giving way to the more commonly used baptismal rite for the dying mentioned above. "So common did its use become in the Middle Ages that it eventually came to serve as the basis for the rite of infant baptism in the Roman Ritual of 1614,"[50] elevating "clinical baptism" to an official status for the first time.

These threads of culture, theology, ritual practice, and ecclesial mandate wove together the reality that the newborn infant was named in public at his or her baptism, sometimes for the first time, sometimes for the only time, depending on their lifespan. But that addition to the Roman Rite and variations on that rite were still not held as essential even in the fourteenth century and beyond. The *Handbook for Curates* (*Manipulus curatorum*) of Guido of Monte Rochen (c. 1330) is a fascinating view into the training of priests with regard to their primary ministry, "the proper administration of the sacraments."[51] The manual asks the question of naming in the following way:

> But should the person to be baptized be named or his name be added or placed before "I", saying "Peter or Maria, I baptize you in the name of the Father, and of the Son, and of the Holy Spirit, Amen"? This is not essential to the form, because baptism can be done without this.

[49] Mark Searle, "Infant Baptism Reconsidered," in *Living Water, Sealing Spirit*, ed. Maxwell E. Johnson (Collegeville, MN: Liturgical Press, 1995), 369.

[50] Cf. Mario Righetti, *Manuale di Storia liturgica*, vol. 4 (Milan: Àncora, 1953), 82–83; Pierre de Puniet, *Le sacrementaire romain de Gellone*, Bibliotheca Ephemerides Liturgicae 4 (Rome: Edizioni Liturgiche, 1938), 90–91. Referenced in Searle, "Infant Baptism Reconsidered."

[51] Guido of Monte Rochen, *Handbook for Curates: A Late Medieval Manual on Pastoral Ministry*, trans. Anne T. Thayer (Washington, DC: The Catholic University of America Press, 2011), xiii. The *Handbook* continued to be reproduced, especially after the invention of the printing press. "Between circa 1468 and 1501, some 122 editions of the *Handbook* rolled off European presses both big and small, making it the eleventh most printed title in the period" (xiii).

Nevertheless it ought to be put into the form for better expression, although it is not necessary that it be placed there.[52]

This flexibility in sacramental form as well as the recognition of elements of primary versus secondary importance makes the demands for the name in the English prayer books (described above) even more striking. Is this a cultural trajectory of kinship expression, as described by Will Coster, which eventually becomes a check against the "wrong types of names" representing the "wrong types of Christianity,"[53] or is it an affirmation of "the emerging modern concept of the person as an autonomous individual"?[54] And how do the changed circumstances of Christianity in the twenty-first century affect these motivating factors and questions?

Back to the Door: Infant Baptism as Christing

In the normative pastoral experiences of American parishes across the ecumenical board, infant mortality rates and popular as well as ecclesial approaches to original sin do not compel practicing Christians (or cultural Christians) to have their infants baptized within the first week of life.[55] Neither is it common for improper names to be changed at will by the officiating clergy in North America.[56] These realities have removed the cultural and legal connections between naming the child

[52] Ibid., 19.

[53] Coster traces the movement in English baptismal names from primarily saints' names to the "Hebrew invasion" of names with the availability of English-language Bibles to the "concept" names of Puritanism (i.e., Temperance, Charity) as a factor in the seventeenth-century episcopal demands for clergy to police the name choices of parents. *Baptism and Spiritual Kinship*, 169–72. See also Fisher, *Christian Initiation*: "In these new circumstances Archbishop Peckham could order the parochial clergy not to allow improper names to be conferred upon infants at their baptism" (152).

[54] Searle, "Infant Baptism Reconsidered," 377, with reference to Louis Dumont, "A Modified View of Our Origins: The Christian Beginnings of Modern Individualism," *Religion* 12, no. 1 (1982): 1–27.

[55] This is still a valid statement, in spite of the instruction of the Roman Rite of Baptism for Children *praenotanda* par. 3, which states that "an infant should be baptized within the first weeks after birth. In the complete absence of any well-founded hope that the infant will be brought up in the Catholic religion, the baptism is to be delayed, in conformity with the provisions of particular law and the parents are to be informed of the reasons."

[56] In contrast to the ecclesial rules of some countries and/or civil rules such as those of France, where only in 1993 were French parents given the freedom to

and baptizing the child in most contemporary Christian ritual contexts.[57]

The kinship bonds of godparents to the infant candidate have also changed from the centuries of the reformations. Rather than functioning as stand-ins for biological parents, whose presence became superfluous as unnecessary reminders of carnal parenthood versus spiritual parenthood,[58] godparents today are often canonically necessary but in actuality background figures, with a renewed stress on the parents as (1) present at the baptism, (2) the primary catechists of their children, and (3) a crucial part of the renewed emphasis on the domestic church.[59]

But perhaps far more important for our consideration is the shift in the concept of reality that is carried from society into the church, resulting in the dislocation between the "we" of liturgical language and ecclesial assumption, and the "I" of contemporary self-understanding. Francis Mannion addressed this issue a number of years ago, calling it one of the most insidious of inculturated values for North Americans. He labeled it "the subjectification of reality" in which "the individual has a primary reality whereas society is a second-order, derived or artificial construct."[60] When brought to liturgy, an uncompromisingly corporate action, "modern Americans 'look for the holy to reveal itself, not in the awe-inspiring rites of baptism and Eucharist, but in the awesome precincts of the self.'"[61] Certainly the infant candidate for

---

name their child without reference to historical calendars and French history, but the registrar still has a legal right to dispute the name and bring in a prosecutor.

[57] The written baptismal record as an official recording of name and often birthdate is still honored, but that is generally a separate action from the liturgy of baptism.

[58] See discussion in Coster, *Baptism and Spiritual Kinship*, 64–68. Particularly interesting is the key role that the midwife played in many medieval baptismal rituals until the 1549 prayer book.

[59] This is not the case across all cultural situations. Certainly in many Hispanic Christian contexts, *los padrinos* play an important and ongoing role in the life of their godchildren.

[60] "Liturgy and the Present Crisis of Culture," *Liturgy and Spirituality in Context: Perspectives on Prayer and Culture*, ed. Eleanor Bernstein (Collegeville, MN: Liturgical Press, 1990), 4. Mannion quotes Robert Bellah, *Habits of the Heart: Individualism and Commitment in American Life* (New York: Harper and Row, 1985), 334.

[61] Mannion, "Liturgy and the Present Crisis of Culture," 7, quoting Nathan Mitchell, "The Sense of the Sacred," in *Parish: A Place for Worship*, ed. Mark Searle (Collegeville, MN: Liturgical Press, 1981), 74.

baptism is free of this self-obsession (or the ability to verbally express it), but new parents are often not. Infant baptism can easily become a videography event of self-absorption for family members and some clergy alike. Part of this critique, however, also needs to be addressed to liturgical churches that have not offered much catechetical help in explaining what it means to "put on Christ," to know that "baptism completely changes a person's status."[62] Whether relying solely on metaphors with no systematic theological underpinnings or adhering to metaphysical categorizations of change, what many parents walk away with is that the child is now joining the congregation rather than the triune God. Kimberly Hope Belcher's new approach to the appropriateness of infant baptism through the theology of "efficacious engagement" is a good start, acknowledging that, "as a work of grace, becoming a Christian is beyond the ability of the initiand: it is the result of election by God and the community."[63] She raises up in multiple ways the need for us to set aside cognitive assent and knowledge as prerequisite and effect of baptism, instead drawing our attention to ritual actions expressive of kenosis and embodiment: "the child's body becomes the space where disappropriation is possible; thus the body is the place of the Spirit."[64] Part of how she calls our theological attention to order is to reiterate a medieval sense of self-emptying, by the baptismal candidate him- or herself, and by the responsible adults in infant baptism. Ritually expressed as offering, Cramer wrote that the child is offered by the parents, released from a primarily familial identity to be filled with an ecclesial identity: "The offering itself is nonetheless an act of personal and social intention; and the child is caught up in intention, despite his own lack of it."[65] Belcher writes in a similar vein by saying, "If the momentum of the rite is a handing over of the infant's identity toward God, the infant himself or herself is the one being handed over. . . . There is a Trinitarian significance to the ritual momentum [because] . . . the child, by being handed over to God in order to complete God's plan for the salvation of humanity, becomes an extension of Christ's mission in

[62] The Venerable Bede. Cited by M. Thomas Aquinas Carroll, "The Venerable Bede: His Spiritual Teachings," (PhD dissertation: Catholic University of America, 1946), 103.

[63] Belcher, *Efficacious Engagement*, 81.

[64] Ibid., 133.

[65] Cramer, *Baptism and Change in the Early Middle Ages*, 135.

the world. The body of the infant . . . becomes the body of Christ."[66] The necessary catechetical issues to bring about greater engagement in this "liturgical pastoral practice" are beyond the scope of this paper, but the ritual expression of this parental self-emptying, engaging the infant as participant offering being offered, would seem to be modestly assisted by place and name differentiation.

First, in the contemporary rites of infant baptism in liturgical churches (and many traditionally "non-liturgical churches"), we see a tremendous similarity in formulae and structure. But none spatially distinguish between the threshold rites of being received except for the Roman Rite of Baptism for Children (RBC; 1969 *editio typica*). There, the introductory rubrics instruct the "celebrating priest or deacon . . . accompanied by the ministers" to go to the "entrance of the church or to that part of the church where the parents and godparents are waiting with the child" (RBC 74).[67] The door, or other place distinct from the font, and the temporal separation from the sacrament of baptism help express and create the liminality of societal and ecclesial identities. Asking for the name—"What name do you give your child? (or: have you given?)" (76)—and welcoming the child at the consignation by name establish a recognition of the cultural, familial identity being brought into the new reality of participation in God. Here, the naming seems deliberate and distinct from the use of the name at the baptismal formula.

The 1979 *Book of Common Prayer* of the US Episcopal Church does not differentiate temporally or spatially with any clarity. The "Presentation and Examination of the Candidates" takes place after the Liturgy of the Word in an undesignated place.[68] The candidates (whether adults or infants) are presented by name, and, unlike the Roman Rite, the name is never used again except at the actual baptism and post-baptismal chrismation.

The new *Evangelical Lutheran Worship* book (2006) instructs "candidates for baptism, sponsors, and parents" to gather "with the ministers

[66] Belcher, *Efficacious Engagement*, 133.

[67] All references to the Roman Rite are taken from *The Rites of the Catholic Church*, vol. 1 (Collegeville, MN: Liturgical Press, 1990).

[68] Although an ancillary rubric in the back of the rite of baptism says "If the Presentation of the Candidates does not take place at the font, then before or during the petitions, the ministers, candidates, and sponsors go to the font for the Thanksgiving over the Water" (*The Book of Common Prayer 1979* [New York: Church Hymnal Corporation, 1979], 312).

at the font." The candidates are then presented by name for baptism, and the name is reiterated by the minister in asking what they want. At that point, the congregation is also asked to support the named candidate. The name is used again at baptism, the bestowal of the gifts of the Spirit, and the optional sealing.[69] There is a second option, however, titled "Welcome to Baptism," which places the presentation of candidates "at the entrance to the church or in front of the assembly." There, the candidate is addressed by name in saying, "gather with this community of faith and hear the word of God with us," but the name is not used at the consignation immediately following.[70]

The *Book of Common Worship* of the Presbyterian Church (USA) follows a similar structure but with presentation through post-baptismal rites all in the same place ("candidates, sponsors, and parents assemble at the baptismal font or pool. Care should be taken to ensure that the baptism is fully visible to the congregation").[71] The candidates are presented by name and the names are used in several questions in this initial ritual. The personal name is not used again until baptism and then again at the laying on of hands and in introducing and welcoming the newly baptized to the congregation. A number of alternative liturgies follow, but the spatial and naming pattern does not change.

In the Episcopal, Lutheran, and Presbyterian samples, there is no differentiation between the use of the personal name at the presentation and the use of the name at baptism and post-baptismal rites. Above all, the presentation seems to be of the child to the congregation, rather than the reception of the child into the space, symbolizing the threshold encounter between identities. Nor do any of these rites use the powerful symbol of the door or threshold to express and create the sense of dynamism in the transformation of identity that Kimberly Hope Belcher describes so well.[72]

Most impoverishing seems to be the indiscriminate use of the personal name throughout the rites, for it ritually obscures the new identity of the child. The baptized child is one who is vulnerable before and within the Body of Christ as the model of both self-emptying and

[69] *Evangelical Lutheran Worship* (Minneapolis, MN: Augsburg Fortress Publishers, 2006), 227–31.

[70] Ibid., 232–33.

[71] *Book of Common Worship* (Louisville, KY: Westminster/John Knox Press, 1993), 403–15.

[72] See footnote 14, p. 177, above.

as a new person in the name of Christ. The baptized child is immersed and forever marked as a participant in the name, and therefore the very essence, of the Trinity.

What if we imagined an infant baptism with a threshold reception, the use of the name asked for and received—the name of the child brought to the ecclesial identity in the christological consignation? What if that meeting of heaven and earth, in which both human and divine identity were recognized, were followed by the Liturgy of the Word celebrated in a different space, followed by movement to the font where the only name was that of the Father and the Son and the Holy Spirit? What if the post-baptismal rites included the movement to the altar, where initiation was completed by the reception of Communion, which has no history of being given by individual name, only the name of Christ? Might we begin from liturgical place, word, action, and actors to invite Christians new and not-so-new into a reinvigorated conversation on what it means to have been named "Christian" and participate in the "authority, the power and the inner character of quality of the person"[73] whose name we share?

[73] Cramer, *Baptism and Change in the Early Middle Ages*, 40.

Part IV

Eucharist

Bryan D. Spinks

Chapter 11

Revisiting Egyptian Anaphoral Development

In 1995 Maxwell Johnson wrote, "No early Christian liturgical tradition has left us with more anaphoral texts and fragments than has the Egyptian tradition, and with the exception of that anaphora called 'Egyptian Basil' (hereafter EgBas) these numerous sources underscore an anaphoral structure which is unique to that tradition."[1]

Although he observed that in the Anaphora of Sarapion the position of the intercessions was that of the "West Syrian" tradition,[2] Johnson noted a possible development from the "praise, offering and supplication" structure of Strasbourg Papyrus Gr.254 (hereafter S) to Greek Mark and Coptic Cyril, and he noted that something like S might lie behind Sarapion too. Undoubtedly, the anaphora attributed to Sarapion of Thmuis, together with a good many Egyptian fragments, witnesses to a pattern of anaphora that is quite distinct. The pattern certainly has some things in common with the Roman *Canon missae*,[3] but its *Sanctus*-epiclesis unit, together with intercessions before the *Sanctus*, and particular phrases and words around the institution narrative have come to be seen as distinctly Egyptian. This essay raises the question of whether in the light of more recent studies this was the only anaphoral pattern that was somehow distinctly Egyptian.

One of the most important elements in discerning Egyptian anaphoral structure has been the contention that S is a complete anaphora.[4]

[1] Maxwell E. Johnson, *Liturgy in Early Christian Egypt*, Alcuin/GROW Liturgical Study 33 (Bramcote/Nottingham: Grove Books, 1995), 20.

[2] Ibid., 22.

[3] M. J. Moreton, "Rethinking the Origin of the Roman Canon," *Studia Patristica* 26 (1993): 63–66; Enrico Mazza, *The Origins of the Eucharistic Prayer* (Collegeville, MN: Liturgical Press, 1995); Walter D. Ray, in papers presented to the North American Academy of Liturgy, and, most recently, "The Strasbourg Papyrus and the Roman Canon: Thoughts on Chapter Seven of Enrico Mazza's *The Origins of the Eucharistic Prayer*," *Studia Liturgica* 39, no. 1 (2009): 40–62.

[4] For the edited Greek text, see Jürgen Hammerstaedt, *Griechische Anaphorenfragmente aus Ägypten und Nubien* (Opladen/Wiesbaden: Westdeutscher Verlag, 1999).

In an article in 1984 I did suggest that this was not the only possible reading of the evidence, though many commentators on early liturgy have preferred to read it as a complete prayer.[5] The idea that it was a complete "*eucharistia*" or anaphora was first hinted at by Edward Kilmartin and subsequently argued by Hermann Wegman, Geoffrey Cuming, and W. H. Bates.[6] Wegman, in particular, argued that it divided neatly into three strophes consisting of praise of God, giving thanks through Christ and offering the reasonable sacrifice, and intercessions for living and dead. He claimed to have found the layer of the most ancient of Egyptian eucharistic prayers and, comparing it with *Didache* 10, concluded that the fragment was no less than a eucharistic *berakah* complete in three strophes.[7] Cuming similarly suggested that the prayer is a "Christian *berakah*" and appealed to the work of Louis Ligier to demonstrate that the *Birkat ha-mazon* was the likely source of the Christian eucharistic prayer.[8] Indeed, following the work of Jean-Paul Audet, Louis Bouyer, Ligier, and Thomas Talley, it became commonplace to regard the Jewish *berakoth*, and more especially the *Birkat ha-mazon*, as the parent of the eucharistic prayer.[9] Talley's and

[5] Bryan D. Spinks, "A Complete Anaphora? A Note on Strasbourg Gr.254," *The Heythrop Journal* 25, no. 1 (1984): 51–55; Walter D. Ray, "The Strasbourg Papyrus," in *Essays on Early Eastern Eucharistic Prayers*, ed. Paul F. Bradshaw (Collegeville, MN: Liturgical Press, 1997), 39–56; Enrico Mazza, *The Origins of the Eucharistic Prayer*.

[6] Edward Kilmartin, "Sacrificium Laudis: Content and Function of Early Eucharistic Prayers," *Theological Studies* 35, no. 2 (1974): 268–87; H. A. J. Wegman, "Une Anaphore Incomplète? Les Fragments sur Papyrus Strasbourg Gr.254," in *Studies in Gnosticism and Hellenistic Religions*, ed. Roelof van den Broek and Maarten J. Vermaseren (Leiden: Brill, 1981), 432–50; Geoffrey J. Cuming, "The Anaphora of St. Mark: A Study in Development," *Le Muséon* 95 (1982): 115–29 (read as a master theme at the Oxford Patristic Conference 1979), also published in *Essays on Early Eastern Eucharistic Prayers*, 57–72; W. H. Bates, "Thanksgiving and Intercession in the Liturgy of St. Mark," in *The Sacrifice of Praise*, ed. Bryan D. Spinks (Rome: CLV–Edizioni Liturgiche, 1981), 107–19.

[7] See Wegman, "Une Anaphore Incomplète," 433: "dans le texte de Str.gr.254 je crois pouvoir trouver la couche la plus ancienne de la prière eucharistique égyptienne."

[8] Cuming, "The Anaphora of St. Mark," 63.

[9] J.-P. Audet, "Literary Forms and Contents of a Normal *Eucharistia* in the First Century," in *Studia Evangelica 1*, Texte uns Untersuchungen zur Geschichte der altchristlichen Literatur, vol. 73, ed. Kurt Aland (Berlin: Akademie, 1959), 643–62; Louis Bouyer, *Eucharist: Theology and Spirituality of the Eucharistic Prayer*, trans. Charles Underhill Quinn (Notre Dame, IN: University of Notre Dame Press, 1968); Louis Ligier, "The Origins of the Eucharistic Prayer: From the Last Supper to the Eucharist," *Studia Liturgica* 9, no. 4 (1973): 176–85; Thomas J. Talley, "The Eucha-

Wegman's suggested evolution became an assured fact of scholarship in the hands of Dennis Smolarski.[10] There is still a hint of this *berakah* evolutionary theory in Enrico Mazza, who describes it as a paleo-anaphora, and Walter Ray, who has developed some of Mazza's arguments.[11]

Many scholars writing in the 1970s and early 1980s (and I would include myself) took it for granted that, whatever may be true of other prayers, direct influence of the *Birkat ha-mazon* on *Didache* 10 had been demonstrated by Louis Finkelstein and that the *berakoth* of Judaism were the bedrock of some early Christian eucharistic prayers. It seemed to be surmised that, if *Didache* 10 was derived from the *Birkat ha-mazon*, then why not other early Christian prayers, and one wonders how far Wegman and Cuming were influenced by the fact that the only praise word that survives in S happens to be "bless." With the appearance of studies by Joseph Heinemann, then James Charlesworth and Stefan Reif, it became clear that Jewish prayer forms were once far more diverse than the "*berakah*" so loved by Audet, Bouyer, and Ligier, that those forms that have come down to us postdate Christian prayers, and also that we have far less knowledge of what was and was not in use at the time of the nascent Church.[12] Paul Bradshaw cautioned of the *Birkat ha-mazon* and *Didache* 10 comparison: "Yet the truth is that the parallels exist only in the very broadest of terms, and in any case are of very dubious value."[13]

Both Jonathan Draper and Aaron Milavec have seriously questioned whether there is any legitimacy in comparing the first-century *Didache* meal prayer with the ninth-century text of the *Birkat ha-mazon*, given Heinemann's strictures. In his 2003 study, Milavec concluded:

ristic Prayer of the Ancient Church according to Recent Research: Results and Reflections," *Studia Liturgica* 11, nos. 3–4 (1976): 138–58.

[10] Dennis C. Smolarski, *Eucharistia: A Study of the Eucharistic Prayer* (Ramsey, NJ: Paulist Press, 1982).

[11] Mazza, *The Origins of the Eucharistic Prayer*, 194; Ray, "The Strasbourg Papyrus and the Roman Canon," 40–62.

[12] Joseph Heinemann, *Prayer in the Talmud: Forms and Patterns* (Berlin/New York: De Gruyter, 1977); James H. Charlesworth, "Jewish Hymns, Odes, and Prayers," in *Early Judaism and Its Modern Interpreters*, ed. Robert A. Kraft and George W. E. Nickelsburg (Atlanta, GA: Scholars Press, 1986), 411–36; Stefan C. Reif, *Judaism and Hebrew Prayer: New Perspectives on Jewish Liturgical History* (Cambridge: Cambridge University Press, 1993). See also Bryan D. Spinks, "Beware the Liturgical Horses! An English Interjection on Anaphoral Evolution," *Worship* 59, no. 3 (1985): 211–19.

[13] Paul F. Bradshaw, *Eucharistic Origins*, Alcuin Club Collections 80 (London: SPCK, 2004), 33.

> Now that I no longer consider that his [Finkelstein] reconstruction is credible, I find it misleading to use it as a possible "source" for the after-meal prayers of the *Didache* (also Vööbus 1968: 166f.). I take it as normative that Heinemann has demonstrated that the prayers of the *Didache* were created at a time when there was a diversity of style and content in Jewish prayers. Hence, it must be supposed that the Eucharistic prayers of the *Didache* had Jewish origins that were refined and defined due to the patterns of preferred usage that gradually emerged among the freely improvised Eucharistic prayers used in *Didache* communities. The same anonymous and obscure origins, of course, stand behind the creation of the Jewish *Birkat Ha-Mazon*.[14]

In his recent study of the *Didache* meal prayers, Jonathan Schwiebert concludes that one can surmise that a threefold after-dinner prayer was traditional (cf. Jubilees 22:1-9) and that the community of the *Didache* simply took that for granted but that "it would be too much to claim that the prayers of *Didache* 10 derive their meaning from a polemical, conscious reorientation of a *fixed* Jewish prayer form."[15] Schwiebert draws attention to the fact that the parallels between *Didache* 9 and *Didache* 10 are far more striking than any echoes of the *Birkat ha-mazon*.[16] Furthermore, one might add that the prayers in the *Acts of Thomas* have no affinity at all to Jewish forms at all. More recent scholarly trends, therefore, have for the most part quietly dropped the *berakoth* foundational argument, though Ray has been one scholar who refuses to be weaned from this now rather passé, if not flawed, approach.[17] This does not invalidate the argument that S could be a complete eucharistic prayer, but analogies with Jewish forms that might be thought to lend support are but a chimera. Finally, although it is quite possible to see S as having a threefold division, it is equally possible to posit a fourfold movement: praise, thanksgiving, beseeching, and remembering. Yet, if S was one early Egyptian form, which was

[14] Aaron Milavec, *The Didache: Faith, Hope and Life of the Earliest Christian Communities, 50–70 C.E.* (New York: Newman Press, 2003), 421. See also Jonathan Draper, "Ritual Process and Ritual Symbol in Didache 7–10," *Vigiliae Christianae* 54, no. 2 (2000): 121–58.

[15] Jonathan Schwiebert, *Knowledge and the Coming Kingdom: The Didache's Meal Ritual and Its Place in Early Christianity* (London/New York: T & T Clark, 2008), 119.

[16] Ibid., 60ff.

[17] Most recently, Walter D. Ray, "The Barcelona Papyrus and the Early Egyptian Eucharistic Prayer," *Studia Liturgica* 41, no. 2 (2011): 211–29. Ray has yet to address the studies of Gabriele Winkler that undermine his a priori assumptions.

subsequently expanded through, for example, the Rylands Library parchment and the wooden tablet in the British Museum (so Cuming) to culminate in the *textus receptus* of Mark/Cyril, was this the only or "original" Egyptian pattern? As Johnson observed, although Sarapion seems to echo parts of S, it also reflects the "West Syrian" pattern in the positioning of the second (albeit Logos) epiclesis and the intercessions. EgBas, the Barcelona Manuscript, and the fragment of an anaphora attributed to Thomas are here pertinent to current reevaluations.

Egyptian Basil

The Coptic Church has in use today three anaphoras: Cyril, Basil, and Gregory. The latter two both follow the "West Syrian" pattern rather than the distinct Egyptian pattern preserved in Cyril. Although "West Syrian" is a convenient term to describe a certain structure of anaphora, it has never actually been determined as to why it should always and everywhere relate to a specific geographical area. Many of the anaphoras classed as "West Syrian" actually postdate EgBas, particularly the Syrian Orthodox anaphoras (mainly post–seventh century), which make up the majority of this group. This, of course, is a matter of taxonomy, but the terminology, useful for family groupings, does tend to reinforce the idea that anywhere other than the Byzantine-Antiochene milieu has borrowed the "West Syrian" structure at a later date, and it is thus an imported pattern.

EgBas is known in Greek, Sahidic, and Boharic recensions, though it is the Sahidic that is regarded as the least developed text. The assumption has been that it migrated in some form to Egypt from Cappadocia —perhaps brought by Basil himself during his visit—and thus is an import. Hieronymus Engberding, Alphonse Raes, and, more recently, Todd Johnson have drawn attention to parts of EgBas that make it distinctly Egyptian, and in terms of paleoanaphoras, it raises the question of whether some earlier Egyptian eucharistic prayer has been fused or thoroughly incorporated into what has become EgBas.[18] The importance of this anaphora in its various recensions has been recently

[18] Hieronymus Engberding, *Das eucharistiche Hochgebet der Basileiosliturgie. Textgeschichtliche Untersuchungen und kritische Ausgabe*, Theologie der christlichen Ostens 1 (Münster: Aschendorff Verlag, 1931); Alphonse Raes, "Un nouveau document de la liturgie de S.Basile," *Orientalia Christiana Periodica* 26 (1960): 401–11; Todd E.

reinforced by the extensive study of Aachim Budde.[19] Budde has not attempted to reconstruct an *Ur-text* but arranges the texts in parallel with the conviction that the variants speak for themselves as to how an anaphoral tradition was localized, or as local examples of "improvisation."[20] He does not suggest that it is an Egyptian composition but that it has been "Egyptianized." Budde has rightly been criticized for ignoring the earliest Armenian version of Basil—something that has been rectified by Gabriele Winkler. Winkler argues, and almost certainly correctly, that the Armenian anaphora under the title of St. Gregory (Arm I) is a very early version of the Basiline anaphora. Her contention for older Syrian traditions underlying the Armenian is speculative and, in the absence of written sources, difficult to substantiate. We lack a critical edition of the Syriac Basiline anaphora, and those known to me in Cambridge Add. 2887 and Cambridge Add. 2917 seem post–seventh century wooden translations of the Byzantine Greek with expansions. Yet even with the priority of Arm I, Winkler admits that the Egyptian version is not unimportant and has its own particular distinctive readings.[21] Among these are the opening *oratio theologica*, with the reference to Psalm 146:6 or Nehemiah 9:6ff., which has parallels in the other Egyptian anaphoras, and the lack of a *Benedictus* following the *Sanctus*. The institution narrative is introduced with "for" or "because," which is an Egyptian characteristic, and the narrative itself is close to that found in Mark/Cyril. The narrative also has *katallangelo* of 1 Corinthians 11 on the lips of Jesus. EgBas has the distinct "Egyptian" aorist form for the offering ("we have offered"), and the doxology is also a distinct form, having parallels in three Coptic sources. The cumulative inference would seem to be that, even if the final pattern of EgBas was not a homegrown Egyptian creation, the anaphora represents a prayer tradition that was honed on Egyptian soil, and at an early date, and perhaps might have influenced the shaping of the Anaphora of Sarapion.

Johnson, "Recovering Ägyptisches Heimatgut: An Exercise in Liturgical Methodology," *Questions Liturgiques* 76, nos. 3–4 (1995): 182–98.

[19] Achim Budde, *Die* ägyptische *Basilios-Anaphora. Text, Kommentar, Geschichte* (Münster: Aschendorff Verlag, 2004).

[20] Ibid., 551.

[21] Gabriele Winkler, *Die Basilius-Anaphora. Edition der beiden armenischen Redaktionen und der relevanten Fragmente, Übersetzung und Zusammenschau aller Versionem im Lichte der orientalischen Überlieferungen* (Rome: Pontificio Istituto Orientale, 2005).

The Barcelona Anaphora

Equally important now in assessing the Egyptian anaphoral tradition is that contained in the Barcelona Papyrus published by Ramón Roca-Puig. For some years scholars were tantalized by the publication of this text in short extracts over prolonged periods. Roca-Puig finally published a full edition of this Greek anaphora in 1994.[22] As the title of his edition indicates, a fourth-century provenance is given to this anaphora, which suggests that it is equally as important as Sarapion and EgBas in assessing the Egyptian tradition. As Michael Zheltov has recently noted, "This papyrus is in fact the oldest manuscript known to contain Christian liturgical prayers conserved in their integrity—while, for example, the famous Strasbourg papyrus, P.Strassb.inv.254, dates from the 4–5th centuries and has many lacunae in its text—giving our codex seminal importance for liturgical scholarship."[23] Zheltov argues that since S is but a fragment, the Barcelona anaphora should be given priority in assessing the Egyptian tradition: "Nevertheless, despite the plain fact that this papyrus, probably connected in some way with the Pachomian monastic community, is the oldest liturgical manuscript containing a full anaphora, its important testimony is almost completely neglected by modern liturgical scholars."[24]

Ray has rightly pointed out that the dating of a manuscript or papyrus should not be confused with the date of its content and thus has defended the "priority" of S over Barcelona.[25] Giving priority to one over the other, however, would seem to rest on prior assumptions and convictions about the shape or content of an anaphora at a given epoch (in Ray's case the wish to interpret S in the light of *Didache* 10 and the *Birkat ha-mazon*), and it may be wiser simply to take both as fourth-century witnesses to more than a simplistic single Egyptian anaphoral tradition rather than attempt a Solomonic judgment.

The anaphora of Barcelona was already known in part in the Coptic parchment Louvain 27, so this anaphora existed in both Greek and

[22] Ramón Roca-Puig, *Anàfora De Barcelona: I Altres Pregàries (Missa del segle IV)* (Barcelona: Grafos, 1994).

[23] Michael Zheltov, "The Anaphora and the Thanksgiving Prayer from the Barcelona Papyrus: An Underestimated Testimony to the Anaphoral History in the Fourth Century," *Vigiliae Christianae* 62, no. 5 (2008): 467–504, here 468.

[24] Ibid., 469.

[25] Ray, "The Strasbourg Papyrus and the Roman Canon," 46.

Coptic. A further Greek fragment is preserved in PVindob. G 41043. Zheltov usefully summarizes its structure:[26]

I. Introductory dialogue
II. Preface with four initial praise verbs, creation narrative, and a christological section
III. Pre-*Sanctus*
IV. Oblation and Epiclesis I
V. Institution narrative
VI. Anamnesis
VII. Epiclesis II
VIII. Concluding doxology

He notes that the *Sanctus*–Epiclesis I–Institution is an Egyptian characteristic, and it also has the short form of the *Sanctus* with no *Benedictus*. Like S and EgBas, it has the quotation from Psalm 146:6/ Nehemiah 9:6, and "O Master, God Pantocrator of our Lord Jesus Christ" which has a parallel in another lesser-known Egyptian anaphora, that of Athanasius. Its close parallels to other Egyptian anaphoras and works even led Zheltov to wonder if Athanasius may have been its author.[27] There are certain elements that are peculiar, such as the interruption of the post-*Sanctus* and Epiclesis I by a christological reference, a lack of intercessions, and the fact that Epiclesis II is a sanctification of the communicants, not the gifts. These may be peculiar but can hardly be deemed "un-Egyptian" or "late" unless one already has a preconception of what is "Egyptian" and "early." Sarapion's anaphora is also "peculiar," but, ultimately, "peculiar" in these documents must just mean "different." One particularly interesting element is the quotation in the Barcelona anaphora from 1 Clement 59:2. While for twenty-first-century scholars this is a quotation from the fathers, in a fourth-century Egyptian context it is, in fact, a quotation from canonical Scripture. It is frequently overlooked in liturgical discussions that both Clement of Alexandria and Didymus the Blind regarded 1 Clement and the *Didache* as sacred texts alongside the gospels and Pauline epistles, and Codex Alexandrinus in-

[26] Zheltov, "The Anaphora and the Thanksgiving Prayer," 493.
[27] Ibid., 497.

cluded 1 and 2 Clement.[28] In the same way, the *Didache* is quoted in Sarapion and Deir Balyzeh. In Egypt both counted as Scripture at this time, and thus the quotations are no more significant than the use of Psalm 146:6/Nehemiah 9:6, other than to indicate that these are Egyptian distinctions. Furthermore, although Barcelona lacks the careful *Sanctus*-Epiclesis unit with a "full-fill" connection, that element is present in the Louvain Coptic fragment and hinted at in the PVindob. G 41043. Sebastià Janeras has suggested the copyist of Barcelona has accidently omitted repeating the phrase "for full is heaven of your holy glory," which is certainly possible.[29] Equally, the other two fragments might suggest that the link phrase was added. Whichever of these might be the case, the cumulative literary evidence shows that some recensions of this anaphora did have the characteristic Egyptian link.

In a recent essay, Paul Bradshaw considered the Barcelona text and Zheltov's arguments.[30] Although he concluded that it probably dates no later than the middle of the fourth century and "thus represents one of the oldest anaphoras known to us, probably as old as the Sacramentary of Sarapion and as the anaphora in the Apostolic Tradition in its fully developed form," his assessment was made with the claim that there is "a growing consensus among liturgical scholars that in other extant early Eucharistic prayers both the Sanctus with its surrounding material and also the institution narrative were usually fourth-century additions to an older core," though this "growing consensus" was footnoted only by reference to a section of Max Johnson's work of 1995 on Sarapion.[31] Max Johnson in turn had referred to the older studies of

[28] Bart D. Ehrman, "The New Testament Canon of Didymus the Blind," *Vigiliae Christianae* 37, no. 1 (1983): 1–21, here 16–18. Bruce M. Metzger, *The Canon of the New Testament* (Oxford: Clarendon Press, 1987), 134, 214, 225. Rufinus was taught by Didymus and he also accords these books a special place. Metzger, *The Canon of the New Testament*, 234. Lee Martin McDonald and James A. Sanders, *The Canon Debate* (Peabody, MA: Henrickson, 2002), 493.

[29] Sebastià Janeras, "Sanctus et Post-Sanctus dans l'anaphore du *P.Monts.Roca inv.no.154b-155a," Studi sull Oriente Christiano* 11, no. 1 (2007): 9–13.

[30] Paul F. Bradshaw, "The Barcelona Papyrus and the Development of Early Eucharistic Prayers," in *Issues in Eucharistic Praying in East and West: Essays in Liturgical and Theological Analysis*, ed. Maxwell E. Johnson (Collegeville, MN: Liturgical Press, 2010), 129–38.

[31] Ibid., 132–33, and footnote 16.

Talley, Cesare Giraudo, Wegman, Cuming, and Mazza on the relationship of the Jewish *berakah* and S.

Where S is regarded as not only a complete anaphora but the touchstone by which all others are measured, then indeed the conclusion cannot be other than that the *Sanctus* and institution narrative are "later" additions. Bradshaw himself, however, in his earlier important review of the study of early Christian worship, had noted that what is most common is not necessarily most ancient, and what is least common is not necessarily least ancient, and the first time something is mentioned is not necessarily the first time it was practiced.[32] This seems pertinent in the discussion of Barcelona relating to S and what constitutes "Egyptian" tradition. It is certainly true that with the dating of the anaphora of the so-called *Apostolic Tradition* once attributed to Hippolytus now seriously questioned (and, in any case, in the sources where the anaphora is present, it is regarded as a prayer at an ordination of a bishop, not a usual Sunday anaphora), we have no evidence for the institution narrative in the eucharistic prayer before the fourth century—presumably now Arm I. This means that it is absent from the few pieces of evidence we have prior to Arm I, including Addai and Mari and possibly MC attributed to Cyril of Jerusalem. That does not mean to say, however, that it was not so used anywhere prior to Arm I but simply that we have no evidence that it was. The origin of the *Sanctus*, though, is rather different, for it does occur in Addai and Mari, which even Wegman felt was as early as S. Furthermore, the philological tour de force of Gabriele Winkler on the *hekhalot* background to the *Sanctus* makes it extremely difficult to continue to maintain that the *Sanctus* is always a later intrusion.[33] What is intriguing in this respect

[32] Paul F. Bradshaw, *The Search for the Origins of Christian Worship* (London: SPCK, 1992), 63, 76.

[33] Gabriele Winkler, *Das Sanctus. Über den Ursprung und die Anfänge des Sanctus und sein Fortwirken*, Orientalia Christiana Analecta 267 (Rome: Pontificio Istituto Orientale, 2002); eadem, "The Sanctus: Some Observations with Regard to Its Origins and Theological Significance," in *Prayer and Spirituality in the Early Church*, vol. 3: *Liturgy and Life*, ed. Bronwen Neil, Geoffrey D. Dunn, and Lawrence Cross (Strathfield, NSW: St. Paul's Publications, 2003), 111–31; eadem, "A New Witness to the Missing Institution Narrative," in *Studia Liturgica Diversa: Essays in Honor of Paul F. Bradshaw*, ed. Maxwell E. Johnson and L. Edward Phillips (Portland, OR: Pastoral Press, 2004), 117–28. With reference to the Ethiopic Anaphora of the Apostles and East Syrian Addai and Mari, Winkler concludes on p. 128: "The interesting fact remains, however, that both the Syriac and the Ethiopic 'Anaphora of

is the fact that both EgBas and Barcelona seem to have an overt reference to *merkavah* or *hekhalot* mysticism. EgBas (retained, but in a much more diffuse context in ByzBas) has "you sit on the throne of your glory." Barcelona has the even more explicit reference (apparently with reference to Christ) "who sits on the chariot, Cherubim and Seraphim before it." It is precisely these references and the hitherto neglected fragment of the Anaphora of Thomas that Mary Farag draws attention to as requiring a reassessment of the origins of the *Sanctus* in the anaphora and, in turn, what constitutes an "Egyptian" pattern.

The Anaphora of Thomas

This anaphoral fragment is found in the Great Euchology of the White Monastery. This manuscript was copied in the tenth or eleventh century and is a compilation of earlier anaphoras. It certainly includes in Coptic the anaphoras of the Syrian Orthodox Church such as Severus of Antioch and John Bostra.[34] It also contains anaphoras of the Coptic Orthodox Church, however, and includes two otherwise unknown anaphoras: the evangelist Matthew, which is an entire anaphora, and the fragment of St.Thomas.[35] I give here the English translation of Thomas by Mary Farag:

> Who can make his mind heavenly and place his thoughts in Paradise and place his heart in the heavenly Jerusalem and see God the invisible, the incomprehensible, the unattainable, the uncreated, the immeasurable?

---

the Apostles' had (=the Ethiopic anaphora) or have (= the Syriac 'Anaphora of the Apostles') no Institution Narrative, but contained the Sanctus from the beginning."

[34] Though for some "Egyptian" elements in Severus, see Bryan D. Spinks, "The Anaphora of Severus of Antioch: A Note on Its Character and Theology," in *Θυσία Αἰνέσεως. Mélanges liturgiques offerts* à *la mémoire de l'archevêque Georges Wagner (1930–1993)*, ed. Job Getcha and André Lossky (Paris: Presses Saint Serge, 2005), 345–51.

[35] Emmanuel Lanne, *Le Grand Euchologie du Monastère Blanc*, Patrologia Orientalis vol. 28, bk. 2 (Paris: Firmin-Didot, 1958). Matthew and Thomas are given in French translations. For the German of Matthew, see Angelicus M. Kropp, "Die Koptische Anaphora des Heiligen Evangelisten Matthäus," *Oriens Christianus* 29 (1932): 111–25; for Italian, see Gabriella Maestri, "Un contributo alla conoscenza dell'antica liturgia egiziana: Studio dell'anafora del santo evangelista Matteo," in *Memoriam Sanctorum Venerantes: Miscellanea in onore di Monsignor Victor Saxer*, Studi Di Antichita Cristiana 48 (Vatican City: Pontificio Istituto di Archeologia Cristiana, 1992), 525–37.

As for He who accurately measured the entire creation, His workmanship no one comprehends, except he Himself and [His] good father and the Holy Spirit. [These] three are one, a single divinity, a single lordship, three hypostases, a perfect Trinity in a single divinity. These three are one: he who collected all the waters that were upon the earth into a single gathering and called it the sea and established the four river-branches flowing into it, (a sea that) can neither become overfilled nor lack (for water), He who bounded the waters in three parts and placed one part in heaven, one part upon the earth, and one part under the earth, He who created the sun and the moon and the stars and appointed the sun to shine upon His creations by day and the moon by night, the evening [star] and Arcturus and the morning star to shine upon the earth. And you also created the angels and the archangels, the principalities and the authorities, the powers and all the powers that are in the heavens. And by Your hands, along with Your good father and the Holy Spirit, You also created man according to Your image and according to Your likeness. And you also created Paradise and placed the man whom You created in it to cultivate it and to praise You,

You whom the angels praise, You whom the archangels worship,

[in Greek] *Those who are seated stand*

You whom the powers hymn, You whose holy glory the authorities sing, You to whom the thrones sing the doxology of victory,

[in Greek] *Look towards the east.*

You before whom stand Your two honored creatures, the Cherubim and the Seraphim, each of them with six wings, with two wings they cover their faces on account of the great glory of Your divinity, and with two they cover their feet on account of the great fire emanating from around Your throne, O God, the Creator,

[in Greek] *Let us attend.*

And with two they fly, while hymning and praising You, glorifying You with unwearying mouth and unceasing tongue and never-silent lips, hymning You, glorifying You, saying,

[in Greek] *Holy,*

Holy are you, holy are you, holy are you, Lord Sabaoth. Truly heaven and earth are full of Your glory. Fill now this sacrifice also with the joy of Your Holy Spirit.

You placed the man whom You had created in the paradise of delight and commanded him that from every tree in . . .[36]

[36] Mary Farag, "The Anaphora of St. Thomas the Apostle: Translation and Commentary," *Le Muséon* 123 (2010): 317–61, here 322–23. My italics, and Farag provides the rest of the text of the presupposed *Sanctus*.

The fragment begins with a trinitarian proclamation of creation, though centered upon the Second Person, and fills out the briefer reference to heaven, earth, the sea, and all that is in them of S, EgBas, and Barcelona. It has the "Egyptian" *Sanctus* and epiclesis unit, with the request "Fill now this sacrifice also with the joy of Your Holy Spirit," though it also has the repetition of the thrice holy, which is usually classed as a "West Syrian" trait. Farag has argued that the prayer fragment reflects the Marcellan and Eunomian christological controversies of the late fourth century and was composed about that time, pointing to the emphasis on God's incomprehensible nature and the unique knowledge of the Son, as well as a reference to the throne of God. She asserts:

> These four reflections of anti-Eunomian polemic in Thomas (use of Ezekiel's vision, the properties of divinity and lordship in the Trinity, Jn 1:18, and the (in)visibility and (in)comprehensibility of God) both reveal the coherence of Thomas' initial lines and provide a benchmark for dating. The Anaphora of Thomas is most likely a composition of the end of the fourth century or of the fifth: that is, no earlier than the Eunomian controversy in the second half of the fourth century, yet no later than the controversy's immediate relevancy, which quickly declined in the first half of the fifth century.[37]

What is of the utmost importance, however, is the commentary she provides on the background to the apparent expansion of the Egyptian concern with Psalm146:6. Noting the echoes of *hekhalot* interests in both EgBas and Barcelona, Farag compares the preoccupation with the details of the creation in the *hekhalot* literature with the account of creation in the Thomas fragment. The opening of the anaphora with a question has a parallel in the anaphora of Matthew, and also in the anaphora of Severus, which has Egyptian elements. Farag calls attention to the questions that are posed in *Ma'aseh Merkavah*, however, both in narrative frames and prayer texts. Farag observes that there is a confluence of a number of themes in both texts:

- Vision of God (and the tension between immanence and transcendence)
- The state of one's heart/mind/thoughts

[37] Ibid., 327–28. See also Thomas Kopecek, *A History of Neo-Arianism*, Patristic Monograph Series, 8, vol. 2 (Cambridge, MA: The Philadelphia Patristic Foundation, 1979), 542–43.

- Knowledge and its endurability
- God as specifically creator
- Creation of heaven and earth
- Angelic retinue including thrones
- Fiery throne
- The glory of God
- Abundant verbs of praise
- Standing facing eastward at sunrise
- Human and angelic participation in the Sanctus/qedussah[38]

Farag suggests that the anaphora was influenced by the prayer corpus of *Ma'aseh Merkavah*, which is regarded as having a Palestinian provenance, and concludes that "By its clear reflection of characteristic *merkavah* speculation, this cosmopolitan anaphora pinpoints Jewish mysticism as the likely influential source not only of the Sanctus, but of the entire unit of *Sursum Corda*, creation-centered preface, and Sanctus."[39]

The *merkavah* influence on some anaphoras was one that I urged in my study on the *Sanctus* and has been strongly defended by Gabriele Winkler.[40] While this may well have implications for the origins of the anaphoral *Sanctus*, the importance of the Anaphora of Thomas is that it widens our understanding of early Egyptian anaphoral patterns. Like the Barcelona anaphora, it has no pre-*Sanctus* intercessory unit, which has been regarded as the hallmark of the Egyptian anaphora. Yet both Thomas and Barcelona *are* genuinely Egyptian anaphoras.

Conclusions

From the above discussion at least the following conclusions can be drawn:

[38] Farag, "The Anaphora of St. Thomas," 353.

[39] Ibid., 357.

[40] Bryan D. Spinks, *The Sanctus in the Eucharistic Prayer* (Cambridge: Cambridge University Press, 1991); Winkler, *Das Sanctus.*

1. The term "West Syrian" is best understood to denote a general shape or structure of an anaphora rather than being limited to a particular geographical origin.
2. Whether S is a complete eucharistic prayer or not, only with *a priori* assumptions about early anaphoral structures can it be claimed that it is "earlier" than Barcelona and that Barcelona is a "later" development. The evidence suggests that it may be more prudent to speak of a variety of anaphoral patterns in Egypt, and they are all "Egyptian." Sarapion, EgBAS, Barcelona, Thomas, Matthew, and Gregory show "West Syrian" traits, but that does not mean they are later importations into Egypt. Here, Sarapion is of the utmost importance. If it is the work of the bishop of Thmuis, and its *terminus ad quem* is mid-fourth century, then we have an Egyptian bishop weaving together patterns that scholars may wish to identify as "Egyptian" and "West Syrian," but it is highly doubtful that the author himself thought he was doing anything other than creating a legitimate expression of the Egyptian anaphoral traditions as he understood it.

What is often left out of scholarly evaluations—mainly because it is so unfathomable—is the human pastoral element in anaphoral composition. The fourth century had no liturgical commissions but rather bishops and presbyters who from time to time authored anaphoras to suit a particular theological context or a pastoral need and exercised the freedom that was theirs to do so. To the best of our knowledge, they did not work with some purist concept of the exact shape of an anaphora. Something along these lines is argued by Alistair C. Stewart in his recent English edition of the Deir Balyzeh and Barcelona Papyri.[41] Stewart observes that certain prayers found independently, such as an *ostraka*, also appear in liturgical collections and also in Egyptian anaphoras; he suggests that in Egypt, rather than talk of interpolations into originally more simple prayers, we should observe a process of agglomeration of prayer units, recognize the independence of the Egyptian liturgical tradition, and abandon any fixed idea

[41] Alistair C. Stewart (a.k.a. Alistair Stewart-Sykes), *Two Early Egyptian Liturgical Papyri: The Deir Balyzeh Papyrus and the Barcelona Papyrus with Appendices Containing Comparative Material*, Alcuin/GROW Study 70 (Norwich: SCM-Canterbury Press, 2010).

of a typical Egyptian anaphora.[42] Sarapion illustrates this, but so does Barcelona and Thomas. Maxwell Johnson's words in 1995 appear to have been prophetic: "The possibility exists, therefore, that either the early Egyptian liturgical tradition knew more than one way to build an anaphora or that, as Raes himself suggested, portions of what was to become EgBAS have their origins not in Cappadocia at all but within the Egyptian tradition itself."[43] That would also seem to be the case with Barcelona and Thomas.

[42] Ibid., 6–7.
[43] Johnson, *Liturgy in Early Christian Egypt*, 32.

Gabriele Winkler

Chapter 12

Attempto: Rethinking the Question of Summaries

Just a few miles away from the pretty medieval buildings of Tuebingen, nestled among hills and rocky slopes, lies the picturesque town of Bad Urach. The impressive castle located in the center of medieval Bad Urach once belonged to the Count of Wuerttemberg, later its first duke, who founded the University of Tuebingen in 1477 under the motto *Attempto*. This remains the university's motto to the present day. For good reason, *Attempto* is invoked as a leitmotiv for this paper.

1. Maxwell Johnson is cherished by many of us not only as a dear and appreciated colleague but also for his broad discussions of a variety of liturgical subjects. Moreover, he should be commended for his many endeavors to utilize German-language studies within his investigations—a practice infrequently witnessed in the United States (and beyond).[1] Additionally, he has encouraged his students to read studies written in German. Thus, his students not only are required to familiarize themselves with the complicated issues and discussions concerning the various liturgical traditions of the Christian East but also have to deal with these difficult topics by studying the various contributions in a language other than their own.

2. Over the years, some of us working in German-speaking countries and publishing our findings in that language have become increasingly concerned that English summaries of German-language

[1] See, for example, the necessary critique of John R. K. Fenwick, *The Anaphoras of St. Basil and St. James: An Investigation into Their Common Origin*, Orientalia Chr. Analecta 240 (Rome: Pontificium Institutum Orientale, 1992), in my review of that work in *Oriens Christianus* 78 (1994): 269–77. Fenwick had not only misunderstood the fundamental conclusions of Hieronymus Engberding's study (written in German) but suggested ameliorations of Engberding's research methods and conclusions (for Engberding's pioneering and groundbreaking study, see note 7 below). In this context also another massive study of some good 950 pages has to be mentioned: Everett Ferguson, *Baptism in the Early Church: History, Theology, and Liturgy in the First Five Centuries* (Grand Rapids, MI/Cambridge: William B. Erdman, 2009), reviewed in *Zeitschrift für Kirchengeschichte*, forthcoming.

studies circulate widely regardless of whether they accurately reflect the discussions and conclusions of these original investigations. It seems to me that this fact requires some attention. In general, summaries should accurately reflect the detailed discussions contained within their sources. But once we realize the momentous repercussions that such inaccurate summaries have on the scholarly community as a whole, the task becomes all the more urgent. Namely, a good many scholars unfamiliar with German depend on what is said in these summaries, and in taking over the alleged conclusions as fact, they implicitly perpetuate these misunderstandings and misrepresentations. Sometimes these summaries are even accompanied by bold assessments of the quality of research (see *inter alia* John Fenwick's inappropriate critique of Hieronymus Engberding).

3. Given the noticeable problems in connection with recent summaries and discussions of research written in German by several different scholars, I have decided to summarize some of the observations and conclusions from my own book-length investigation of the Anaphora of Basil.[2] For this paper I have focused on the Epiclesis in the various versions of the Anaphora of Basil as well as partially including the Institution Narrative (as its central vocabulary is dependent on the Epiclesis).[3] I spoke about this theme at the 2007 Moscow Conference, which was subsequently published in Russian in the *Acta* of this conference under the following heading: "The Epiclesis and Institution Narrative of the Anaphora of Basil: Some Philological Considerations Concerning Their Evolution and Theological Meaning."[4] Since Russian belongs, even less than German, to those languages used in Western scholarship, I herewith thank Michael Zheltov, the organizer of the memorable Moscow Conference, for giving me permission to publish my paper now in the original English language.

[2] Gabriele Winkler, *Die Basilius-Anaphora. Edition der beiden armenischen Redaktionen und der relevanten Fragmente, Übersetzung und Zusammenschau aller Versionen im Licht der orientalischen Überlieferungen*, Anaphorae Orientales 2, Anaphorae Armeniacae 2 (Rome: Pontificio Istituto Orientale, 2005).

[3] Ibid., 753–830; see in addition the vocabulary of the various versions of the Anaphora of James: Gabriele Winkler, "Preliminary Observations about the Relationship between the Liturgies of St. Basil and St. James," *Orientalia Chr. Periodica* 76 (2010): 5–55, here 28–40.

[4] I also want to take this opportunity to thank Michael Zheltov for his Russian translation of my paper, published in *Orthodox Teaching on the Sacraments of the Church: The Acts of 5th International Theological Conference of the Russian Orthodox Church (Moscow, 13–16 November 2007)*, vol. 1 (Moscow, 2009 in Russian), 382–99.

Among those familiar with the Eastern anaphoral tradition, it is well known that the Anaphora of Basil took center stage for many centuries, not only in the Byzantine and Armenian Rites, but also in other eucharistic traditions such as the Alexandrian Rite. Only at the turn of the tenth to eleventh century did the Anaphora of Chrysostom supplant the Anaphora of Basil in significance within the Byzantine tradition,[5] taking over first place from the Anaphora of Basil as the principal liturgy, just as the Anaphora of Athanasius assumed priority over the Anaphora of Basil in the Armenian Rite from the ninth to tenth century onward.[6]

Thus, as its central position in the Antiochene *and* Alexandrian liturgical tradition clearly demonstrates, the Anaphora of Basil is one of the most important Eucharistic Prayers of all Christendom. Likewise, the fact that the Anaphora of Basil has come down to us in virtually all languages of the Christian East is indicative of its central place in the eucharistic tradition.

Introduction to the Editions and Studies of the Anaphora of Basil

It is also common knowledge among specialists that it was Engberding who first established the prominence of the four most important versions of this Anaphora in his groundbreaking study of 1931:[7]

[5] For a new assessment of the date, see the forthcoming important contribution of Michael Zheltov, "The Rite of the Eucharistic Liturgy in the Oldest Russian Leitourgika (13th–14th centuries)" in *Inquiries into Eastern Christian Worship: Selected Papers of the Second International Congress of the Society of Oriental Liturgies, Rome, 17–21 September 2008*, ed. Basilius J. Groen, Stephen Hawkes Teeples, and Stefanos Alexopoulos (Leuven: Peeters, 2012), 293–309.

[6] For the hitherto held position with regard to the date of the shift in the Byzantine tradition, see Robert F. Taft, *The Great Entrance: A History of the Transfer of Gifts and Other Preanaphoral Rites of the Liturgy of St. John Chrysostom*, Orientalia Chr. Analecta 200, 2nd ed. (Rome: Pontificio Istituto Orientale, 1994), xxxii; for the Armenian tradition, see Hans-Jürgen Feulner, *Die armenische Athanasius-Anaphora. Kritische Edition, Übersetzung und liturgievergleichender Kommentar*, Anaphorae Orientales 1, Anaphorae Armeniacae 1 (Rome: Pontificio Istituto Orientale, 2001), 79; Gabriele Winkler, "On the Formation of the Armenian Anaphoras: A Completely Revised and Updated Overview," *Studi sull'Oriente Cristiano* 11, no. 2 (2007): 97–130, here 121–22 with n. 136.

[7] Hieronymus Engberding, *Das Eucharistische Hochgebet der Basileiosliturgie. Textgeschichtliche Untersuchung und kritische Ausgabe*, Theologie des Christlichen Ostens. Texte und Untersuchungen (Münster: Aschendorff, 1931): LXXXVII; for an overview and assessment of Engberding's major pioneering study, see Winkler, *Die Basilius-Anaphora*, 9–21.

1. the *short* Egyptian Anaphora of Basil (in Greek, Coptic, Ethiopic)
2. the *longer* redaction based on a lost archetype Ω, from which the first Armenian version emerged
3. the lost archetype Ψ, also dependent on Ω, from which the Syriac redaction derives
4. the Byzantine version, also derived from Ψ, which, according to Engberding, is one of the youngest redactions

Since then, the Anaphora of Basil has become the focus of various significant new editions and major monographs:

1. The *short* Egyptian Basil (extant in Greek, Coptic, and Ethiopic) was the main focus of an extensive and highly interesting study by Achim Budde. His investigation, based on the extant Greek and Coptic manuscripts, appeared in 2004.[8]
2. The *longer* redaction of Ω has survived in two Armenian redactions published partially by Erich Renhart[9] and entirely by Gabriele Winkler.[10]

[8] Achim Budde, *Die ägyptische Basilius-Anaphora. Text – Kommentar – Geschichte*, Jerusalemer Theologisches Forum 7 (Münster: Aschendorff, 2004); for a detailed review, see *Oriens Christianus* 89 (2005): 264–75; eadem, *Die Basilius-Anaphora*, 30–37. For the Sahidic version, see Jean Doresse and Emmanuel Lanne, "Un témion archaïque de la liturgie copte de S. Basile. En annexe: les liturgies 'basiliennes et saint Basile' par B. Capelle," *Bibliothèque du Muséon* 47 (Leuven: Peeters, 1960): 10–75; for the Ethiopic version, see Sebastian Euringer, "Die äthiopische Anaphora des hl. Basilius nach vier Handschriften herausgegeben, übersetzt und mit Anmerkungen versehen," *Orientalia Christiana* 36, no. 98 (1934): 135–223.

[9] In 2001 Erich Renhart published an edition of the older Armenian version (surprisingly based on the Codex of Lyons instead of the better Munich Codex) accompanied by a German translation without any commentary: Erich Renhart, "Die älteste armenische Anaphora. Einleitung, kritische Edition des Textes und Übersetzung," in *Armenische Liturgien. Ein Blick auf eine ferne christliche Kultur*, ed. Erich Renhart and Jasmine Dum Tragut, Heiliger Dienst, Ergänzungsband 2 (Graz/Salzburg: Schnider, 2001), 93–241. For a review of Renhart's publication, see Winkler, *Die Basilius-Anaphora*, 25–27.

[10] Renhart's publication became then superseded in 2005 by the edition and translation of both Armenian redactions, including the pertinent fragments of the Anaphora of Basil, combined with a comprehensive commentary on the basis of the most important versions of the Anaphora of Basil: see Winkler, *Die Basilius-Anaphora*: Foreword (v–viii); Table of Content (ix–xxiv); Bibliography (xxv–lx); Status Quaestionis (1–37); Methodology (38–52); Overview on the Extant Armenian Manuscripts and Fragments (53–132); Edition and Translation of the First

3. With regard to the versions of Ψ in Syriac and Byzantine Greek, a critical edition of the oldest Greek manuscript (*Barb. gr. 336*, eighth century) was provided by Stefano Parenti and Elena Velkovska in 2000.[11] The Syriac version still awaits further scrutiny; so far we remain dependent on the Syriac edition by Ignatius Rahmani.[12] (For the Georgian redaction dependent on the Byzantine recension, we have a preliminary assessment by Nino K'aǰaia on the basis of the Georgian manuscripts.[13])

After my 2005 edition of the extant Armenian evidence and an extensive investigation of the most important versions of the Anaphora of Basil, I have turned my attention to particular problems of this Anaphora,[14] publishing them predominantly in English.

Armenian Redaction (135–97); Edition and Translation of the Second Armenian Redaction (199–275); Comprehensive Commentary (277–861); Summaries (862–82); Indices (885–901).

[11] Stefano Parenti and Elena Velkovska, eds., *L'Eucologio Barberini gr. 336*, BELS 80, 2nd ed. (Rome: Edizioni Liturgiche, 2000).

[12] Ignatius E. Rahmani, *Missale iuxta Ritum Ecclesiae Apostolicae Antiochenae Syrorum* (Sharfé: Typis patriarchalibus in Seminario Sciarfensi de Monte Libano, 1922).

[13] Nino K'aǰaia, *Basili Kesarielis t'xzulebat 'a jveli k'art'uli t'argmanebi* [= The Old-Georgian translations of the works of Basil of Caesarea] (Tbilisi: Mec'niereba, 1992).

[14] For the investigation of the *Sancta sanctis*, see now Gabriele Winkler, *Die armenische Liturgie des Sahak. Edition des Cod. arm. 17 von Lyon, Übersetzung und Vergleich mit der armenischen Basilius-Anaphora*, Anaphorae Orientales 3, Anaphorae Armeniacae 3 (Rome: Pontificio Istituto Orientale, 2011); eadem, "The Precommunion Rites and the Problem of the *Sancta Sanctis* in the Various Redactions of the Liturgy of Basil and Other Traditions," *Orientalia Chr. Analecta* (forthcoming); for other problems, see eadem, "Which Is Older: The *Short* Egyptian Redaction of the Anaphora of Basil or the *Longer* Armenian, Syriac, and Byzantine Text" (Paper read at the first SOL-Conference held in Eichstätt, subsequently published in German): "Fragen zur zeitlichen Priorität der ägyptischen Textgestalt gegenüber den längeren Versionen der Basilius-Anaphora," in *Acts of the First International Congress of the Society for Oriental Liturgies* [= *Bollettino della Badia Greca di Grottaferrata* 3, no. 4 (2007)]: 243–73; eadem, "Unsolved Problems Concerning the Background and Significance of the Vocabulary of Praise in Some of the Oldest Eucharistic Prayers," in Groen, Hawkes Teeples, and Alexopoulos, eds., *Inquiries into Eastern Christian Worship*, 135–72; eadem, "Preliminary Observations about the Relationship between the Liturgies of St. Basil and St. James," 5–55 (as in n. 3 above); eadem, "The Antiochene Synods and the Early Armenian Creeds Including the '*Rezeptionsgeschichte*' of the Synod of Antioch 341 in the Armenian Version of the Anaphora of Basil," *Bollettino della Badia Greca di Grottaferrata* 3, no. 3 (2006): 275–98; eadem, "Armenia's Liturgy at the Crossroads of Neighbouring Churches," *Orientalia Chr. Periodica* 74 (2008): 363–87; eadem, "On the Formation of the Armenian Anaphoras: A Completely

The Evolution of the Epiclesis in the Anaphora of Basil[15]

This study of the Epiclesis of this Anaphora is based on my analysis of the most important redactions of the Anaphora of Basil, namely, the Egyptian[16] and both Armenian versions,[17] including the Byzantine Greek text.[18]

Revised and Updated Overview," 97–130 (as in n. 6 above); eadem, "L'anamnèse dans les diverses versions de l'anaphore de St. Basile: leur liens avec le symbole d'Antioche et leur signification théologique," in *"Faire mémoire": l'anamnèse dans la liturgie: conférences Saint-Serge, LVIe Semaine d'études liturgiques, Paris, 29 juin–2 juillet 2009*, ed. André Lossky and Manlio Sodi (Città del Vaticano: Libreria Editrice Vaticana, 2011), 149–61; eadem, "Über das christliche Erbe Henochs und einige Probleme des Testamentum Domini," *Oriens Christianus* 93 (2009): 201–47.

[15] For the general study of the Epiclesis, two investigations of Sebastian P. Brock should be singled out: "Invocations to/for the Holy Spirit in Syriac Liturgical Texts: Some Comparative Approaches," in *Acts of the International Congress Comparative Liturgy Fifty Years after Anton Baumstark (1872–1948), Rome, 25–29 September 1998*, ed. Robert F. Taft and Gabriele Winkler, Orientalia Chr. Analecta 265 (Rome: Pontificio Istituto Orientale, 2001), 377–406; and "Towards a Typology of the Epicleses in the West Syrian Traditions," in *Crossroad of Cultures: Studies in Liturgy and Patristics in Honor of Gabriele Winkler*, ed. Hans-Jürgen Feulner, Elena Velkovska, and Robert F. Taft, Orientalia Chr. Analecta 260 (Rome: Pontificio Istituto Orientale, 2000), 173–92; for the Anaphora of Basil in its various redactions, see Winkler, *Basilius-Anaphora*, 753–830: part 1: The κατὰ πάντα and the praise of God by the people, with which the Epiclesis begins (pp. 753–74); part 2: The Epiclesis proper (pp. 775–836): Presentation of the text of the various redactions (pp. 777–87); Overview on the central verbs (pp. 778–89); Analysis of the Epiclesis: the transition to the Invocation of the Holy Spirit (pp. 790–92); The nucleus of the Epiclesis: The Verbs of Sanctification and their background (pp. 793–804); The Interpolation of the Consecratory Verb 'to make' (pp. 805–7); The Verb ἐλθεῖν combined with the Verbs of Sanctification and their background (pp. 809–17); the Verb '*to send*' in the older Armenian and Ethiopic witness and its background (pp. 818–22); The addressee of the Epiclesis in the Anaphora of Basil (pp. 822–26); The fruits of the Epiclesis (pp. 827–30).

[16] For the Egyptian tradition, see Budde, *Die ägyptische Basilius-Anaphora*, 378–430. For a comparative study of the most important versions, see Winkler, *Die Basilius-Anaphora*, 753–830, in particular 775–830.

[17] Winkler, *Die Basilius-Anaphora*, 783–85, 788–89, 795, 797–99, 801–4, 809–10, 817–19, 821–22, 829.

[18] For an overview of the pertinent texts, see Winkler, *Die Basilius-Anaphora*, 777–78 (= *Sahidic text* according to Doresse and Lanne, 20, 22); 779–80 (= *Egyptian Greek text* according to W. F. Macomber, "The Greek Text of the Coptic Mass and of the Anaphoras of Basil and Gregory according to the Kacmarcik Codex," *Orientalia Chr. Periodica* 43 [1977]: 323–24; Eusèbe Renaudot, *Liturgiarum Orientalium Collectio* I, 2nd ed. [Frankfurt/London: Joseph Baer, 1847, photomech. reprint: Farnborough: Gregg, 1970], 67–68 [Budde, *Die ägyptische Basilius-Anaphora*, 160,162, 164]); 781–82 (= *Bohairic text* according to Tukhi, 114–16 [Budde, *op. cit.*, 161, 163, 165]); 783–85

The Epiclesis of the Anaphora of Basil, introduced by the petition "we implore [δεόμεθα] you,"[19] consists of several building blocks:[20]

1. the *Petition* (addressed to whom?) for the invocation of the Holy Spirit *"to come"* (ἐλθεῖν)[21] first upon the people (!) and then also upon the gifts of bread and wine
2. the *Reason* why the Holy Spirit should come, consisting of two groups of verbs:
   (1) The verbs of *Sanctification*: εὐλογῆσαι, ἁγιάσαι, ἀναδεῖξαι (with varying combinations);[22] the term ἀναδεῖξαι requires special attention (see below)
   (2) The verb of *Consecration*: "to make" (in the grammatical form of ποιήσῃ)[23]
3. the *Fruits* of the Epiclesis: (1) the remission of sins and life eternal because of having received the gifts of bread and wine, serving as a transition to (2) eschatological outlook: the partaking in the life of the saints (transition to the Intercessions).

The term ἀναδεῖξαι has to be analyzed in connection with its context:

(i) it is imbedded in the verb(s) of *Sanctification*

(ii) it is concatenated with ἅγια ἁγίων in the oldest text:[24]

(= *Armenian text*, both versions), 786–87 (= *Byzantine Greek text* according to the edition of *Codex Sevastianov* 474 by Stephan Josef Koster, *Das Euchologion Sevastianov 474 [X/XI Jhdt.] der Staatsbibliothek in Moskau*, Excerpta ex Dissertatione ad Doctoratum, Pont. Institutum Orient. Stud., Sectio Liturgica [Rome: Pontificio Istituto Orientale, 1996], 54).

[19] For this petition, which *introduces* the Epiclesis, see Winkler, *Die Basilius-Anaphora*, 753–57, 775, 791–92.

[20] Ibid., 775, 793–94.

[21] Two versions, namely, arm Bas I + Ethiop Bas, deviate from the genuine tradition of Bas with the imperative: "send!"; see ibid., 818–22.

[22] The *verbs of sanctification*: Egypt Bas: ἁγιάσαι–ἀναδεῖξαι (= typical for Egypt); byz Bas + arm Bas II have: εὐλογῆσαι–ἁγιάσαι (= typical for the Syriac tradition); both versions add to this pair of verbs ἀναδεῖξαι seemingly deriving from Egypt Bas; in arm Bas I the verbs of *sanctification* are missing = secondary manipulation. For the entire evidence, see ibid., 788–89.

[23] The *verb of consecration* (ποιήσῃ) is still missing in sah Bas (= oldest form of Egypt Bas) and byz Bas (= in this context oldest form of Ω). For the entire evidence, see ibid., 788–89.

[24] Ibid., 794–96.

Egypt Bas has: καὶ ἁγιάσαι καὶ ἀναδεῖξαι ἅγια ἁγίων (= original place of ἅγια ἁγίων); in the secondary Byz Bas + Arm Bas II, the ἅγια ἁγίων is *not* combined with ἀναδεῖξαι but is used as an address at the beginning of the Epiclesis: καὶ σε παρακαλοῦμεν ἅγιε (!) ἁγίων . . .

Observations:

My observations are centered *first* on the various building blocks of the Epiclesis, *second* on the central verbs of Sanctification in the Epiclesis and their Syriac parallels, and *third* on the meaning of the verb ἀναδεῖξαι, typical of the Egyptian tradition.

1. The Epiclesis of the Anaphora of Basil consists of various building blocks deriving from different regional traditions. Not all of them belong to the genuine tradition of the Anaphora of Basil.[25]
2. The Epiclesis seemingly consists above all of two larger sections:

   (1) An *older* layer:

   ἐλθεῖν ("to come") *combined with the verbs of Sanctification*:

   either: εὐλογῆσαι – ἁγιάσαι (= typical of the Syriac tradition[26])

   or: ἁγιάσαι – ἀναδεῖξαι (= typical for Egypt[27]);

   the transition to the Intercessions also pertains to the original layer. (At this transition also the scene of Jesus' baptism in the Jordan is invoked; cf. the presence of εὐδοκία![28]) There are signs which suggest that *this older section was once possibly addressed to the Son*.[29]

   (2) A *later* stage:

   the interpolation of the verb of Consecration, "to make" (in the grammatical form of ποιήσῃ), deriving probably from Jerusalem;[30]

[25] Ibid., 793–94.

[26] See Brock, "Invocations" (as n. 15 above), 390–91; and Winkler, *Die Basilius-Anaphora*, 788, 799–801, 803.

[27] Winkler, *Die Basilius-Anaphora*, 778, 794–99.

[28] See, for example, the wording of arm Bas II: "we . . . implore you, Holy [One] of the Holy [Ones] (*surb srboc'*), for your Holy Spirit to come in your benevolence (= εὐδοκία)"; ibid., 244/45, 783, 824; or byz Bas: . . . καὶ σὲ παρακαλοῦμεν, ἅγιε ἁγίων, εὐδοκίᾳ τῆς σῆς ἀγαθότητος, ἐλθεῖν τό πνεῦμα σου τό ἅγιον, see ibid., 786. For the evocation of Jesus' baptism see, 822–25.

[29] Ibid., 822–26.

[30] Ibid., 779 note 6, 789, 805–7.

moreover, in addition the fruits of the Epiclesis (first part only), namely, the remission of sins and life everlasting. *This section is addressed to the Father*.[31]

Behind the first part of the Epiclesis, namely, the older layer, seemingly lies a common tradition, shared by the Anaphora of Basil, plus the East Syrian Anaphora of Nestorius *and* the East Syrian Anaphora of Addai and Mari. They have apparently a common root consisting of the invitatory verb ἐλθεῖν ("to come") *combined with the verb-pair of Sanctification*: εὐλογῆσαι–ἁγιάσαι ("bless–sanctify").[32]

The verbs of the Epiclesis in the East Syrian Anaphoras (and *Sharrar*) comprise:

I. the verb *"to come,"* to which later on one or two other verbs (*"to rest" / "to dwell"*) were added;

II. the *verb-pair of Sanctification*: *"bless–sanctify"* (still absent in *Sharrar* [= syr Pet III][33]);

III. the *verb of Consecration*: *"to make,"* present in the Anaphora of Nestorius,[34] yet *still absent in* Addai and Mari (since there is no Institution Narrative)[35] and in *Sharrar* (= syr Pet III).[36]

Here is an overview of the verbs in the Epiclesis of the Anaphora of Basil, comparing them to the East Syrian Anaphora of Addai and Mari, the Maronite Anaphora *Sharrar* (= syr Pet III) and the East Syrian

[31] Ibid., 822–26.

[32] Ibid., 799–801, 812–13.

[33] Josephus-Maria Sauget, *Anaphora syriaca sancti Petri Apostoli III*, Anaphorae Syriacae II/3; Nr. XVIII (Rome: Pontificium Institutum Orientale, 1973), 273–323, here 308–9; Brock, "Invocations," 390–91, 401–2 (as n. 15 above); Winkler, *Die Basilius-Anaphora*, 802, 812–13.

[34] Sébastien Naduthadam, *L'Anaphore de Mar Nestorius. Edition critique et étude* (PhD dissertation, Institut Catholique, Paris, 1992), 224/269; Winkler, *Die Basilius-Anaphora*, 812–13.

[35] W. F. Macomber, "The Oldest Known Text of the Anaphora of the Apostles Addai and Mari," *Orientalia Chr. Periodica* 37 (1966): 335–71, here 368–69; Anthony Gelston, *The Eucharistic Prayer of Addai and Mari* (Oxford: Clarendon Press, 1992), 54–55; Winkler, *Die Basilius-Anaphora*, 812.

[36] Sauget, *Anaphora syriaca sancti Petri Apostoli III*, 308–9; Brock, "Invocations," 390–91, 401–2 (as n. 15 above); Winkler, *Die Basilius-Anaphora*, 802, 812–13.

Anaphora of Nestorius (syr Nest).[37] We begin with Addai and Mari and relate with it *Sharrar*, followed by syr Nest and Bas:

Addai and Mari	***Sharrar* (= syrPet III)**
I. *Invitatory Petition*: . . . and *may* your	. . . and *may* your
Holy Spirit	living and holy Spirit
come, Lord,	*come*
and be rested	and reside and be rested
upon this offering . . .	upon this offering . . .
II. *The Verb-Pair of Sanctification*: . . . and *bless* it *and sanctify* it	—
III. *The Consecratory Verb*: —	—

syr Nest	**Basilius-Anaphora**
I. *Invitatory Petition*: . . . and *may*	
the grace of the Spirit of Holiness	the Holy Spirit
Come	ἐλθεῖν ("*to come*")
and reside and be rested	—
upon this offering . . .	upon . . .
II. *The Verb-Pair of Sanctification*: and *bless* it *and sanctify* it	*bless* (εὐλογῆσαι) *and sanctify* (ἁγιάσαι) (+ ἀναδεῖξαι = byz Bas)[38]
III. *The Consecratory Verb*: *and make* . . .	*still missing in the oldest versions*: sah Bas + byz Bas[39]

[37] Brock, "Invocations," 390–91, 401–2 (as n. 15 above); Winkler, *Die Basilius-Anaphora*, 799–804, 814–15.

The overview demonstrates the remarkable congruency between the invitatory verb ἐλθεῖν ("to come") *combined with the verb-pair of Sanctification*: εὐλογῆσαι–ἁγιάσαι ("bless–sanctify") and the still-missing *Consecratory verb "to make"* in several Syrian Anaphoras and the oldest form of the Anaphora of Basil.[40] Both traditions have in common the following verbs (albeit in different grammatical forms):

ἐλθεῖν plus: εὐλογῆσαι – ἁγιάσαι ("bless – sanctify");

absence of the verb "to make" in *Sharrar* (syr Pet III) and the oldest versions of Bas.

With the evolution of the Epiclesis, both traditions then go different ways:

- The Syriac tradition expands the invitatory verbs (cf. I), namely, adding to the verb "come" one or two additional verbs ("to reside" / "to dwell");
- The Anaphora of Basil expands the verbs of Sanctification (II) with one or two verbs. In other words:

I. The Syriac evolution of the Epiclesis tends to expand the initial invitation of the Spirit "to come" by adding additional verbs, whereas the Epiclesis of the Anaphora of Basil remains restricted to the invitatory verb "come."

II. Concerning the verbs of *Sanctification*, the Syrians tend to leave the initial verb-pair "bless–sanctify" intact, whereas the Anaphora of Basil (e.g., byz Bas) has created a *combination* of:

- the verb-pair "bless–sanctify," deriving from the Syrian tradition, plus:
- ἀναδεῖξαι typical of the Egyptian tradition.

III. Moreover, there existed initially no *Consecratory* verb ("to make") in *both* traditions.

[38] The Armenian version (arm Bas II) has two additional verbs, in contrast to byz Bas (*Cod. Sevastianov 474*) with only one additional verb; see Winkler, *Die Basilius-Anaphora*, 786, 788, 798 (= byz Bas), 783, 788, 798–99 (= arm Bas II).

[39] In the oldest witnesses (here sah Bas + byz Bas) the verb "to make" in the grammatical form of ποιήσῃ) is still absent; Winkler, *Die Basilius-Anaphora*, 789, 798, 812–15.

[40] Ibid., 814–15.

3. We have to turn now to the meaning of ἀναδεῖξαι ἅγια ἁγίων in Egypt Bas.[41] Here we have to point out once more:

(1) that the verb ἀναδεῖξαι forms part of the verb(s) of *Sanctification*: καὶ ἁγιάσαι καὶ ἀναδεῖξαι ἅγια ἁγίων;

(2) that Egypt Bas presents the original place of the ἅγια ἁγίων, in contrast to byz Bas + arm Bas II, where the ἅγια ἁγίων is *not* combined with ἀναδεῖξαι, but is used as an address at the *beginning* of the Epiclesis: καὶ σὲ παρακαλοῦμεν ἅγιε (!) ἁγίων . . .

We have to remember that originally there existed *no verb of Consecration* (= the verb ποιήσῃ) in the Anaphora of Basil. Originally the Epiclesis was restricted to the invitation of the Holy Spirit "to come" (ἐλθεῖν) *upon both* the people and the gifts of bread and wine, so that *both*, the community and the gifts alike, may be "sanctified," as expressed by the verb-pair of *Sanctification*: εὐλογῆσαι–ἁγιάσαι ("bless–sanctify"). In the Egyptian tradition this apparently becomes, on the one hand, altered and, on the other, even more emphasized.

Once the Antiochene Anaphora of Basil was taken over in Egypt, the text was altered by seemingly dropping the verb εὐλογῆσαι ("bless") while adding (1) the verb ἀναδεῖξαι and (2) clarifying, moreover, the concept of Sanctification by joining the ἅγια ἁγίων to the verb ἀναδεῖξαι (which reminds us immediately of the "*Sancta sanctis*" before receiving Communion).[42] In the Egyptian Greek text the people

[41] Ibid., 794–96.

[42] For the "*Sancta sanctis*"–cycle, see Winkler, *Die armenische Liturgie des Sahak. Edition des Cod. arm. 17 von Lyon, Übersetzung und Vergleich mit der armenischen Basilius-Anaphora* (as n. 14 above) with the following detailed investigation of the "*Sancta sanctis*"–cycle in the various redactions of the Liturgy of Basil and the Liturgy of James: "Das Sancta sanctis und sein unmittelbares Umfeld; Einleitung: Die strukturellen Bestandteile des Sancta sanctis; 1. Die Proskynese; 2. Das Inklinations-Gebet des Priesters in der Basilius-Liturgie im Vergleich mit verwandten Texten und ihr Hintergrund: a. Die Oratio I (= Inklinations-Gebet): Δέσποτα Κύριε; b. Die Oratio II: Πρόσχες Κύριε; 3. Das Πρόσχωμεν im Kontext des Sancta sanctis: a. Der unterschiedliche strukturelle Ablauf zu Beginn; b. Der Hintergrund des Πρόσχωμεν und seine Bedeutung beim Sancta sanctis; Über die Bedeutung des Πρόσχωμεν beim Sancta sanctis und seine syrische und äthiopische Übersetzung; 4. Die Oratio Πρόσχες Κύριε und ihre Bedeutung als Elevations-Gebet: a. Die Rubriken; b. Die Aussagen in der Oratio Πρόσχες Κύριε: (1) Die Gemeinsamkeit mit einer zentralen Aussage der Oratio ante Sanctus; (2) Die Gemeinsamkeit mit

and the gifts of bread and wine are to be "sanctified" in such a way that they "show forth" / "make manifest" (ἀναδεῖξαι) this Sanctification: "showing forth" / "making manifest" the gifts of bread and wine *as "holy"* for those who have become equally "holy" *because of the coming of the Holy Spirit* upon them, in order "to sanctify" the gifts and the people alike.

This verb ἀναδεῖξαι surely belonged primarily to the Epiclesis where its function seems to embrace both aspects of the invocation: "showing forth" / "making manifest" (ἀναδεῖξαι) the holiness not only of the gifts of bread and wine *but of the people as well.*

This understanding of the Epiclesis should not remain in this pristine "fluidity." The further evolution of the Epiclesis went in two directions, and both have to do with the clarification of the concept of "Sanctification." First, the attention became restricted to the gifts, as in byz Bas: . . . καὶ *ἀναδεῖξαι τὸν μεν ἄρτον* τοῦτον αὐτὸ τὸ τίμιον σῶμα τοῦ κυρίου. This restriction to the gifts is still absent in sah Bas: there is no claim that bread (and wine) "should become manifest" (ἀναδεῖξαι) *as the "body" (and "blood") of the Lord.*[43]

And finally, even the *"Consecratory"* verb "to make" (in the grammatical form of ποιήσῃ) was added.

The Formation of the Institution Narrative[44]

Structurally, the Institution Narrative consists of (1) an Introduction (on the basis of John 6:51 and/or 1 Cor 11:23), (2) the Words of Bread and Wine, (3) ending with the Command to do as the Lord has done. I shall restrict myself here to the central part, namely, to the verbs introducing the formulations in connection with the gifts of bread and wine.

First, we shall look into the introduction to the Bread-Words and then into the Words connected with the Chalice.

zentralen Verben der Epiklese; 5. Überleitung zum Sancta sanctis; 6. Das Τὰ ἅγια τοῖς ἁγίοις und seine Übersetzungen: a. Die armenischen Übersetzungen; b. Anmerkungen zur syrischen und äthiopischen Übersetzung; 7. Die Antwort des Volkes auf das Sancta sanctis: a. Die christologische Formulierung; b. Die trinitarische Formulierung; c. Die aus Εἷς ἅγιος hervorgegangenen Zeugen"; etc.; eadem, "The Precommunion Rites and the Problem of the *Sancta Sanctis* in the Various Redactions of the Liturgy of Basil and Other Traditions."

[43] For the details, see Winkler, *Die Basilius-Anaphora*, 794–96.

[44] Ibid., 693–721.

1. The Introduction to the Bread-Words of the Lord[45]

The Bread-Words are inaugurated by the verb "he took" (ἔλαβεν) or "taking" (λαβών) followed by the central introductory verbs:

ἀναβλέψας (= Egypt Bas)[46] or ἀναδείξας (= all other versions), combined with:

[εὐχαριστήσας *still missing in the oldest witness*: sah Bas!—present in all other versions[47]]

εὐλογήσας + ἁγιάσας

ending with: "breaking" (κλάσας) and "he gave" (ἔδωκεν).

2. The Introduction to the Lord's Words in Connection with the Chalice[48]

The Words associated with the Chalice comprise:

["taking" (λαβών) is missing in Egypt Bas, present in all other versions in imitation of the inauguration of the Bread-Words[49]]

κεράσας (missing in the Armenian tradition[50])

combined with:

εὐχαριστήσας + εὐλογήσας (in arm Bas I inversion: "he blessed – he thanked"[51])

ἁγιάσας

ending with "he gave" (ἔδωκεν).[52]

Observations

1. Introductory Remarks:

(1) Egypt Bas offers in connection with the Bread-Words the verb ἀναβλέψας ("looking up"),[53] whereas all the longer versions of the Anaphora of Basil have ἀναδείξας.

[45] Ibid., 699.

[46] In sah Bas this verb is still missing; ibid., 699 with note 17, 701.

[47] Ibid., 699 with note 20.

[48] Ibid., 700 (arm Bas II deviates here from the genuine tradition of the Anaphora of Basil).

[49] Ibid.

[50] Ibid. (with details concerning the manuscripts in note 24).

[51] Ibid.

[52] The Egyptian version (+ syr Bas) have added γευσάμενος before ἔδωκεν; ibid.

[53] The verb is missing in sah Bas; see ibid., 699.

Interestingly enough, the verb ἀναδείξας is still missing in the oldest witness, sah Bas![54] This verb seemingly belongs not to the Institution Narrative but to the Epiclesis from where it was taken over.[55] (For ἀναδείξας and its context, see my comments in connection with the Epiclesis.)

(2) The central verbs in both the introduction to the Bread-Words plus those for the Chalice comprise:

εὐχαριστήσας

εὐλογήσας + ἁγιάσας

The latter two verbs εὐλογήσας + ἁγιάσας occur as well in the Epiclesis, as we have seen. But we have to investigate the matter in greater detail before drawing any conclusions.

2. Analysis of the Bread-Words and Their Syriac Parallels

(1) We have to begin with the New Testament and remember the well-known fact that the oldest gospel is the Gospel of Mark and that the Gospel of Matthew has Aramaic traits. Now, both of these gospel texts make a clear distinction between the verb for the bread and for the wine (Mark 14:22-23; Matt 26:26-27):

– the bread is *blessed* (εὐλογήσας) [plus ἔκλασεν / "he broke"]

– for the wine, *thanks is given* (εὐχαριστήσας [so also *syr* Matt 26:26-27]).

Turning, however, to John 6:11, the *Greek* text says: Jesus took the bread "and *gave thanks* (καὶ εὐχαριστήσας)," whereas the *Syriac* text (both: Vet Syr + Pesh) still has "and *blessed* it." The same is true for 1 Corinthians 11:24: the Greek version has "he took the bread and *gave thanks* (εὐχαριστήσας); Pesh, however, says "and *blessed it*."[56]

This shows that the Syriac tradition made a clear distinction between the "*blessing*" of the bread, while "*giving thanks*" for the wine.[57]

(2) Moreover, the Syrians preserved this distinction in their Anaphoras as, for example, the Maronite *Sharrar* (= syr Pet III) and the East Syrian Anaphora of Theodore (syr TheoMop) demonstrate: the verb "*he blessed*" is used *for the bread*, and "*he gave thanks*" *for the*

[54] Ibid., with note 17.

[55] Ibid., 701.

[56] Ibid., 702–3.

[57] Ibid.

wine.[58] Also, the oldest witness of the Anaphora of Basil seemingly knew that the bread was blessed, *not given thanks* for it: the verb εὐχαριστήσας is still missing in sah Bas, the oldest witness.

Another fact is indicative as well. The position of the verb εὐχαριστήσας varies once it is present: the norm is εὐχαριστήσας–εὐλογήσας (in that order). Arm Bas I provides the exception: in arm Bas I we observe an inversion of these verbs: "he blessed–he thanked."[59] Given the facts (i) that in the oldest witness of the Anaphora of Basil εὐχαριστήσας is still missing in connection with the Bread-Words and (ii) that, once the verb is attested, it is interpolated before (= the norm) *or* after εὐλογήσας (= rare), it may hypothetically be suggested that the *Urtext* had no εὐχαριστήσας in connection with the introduction to the Bread-Words.

(3) The verb-*pair*: εὐλογήσας–ἁγιάσας (persistently in that order) belongs *primarily* to the Epiclesis and via the influence of the Epiclesis it became introduced to the Institution Narrative as well.

In this connection the Institution Narrative in arm Bas I is of greatest interest, for arm Bas I has only *"he blessed"* (to which the secondary verb "he thanked" was added) while the verb "he sanctified [ἁγιάσας]" is still missing! This allows the conclusion that the *primary* verb in the Institution Narrative, attested in *all* versions of the Anaphora of Basil in connection with the bread, is *"he blessed* [εὐλογήσας]," not the verb-pair εὐλογήσας–ἁγιάσας, which was taken over from the Epiclesis (or: εὐλογήσας–εὐχαριστήσας [only in arm Bas I]).

The evident conclusion that the *primary* verb in connection with the bread in the Anaphora of Basil is *"he blessed* [εὐλογήσας]" corresponds with the early Syriac tradition where the verb associated with the bread is exclusively "he blessed" (and not "he thanked") as, for example, in syr Pet III (= *Sharrar*) or syr TheoMop.

3. Analysis of the Words in Connection with the Chalice

(1) The Armenian versions have deliberately purged any reference to the mixing (κεράσας) of the wine with water, so that the text of the Anaphora reflects their tradition.

(2) The presence of the verb-pair εὐλογήσας–ἁγιάσας is due to the influence of the Epiclesis, where this verb-pair has its original *Sitz im Leben*.

[58] Sauget, *Anaphora syriaca sancti Petri Apostoli III*, 300 [= text], 301 [= trans.] (as in n. 33 above); Winkler, *Die Basilius-Anaphora*, 703–4.

[59] Winkler, *Die Basilius-Anaphora*, 700.

(3) The additional verb of "tasting" (γευσάμενος), present in Egypt Bas + syr Bas, is a secondary element, which was introduced in order to form an exact symmetry with the verb "breaking" (κλάσας) of the bread. (The actual Words of the Lord over bread and wine were predominantly taken from Matt 26:26-28 [including some expressions from Luke 21:19-20 + 1 Cor 11:24-25]).

4. Summary[60]

It can hypothetically be surmised that whoever compiled the original text of the Institution Narrative of the Anaphora of Basil may have been fully aware that with the bread only the "blessing" was associated and that "giving thanks" was restricted to the wine. Hence we can draw the following hypothetical conclusions concerning the evolution of the introduction to the Institution Narrative proper:

(1) With regard to the Bread: The verb "he took" (ἔλαβεν) or "taking" (λαβών) inaugurates the text, followed by:

(i) *primarily* εὐλογήσας to which ἁγιάσας was appended due to the influence of the Epiclesis, for which the verb-pair εὐλογῆσαι–ἁγιάσαι ("bless–sanctify") is normative.

The verb εὐχαριστήσας is an interpolation due to the formation of symmetry with the words connected with the Wine.

(ii) "breaking" (κλάσας) of the bread.

(iii) "he gave" (ἔδωκεν).

Traces of the oldest layers are still detectable in sah Bas, where the εὐχαριστήσας is still missing (!), and arm Bas I, where the ἁγιάσας is still absent!

(2) With regard to the Chalice: The verb "taking" (λαβών) is seemingly secondary due to the formation of symmetry with the Bread-Words. The initial "mixing" (κεράσας) was followed by:

(i) *primarily* εὐχαριστήσας, then expanded to εὐλογήσας – ἁγιάσας in order to form a symmetry with the Bread-Words.

(ii) "he gave" (ἔδωκεν).

If we prescind from the secondary purgation of the verb "mixing" (κεράσας) in arm Bas I, then arm Bas I seemingly, in this context, has kept closest to the original text of Bas.

[60] Ibid., 719–21.

Theological Considerations Concerning the Institution Narrative Proper and the Epiclesis

The function and meaning of the Words of Institution in the Anaphora of Basil are still "narrative," that is to say, the Words are not "consecratory" in meaning: the story of the Institution is told without it being a consecratory formula.

Moreover, the emphasis lies rather on the Epiclesis. But here again, caution is required. The original text of the Anaphora of Basil did not contain the *Consecratory* verb "to make" but was restricted to the verb-pair of *Sanctification*, εὐλογῆσαι–ἁγιάσαι ("bless–sanctify").

The Egyptian version seemingly altered the shape of the Epiclesis in the Anaphora of Basil once they took over this *Antiochene* Eucharistic Prayer (as they also did with other sections of the Anaphora). It was in particular the concept of Sanctification that they apparently reshaped and sought to clarify by adding the verb ἀναδεῖξαι (while seemingly dropping the verb εὐλογῆσαι) and joining, moreover, the ἅγια ἁγίων to the verb ἀναδεῖξαι.

The Byzantine Greek text went even a step further in clarifying that the verb ἀναδεῖξαι is now restricted to the gifts of bread and wine: the coming of the Holy Spirit serves as a manifestation for the gifts of bread and wine *as the body and blood* of the Lord: bread and wine "are made manifest" (ἀναδεῖξαι) *as the body and blood* of the Lord. This is not the case in the Egyptian Greek text: here, the Spirit is asked to come, so that he "sanctifies" both the people and the gifts alike, "making" their holiness "manifest" (ἀναδεῖξαι).

At the end of the process, the Consecratory verb "to make" (the bread and wine the body and blood of Christ) is finally interpolated into the Epiclesis.

Given the difficulties that many have with publications in German, I want to mention briefly as well that I have myself written several summaries while including the ongoing discussion. All the Praise-Verbs have now been systematically collected and analyzed in the respective original languages: (1) the Praise-Verbs in connection with the *Sanctus and* the Epiclesis of all the versions of Basil, including the evidence in Addai and Mari, were originally investigated and discussed (in German) in my study: *Die Basilius-Anaphora*, 419–51 (= before the *Sanctus*), 753–74 (= before the Epiclesis); (2) an English summary of the research with an expansion of the analysis to other early eucharistic prayers has been recently published;[61] (3) the systematic inclusion of the Praise-Verbs before the *Sanctus* in the extant versions of the Anaphora of Basil *and* James was published recently in English;[62] (4) moreover, the study of the Praise-Verbs of the *ante Sanctus* in Basil, James, and in all the Ethiopic Anaphoras, including the evidence in Enoch and in the Testamentum Domini, has now come out (in German).[63]

In addition, a French summary of the analysis of the Anamnesis in the various versions of Basil, all of which reflect the formulae of the Antiochene creed of 341, will probably come out in 2012.[64]

A final remark concerning this survey may further clarify some aspects of this paper, which is headed by our university's motto, *Attempto*, for good reason: (1) Such a summary always entails simplifications of highly complicated issues and they are thereby *no substitute* for the detailed presentation of the evidence, either on the basis of the manuscripts themselves or critical editions thereof in the respective original languages, followed by an analysis and discussion. (2) A distinction ought to be made between observations and conclusions. (3) Some conclusions are hypothetical while others reflect the final assessment of the evidence.

"Rethinking the Question" of summaries under the motto of *Attempto* seemingly is a necessary exercise.

[61] Winkler, "Unsolved Problems Concerning the Background and Significance of the Vocabulary of Praise in Some of the Oldest Eucharistic Prayers" (as n. 14 above).

[62] Winkler, "Preliminary Observations about the Relationship between the Liturgies of St. Basil and St. James" (as n. 3 above), 18–27.

[63] Winkler, "Über das christliche Erbe Henochs und einige Probleme des Testamentum Domini" (as n. 14 above).

[64] Winkler, "L'anamnèse dans les diverses versions de l'anaphore de St. Basile: leur liens avec le symbole d'Antioche et leur signification théologique" (as n. 14 above).

Anne McGowan

Chapter 13

The Epiclesis in Eucharistic Praying Reconsidered: Early Evidence and Recent Western Reforms

The widespread "recovery" of the pneumatic epiclesis in contemporary Western eucharistic praying can be attributed to the combined influence of a number of factors, especially the confluence of liturgical, ecumenical, and pastoral concerns. Historical liturgical scholarship in particular played an important role during the first half of the twentieth century, even before a more general resurgence of interest in trinitarian theology in general and pneumatology in particular took hold in the latter half of the century. John R. K. Fenwick and Bryan D. Spinks credit the Liturgical Movement's interest in "renewal and rediscovery" at a pastoral level with influencing the trajectory of historical liturgical scholarship. While scholars of previous generations had long been interested in investigating the origins of liturgical rites, they typically refrained from using this knowledge to critique contemporary liturgical practice. As the influence of the Liturgical Movement grew in the early twentieth century, however, a "new type of scholarship began to emerge . . . scholarship that questioned the current practices."[1] Paul Bradshaw has suggested that historical research contributed to the perception "that some reference to the work of the Spirit had been a standard feature of early eucharistic prayers, and so needed to be

[1] John R. K. Fenwick and Bryan D. Spinks, *Worship in Transition: The Liturgical Movement in the Twentieth Century* (New York: Continuum, 1995), 30. For example, studies of early eucharistic prayers, such as the *Apostolic Tradition* (then generally thought to be a composition by Hippolytus of Rome from the early third century), led scholars to question why later Roman prayers had no comparable invocation of the Holy Spirit.

replicated in modern revisions that were attempting to get back to the historical roots of Christian liturgy."[2]

Although the location and language of the epicleses incorporated into Western eucharistic prayers during the last half century have varied, many of these pneumatic invocations on eucharistic bread, wine, and people were influenced at some stage of their development by early models (and often early *Eastern* models) of eucharistic praying. The unearthing of "new" sources (e.g., the *Didache* and the *Apostolic Tradition*) and the greater accessibility of critical editions of ancient texts made it much more possible than it had been in the sixteenth century to reform Christian worship in light of the perceived practices of the early church, the epiclesis among them. Contemporary scholarship on ancient liturgical texts in general and the epiclesis in particular during the past few decades, however, has since challenged some of the interpretations that grounded the formulations of the epicleses in contemporary Western eucharistic prayers. Recent studies have even, to some degree, called into question the function the framers of these new texts intended for the epicleses they contain. Thus, these epicletic prayer texts provide an interesting case study of the application of historical liturgical scholarship to contemporary pastoral practice. Three trends related to the modern use of ancient epicleses will be considered here as examples of this phenomenon: (1) the status of the "split epiclesis" in the early Alexandrian tradition of eucharistic praying and in recent Western reforms, (2) the dominance of the West Syrian or Antiochene "shape" of eucharistic praying that served to introduce a trinitarian pattern of prayer to Western churches (and often an epiclesis following the anamnesis), and (3) some noteworthy differences between ancient and modern "diversity" with regard to epicletic prayer patterns.

The Split Epiclesis: Reconsidering the Alexandrian Synthesis

Several modern anaphoras feature a "split epiclesis," typically consisting of a supplication for the Spirit's presence (and possible cooperation in the work of sanctifying the eucharistic bread and wine)

[2] Paul F. Bradshaw, "The Rediscovery of the Holy Spirit in Modern Eucharistic Theology and Practice," in *The Spirit in Worship—Worship in the Spirit*, ed. Teresa Berger and Bryan D. Spinks (Collegeville, MN: Liturgical Press, 2009), 91.

preceding the institution narrative and a further petition, often oriented toward the Spirit's role of realizing the fruits of communion in those who partake of the eucharistic bread and wine, after the anamnesis.[3] The principal employment of this structure is found in Roman Catholic eucharistic prayers composed since the conclusion of the Second Vatican Council; these prayers locate an explicit pneumatic consecratory epiclesis in a location equivalent to the Roman Canon's *Quam oblationem*.[4] The heritage of the Alexandrian tradition is often cited as precedent for this development. For example, Cipriano Vagaggini, an individual intimately involved with composing the new prayers that appeared in the *editio typica* of the Roman Missal promulgated in 1969,[5] commented on the structural parallels between early Egyptian prayers and the Roman Canon: "Dêr-Balizeh and the Louvain fragment separate the two ideas contained in an epiclesis, and put the prayer for consecration before the institution, and the prayer for a fruitful communion after the anamnesis, as is the practice of the Roman canon (*Quam oblationem; Supplices . . . ut quotquot*)."[6] Although a number of Egyptian anaphoras do contain epicletic petitions both before and after the institution narrative, a close examination of the early Egyptian evidence raises the question of whether the Alexandrian pattern can really serve to justify the modern epicleses that claim it as inspiration.

[3] This arrangement is also sometimes referred to as a "double epiclesis," emphasizing the fact that prayers of this type feature two distinct petitions for the Spirit's presence and activity in the eucharistic context. The term "split epiclesis," on the other hand, draws attention to the perception that the consecratory and communion aspects of the epiclesis are really two dimensions of a single reality, whether the invocations for consecration and communion are conjoined or separated in the prayer. Prime examples of "split epicleses" include those in the prayers of the Roman Catholic Church (in addition to the Roman Canon) and Eucharistic Prayers A and B of the Church of England's *Common Worship*.

[4] Although the Holy Spirit is not mentioned in the pre-institution portion of the English translation of Eucharistic Prayer for Masses with Children III, the Latin text on which the 1975 ICEL translation is based does reference the Spirit's action at this point in the prayer. Presumably, the revised English translation currently in preparation will resemble the Latin text more closely.

[5] For the role of Vagaggini in the reform of the Roman eucharistic prayers, see Annibale Bugnini, *The Reform of the Liturgy 1948–1975*, trans. Matthew J. O'Connell (Collegeville, MN: Liturgical Press, 1990), 450.

[6] Cipriano Vagaggini, *The Canon of the Mass and Liturgical Reform*, trans. Peter Coughlan (Staten Island, NY: Alba House, 1967), 69.

The primary problem here for the theory—based on historical evidence—is that early Egyptian texts do not contain *both* (1) a preliminary pneumatic epiclesis before the institution narrative oriented toward consecration of the gifts and (2) a subsequent invocation of the Spirit whose emphasis is communion.[7] While the Dêr Balyzeh Papyrus (ca. 500–700) does frame the connection between the *Sanctus* and the institution narrative as a consecratory epiclesis, nothing is known about the content of a "second" epiclesis in this document—or even if there was a second epiclesis at all.[8] The testimony of the Louvain Coptic Papyrus (ca. 600), which contains a portion of an anaphora extending from the conclusion of the *Sanctus* through the institution narrative, likewise is not complete enough to testify to a consecratory epiclesis preceding the institution narrative *and* a communion epiclesis following it.[9]

In a recent article, Michael Zheltov has drawn renewed attention to a fourth-century papyrus containing a complete anaphora and

[7] Some of the issues discussed below were previously raised by Aidan Kavanagh, "Thoughts on the New Eucharistic Prayers," *Worship* 43, no. 1 (1969): 5–6, 9–12; and Thomas J. Talley, "The Literary Structure of the Eucharistic Prayer," *Worship* 58, no. 5 (1984): 416–17.

[8] The post-*Sanctus* section of the Dêr Balyzeh fragment reads:

> Both fill us with the glory which comes from you, and deign to send your Holy Spirit upon these creatures, and make the bread the body of our Lord and Saviour Jesus Christ, and the cup the blood of the new covenant of our same Lord and God and Saviour Jesus Christ. . . .

There is a second mention of the Holy Spirit after the institution narrative that may have comprised part of an epiclesis, but the fragmentary nature of the manuscript evidence permits little clarity regarding either the content or function of this part of the prayer:

> . . . . and give to us your servants in the power of the Holy Spirit for the strengthening and increase of faith in the hope of eternal life to come.

Translation from Bridget Nichols and Alistair MacGregor, *The Eucharistic Epiclesis* (Durham: Ushaw College Library, 2001), 4–5. Unless otherwise indicated, all epicleses quoted in this essay are addressed to God (the Father), the first person of the Trinity.

[9] The text of the post-*Sanctus* epiclesis is: "We pray and beseech you to send out over them [i.e., this bread and this cup] your Holy Spirit, the Paraclete, from heaven . . . to make (?) the bread the body of Christ and the cup the blood of Christ of the new covenant." Translation from R. C. D. Jasper and G. J. Cuming, eds., *Prayers of the Eucharist: Early and Reformed*, 3rd ed. (Collegeville, MN: Liturgical Press, 1990), 81.

thanksgiving prayer that is an earlier Greek version of the prayer of the Louvain Papyrus. While this "Barcelona Papyrus" definitely does contain a consecratory epiclesis preceding the institution narrative, once again, the evidence for an explicitly pneumatic communion epiclesis following the narrative is lacking. The epiclesis prior to the institution narrative reads: "Through Him [Jesus Christ] we offer You these Your creations, the bread and the cup: we ask and beseech You to send onto them Your Holy and Comforter Spirit from Heaven, to represent them materially and to make the bread the Body of Christ and the cup the Blood of Christ, of the New Covenant."[10] After the anamnesis, there is a prayer for worthy communion that mentions "communion of the Holy Spirit" as one of the benefits of communion, but the epicletic petition itself is *not* framed as an invocation of the Spirit: "Even so, we pray to You, Master, that in blessing You will bless and in sanctifying sanctify . . . for all communicating from them for undivided faith, for communication of incorruption, for communion of the Holy Spirit, for perfection of belief and truth, for fulfillment of all Your will."[11]

Among the peculiarities Zheltov detects in this anaphora, two relate specifically to the epiclesis. The characteristic link between the *Sanctus* ("full are heaven and earth . . .") and the first epiclesis ("fill . . .") in the Alexandrian tradition is disrupted by a christological post-*Sanctus* section (a feature commonly found in Antiochene anaphoras), and the second epiclesis requests the sanctification of the communicants but not the gifts.[12] Furthermore, the petition of the first epiclesis is not "fill" at all but rather "send," a construction of the epiclesis not certainly attested in Egypt—or anywhere else—before the second half of the fourth century.[13] Drawing attention to this and other features of

[10] Michael Zheltov, "The Anaphora and the Thanksgiving Prayer from the Barcelona Papyrus: An Underestimated Testimony to the Anaphoral History in the Fourth Century," *Vigiliae Christianae* 62, no. 5 (2008): 490.

[11] Ibid., 491.

[12] Ibid., 494. Zheltov suggests the need, based on this anaphoral witness, to distinguish between *two* types of the Egyptian anaphora based on the content of the section between the *Sanctus* and the institution narrative: (1) *Sanctus* → Epiclesis → Institution narrative (represented, e.g., by the Anaphora of Mark); and (2) *Sanctus* → Post-*Sanctus* → Epiclesis → Institution narrative (as in the prayer of the Barcelona Papyrus).

[13] On the significance of the verbs used in the epiclesis, see Sebastian P. Brock, "The Epiklesis in the Antiochene Baptismal Ordines," *Symposium Syriacum 1972*, Orientalia Christiana Analecta 197 (Rome: Pontificium Institutum Studiorum Ori-

this anaphora whose Egyptian provenance is doubtful, Paul Bradshaw concludes that, together, "these differences suggest that the original nucleus of the prayer either was not composed in Egypt or alternatively represents a variant tradition there that was probably subject to some significant influence from elsewhere."[14]

Other Egyptian anaphoras do not lend much more support to a primitive Egyptian pattern resembling that of the split epiclesis found in current Western eucharistic prayers. Twentieth-century scholars viewed the Anaphora of Sarapion of Thmuis as something of an anomaly[15] and did not draw upon it specifically as a model for contemporary prayers. Nonetheless, considering the epicleses of this prayer does contribute to a portrayal of the Egyptian invocation that is much more complex than a classification of epicleses into the categories of "consecration" or "communion" can easily accommodate. In Sarapion's anaphora, there is a request in the post-*Sanctus* section that the Father "Fill also this sacrifice with your power and with your

---

entalium, 1974), 183–218; idem, "Towards a Typology of the Epicleses in the West Syrian Anaphoras," in *Crossroad of Cultures: Studies in Liturgy and Patristics in Honor of Gabriele Winkler*, ed. Hans-Jürgen Feulner, Elena Velkovska, and Robert F. Taft, Orientalia Christiana Analecta 260 (Rome: Pontificio Istituto Orientale, 2000), 173–92; and idem, "Invocations to/for the Holy Spirit in Syriac Liturgical Texts: Some Comparative Approaches," in *Comparative Liturgy Fifty Years after Anton Baumstark (1872–1948)*, Orientalia Christiana Analecta 265 (Rome: Pontificio Istituto Orientale, 2001), 377–406. Gabriele Winkler has developed Brock's insights in a series of articles: "Nochmals zu den Anfängen der Epiklese und des Sanctus im Eucharistischen Hochgebet," *Theologische Quartalschrift* 174, no. 3 (1994): 214–31; "Further Observations in Connection with the Early Form of the Epiklesis," in *Le Sacrement de l'Initiation: Origines et Prospective, Patrimoine Syriaque. Actes du Colloque III* (Antelias, Lebanon: Centre d'Etudes et de Recherches Pastorales, 1996), 66–80 [reprinted in Gabriele Winkler, *Studies in Early Christian Liturgy and Its Context* (Aldershot/Brookfield, VT: Ashgate, 1997)]; and "Weitere Beobachtungen zur frühen Epiklese (den Doxologien und dem Sanctus). Über die Bedeutung der Apokryphen für die Erforschung der Entwicklung der Riten," *Oriens Christianus* 80 (1996): 177–200.

[14] Paul F. Bradshaw, "The Barcelona Papyrus and the Development of Early Eucharistic Prayers," in *Issues in Eucharistic Praying in East and West: Essays in Liturgical and Theological Analysis*, ed. Maxwell E. Johnson (Collegeville, MN: Liturgical Press, 2010), 132.

[15] Vagaggini deemed it "not in the least typical" (see 67) although Louis Bouyer supplies a more circumspect discussion in idem, *Eucharist: Theology and Spirituality of the Eucharistic Prayer*, trans. Charles Underhill Quinn (Notre Dame, IN: University of Notre Dame Press, 1968), 203ff.

participation";[16] however, besides lacking specifically pneumatic content, this request need not be read as implying "consecration" in the sense of transforming the gifts of bread and wine. The case for this interpretation is strengthened by the presence of an invocation of the *Logos* for the consecration of the bread and cup *after* the institution narrative: "God of truth, let your holy Word come [ἐπιδημησάτω] upon this bread in order that the bread may become body of the Word, and upon this cup in order that the cup may become blood of truth."[17] In fact, the only possible explicit invocation of the Spirit in this anaphora *precedes* the *Sanctus*. Its content resembles neither "consecration" nor "communion" intentions but serves instead as a petition for the realization of the trinitarian mystery in the midst of the gathered assembly: "Give us holy Spirit, in order that we may be able to proclaim and describe your inexpressible mysteries. Let the Lord Jesus speak in us and let holy Spirit also hymn you through us."[18]

Although the more developed forms of the Alexandrian anaphora (e.g., the Coptic and Greek recensions of the Anaphora of Mark) display some parallels to the modern "split epiclesis" pattern, even this evidence is not as conclusive as has sometimes been supposed. While the epiclesis preceding the institution narrative may or may not be consecratory,[19] the second epiclesis located after the narrative clearly contains *both* consecratory and communion dimensions:

[16] Translation from Maxwell E. Johnson, *The Prayers of Sarapion of Thmuis: A Literary, Liturgical, and Theological Analysis*, Orientalia Christiana Analecta 249 (Rome: Pontificio Istituto Orientale, 1995), 47.

[17] Ibid., 49. For a discussion of the translation of the verb, see Maxwell E. Johnson, "The Origins of the Anaphoral Use of the Sanctus and Epiclesis Revisited: The Contribution of Gabriele Winkler and Its Implications," in Feulner et al., *Crossroad of Cultures*, 437ff.

[18] Johnson, *The Prayers of Sarapion of Thmuis*, 47. On this point, Johnson observes that "Sarapion's anaphora does not say that the Son and Holy Spirit are praised by the sanctus of both the seraphim and the community. What it does say is that the Son and Holy Spirit themselves are to 'speak in' the community and 'hymn' *God* through the sanctus" (213); emphasis his.

[19] Even in the thirteenth-century manuscript tradition, the pre-institution epiclesis petition of Greek Mark, which reads, "Make this sacrifice also full of your blessing through the coming of your Holy Spirit," need not be read as explicitly consecratory in intent. As Nichols and MacGregor note, much depends on whether "sacrifice" here is to be read as a specific reference to the eucharistic elements or more generally as referring to a sacrifice of praise and thanksgiving; see Nichols and MacGregor, *The Eucharistic Epiclesis*, 8. Geoffrey Cuming deems this epiclesis

For we pray and beseech you, generous lover of the human race, that you would send from your holy height, from your prepared dwelling-place, from your embrace that cannot be circumscribed, the Paraclete himself, the Holy Spirit [of truth], the life-giving Lord, who has spoken in the law and through the prophets and apostles; who is . . . consubstantial with you, proceeding from you, sitting with you on the throne of your kingdom and with your only-begotten Son, our Lord and God and Saviour Jesus Christ. [Look] upon us and send upon these loaves and cups your Holy Spirit to sanctify and consecrate them,[20] [as Almighty God], and make the bread the body, and the cup the blood of the new covenant of our Lord and God and Saviour and supreme King, Jesus Christ, that they may become to all of us who partake of them for faith, for sobriety, for healing, for temperance, for sanctification, for renewal of soul, body, and spirit, for fellowship in the blessedness of eternal life and immortality, for the glorification of your most holy name, and for the remission of sins; so that in this as in all things your most holy, precious, and glorious name may be glorified, praised and sanctified with Jesus Christ and the Holy Spirit.[21]

Thus the neat distinction placing consecration before the institution narrative and concerns for communion afterward is simply not to be found in the textual record of early (or even relatively late) Alexandrian anaphoras.

Finally, the question must be raised as to whether the epiclesis structure in some of these prayers is ultimately "Egyptian" at all. Several scholars have suggested that the second epiclesis may be a West Syrian interpolation since its location corresponds to that of the

"so vague"; see Geoffrey J. Cuming, *The Liturgy of St. Mark*, Orientalia Christiana Analecta 234 (Rome: Pontificium Institutum Studiorum Orientalium, 1990), 125. The petition of the Coptic version is more explicitly consecratory with its specification of the eucharistic elements as the objects of blessing and sanctification: "and in blessing bless, and in sanctifying sanctify, these your precious gifts which have been set before your face, this bread and this cup" (trans. from Nichols and MacGregor, *The Eucharistic Epiclesis*, 7.

[20] The Coptic reads here: "that they may be sanctified and changed." Jasper and Cuming, *Prayers of the Eucharist*, 66.

[21] Translation from Nichols and MacGregor, *The Eucharistic Epiclesis*, 7–8 (rubrics omitted); cf. Jasper and Cuming, *Prayers of the Eucharist*, 65–66. The material in square brackets is present in the Greek text of the anaphora but absent from the Coptic version.

sole epiclesis in the Antiochene form.[22] More recently, the claim has been made that West Syrian influence might have shaped the "Alexandrian" anaphora from the *Sanctus* to the final doxology. The most primitive form of the Alexandrian eucharistic prayer would then have been similar to that which survives in the Strasbourg Papyrus 254 (ca. 300–500), a likely predecessor of the developed form of the Anaphora of St. Mark. Both of these anaphoras begin by praising God who created all things in Christ and continue with an offering of "sacrifice" (whose most likely connotations are that of a sacrifice of praise and thanksgiving) and intercessions. Then the two forms diverge. Whereas the "developed" form of Mark introduces the *Sanctus* at this point, the Strasbourg Papyrus continues with a doxology that may represent the conclusion of the prayer, making the earliest Egyptian core a simple structure of praise, offering, and intercession.[23]

An extensive role for Syrian traditions in this prayer, especially as far as the epiclesis is concerned, could lend support to Gabriele Winkler's recent theories about the geographic origin of the epiclesis in Syria. A perennial problem in the Alexandrian anaphoral tradition has been explaining the presence of the *two* epicletic units in the

[22] Hans Lietzmann, for example, considered this epiclesis a *Fremdkorper* within the prayer. See idem, *Mass and Lord's Supper: A Study in the History of the Liturgy* (Leiden: E. J. Brill, 1979), 63.

[23] See Talley, "Literary Structure," 416. The status of the Strasbourg Papyrus as a complete anaphora in itself was suggested by Edward Kilmartin, "Sacrificium Laudis: Content and Function of Early Eucharistic Prayers," *Theological Studies* 35, no. 2 (1974): 268–87; and developed further in Geoffrey J. Cuming, "The Anaphora of St. Mark: A Study in Development," *Le Muséon* 95 (1982): 115–29. Zheltov has recently criticized this view, contending that, "as a liturgical text, the prayer from the Strasbourg papyrus should have been mirroring the current Egyptian liturgical practice, which by the time of creation of this papyrus already knew the anaphoral Sanctus, epiclesis, etc. . . . [T]he discovery of the Barcelona papyrus leaves the hypothesis of the Strasbourg papyrus' integrity unfounded . . . [and] it leaves the different variants of the '4th-century interpolations' theory without any actual documentary proof" (Zheltov, "The Anaphora," 502). Much would seem to depend on the relative dating of the Strasbourg and Barcelona Papyri. Zheltov suggests that the contents of the Barcelona Papyrus predate those of the Strasbourg Papyrus —as the text of the Barcelona Papyrus "is not younger than the mid-4th century and may go back to the 3rd" (502). The first half of the fourth century, however, falls within the two hundred–year span to which the Strasbourg Papyrus is commonly dated as well. If the two texts are roughly contemporaneous, it becomes more difficult to dismiss the seemingly "primitive" pattern of the Strasbourg Papyrus as an anachronism.

prayer. While West Syrian origin has been logical for the latter, Winkler's theory of the *Sanctus* and epiclesis originating (and perhaps initially circulating) as an integral unit[24] may lend credence to the idea that the earlier section could possibly have its origins in Syria as well. While the first epiclesis in the developed Alexandrian anaphoras had been difficult to dismiss as a late interpolation, given its intimate link with the *Sanctus*,[25] this does not rule out the possibility that it could have been one component of a relatively *early* interpolation of the *Sanctus*-epiclesis unit into a structure that previously lacked both of these components.

Given Winkler's contention that both the *Sanctus* and epiclesis arose in Syria and that by the middle of the fourth century, "the initial epiklesis is steadily making room for doxologies, eventually including the Sanctus as well,"[26] it is curious that a close literary or structural link between the *Sanctus* and epiclesis is *not* a characteristic of later Syrian prayers. Rather, in the developed Antiochene or West Syrian pattern, following the *Sanctus* (with *Benedictus*), the post-*Sanctus* section focuses on thanksgiving to God the Father for redemption in Christ (culminating in the institution narrative) with a Spirit-epiclesis following in the third part of the prayer, providing a tidy trinitarian framework for the whole. Winkler has argued that the situation of epicleses within a trinitarian framework was a later reworking of a more original petition addressed to the Spirit.[27]

Regardless of the ultimate origin of the *Sanctus* and epiclesis, if the *Sanctus* and epiclesis ever *did* travel together and if Winkler's theory about an original layer of pneumatic eucharistic epicleses being subsequently reworked to accommodate their placement in a broader trinitarian context is correct, the Anaphora of Mark could provide an example of a case where this unit had not yet been worked into an explicitly trinitarian framework. This possibility in itself might suggest the relatively early origin of the first epiclesis in Egyptian texts. This could explain why the first epiclesis seems much more integral to the

[24] See, e.g., Winkler, "Further Observations," 79–80.

[25] This connection has been dubbed the "*pleni-vereplenum-imple*" construction, with the "full is heaven and earth of your glory" of the Egyptian *Sanctus* (which lacks the *Benedictus*) providing a logical transition to the following epicletic petition, "Fill . . ."

[26] Winkler, "Further Observations," 79.

[27] See ibid. and also Winkler, "Weitere Beobachtungen," 192ff.

anaphora than the second epiclesis following the anamnesis—which could more logically be a later interpolation under West Syrian influence.

From this brief survey, it seems that the Alexandrian anaphoral tradition tended to keep consecration and communion dimensions of the epiclesis together after the anamnesis, whatever the epicletic content preceding the narrative. In contrast, modern eucharistic prayers containing a "split epiclesis" overtly separate the consecration and communion dimensions of the anaphora by relegating these aspects of the Spirit's work to different sections of the anaphora. Insofar as these newer epicleses are inconsistent, in this way, with their supposed predecessors in the Alexandrian anaphoral tradition, the modern split epicleses raise theological issues that the older Egyptian epicleses do not. Some have argued that a split epiclesis obscures the inherent unity of the Spirit's activity in the eucharistic context, namely, that the Spirit is invoked on the eucharistic gifts *so that* all who share in them may in turn be brought together in unity in the one body of Christ.[28] Another way to put this is that the connection between the pneumaticized Body of Christ consumed in the eucharistic species and the pneumaticized Body of Christ that the church is called to be is downplayed. Furthermore, as Aidan Kavanagh notes, locating a pneumatic epiclesis immediately before the institution narrative has inevitable and undesirable consequences insofar as it "not only welds both sections into a unit that is longer and more strongly consecratory than before: it also interrupts the flow of sequence in narrating the divine mercies for which eucharistic prayer is made and sets the institution account off from this cursus."[29] Therefore, the phenomenon of the "split epiclesis" is one that might fruitfully be revisited in future reforms of eucharistic praying. In addition to the "Alexandrian" split epiclesis, however, Western churches picked up other prayer patterns from the practice of ancient churches, including a preference for the West Syrian or Antiochene "shape" of the eucharistic prayer.

[28] See, e.g., John H. McKenna, "Eucharistic Epiclesis: Myopia or Microcosm?," *Theological Studies* 36, no. 2 (1975): 283; and Bradshaw, "The Rediscovery of the Holy Spirit," 88.

[29] Kavanagh, "Thoughts on the New Eucharistic Prayers," 9. For similar critiques, see John H. McKenna, *The Eucharistic Epiclesis: A Detailed History from the Patristic to the Modern Era*, 2nd ed. (Chicago, IL: Hillenbrand Books, 2009), 227; and Frank C. Senn, "Toward a Different Anaphoral Structure," *Worship* 58, no. 4 (1984): 348.

Reshaping Eastern Prayers: Ancient West Syrian Influence on Modern Western Christianity

Ecumenical consensus increasingly affirms the role of the Spirit in the eucharistic action as a whole and more cautiously assigns some effect to the invocation of the Spirit in eucharistic prayers. A good example can be found in the agreed ecumenical statement *Baptism, Eucharist, and Ministry* (1982) produced by the Faith and Order Commission of the World Council of Churches.[30] The commentary associated with a subsection of the document titled "The Eucharist as Invocation of the Spirit" assigns an important role to the eucharistic epiclesis in connection with the words of institution and the promise of Christ's presence realized in the liturgical context, claiming that a renewed appreciation of the epiclesis in light of the eucharistic encounter as a whole might even help to resolve present theological difficulties: "In the early liturgies the whole 'prayer action' was thought of as bringing about the reality promised by Christ. The invocation of the Spirit was made both on the community and on the elements of bread and wine. Recovery of such an understanding may help us overcome our difficulties concerning a special moment of consecration."[31]

While the latter statement may indeed be true, the implied link between the words of institution and the epiclesis may have set up a temporal expectation for the sequence of these elements within the anaphora that led to West Syrian structure being somewhat selectively employed to serve the ends of Western theology—with its traditional emphasis on the consecratory efficacy of the words of Christ. The tension between these two approaches is similarly expressed in this comment from Philip Pfatteicher: "The whole Eucharist has an epicletic character because it all depends on the work of the Holy Spirit. In the liturgy the presence of the risen and reigning Lord—Christ filled with the Spirit—is actualized. Specifically at this point in the prayer the

[30] *Baptism, Eucharist, and Ministry*, Faith and Order Paper no. 111 (Geneva: World Council of Churches, 1982). The text is also available online: http://www.oikoumene.org/en/resources/documents/wcc-commissions/faith-and-order-commission/i-unity-the-church-and-its-mission/baptism-eucharist-and-ministry-faith-and-order-paper-no-111-the-lima-text.html. See especially nos. 14–18 in the "Eucharist" section.

[31] Ibid., "Eucharist," no. 14.

epiclesis asks God's response to the church's obedience to the command of Christ to 'Do this in *anamnesis* of me.'"[32]

This lends support to Bryan Spinks's claim that the West Syrian pattern of eucharistic praying has been touted "not only [as] the perfect and only paradigm for authentic eucharistic prayers" but also as a form that "can be traced back directly to the Jewish euchology used by Jesus at the Last Supper, and implied by him in the words 'Do this in remembrance of me.'"[33] Many of the new Western eucharistic prayers did, in fact, adopt what has come to be known as an "Antiochene" or "West Syrian" structure, which traditionally contains the following elements:[34]

1. *Sursum corda*
2. Preface
3. Pre-*Sanctus*
4. *Sanctus*
5. Post-*Sanctus*
6. Institution Narrative
7. Anamnesis
8. Offering
9. Epiclesis
10. Intercessions
11. Doxology

Although it does not seem that contemporary Western prayers, for the most part, were deliberately patterned after this structure per se,[35] Frank Senn has provided several plausible reasons why this format might have proved quite attractive to those involved in the reform of

[32] Philip H. Pfatteicher, *Commentary on the Lutheran Book of Worship: Lutheran Liturgy in Its Ecumenical Context* (Minneapolis, MN: Augsburg Fortress, 1990), 167. Pfatteicher is commenting here specifically on the epicleses of the *Lutheran Book of Worship* (1978), which are found in the standard "West Syrian" post-anamnesis location.

[33] Bryan D. Spinks, "Berakah, Anaphoral Theory and Luther," *Lutheran Quarterly* 3, no. 3 (1989): 267–68.

[34] As outlined by Jasper and Cuming in the introduction to *Prayers of the Eucharist*, 6. Ancient anaphoras that fit this pattern, thought to have emerged by the late fourth century, include the Anaphoras of St. Basil, St. James, and St. John Chrysostom as well as the *Apostolic Constitutions*.

[35] Fenwick and Spinks remark that "no really sound argument has been advanced as to why West Syrian fifth-century forms should be the basis for twentieth-century prayers" (*Worship in Transition*, 131).

eucharistic prayers in the late twentieth century.[36] First, this structure had the benefits both of antiquity and orthodoxy, "represent[ing] a post-Nicene synthesis of archaic form and developed Trinitarian theology." Second, "wittingly or unwittingly, the West Syrian anaphoras follow a tripartite scheme similar to the Jewish *birkat ha-mazon*." Although Senn does not make this connection explicit, it should be noted that many of the new eucharistic prayers were written in an era when the theory that Christian eucharistic prayers developed from Jewish table prayers such as the *birkat ha-mazon* had wide currency.[37] It was thought that this Jewish prayer (with its tripartite structure featuring praise of God for creation, thanksgiving in memory of God's saving acts, and petition for God's fulfillment of promises made to the people of Israel) was adapted and reworked into a threefold Christian prayer of praise, remembrance, and supplication, with the works of the Father, Son, and Spirit as the dominant focus, respectively, of each section of the prayer. Third, the West Syrian anaphoral form held narrative appeal for reformers and congregations of the late twentieth century faced with the challenge of fitting the story of salvation history into the form of a prayer. Elsewhere, Senn suggests that the Antiochene form of eucharistic praying also provided the necessary flexibility to accommodate a compromise between traditional prayer forms and the requirements of contemporary vernacular liturgical language. Given this context, Senn suggests that the inclination toward the West Syrian structure "was because its narrative style allowed for including issues from contemporary life within the scope of salvation history, or for retelling the biblical story in such a way as to address it to the concerns of contemporary life."[38] Finally, this structure made it

[36] The following ideas are presented in Senn, "Toward a Different Anaphoral Structure," 347.

[37] Discussion of possible Jewish precedents for the use of epicleses in Christian anaphoras can be found in, e.g., Louis Ligier, "De la Cène de Jésus à l'Anaphore de l'Église," *La Maison-Dieu* 87 (1966): 7–51; Bouyer, *Eucharist*, 106ff.; and William R. Crockett, *Eucharist: Symbol of Transformation* (New York: Pueblo Publishing Co., 1989), 54–63. For a more recent assessment of Jewish influences on early Christian worship, see Paul F. Bradshaw, *The Search for the Origins of Christian Worship: Sources and Methods for the Study of Early Liturgy*, 2nd ed. (Oxford/New York: Oxford University Press, 2002), 23ff.

[38] Frank C. Senn, "Introduction," in *New Eucharistic Prayers: An Ecumenical Study of Their Development and Structure*, ed. Frank C. Senn (New York: Paulist Press, 1987), 5.

easy to introduce congregational acclamations within the prayer—acclamations that were consistent with the reformers' desire to promote the active participation of the whole community in the Eucharist.

In an article titled "Toward a Different Anaphoral Structure," Senn notes the theological difficulties Western churches have encountered with respect to the location and language of the epiclesis of Eastern anaphoras of the West Syrian type, such as the Egyptian Anaphora of Basil, concluding that "it would be problematic in this tradition for the church to petition the Holy Spirit to do what the authoritative and creative words of Christ do with regard to the gifts, notwithstanding a generally appreciative regard for the role of the Holy Spirit in the Eastern eucharist on the part of Western theologians since the sixteenth century."[39] Some of the solutions adopted do not respect the integrity or internal logic of West Syrian prayers. An epiclesis preceding the institution narrative, as noted above, disrupts the account of salvation history located in the post-*Sanctus* of prayers of the West Syrian type. On the other hand, leaving the epiclesis in its traditional post-anamnesis location—while excising language that might be interpreted as asking the Spirit to sanctify the gifts at this point in the prayer—results in an attenuated epiclesis in which the inherent unity of the consecration and communion dimensions is lost. Furthermore, the epiclesis itself becomes a minor component whose purpose is reduced to little more than a transition between the anamnesis and intercessions. For the most part, "it is evident that the Western churches are not yet prepared to import Eastern anaphoras without altering them to suit Western stylistic and theological preferences."[40]

However compelling reasons for favoring the West Syrian structure may have been for liturgical reformers of the late twentieth century, alternative models of eucharistic praying (some derived from very early prayers and some from later Western models) might profitably be tapped to enrich the euchological repertoire of Western churches in the future—without selectively appropriating Eastern frameworks that happen to be amenable to accommodating Western concerns. The first (and simplest) solution with regard to the epiclesis would be to take a cue from very early texts, no matter what the precise location of the epiclesis in the prayer. Sebastian Brock and Gabriele Winkler have

[39] Senn, "Toward a Different Anaphoral Structure," 348–49.
[40] Ibid., 349.

argued that the most primitive form of the epiclesis simply asked that the Holy Spirit "come" without any further specificity regarding the objects and/or persons who might benefit from this coming or even any elaboration about the effects that this coming might have on anyone or anything; there was certainly no petition for "consecration" contained in such epicleses.[41] Maxwell Johnson highlights the potential of such a solution to address discomfort in ecumenical dialogue with a high degree of specificity regarding how or when the Spirit acts in the context of the eucharistic action. "Indeed, such an 'epiclesis,' such an invocation of the Holy Spirit in the liturgical assembly, is an ancient petition merely for the Spirit's divine presence and, as such, transcends the confession-specific concerns about theories of consecration."[42]

Senn suggests that Western Christians might look to the bipartite anaphoral structure of praise and supplication (which is perhaps even more ancient than the tripartite praise-thanksgiving-supplication structure that received its fullest expression in the West Syrian anaphoras) as a way around the Western theological impasse with West Syrian structure. This bipartite pattern can be found in ancient texts as diverse as *Didache* 10, *Apostolic Tradition* 4, and the Mar Esha'ya text of the Anaphora of Addai and Mari—and possibly also in the Roman Canon if the *Sanctus* is considered as the division between the two main sections of the prayer. Some of the first examples of reformed liturgies from the sixteenth century adopted a bipartite structure as well, including Martin Luther's *Formula Missae et Communionis* (1523), Diebold Schwarz's German Mass (1524–25), the Brandenburg Church Order (1540), and Thomas Cranmer's first *Book of Common Prayer* (1549). Senn remarks, "It is noteworthy that these examples,

[41] Robert Taft provides a helpful caveat, however, noting that "any prayer for the power of God to come upon something in order that it be unto salvation for those who partake of it or participate in it as God intended, necessarily implies that God do something by his coming to make that object salvific"; one should not therefore infer that "a more primitive, less explicit epicletic prayer is not, in fact, implicitly consecratory" since considerations of this kind reveal more about the structure of a text than its theology. See Robert F. Taft, "From Logos to Spirit: On the Early History of the Epiclesis," in *Gratias Agamus: Studien zum eucharistischen Hochgebet. Für Balthasar Fischer*, ed. Andreas Heinz and Heinrich Rennings (Freiburg: Herder, 1992), 493.

[42] Johnson, "The Origins of the Anaphoral Use of the Sanctus and Epiclesis Revisited," 435.

progenitors of the Reformed, Lutheran, and Anglican eucharistic traditions . . . still followed the pattern of the Roman canon even though the reformers eschewed the use of the Roman canon itself. This is significant because the reformers were increasingly familiar with editions and translations of the Greek anaphoras."[43] Senn's proposed anaphoral structure introduces the congregational acclamation, "Amen. Come, Lord Jesus," in imitation of the ancient *maranatha* as a division between the praise and supplication sections of the prayer, followed by an epiclesis (although not necessarily a pneumatic one) and a petition for the fruits of communion.[44]

John McKenna's reflections on whether or not an "epiclesis proper" (i.e., an explicit petition for the Holy Spirit to sanctify the gifts and/or the faithful) is an absolutely necessary component of eucharistic prayers suggest a third potential alternative to the West Syrian pattern that could open Western churches to a greater degree of structural flexibility in their official eucharistic prayer texts. Of course, historical evidence from the early centuries (and the practice of many major Western Christian traditions until relatively recently) and hesitancy to elevate *any* prayer formula (whether the institution narrative or the epiclesis) into a sort of liturgical *sine qua non* argue against the view that an epiclesis proper is necessary. Nonetheless, a case could be made for the necessity of an "epiclesis attitude" whether an explicit epiclesis is present in a community's eucharistic prayers or not. "It is a practical necessity for the eucharistic assembly to express its awareness, for instance, of the necessary intervention of the Holy Spirit and of its own need for a praying or 'epiclesis' attitude."[45] Granting that the epiclesis, conceived in this way, is indispensable, it may not be necessary for a particular praying community to include an explicit pneumatic epiclesis in *all* of its eucharistic prayers or to frame all of its

[43] Senn, "Toward a Different Anaphoral Structure," 349ff.; quote from 352. Greek editions of the Liturgies of St. John Chrysostom and St. Basil were published in Europe in 1526, and occasional allusions and citations from Greek anaphoras can be found in Reformation liturgies. Senn discusses in some detail the Liturgy of King Johan III of Sweden (1576), which borrows phrases from book 8 of the *Apostolic Constitutions* and the Anaphora of St. John Chrysostom—while nonetheless maintaining the twofold pattern of praise and supplication found in the Roman Canon.

[44] See ibid., 356, 357–58.

[45] See McKenna, *The Eucharistic Epiclesis*, 224–27; quote from 225.

epicleses in a similar way (in terms of location within the prayer, benefits requested, etc.).

Yet another option would be to focus less on either the words of institution or the epiclesis as consecratory and instead emphasize that the *whole* eucharistic prayer is consecratory, once again along the lines of the early church's emphasis on the sacrifice of praise and thanksgiving. For, as Senn observed, "The early liturgical tradition was simply uninterested in pinpointing a 'moment of consecration' and identifying that either with the words of institution or with the invocation of the Holy Spirit. There are early Christian traditions that had neither an institution narrative nor a consecratory epiclesis, without thereby losing a sense of communion with Christ in, with, and through the bread and cup."[46] Even though concerns about the "moment of consecration" were not an issue for the framers of early eucharistic prayers, it may, however, represent an insurmountable obstacle in practice to expect this sort of second naiveté from modern liturgical revisers. As W. Jardine Grisbrooke notes, once such concerns arose, "even the attempt to abandon such a concept by saying that the whole prayer consecrates merely results, in practice, in regarding the conclusion of the prayer as that moment."[47]

Employing some of these strategies may result in prayers with a greater range and nuance of epicletic patterns than those presently printed in current official liturgical books. Meanwhile, it should also be emphasized that considerable diversity in terms of the epicleses themselves already exists among Western eucharistic prayers. The influence of more contemporary theological concerns, however, makes this diversity of a different sort than that which is characteristically found in early eucharistic prayers.

"Common" Prayers? Ancient and Modern Epicletic Diversity

Regardless of the process by which older prayers were adapted and new ones created, the prayers that resulted have much in common with each other, both within and across denominational boundaries.

[46] Frank C. Senn, *Christian Liturgy: Catholic and Evangelical* (Minneapolis, MN: Fortress Press, 1997), 85.

[47] W. J. Grisbrooke, "Anaphora," in *A New Dictionary of Liturgy and Worship*, ed. J. Gordon Davies (London: SCM Press, 1986), 20.

Upon closer examination, however, the current Western euchological consensus on the role of the epiclesis in the eucharistic prayer is not as consistent as it might initially appear. Even among contemporary prayers modeled on the *same* ancient text, the epicletic language of the "common" prayers that have resulted sometimes sounds quite different theologically. Diversity is also to be found in the somewhat selective incorporation of ancient themes and language into modern prayers. [48] Examples of each of these cases will be considered here.

Example 1: Apostolic Tradition *and Its Contemporary Incarnations*

Although drawing on ancient texts was a common project in the recent decades of liturgical reform, two early prayers in particular served as models for many modern compositions: *Apostolic Tradition* 4 and the Egyptian version of the Anaphora of Basil have both entered the repertoire of eucharistic praying in a number of Western churches. The modifications made were typically more drastic than translating these texts into modern vernacular languages, and in many cases the prayers were "adapted" so extensively that they might be almost unrecognizable to the communities that originally produced and prayed them. While elements of these eucharistic prayers are now held in "common" across modern traditions, the means of modification were not as common—and the inconsistencies suggest other theological motives at work. A comparison of the epiclesis of *Apostolic Tradition* 4 with some modern renditions of this text is revealing.

[48] Adrien Nocent has suggested at least two forces operative behind the Western reworking of what were largely Eastern eucharistic prayers. First, there was a "desire for similarity in the wording of the various Eucharistic prayers." In some cases (especially Roman Catholic), the text of the original may have been altered beyond the requirements of a simple translation out of a desire to harmonize the wording of certain parts of the prayer among all the eucharistic prayers in a particular tradition's repertoire. This explains, for example, the changes the Roman Catholic Church introduced to the doxology of *Apostolic Tradition*. Second, modifications were made out of "fear of being outside the orthodoxy of the faith." This can be seen in the introduction of an epiclesis *before* the institution narrative in Roman Catholic Eucharistic Prayer II, producing a "split epiclesis." See Nocent, *A Rereading of the Renewed Liturgy*, trans. Mary M. Misrahi (Collegeville, MN: Liturgical Press, 1994), 46–47.

The epiclesis in chapter 4 of the *Apostolic Tradition* reads as follows: "And we ask that you would send your Holy Spirit in the oblation of [your] holy church, [that] gathering [them] into one you will give to all who partake of the holy things [to partake] in the fullness of the Holy Spirit, for the strengthening of faith in truth, that we may praise and glorify you through your Child Jesus Christ."[49] Although there has been scholarly debate over whether this petition requests any specific transformation of the eucharistic gifts (with recent consensus favoring the opinion that it does not),[50] it is clear that its author sought to make a connection between the community's celebration of the Eucharist, the unity of this community, and the strengthening of the community's faith.

While still recognizable as deriving from *Apostolic Tradition*, contemporary Western prayers that use this ancient prayer as a model mold the epiclesis in certain ways that reflect theological concerns of their own times and traditions. Contemporary prayers derived from the *Apostolic Tradition* include Roman Catholic Eucharistic Prayer II, Eucharistic Prayer IV in *Lutheran Book of Worship* (cf. Great Thanksgiving XI in *Evangelical Lutheran Worship*), Great Thanksgiving G in the Presbyterian *Book of Common Worship*, and Eucharistic Prayer B in the Church of England's *Common Worship*:

[49] Paul F. Bradshaw, Maxwell E. Johnson, and L. Edward Phillips, *The Apostolic Tradition: A Commentary* (Minneapolis, MN: Fortress Press, 2002), 40. The Latin text reads:

> Et petimus, ut mittas spiritum tuum sanctum in oblationem sanctae ecclesiae; in unum congregans des omnibus qui percipiunt sanctis in repletionem spiritus sancti ad confirmationem fidei in veritate, ut te laudemus et glorificemus per puerum tuum Iesum Christum . . .

Text from Erik Tidner, ed., *Didascaliae Apostolorum Canonum Ecclesiasticorum Traditionis Apostolicae Versiones Latinae*, Texte und Untersuchungen zur Geschichte der altchristlichen Literatur, vol. 75 (Berlin: Akademie-Verlag, 1963), 125–26.

[50] See, e.g., Senn, *Christian Liturgy*, 79: "[T]here is no suggestion that consecration is associated with either the institution narrative or the epiclesis. Rather, the communicants receive the fruits of Holy Communion through the operation of the Holy Spirit: unity with God, being filled with the Spirit of Christ, and being confirmed in true faith."

Roman Missal (Roman Catholic) Eucharistic Prayer II[51]	***Lutheran Book of Worship*** **Eucharistic Prayer IV**[52]	***Book of Common Worship*** **(Presbyterian) Great Thanksgiving G**[53]	***Common Worship*** **(Church of England) Eucharistic Prayer B**[54]
(I): Make holy, therefore, these gifts, we pray, by sending down your Spirit upon them like the dewfall, so that they may become for us the Body (+) and Blood of our Lord, Jesus Christ. (II): Humbly we pray that, partaking of the Body and Blood of Christ, we may be gathered into one by the Holy Spirit.	And we ask you: Send your Spirit upon these gifts of your Church; gather into one all who share this bread and wine; fill us with your Holy Spirit to establish our faith in truth, that we may praise and glorify you through your Son Jesus Christ.	We ask you to send your Holy Spirit upon the offering of the holy church. Gather into one all who share these holy mysteries, filling them with the Holy Spirit and confirming their faith in the truth, that together we may praise you and give you glory, through your Servant, Jesus Christ.	(I): Lord, you are holy indeed, the source of all holiness; grant that by the power of your Holy Spirit, and according to your holy will, these gifts of bread and wine may be to us the body and blood of our Lord Jesus Christ; (II): Send the Holy Spirit on your people and gather into one in your kingdom all who share this one bread and one cup, so that we, in the company of [*N and*] all the saints, may praise and glorify you for ever, through Jesus Christ our Lord;

In Roman Catholic Eucharistic Prayer II, the integral connection between Eucharist, unity, and the faith of the community is disrupted by the introduction of a consecratory epiclesis before the institution narrative, which does explicitly request a transformation of the gifts, and subsequent modification of the communion aspect of the epiclesis after the institution narrative. In this section, *Apostolic Tradition*'s concern for unity is maintained; the petition for the strengthening of the community's faith in truth is not.

[51] From the English translation of the Roman Missal, © 2010, International Commission on English in the Liturgy, Inc., at http://www.usccb.org/romanmissal/samples-priest-prayer2.shtml.

[52] Inter-Lutheran Commission on Worship, *Lutheran Book of Worship*, Ministers Desk Edition (Minneapolis, MN: Augsburg Publishing House, 1978), 298.

[53] The Theology and Worship Ministry Unit for the Presbyterian Church (USA) and the Cumberland Presbyterian Church, *Book of Common Worship* (Louisville, KY: Westminster/John Knox Press, 1993), 151.

[54] The Church of England, "Eucharistic Prayers for Use in Order One," http://www.churchofengland.org/prayer-worship/worship/texts/principal-services/holy-communion/epsforonefront/prayerb.aspx.

In *Common Worship*, Eucharistic Prayer B follows a similar pattern, with mention of the Holy Spirit's action on the gifts before the institution narrative and mention of the Spirit's action in relation to the people afterward. The reference to strengthening in faith has likewise disappeared, and the sense of unity conveyed here ("in your kingdom") could be heard in an eschatological rather than in an immediate sense.

Lutheran Book of Worship and the Presbyterian *Book of Common Worship* both follow the structure of the ancient prayer with regard to the epiclesis, leaving it intact after the anamnesis.[55] Both translations retain the original's connections between the eucharistic context, the unity of the community, and the nourishment of the community's faith. Presbyterian Great Thanksgiving G is the only prayer that renders *oblationem* in English as "offering." The other churches opted to translate the object of the invocation as "gifts," although the Lutheran translators in particular might have been especially concerned with avoiding the connotations of "offering" the eucharistic gifts in this instance. The Presbyterian version likewise retains the more primitive language of Christ as servant/child (*puerum* in Latin or *pais* in Greek) of God in the transition to the concluding doxology.

Example 2: Modern Rereading of Ancient Intent?

Furthermore, while the current diversity in the wording of the epiclesis among various traditions has a long history, Paul Bradshaw has remarked that "at least some of this diversity seems to stem from a theological uncertainty as to what it is precisely that the Holy Spirit is expected to do in relation to the Eucharist, or alternatively from a fear of saying something that might imply a belief that the framers [of the prayers] did not wish to articulate."[56] As John McKenna has similarly

[55] Frank Senn notes that it is *only* in *Lutheran Book of Worship*, Ministers Edition, that *Apostolic Tradition* is used according to the pattern preserved in ancient texts (i.e., without the addition of the *Sanctus* or other acclamations). *With One Voice* (Minneapolis, MN: Augsburg Fortress, 1995) changed the earlier precedent of the 1978 book by framing *Apostolic Tradition* as a post-*Sanctus* prayer. See Senn, *Christian Liturgy*, 79, note 72. *Evangelical Lutheran Worship* (Minneapolis, MN: Augsburg Fortress, 2006) also follows this latter pattern.

[56] Bradshaw, "The Rediscovery of the Holy Spirit," 96.

noted, a survey of modern expressions of the epiclesis "is revealing liturgically, theologically, and ecumenically."[57]

While not wishing to take early eucharistic prayers as an "inflexible norm," McKenna has highlighted several ways in which the emphases in these texts can serve as a standard against which modern prayers could be compared. In early Christian prayers that feature the fully developed form of the eucharistic epiclesis, most expect some sort of change of the bread and wine, if not into, at least "in the direction of" Christ's Body and Blood.[58] The eschatological aspect of the Eucharist is often highlighted in ancient prayers, alongside a diverse collection of additional graces flowing forth as fruits of Communion. Last, some mention of sharing in the eucharistic gifts is almost invariably present.[59]

While an exhaustive survey is not possible here, it can be observed that the four aspects just mentioned—change in/of bread and wine, eschatology, fruits of Communion, and sharing in the eucharistic gifts—are not *consistently* found together in the epicleses of contemporary prayers:[60]

[57] John H. McKenna, "Eucharistic Prayer: Epiclesis," in Heinz and Rennings, eds., *Gratias Agamus*, 288.

[58] Of course, language that requests some sort of conversion or change of the elements need not, at this early stage, imply anything approaching a change of "substance" similar to the concerns that would arise in later Western theology. The question could be posed whether the change in view here is one of substance or rather one of use (a question raised by G. W. H. Lampe in R. E. Clements and others, *Eucharistic Theology Then and Now* [London: SPCK, 1968], 51). For a fuller discussion of this issue, see Donald Macleod, "Calvin into Hippolytus?," in *To Glorify God: Essays on Modern Reformed Liturgy*, ed. Bryan Spinks and Iain Torrance (Grand Rapids, MI: William B. Eerdmans Publishing Company, 1999), 266–67.

[59] McKenna, "Eucharistic Prayer: Epiclesis," 288. For a presentation of these elements in early eucharistic texts, see "Table 1.1: The Epiclesis in the Ancient Anaphoras," in McKenna, *The Eucharistic Epiclesis*, 40–41.

[60] The Prayers of Rite I in the Episcopal *Book of Common Prayer* are not "new" compositions per se but rather are framed in traditional Prayer Book idiom. For purposes of the table, the designation "some" indicates that a particular feature is not absent from a particular tradition's prayers but is present in less than half of the eucharistic prayers in this church's official worship book(s). "Most" means that a feature is present in the majority (i.e., more than half) of a tradition's prayers (but not in all of them).

Tradition (Text)	Change in Bread/Wine → Christ's Body/ Blood?	Eschatological References?	Fruits of Communion?	Sharing in Gifts?
Roman Catholic (Roman Missal)	Yes ("may become")	No	Yes	Yes
Evangelical Lutheran Church in America & Evangelical Lutheran Church in Canada (*Lutheran Book of Worship, Evangelical Lutheran Worship*)	No (Some prayers in *ELW* ask God to send the Spirit to "bless" the gifts and/or the meal, but no change of the bread and wine is mentioned specifically.)	Yes (in some)	Yes	Yes (in most)
Episcopal Church in the United States of America (*Book of Common Prayer*)	Yes (expression varies) in all but Rite I, Prayer I	*Rite I: No Rite II: Yes (in some)	*Rite I: No Rite II: Yes (in all but Prayer C, which has a pre-institution epiclesis only)	Yes (in some)
United Methodist Church (*United Methodist Book of Worship*)	Yes ("be for us") in all but IV	Yes (in most)	Yes	Yes (in some)
Presbyterian Church (USA) (*Book of Common Worship*)	Yes (?) ("may be a/the communion of") in most	Yes (in some)	Yes (in most)	Yes (in most)
Church of England (*Common Worship*)	Yes ("be to [or for] us") in most	Yes (in some)	Yes (in most)	Yes (in most)

While one would not expect any single prayer to touch upon all of these elements thoroughly, the complete absence of certain of these dimensions from *all* of a tradition's prayers could be telling theologically. Hence the lacunae in the chart above are the most interesting. For instance, Lutheran prayers do not directly attribute any change in the gifts to the power of the Spirit. McKenna wonders, "Is its absence due to an emphasis on the institution narrative as 'consecratory' or a desire to avoid the implications of certain terms, e.g., 'make them be for us the body and blood of Christ', 'may they be for us . . .', '. . . that they become . . .', '. . . to change . . .'—or both?"[61] While "be" (the typical verb in the Episcopal Eucharistic Prayers and the Methodist Great Thanksgivings) conveys the idea of change less forcefully

[61] McKenna, "Eucharistic Prayer: Epiclesis," 289.

than "become" (the typical request in the Roman Catholic prayers), there is still suggested the idea of some difference, perceptible at least by faith, in the eucharistic elements in connection with the prayer for the coming of the Spirit upon them. The Presbyterian Great Thanksgivings' characteristic request that the Spirit come upon the people and gifts so that the gifts (or the meal) "may be a communion" in or of Christ's Body and Blood may or may not imply consecration of the gifts.

In terms of eschatology, at least some of the epicleses of most traditions considered here do look with hope toward the kingdom Christ proclaimed or hint at the relation between the sacrament shared by the community in the present in memorial of Christ's past sacrifice as an anticipation of future sharing in the messianic banquet. Other traditions have fairly little eschatology in their epicleses or none at all. The only definite hint of final fulfillment in the Roman Catholic prayers is the epiclesis of the four Eucharistic Prayers for Various Needs: "[G]rant that, by the power of the Spirit of your love, we may be counted now and until the day of eternity among the members of your Son, in whose Body and Blood we have communion"—a rather meager reference indeed.[62]

As the examples above have indicated, the role of the epiclesis in a specifically eucharistic context is not understood in the same way in every tradition. Major differences include location of the epiclesis within the eucharistic prayer as a whole (particularly in relation to the institution narrative) and the language used to articulate how the community requests the Holy Spirit to act on the people, the gifts, or both. Reconsidering the epicleses of ancient anaphoras will not necessarily provide easy solutions to more modern dilemmas. Nonetheless, reflection on the diversity of early epicleses might inspire openness toward a greater variety of prayer patterns and a broader range of theological resonance within which eucharistic epicleses might legitimately be interpreted.

All this is not to suggest that insights from ancient anaphoras should not be adapted for modern liturgies. Through their continued use in changing contexts, early traditions and texts can connect con-

[62] In this tradition and others, eschatology does figure prominently in the intercessions that follow the post-anamnesis epiclesis and thus is not absent from the eucharistic prayer as a whole. From the English translation of *The Roman Missal* © 2010, ICEL.

temporary Christian congregations with the wider tradition of their faith as past reality, present participation, and future hope. Prayers incorporating aspects of early euchology have become part of the current "tradition" of eucharistic praying and are meeting the pastoral needs of Western Christians. Ancient examples should not, however, be used as uncritical justification for positions that these very texts cannot be read as supporting. In this respect, emerging knowledge of the historical development of early liturgies can be used both to illuminate and to critique later developments. While the emphases of modern Western epicleses are perfectly acceptable within their own denominational frameworks, they do not necessarily represent unbroken continuity with any one particular "ancient tradition" of eucharistic praying.

As Bradshaw has noted, some degree of tension between tradition and innovation seems to be essential to ongoing liturgical development: "Quite clearly what is required is . . . some sort of 'creative tension' between adhering to tradition and following contemporary trends, in order to avoid the unacceptable extremes of either position. . . . But we have to risk letting liturgy go wrong if it is to develop naturally at all, if it is to have any real chance of getting it right. For, in the end, the only real test of good liturgy is the test of time."[63] Perhaps one fruit of such tension in the realm of eucharistic praying will be the incorporation of a more diverse and robust pneumatology into the eucharistic prayers of Western traditions in the future, both within the epiclesis proper and elsewhere in the prayers.

[63] Paul F. Bradshaw, "The Liturgical Use and Abuse of Patristics," in *Liturgy Reshaped*, ed. Kenneth Stevenson (London: SPCK, 1982), 145.

Stefanos Alexopoulos

Chapter 14

"Ὅλοι μαζί": Liturgical Practice and Liturgical History*

Ritual practice and its meaning in popular understanding oftentimes vacillate between two extreme positions: (1) on the one hand, seeing *all* current practices as normative, normal, and historical, clothing them with the romantic veil of "changelessness" and branding them "traditional," even if they reflect very recent changes in worship; or (2) seeing *no* practice as normative, normal, and historical but rather seeking to change, alter, and reform worship so that it fits the tastes, trends, and whims of any individual or group, so that worship may become "relevant," whatever that might mean.[1] Can the study of liturgical history play any role in this tension? According to Maxwell Johnson, "it is the Christian liturgical tradition as known from the texts of that tradition that is primary, and our 'experience' of the contemporary use or misuse of that tradition that is secondary. To actually 'know what we are talking about' . . . means that we have to study history. There is no other way. . . . The pastoral practice of liturgy itself, I am convinced, must also flow from . . . a historical and theological approach."[2]

* Many thanks to Jonathan Swarts, Gabriel Galadza, David Pitt, and Melita Mudri-Zubacz for their help and comments.

[1] On the tension between "normative" and "relative" in worship, see Maxwell E. Johnson, "Can We Avoid Relativism in Worship? Liturgical Norms in the Light of Contemporary Liturgical Scholarship," *Worship* 74, no.2 (2000): 135–55. In Greek liturgical scholarship, see Evaggelos Theodorou, "Τὸ σταθερὸ καὶ μεταβλητὸ στὴν Ὀρθόδοξη λατρεία," *Θεολογία* 70 (1999): 7–55; and George Filias, *Παράδοση καὶ Ἐξέλιξη στὴ Λατρεία τηχς Ἐκκλησίας* (Athens: Gregoris, 2006).

[2] Maxwell E. Johnson, *The Rites of Christian Initiation: Their Evolution and Interpretation*, 2nd ed. (Collegeville, MN: Liturgical Press, 2007), xxi. Of course, the context of discussion here is baptism, but the principle is general.

The study of liturgical history, then, is of paramount importance, not only because it allows us to explore the origins, the evolution, and the history of a particular rite, but also because it can simultaneously guide us through conceptions and misconceptions about current liturgical practice. Paying tribute to Maxwell Johnson, my "Doktorvater," my teacher, and my friend, a person who combines scholarly excellence with paternal warmth, academic recognition with Christian humility, amazing teaching skills with love and dedication to his students, I offer this short case study as an example of how history can prove to be a guide for the pastoral practice of liturgy, in this particular case within the Byzantine liturgical tradition.

The Case Study

Every Sunday morning at a parish in the city of Athens, at specific times, the cantor, following the practice of the parish, proceeds to the middle of the solea[3] of the church and leads the congregation in reciting in unison the Creed and, later, the Lord's Prayer, inviting their participation by saying, "ὅλοι μαζί," that is, "all together." Some visitors—*not* members of the parish—have reacted to this practice, characterizing it an "innovation," and especially taking to task the cantor's directive to the people to join in the recitation of the Creed and the Lord's Prayer by saying, "ὅλοι μαζί." They go on to comment that such practices are not "Orthodox" but "Catholic" or "Protestant," that people should not recite things in unison because they "spoil" the atmosphere, and suggest that at a minimum the cantor ceases to make the exhortation "ὅλοι μαζί" before the recitation of the Creed and the Lord's Prayer. The parish priests respond by saying that they have introduced this "innovation," a temporary measure, in order to encourage and promote liturgical participation among the people. They also point to the fact that people need this encouragement to join in and that they have observed a gradual but steady increase in participation due to this "encouragement."[4] These visitors, however, insist they are right!

[3] The solea is the raised sanctuary platform that lies outside the icon screen. For more information, see Alexander P. Kazhdan, ed., *The Oxford Dictionary of Byzantium* (New York/Oxford: Oxford University Press, 1991), 3:1923.

[4] This is a true event. The names of these visitors and location of the church are withheld.

The immediate questions that I particularly want to address in this essay are the following: (1) Is it an "innovation" to encourage people to recite the Creed and the Lord's Prayer in unison? And (2) is the exhortation "ὅλοι μαζί" an innovation, a result of "Protestant" or "Catholic" influence? It is evident that behind these questions is the issue of congregational participation and its place in the current Greek Orthodox liturgical setting. Let us turn then to the study of liturgical history to see if answers may be found to the questions posed above.

The Manuscript Evidence

The Creed entered the Divine Liturgy during the Patriarchate of Timothy (511–18), occupying its present place,[5] just before the anaphora. The whole breadth of the manuscript evidence assigns the Creed to the people or to the clergy and the people jointly.[6] In a few cases, it is directed that the people chant the Creed,[7] while two note that the archdeacon begins to chant the Creed and the people follow:

Ὁ διάκονος. Πρόσχωμεν· καὶ τὸ σύμβολον ψάλλωμεν. Καὶ τοῦ Ἀρχιδιακόνου ἀρχομένου, πάντες τὸ σύμβολον ψάλλουσι.[8]	The deacon: Let us be attentive, and let us chant the symbol. And after the archdeacon has begun [it], everyone chants the symbol [i.e., the Creed].[9]

While in only two cases the archdeacon is identified as the person leading the recitation of the Creed by all, we can assume that in the absence of a deacon—keep in mind that the two sources mentioned above are Ἀρχιερατικά (Pontificals)—someone would coordinate and lead the people in order to achieve an orderly recitation of the Creed. And even if we accept that all the responses assigned to the people

[5] Robert F. Taft, *The Great Entrance: A History of the Transfer of Gifts and Other Pre-anaphoral Rites of the Liturgy of St. John Chrysostom*, Orientalia Christiana Analecta 200, 2nd ed. (Rome: Ponticium Institutum Studiorum Orientalium, 1978), 398–403.

[6] Ibid., 417. See footnote 214 for details. See also Panayiotis Trempelas, *Αἱ Τρεῖς Λειτουργίαι κατὰ τοὺς ἐν Ἀθήναις Κώδικας*, 2nd ed. (Athens: Soter, 1982), 92. See also Melita Mudri-Zubacz, "Congregational Singing in the Rus' Liturgical Tradition," *Logos* 46 (2005): 347–453, here 351–62; I would like to thank Daniel Galadza for referring me to this article and to Melita Mudri-Zubacz for sending it to me.

[7] Taft, *The Great Entrance*, 417; Trempelas, *Αἱ Τρεῖς Λειτουργίαι*, 92. The Slavic tradition still adheres to this practice.

[8] Taft, *The Great Entrance*, 378–79 and note 17.

[9] Translation from ibid., 378–79.

were gradually taken over by the choir,[10] the fact that the manuscript sources have the people recite the Creed is significant. They retain the principle of congregational participation, even if in practice that principle was not generally upheld.

Even though a shift is noted in the *editio princeps* of Doucas where the Creed is assigned to the choir,[11] this change is not reflected in most of the printed editions of the three liturgies I have had the chance to examine.[12] The shift is reflected, however, in the Athens editions of the *Ἱερατικόν* from the second half of the twentieth century. In these editions, the rubric directs the bishop or the senior clergyman attending (i.e., not celebrating) or the reader to recite the Creed, the implication being that the congregation remains silent, with the choirs sealing the recitation with the "Amen."[13] What we see here is the decline of congregational participation codified.

It is exactly that which is undone in the most recent edition of the *Ἱερατικόν* of 2002 in which we observe a return to the ancient order, a return to the principle of congregational participation: "Ὁ λαός· Πιστεύω εἰς ἕνα Θεόν . . ." (The people: I believe in one God . . .) with a footnote reminding that the Creed (and the Lord's Prayer) should be recited by the people at the beckoning of the deacon or the first cantor.[14] After all, the whole Divine Liturgy and the anaphora in

[10] Evaggelia Spyrakou, *Οἱ Χοροὶ Ψαλτῶν κατὰ τὴν Βυζαντινὴ Παράδοση*. Μελέται 14 (Athens: Institute for Byzantine Musicology, 2008), 161–64.

[11] *Αἱ Θεῖαι Λειτουργεῖαι τοῦ ἁγίου Ἰωάννου τοῦ Χρυσοστόμου, Βασιλείου τοῦ Μεγάλου καὶ ἡ τῶν Προηγιασμένων, Γερμανοῦ ἀρχιεπισκόπου Κωνσταντινουπόλεως. Ἱστορία Ἐκκλησιαστικὴ καὶ Μυστικὴ Θεωρία* (Rome: Demetrios Doukas, 1526), as cited in Taft, *The Great Entrance*, 417.

[12] The Creed (and the Lord's Prayer) is assigned to the people (Λαός) in the editions of the three liturgies of Venice 1760, 13; Venice 1773, 13; Venice 1814, 15; Constantinople 1820, 17; Athens 1835, 37; Venice 1852, 16; Athens 1856, 19; Venice 1859, 16; Athens 1864, 22; Tripoli 1892, 46. The Creed (and the Lord's Prayer) is assigned to the choir in the editions of the three liturgies of Constantinople 1875, 31; and Athens 1877, 23.

[13] *Ἱερατικόν* Athens 1951, 85 (as cited in Taft, *The Great Entrance*, 416); *Ἱερατικόν* Athens 1995, 123: "Ὁ προεστὼς ἐκτὸς τοῦ ἱεροῦ Βήματος, ἢ ὁ Ἀναγνώστης, τρανῶς καὶ εὐκρινῶς, καὶ ἕκαστος τῶν ἐκκλησιαζομένων ἰδίᾳ καθ' ἑαυτόν, ἀπαγγέλει τὸ ἱερὸν Σύμβολον τῆς Πίστεως· Πιστεύω εἰς ἕνα Θεόν, πατέρα, παντοκράτορα. . . . Ὁ Χορός· Ἀμήν."

[14] "Τὸ Σύμβολον τῆς πίστεως καὶ ἡ Κυριακὴ προσευχὴ δὲον ν' ἀπαγγέλωνται ὑπὸ σύμπαντος τοῦ λαοῦ τῷ νεύματι τοῦ διακόνου ἢ τοῦ πρωτοψάλτου." *Ἱερατικόν* 2002, 130. What is striking, however, is that the same editor, in the latest edition of the

particular have a dialogical structure, a statement-response framework that demands the participation of the people, sealed by the great "Amen" at the end of the anaphora.[15]

Things are less complicated regarding the Lord's Prayer. It "is a fact that from Cyril/John II of Jerusalem on, in most traditions East and West, the people have recited the Our Father in the Eucharist,"[16] a tradition that is reflected in the vast majority of the manuscript and printed tradition.[17] This is clear in the invitation to the Lord's Prayer in the Byzantine Rite:[18]

Καὶ καταξίωσον *ἡμᾶς*, Δέσποτα, μετὰ παρρησίας ἀκατακρίτως τολμᾶν ἐπικαλεῖσθαι σὲ τὸν ἐπουράνιον Θεὸν Πατέρα καὶ λέγειν·[19]	And make *us* worthy, Master, with confidence and without fear of condemnation, to dare call You, the heavenly God, Father, and to say:[20]

The "us" above obviously refers to the whole congregation, clergy and laity. It is an invitation *for all* to join in and recite the Lord's Prayer.[21]

Ἐγκόλπιον Ἀναγνώστου καὶ Ψάλτου (Athens, 2005), assigns both the Creed and the Lord's Prayer to the senior clergyman attending who is supposed to recite it with the people: "Ὁ προεστὼς ἀπαγγέλλει μετὰ τοῦ λαοῦ τὸ Σύμβολον τῆς πίστεως" (p. 189); "Καὶ ἀπαγγέλλεται ὑπὸ τοῦ προεστῶτος καὶ τοῦ λαοῦ ἡ Κυριακὴ προσευχὴ" (p.192). Given the explicit directions in the *Ἱερατικόν* presented above encouraging the participation of the faithful in the recitation of the Creed and the Lord's Prayer, one would expect similar directions in the *Ἐγκόλπιον*, a liturgical book that is exclusively used by the readers and cantors. The participation of the people in the *Ἐγκόλπιον* is mentioned but unfortunately not encouraged. Priority is given to the senior clergyman attending, more in line with the older versions of the *Ἱερατικόν* (see footnote 13).

[15] David Drillock, "Liturgical Song in the Worship of the Church," *St Vladimir's Theological Quarterly* 41 (1997): 183–218.

[16] Robert F. Taft, *The Precommunion Rites*, Orientalia Christiana Analecta 261 (Rome: Pontificio Istituto Orientale, 2000), 143.

[17] See Trempelas, *Αἱ Τρεῖς Λειτουργίαι*, 127–28; and footnote 12 above. See also Melita Mudri-Zubacz, "Congregational Singing," 351–62.

[18] On the Lord's Prayer in the Divine Liturgy, see Taft, *The Precommunion Rites*, 129–54.

[19] *Ἱερατικόν* 2002, 137. Emphasis added.

[20] The English text is from the translation of the Holy Cross Greek Orthodox School of Theology Faculty, available at http://www.goarch.org/chapel/liturgical_texts/liturgy_hchc.

[21] In all the sources examined, those that assign the Creed to the people (λαός), also assign the Lord's Prayer to the people. On the other hand, those that assign

Directing the People

The sources confirm that the people recited the Creed and the Lord's Prayer but they are largely silent as to who directed the people in the recitation of the Creed and the Lord's Prayer, from where, and how (with the two exceptions mentioned above). We have evidence, however, that participation of the people in services was not only encouraged but also guided. Elements from the extinct cathedral office of Hagia Sophia of Constantinople have been preserved in the sources that point to the fact that the people were guided in chanting responses in unison by hand gestures (μετὰ χειρονομίας) of a cantor from the ambo in the middle of the church.

Although the Studite Evergetis Typikon of the twelfth century reflects monastic usage, it preserves elements of the cathedral office such as the following case, where it offers guidelines as to how a hymn of the Second Sunday before Christmas is to be chanted during Orthros:

Ψάλλεται δὲ οὕτως· πρῶτον ὁ ψάλτης, ἔπειτα ὁ λαὸς μετὰ χειρονομίας, εἶτα ὁ ψάλτης τὸν στίχον. . . . Μετὰ δὲ τὸν στίχον, ψάλλει ὁ λαὸς πάλιν τὸ τέλος τῆς ὑπακοῆς.	And it is chanted like this: first the cantor, next the people *with hand gesture*;[22] then the cantor [chants] the stichos.[23] . . . After the stichos, the people chant the end of the hypakoe again.[24]

the Creed to the choir (χορός), also assign the Lord's Prayer to the choir. See footnote 12.

[22] Translation of term is by the author, as in this and the following example the original translator does not offer a translation for the term "μετὰ χειρονομίας." Rather, Robert Jordan only transliterates the term: *cheironomia*.

[23] Psalm verse.

[24] Text and translation by Robert H. Jordan, *The Synaxarion of the Monastery of the Theotokos Evergetis: September–February*, Belfast Byzantine Texts and Translations 6.5 (Belfast: The Institute of Byzantine Studies, Queen's University, 2000), 285, emphasis added. For the Greek, see also A. Dmitrievskij, *Opisanie litugiceskix rukopisej xranjascixsja v bibliotekax pravoslavnago vostoka*, vol. 1 (Kiev, 1895), 339–40. For a discussion of the examples presented here in terms of responsorial and antiphonal chanting in the cathedral liturgy, see Juan Mateos, *La célébration de la parole dans la liturgie byzantine*, Orientalia Christiana Analecta 191 (Rome: Pontificium Institutum Studiorum Orientalium, 1971), 7–26; and Dimitri E. Conomos, *The Late Byzantine and Slavonic Communion Cycle: Liturgy and Music*, Dumbarton Oaks Studies 21 (Washington, DC: Dumbarton Oaks Research Library and Collection, 1985), 16–19. Drillock, "Liturgical Song," 183–93.

The same Typikon offers guidelines as to how to chant the hymn "Λαθὼν ἐτέχθης" on Christmas Eve:

Καὶ μετὰ τὸ ἀναγνωσθῆναι ἀναγνώσματα γ λέγει εὐθὺς ὁ ψάλτης τροπάριον ἦχος πλ. β´ Λαθὼν ἐτέχθης ὑπὸ τὸ σπήλαιον, ψάλλεται δὲ ἐν τῷ μέσῳ μετὰ χειρονομίας. Εἶτα λέγει στίχον ὁ ψάλτης, ψαλμὸς πς' Οἱ θεμέλιοι αὐτοῦ . . . Ὁ λαός Καὶ μάγους σοι προσήνεγκεν. Καὶ ἰδοὺ ἀλλόφυλοι καὶ Τύρος . . . Ὁ λαός· Καὶ μάγους σοι προσήνεγκεν. Κύριος διηγήσεται . . . καὶ πάλιν ὁ λαός· Καὶ μάγους σοι προσήνεγκεν. Εἶτα πάλιν ὁ ψάλτης τὸ αὐτὸ τροπάριον Λαθὼν ἐτέχθης ὑπὸ τὸ σπήλαιον.	And after three readings have been read, the cantor immediately recites in plagal mode 2 troparion: Λαθὼν ἐτέχθης ὑπὸ τὸ σπήλαιον *and it is chanted in the middle with hand gesture*. Then the cantor recites a stichos, psalm 86: His foundations . . . [Ps 86:1-4]. The people καὶ μάγους σοι προσήνεγκαν. And behold, Philistines and Tyre . . . [Ps 86:4-5]. The people καὶ μάγους σοι προσήνεγκαν. The Lord will describe . . . [Ps 86:6-7] and again the people καὶ μάγους σοι προσήνεγκαν. Then again the cantor [recites] the same troparion: Λαθὼν ἐτέχθης ὑπὸ τὸ σπήλαιον.[25]

For the same hymn and day another twelfth-century source, the Typikon of the Monastery of the Holy Savior in Messine provides similar directions for how the singing of the hymn is to be executed with an interesting detail: the people are directed to "keep it simple" in their responses, avoiding the elaborate execution of the cantors: "καὶ ψάλλουσιν αὐτὸ λιτῶς καὶ οὐ ψαλτικῶς."[26] This source also informs us that this manner of singing is applicable also to all the *troparia* of Christmas and Epiphany: "Οὕτως οὖν ψάλλονται καὶ τὰ λοιπὰ τροπάρια τῶν Χριστουγέννων καὶ τῶν Φώτων."[27]

The examples mentioned above are of special value since, even though they are of monastic origin, they give us glimpses into the manner in which the congregation would participate in the chanting of the cathedral office. It is no accident that within these descriptions of "congregational singing" in the Byzantine liturgical tradition the technical term "μετὰ χειρονομίας" appears, designating hand gestures of rhythmic and musical value performed by the head of the choir.[28]

[25] Text and translation from Jordan, *The Synaxarion of the Monastery of the Theotokos Evergetis*, 330–31. Emphasis is added. The editor provides the full psalm verses. See also Dmitrievskij, *Opisanie*, vol. 1, 354.

[26] Miguel Arranz, *Le Typikon du Monastère du Saint-Sauveur à Messine*, Orientalia Christiana Analecta 185 (Rome: Pontificium Institutum Orientalium Studiorum, 1969), 80.

[27] Ibid., 80–81.

[28] Jordan, *The Synaxarion of the Monastery of the Theotokos Evergetis*, 573. In the definition provided in the glossary, Jordan erroneously assigns the hand gesturing

This practice disappeared together with the cathedral office, as the monastic office gradually took over,[29] introducing monastic practices in chanting that limited the participation of the people, replacing the cantors on the ambo with the two choirs, who also took over the parts traditionally assigned to the people.[30] This is the end of a long process that began after Iconoclasm when one observes the slow but gradual limitation of popular participation in chanting.[31]

Exhortations to Participation

We have established, I believe, the fact that within the history of the Byzantine Rite the congregation was expected to participate in the responses and in the recitation of the Creed and Lord's Prayer and that, in order to coordinate their participation, they were directed by a person leading them in their responses. But what about the exhortation "ὅλοι μαζί" said by the cantor before the recitation of the Creed and the Lord's Prayer in the practice of the aforementioned parish in Athens? Is that an "innovation"?

It is true that, in looking at our sources, we have not found any such exhortation associated with the recitation of the Creed and the Lord's Prayer, although it is clearly mentioned that the cantor or the deacon is to direct the people in the recitation. In examining the validity of the exhortation "ὅλοι μαζί," then, we will focus on two questions:

---

to *all* members of the choir: "(literally, 'hand law') hand gestures performed by all singers of the choir in certain, preferably more solemn, pieces. Each conventional musical formula had its own cheironomia, involving various positions (flexions) of fingers and hand. Cheironomia is a phenomenon of a semi-oral musical tradition like the Byzantine one and can be described as a gestic or mnemonic notation rather than conducting in the modern sense." Juan Mateos translates the term "μετὰ χειρονομίας" as "sous la direction rythmique du psalmiste." See Mateos, *La célébration*, 20. For further discussion on the "cheironomia," see Dimitri E. Conomos, *Byzantine Trisagia and Cheroubika of the Fourteenth and Fifteenth Centuries: A Study of Late Byzantine Liturgical Chant* (Thessaloniki: Patriarchal Institute for Patristic Studies, 1974), 325–67; Neil K. Moran, *Singers in Late Byzantine and Slavonic Painting*, Byzantina Neerlandica 9 (Leiden: E. J. Brill, 1986), 38–47. Moran defines "cheironomia" as the "art of directing a choir by means of movement of the hand"; Spyrakou, *Οἱ Χοροὶ Ψαλτῶν*, 468–84.

[29] For the standard introduction to the history of the Byzantine Rite, see Robert F. Taft, *The Byzantine Rite: A Short History*, American Essays in Liturgy (Collegeville, MN: Liturgical Press, 1992).

[30] Spyrakou, *Οἱ Χοροὶ Ψαλτῶν*, 483–84.

[31] Ibid., 161–64.

(1) how do we encourage people to actively participate in worship, and (2) are there antecedents of such an exhortation in the Byzantine liturgical tradition?

Modern Greek liturgical studies recognize the lack of congregational participation as one of the important issues that needs to be addressed. As frequently noted, the congregation is often relegated to the role of the observer rather than participant,[32] and the tendency is to see worship as an opportunity for private meditation and as an expression of personal piety rather than conscious and active participation in the *common* worship.[33] The call to undo this unfortunate situation and return to the tradition and the ancient practice of the church is, however, stronger than ever. In this context the theological and liturgical consequences of the royal priesthood of the faithful are being reexamined,[34] the practice of the inaudible recitation of the priestly prayers has been challenged,[35] and the active participation of the people in worship is being increasingly encouraged and cultivated.[36]

It is within the context and framework of this last statement that the exhortation "ὅλοι μαζί" needs to be examined. The reality is that for

[32] This is also demonstrated in the expression used to describe church going: When asked what they do in church, most people (even clergy) respond, "παρακολουθῶ τὴ Θεία Λειτουργία" (I observe/watch the Divine Liturgy, literally, "follow on the side"), rather than, "συμμετέχω στὴ Θεία Λειτουργία" (I participate in the Divine Liturgy). I will not deal here with another burning issue, that of infrequent reception of the Eucharist. On this issue, see, for example, Elias Mastrogiannopoulos, "Ἡ συμμετοχὴ τῶν πιστῶν στὴν Θεία Κοινωνία," in Τὸ μυστήριο τῆς Θείας Εὐχαριστίας. Πρακτικὰ Γ´ Πανελληνίου Λειτουργικοῦ Συμποσίου (Athens: Apostoliki Diakonia, 2004), 373–96. (The whole volume is available in PDF format from the web site of the Holy Synod of the Church of Greece: http://www.ecclesia.gr/greek/holysynod/commitees/liturgical/eyxarist.pdf). See also the Encyclical of the Holy Synod of the Church of Greece No. 2785 (March 31, 2004). For the text, see http://www.ecclesia.gr/greek/holysynod/egyklioi/egkyklios2785.html.

[33] Demetrios Tzerpos, "Τὸ αἴτημα τῆς ἐνεργοῦς συμμετοχῆς τοῦ λαοῦ κατὰ τὴν τέλεση τῆς Θείας Λατρείας," in *«Λατρεύσωμεν εὐαρέστως τῷ Θεῷ»: Τὸ Αἴτημα της Λειτουργικης Ανανεωσεως στην Ορθόδοξη Εκκλησια*. Πρακτικὰ Β´ Πανελληίου Λειτουργικοῦ Συμποσίου (Athens: Apostoliki Diakonia, 2003), 361–86, 362. (The whole volume is available in PDF format from the website of the Holy Synod of the Church of Greece: http://www.ecclesia.gr/greek/holysynod/commitees/liturgical/latrefsomen.pdf).

[34] Tzerpos, "Τὸ αἴτημα τῆς ἐνεργοῦς συμμετοχῆς," 364–68 and the footnotes for further Greek bibliography.

[35] Ibid., 368–71 and the footnotes for further Greek bibliography.

[36] Ibid., 371–77 and the footnotes for further Greek bibliography.

centuries the congregation has been accustomed to a passive attendance of services rather than active participation, and even if they are convinced that participation is theologically, traditionally, and liturgically valid, they often need active encouragement to break the old habits of nonparticipation. In other words, the return to the common recitation of the Creed and the Lord's Prayer as preserved in the totality of the manuscript and the majority of the printed tradition needs extra encouragement, a "push" that will help people act on the theological and liturgical tradition of the church.

I see the exhortation "ὅλοι μαζί" as a necessary call to the people, reminding them that the recitation of the Creed and the Lord's Prayer is *their* part too. Obviously, if we lived in an ideal world, no such exhortations would be needed for our faithful; they would know what to do and what to say at what moment. But throughout the history of the church, that has not been the case. If we examine the liturgical texts of the Byzantine liturgical tradition, we will observe that many of the diaconal petitions are either exhortations calling for a proper body posture and movement, calling for a proper prayerful attitude among the assembly, and even reminding the priest what to do and what to say. So, for example, taking just the text of the Divine Liturgy of Chrysostom, I have grouped the deacon's petitions into the following categories, with a representative example in each category (the list is not exhaustive):[37]

(1) Guidance as to what to pray for:

> Ὑπὲρ τῆς εἰρήνης τοῦ σύμπαντος κόσμος, εὐσταθείας τῶν ἁγίων τοῦ Θεοῦ Ἐκκλησιῶν καὶ τῆς τῶν πάντων ἑνώσεως τοῦ Κυρίου δεηθῶμεν (112) / For peace in the whole world, for the stability of the holy churches of God, and for the unity of all, let us pray to the Lord

(2) Guidance as to what to do:

> Πληρώσωμεν τὴν δέησιν ἡμῶν τῷ Κυρίῳ (128) / Let us complete our prayer to the Lord

[37] The Greek text is from the 2002 *Ἱερατικόν* of the Church of Greece. Page numbers after the Greek text refer to this edition. The English text is from the translation of the Holy Cross Greek Orthodox School of Theology Faculty, available at http://www.goarch.org/chapel/liturgical_texts/liturgy_hchc. This text relegates the deacon's parts to the priest, as in the American context it is rare for a priest to celebrate with the assistance of a deacon.

(3) Guidance as to the proper body posture and movement:

Τὰς κεφαλὰς ἡμῶν τῷ Κυρίῳ κλίνωμεν (138) / Let us bow our heads to the Lord

(4) Guidance as to the proper prayerful attitude in the assembly:

Πρόσχωμεν (139) / Let us be attentive

(5) Reminders to the priest

Εὐλόγησον, Δέσποτα (111) / Bless, Master[38]

(6) Combined cases:[39]

Σοφία (#4)· ὀρθοί (#3)· ἀκούσωμεν τοῦ ἁγίου εὐαγγελίου (#2) (119) / Wisdom (#4). Arise (#3). Let us hear the holy Gospel (#2)

And if we carefully go through liturgical texts of the early church, we find diaconal petitions and admonitions that may sound strange to our modern ears. One example that stands out is a petition in the *Apostolic Constitutions*, an early church order from about AD 380 from the environs of Antioch that could fall under a different category that I would call guidance as to the proper conduct in the assembly. There, in the context of the celebration of the Divine Liturgy, we find the following diaconal exhortation: "Τὰ παιδία προσλαμβάνεσθε αἱ μητέρες" / "Mothers, take care of your children!"[40]

The deacon's petitions and exhortations demonstrate that we do *not* live in an ideal world; on the contrary, the members of the congregation need continuous reminders as to their proper attitude and conduct within the liturgical celebration of the church.[41] For example, the exhortation "Πρόσχωμεν" / "Let us be attentive" is said six times in the context of a single celebration of the Divine Liturgy, four times in the context of the readings alone! Therefore, the exhortation "ὅλοι

[38] Translated by the author. Not translated in the online edition (see previous footnote) as this is not said when there is no deacon. In the Greek-American practice it is sometimes said by the choir.

[39] Numbers in parenthesis with the symbol # refer to the above five categories.

[40] *Apostolic Constitutions* 8.12.2. For the English translation, see W. Jardine Grisbrooke, *The Liturgical Portions of the Apostolic Constitutions: A Text for Students*, Alcuin/GROW Liturgical Study 13–14, Grove Liturgical Study 61 (Bramcote/Nottingham: Grove Books, 1990), 31.

[41] On the interplay between the diaconal petitions and the conduct of the faithful during the Divine Liturgy, see Panayiotis Skaltsis, "Τὰ Διακονικὰ Παραγγέλματα καὶ ἡ Στάση τῶν Πιστῶν στὴ Θεία Λειτουργία," in idem, *Λειτουργικὲς Μελέτες II* (Thessaloniki: Pournara, 2006), 119–72.

μαζί" to remind the people to recite in unison the Creed and the Lord's Prayer is *not* an innovation; rather, it reflects the effort to instill a particular way of thinking in the mentality of the congregation that is squarely within the theological and liturgical tradition of the church.

It is neither a "Protestant" nor a "Catholic" influence. It is very Orthodox indeed, still used quite often in the liturgy of the Orthodox Church, albeit linguistically in a more ancient form. "Ὅλοι μαζί" is nothing more than the opening words of the *ektene* litany, "εἴπωμεν πάντες,"[42] rendered in Modern Greek:

Διάκονος: Εἴπωμεν πάντες ἐξ ὅλης τῆς ψυχῆς καὶ ἐξ ὅλης τῆς διανοίας εἴπωμεν.	Deacon: *Let us all say* with our whole soul, and with our whole mind, *let us say*.[43]
Λαός: Κύριε ἐλέησον	People: Lord have mercy

In reality, this opening petition is a strong exhortation to the people to respond to the petitions coming next with the "Κύριε ἐλέησον" / "Lord have mercy." It is a pointer not only to the response but also to the manner of the response: ". . . with our whole soul, and with our whole mind." And our case becomes even stronger when we examine the opening of the *ektene* litany in its earlier form, where we see that this opening was composed of originally two petitions, now collapsed into one. When looking at some of the early sources for this litany, the original two petitions are obvious, and it becomes evident that their role is to guide the people to use the appropriate response and encourage their heartfelt participation:

Codex Pyromalus: [44]

Εἴπωμεν πάντες τὸ κύριε ἐλέησον / Let us all say the Lord have mercy

Ἐξ ὅλης τῆς ψυχῆς / With all our soul

[42] On the *ektene* litany, see Mateos, *La célébration*, 148–56; Stefano Parenti, "L'*Ektenê* della Liturgia di Crisostomo nell'eucologio St. Peterburg gr. 226," in *ΕΥΛΟΓΗΜΑ: Studies in Honor of Robert Taft, SJ*, ed. Ephrem Carr, Stefano Parenti, Abraham-Andreas Thiermeyer, Elena Velkovska, Studia Anselmiana 110, Analecta Liturgica 17 (Rome: Pontificio Ateneo S. Anselmo, 1993), 295–318; Stefanos Alexopoulos, *The Presanctified Liturgy in the Byzantine Rite: A Comparative Analysis of Its Origins, Evolution, and Structural Units*, Liturgia Condenda 21 (Leuven: Peeters, 2009), 197–202.

[43] Translation from http://www.goarch.org/chapel/liturgical_texts/vespers.

[44] As cited in Parenti, "L'*Ektenê*," 303. I quote here, as in the following examples, only the two first petitions, relative to our topic.

St. Petersburg gr. 226:[45]

> Εἴπωμεν πάντες Κύριε ἐλέησον / Let us all say Lord have mercy
> Ἐξ ὅλης τῆς ψυχῆς καὶ ἐξ ὅλης τῆς διανοίας. / With all our soul and all our mind

Actually, the *ektene* litany from the Johannesberg Latin translation of the Liturgy of Basil demonstrates our case very clearly:[46]

Dicamus omnes kyrieeleison	Let us all say Lord have mercy
Pop(ulus): kyrieeleison	People: Lord have mercy
Diac(onus): Ex omni anima, & ex omni mente dicamus omnes kyrieeleison	Deacon: From all our soul and all our mind let us all say Lord have mercy
Pop. kyrieeleison	People: Lord have mercy[47]

It is without doubt that the role of the deacon here is not only to indicate the correct response for the following petitions but to encourage *the full and active and lively participation* of the faithful! That is exactly the purpose of the exhortation "Ὅλοι μαζί" before the recitation of the Creed and the Lord's Prayer.

Changing Attitudes

This is what the late Archbishop Christodoulos (d. 2008) pushed for. He actively supported the movement of liturgical renewal within the Greek Orthodox Church. He saw liturgical renewal not as a "reform" or "innovation" but as the "return to our traditional liturgical roots."[48] Within this context, he urged for the participation of the people in the Divine Liturgy and in the recitation of the Creed and the Lord's Prayer in particular, "under the supervision either of the deacon (if present) or one of the cantors."[49] In an encyclical addressed to the cantors of the Archdiocese of Athens, the late Archbishop Christodoulos strongly supported the participation of the people in the chanted parts and the recitation of the Creed and the Lord's Prayer. He noted that people need encouragement and pointed to the example of the late Spyridon Peristeris (d. 1998), head cantor of the Cathedral of Athens, who "*with*

[45] As cited in ibid., 306.

[46] As cited in ibid., 304.

[47] Translated by the author.

[48] Encyclical 9 – 2292/16.10.1998. See Christodoulos, Archbishop of Athens, *Ἔργα, Τόμος Β΄: Λειτουργικαὶ Ἐγκύκλιοι* (Athens: Kyriakidis, 2010), 299.

[49] Ibid., 303.

his hands" would invite the people to join in the chanting.[50] Whenever the late archbishop would serve the Divine Liturgy, at the specific times his archdeacon would face the people and direct with his hands the recitation of the Creed and the Lord's Prayer.

Another instance where one may observe the celebrating bishop encouraging the participation of the faithful by hand movements and sometimes by saying "ὅλοι μαζί" is within the context of festal vespers, where the people are invited to join the clergy in chanting the vesperal hymn "O Joyful Light," the Prokeimenon of the day,[51] and Psalm 33:11 (LXX) in the context of the Artoklasia (Blessing of the Five Loaves). In these cases, because these hymns are well known *and* the people are encouraged to join in, the vigor of their participation is overwhelming, a stark contrast to the generally passive congregation that one witnesses when visiting a Greek Orthodox parish.

The above examples are *not* the norm; they represent the few exceptions to the rule and reflect a very slow process of changing attitudes toward congregational participation within the Greek Orthodox Church. Notwithstanding the number of studies published in Greece over the last fifty years on the issue of congregational participation, a present evaluation of the current situation is that "there is no systematic action, no substantial progress and almost no or minimal application"[52] to the call for congregational participation.

Conclusions

Having examined this case study through the lens of liturgical history (and it could be approached in many different ways) we can reach the following conclusions:

1. It is *not* an innovation to encourage the faithful in reciting the Creed and the Lord's Prayer in unison. In fact, the overwhelming majority of sources assign these to the people.

[50] Encyclical Ζ/465/19.02.2001. See Christodoulos, *Λειτουργικαὶ Ἐγκύκλιοι*, 407–21, here 418–19. Emphasis added. On a first evaluation of the liturgical encyclicals of the late archbishop, see the introduction of George Filias in the aforementioned, 13–68.

[51] For an English translation of the hymn "O Joyful Light" and for the Prokeimena of the week, see http://goarch.org/en/chapel/liturgical_texts/vespers.

[52] Christophoros Stavropoulos, *Ἡ Θεία Εὐχαριστία Κέντρον τῆς Ποιμαντικῆς Διακονίας* (Athens: Athos, 2006), 181. For the Russian tradition, see Melita Mudri-Zubacz, "Congregational Singing," 362–453.

2. The participation of the people necessitates that someone directs them. Throughout history we have evidence that either one of the cantors or the deacon would direct the people.
3. Exhortations of all sorts existed and exist within the Divine Liturgy, reflecting real pastoral needs, guiding the people to the proper participation in the Divine Liturgy, moving the community toward the ideal world that is celebrated in the Divine Liturgy.
4. The exhortation "ὅλοι μαζί" is just that! It is an exhortation to encourage people to break the old habit of nonparticipation and join in, to make the Divine Liturgy their own.
5. The exhortation "ὅλοι μαζί" is similar in function and meaning with the opening petition of the *ektene*, "εἴπωμεν πάντες."
6. The pastoral practice of liturgy can easily fall prey to misconceptions about what liturgy is, what liturgy does, and how one participates in it, *if* the study of liturgical history is ignored.

Contributors

Stefanos Alexopoulos is assistant professor of liturgy at the Ecclesiastical Academy of Athens, Greece.

Paul F. Bradshaw is professor of liturgical studies in the Department of Theology at the University of Notre Dame, Indiana.

Michael Daniel Findikyan is dean and professor of liturgical studies at St. Nersess Armenian Seminary in New Rochelle, New York.

Ruth Langer is associate professor in the Theology Department and associate director of the Center for Christian-Jewish Learning at Boston College, Massachusetts.

Lizette Larson-Miller is professor of liturgical leadership and dean of the Chapel at the Church Divinity School of the Pacific, Berkeley, California.

Christian McConnell is assistant professor of liturgical studies at the University of St. Michael's College in Toronto, Ontario.

Anne McGowan is a postdoctoral associate at the Yale Institute of Sacred Music, New Haven, Connecticut.

David A. Pitt is associate professor of liturgical and sacramental theology at Loras College in Dubuque, Iowa.

Walter D. Ray is assistant professor and political papers archivist at Southern Illinois University, Carbondale, Illinois.

Nicholas V. Russo is assistant dean for undergraduate studies at the University of Notre Dame, Indiana.

Bryan D. Spinks is professor of liturgical studies and pastoral theology and chair of the program in liturgical studies at the Yale Divinity School and Yale Institute of Sacred Music, New Haven, Connecticut.

Robert F. Taft, SJ, FBA, is professor emeritus of Oriental Liturgy at the Pontifical Oriental Institute in Rome.

Jeffrey A. Truscott is lecturer in liturgy and worship and chaplain at Trinity Theological College, Singapore.

Gabriele Winkler is professor emerita at the University of Tübingen, Germany.